THE

CONQUEST OF KANSAS,

BY

MISSOURI AND HER ALLIES.

A HISTORY OF THE TROUBLES IN KANSAS, FROM THE PASSAGE OF THE ORGANIC ACT UNTIL THE CLOSE OF JULY, 1856.

BY WILLIAM PHILLIPS,
SPECIAL CORRESPONDENT OF THE NEW YORK TRIBUNE, FOR KANSAS.

"Come on, then, gentlemen of the slave States; since there is no escaping your challenge, I accept it in behalf of Freedom. We will engage in competition for the virgin soil of Kansas, and God give the victory to the side that is stronger in numbers as it is in right!" —*Speech of* Wm. H. Seward, *in the U. S. Senate*, 1854.

BOSTON.
PHILLIPS, SAMPSON AND COMPANY.
1856.

Stereotyped by
HOBART & ROBBINS,
New England Type and Stereotype Foundery,
BOSTON.

PREFACE.

THE writer deems no apology necessary in submitting the early and unhappy history of Kansas to the public. A conviction of its importance impelled him to the task, and he assumed the duty of historian under the belief that his opportunities for observation, and participation in much of what has occurred, gave him advantages over other writers less conversant with the subject.

It is not the intention of this preface to make an elaborate assertion of impartiality. What is written is offered to the public as the simple TRUTH, and a fair record of the events it chronicles. The writer does not claim to be impartial on the *cause* of quarrel, nor would he regard such a profession as very creditable in any other person; yet he believes that his convictions could neither induce him to wrong an enemy, nor do a friend more than justice. The future will fully vindicate the truth of all that is written; and, if there is one generous mind which, with the lights now before it, would incline to charge the author with perversion, let such a doubter know that the author, while he values the good opinion of all good men, would rather thus be suspected, than purchase a doubtful reputation for impartiality, at the sacrifice of a truthful record. The common trick of authors who lack independence, is, to compound between "God and mammon," and, in steering exactly between two opinions, to claim all the virtues, and exemption from all the vices, of both. Such a course the author does not desire to imitate.

In this narrative there is a faithful record of all the important documents, and the opinions of both sides have been given on many important points, although the design was to have a connected narrative, rather than a collection of statements. In the biographical sketches contained in the work the writer has treated the leaders on both sides with that close scrutiny which is the public right as regards public men. A perusal will probably exonerate from the charge of "puffing;" and if some friends regard their handling as rather "candid," let them know that it was, at least, without malice.

In descriptions of the battles, skirmishes, and other striking incidents, great pains has been taken to have the outlines and the facts correct, and to make the picture as true to nature as possible. As it was the design to give a history of the struggle, rather than a condensation or collection of outrages, very many important and outrageous occurrences have been necessarily omitted.

Finally, reader, after having perused it, criticize, and censure it as much as you think you *conscientiously* can. In the history thus submitted, the privilege of judging men and things has been too freely exercised to be grudged to any careful reader by

THE AUTHOR.

CONTENTS.

CHAPTER I.

INTRODUCTORY CHAPTER.

Kansas before the Passage of the Organic Act — Indians and Indian Reserves — Santa Fe and California Roads — Religious Missions — Slavery Introduced — Kansas Nebraska Bill — Emigration — Federal Appointments — Indian Treaties — Rival Interests, ... 11

CHAPTER II.

THE FIRST INVASION.

Eastern Emigration — Threatened Attack — Border Ruffians — A Warning — Another — Prudent Valor — A Retreat — A Sharp Joke — Bogus "Nigger Hunter" — "Right on the Records," 27

CHAPTER III.

GOV. REEDER — FIRST ELECTION — BLUE LODGE.

Federal Appointees — A Missouri View of Reeder — Flenniken — Whitfield — Wakefield — Fall Election — Blue Lodge operates in Missouri as well as Kansas — Mr. Prince — Having Friends in Missouri — A Cross Examination, ... 37

CHAPTER IV.

SMART ELECTIONEERING TRICK.

A Resolve — Abstract Democracy — Simon Pure Know-Nothing — Another — How Electioneering with Indians goes — Slavery Established by Missouri and Territorial Judges — Slavery Vindicated, ... 53

CHAPTER V.

THE MARCH ELECTION.

Kind of Population — Old-fashioned Pioneers — Modern Pioneers — Squatter Sovereignty — The Census — The Election — The Men Elected — The Fraud as certified to, ... 63

1*

CHAPTER VI.

WHAT KANSAS AND MISSOURI THOUGHT OF IT — PROTEST — MAY ELECTION.

Kansas to be "kept Conquered" — Lynching of Phillips — Death of Clark — Proceedings in Missouri — Free Press and Speech Tabooed — The Pulpit under Censorship — An Original Specimen on the Stand — Parkville Press thrown into the Missouri, ... 83

CHAPTER VII.

THE BOGUS LEGISLATURE.

Missouri Wars on Reeder — Legislature Meets — Legal Members Ejected, July 4th — Legislation — Laws relative to Slave Property — Election of Local Officers — Bogus Legislature help Themselves — Federal Courts pronounce in Favor of Bogus Laws in Advance — A Memorial — An Office-seeker on the Stool of Repentance, ... 98

CHAPTER VIII.

REEDER DISMISSED — SHANNON APPOINTED — BIG SPRINGS CONVENTION.

The Excuse — Shannon — His Reception and Speech — The People Murmur — The State Movement — Reeder nominated for Delegate — His Acceptance and Speech — Resolutions — The Platform, ... 114

CHAPTER IX.

THE TOPEKA CONSTITUTION.

The First Topeka Convention — A County Seat Election — October Election — The Constitutional Convention — The Constitution — Sketches of the Topeka Delegates, ... 125

CHAPTER X.

PAT LAUGHLIN — PARDEE THE MARTYR — LAW AND ORDER CONVENTION.

Pat's Conversion — His Zeal — His Repentance — Death of Collins — Atchison — Border Ruffian Story — Law and Order in Leavenworth — The Governor as a Popular Delegate — Law and Order Speeches — Bogus Laws to be Enforced, ... 141

CHAPTER XI.

RESCUE OF BRANSON.

Origin of the Difficulty — Murder of Dow — Flight of the Murderer — Meeting at Hickory Point — A Plot — Jones enters the Territory with Coleman — A

Justice Manufactured — Branson Arrested — Big Threats — The Rescue — Impending War, ... 151

CHAPTER XII.

WAKARUSA WAR — PREPARATIONS.

Jones Fulminates — The Governor Assists — Military Orders — Proclamation — Secret Orders — Col. Boone's Despatches — Missouri in the Field, . . 162

CHAPTER XIII.

WAKARUSA WAR — INCIDENTS OF THE SIEGE.

The First Impulse — A more Prudent Position — Organized Defence — An Alarm — An Expedition — The Invaders — Queries about "Sharpe's" Rifles — The Fillibuster Flag — An Effort to prevent the "Effusion of Blood" — The Demand for Arms, ... 174

CHAPTER XIV.

ADVENTURES WITH THE BORDER RUFFIAN CHIEFS.

Expedition — A Free and Easy Guard — A Ruffian Chief — Careful Guard and a Capture — Wakarusa Camp again — A Vermonter — A Journey — Another Arrest — An Odd-Fellow — Gen. Pomeroy — The Return — How we swam the River, ... 187

CHAPTER XV.

WAKARUSA WAR — DEATH OF BARBER.

Preparations for Defence — A Patrol Incident — A Spy — Indians offer their Services — The Brass Howitzer — The Ladies of Lawrence — Jones as a Scribe — A Threatening Letter — The Murder of Barber, ... 203

CHAPTER XVI.

THE "PEACE-MAKERS."

The Deputation — Shannon comes up — In Trouble — A Cautious Colonel — The Governor and his Friends — The Ghost of Banquo — Negotiations — Speeches — The Treaty — What they treated about — "Militia" Disbanded — A Row — A Storm — Breaking up of the Invading Camp — The Governor "when you know him," 216

CHAPTER XVII.

MOBBING THE BALLOT-BOXES.

Prisoners of War — Fruits of the War — The Peace Banquet — Volunteers Disbanded — Vote on the State Constitution — "Emigration" on the "Squatter Sovereignty" Plan — Two Heroes — An Attack — Successful — Further Threats — "Militia" Disbanded — Law and Order Speeches — Fears for a Night Attack, ... 229

CHAPTER XVIII.

SKIRMISH AT EASTON.

Election Forbidden in Leavenworth — Held at Easton — Voters Molested and Polls Threatened — An Attack — A Rescue — A Fight — Taken Prisoner — Death of Capt. Brown — Nominating Convention Election, ... 240

CHAPTER XIX.

STATE LEGISLATURE — DRAGOONS — SHERIFF JONES SHOT.

Treason — President's Poclamation — Response to it — Assemblage of the Legislature — Governor's Speech — Committee of Congress — Attempted Arrests — Dragoons under Orders of Jones — Military Correspondence — Arrests — The "Assassin" — "Passin' Resolutions" — A Trick Suspected — Missouri Indignant — Outrages not mentioned by Authority — The War Begun, . 248

CHAPTER XX.

MARSHAL DONALDSON DECLARES WAR.

Missouri receives Allies — A Couple of Deputies — A Marshal — A Federal Court in Kansas — An Indictment against Mortar, Iron, and Paper — Attempt to arrest Reeder — Gov. Robinson starts for the East — His Capture — Reeder's Flight — Committee leave Lawrence — Proclamation — Protests — Proposals for Defence Overruled — A New Committee of Safety — A Threatening Letter — Adventures of Free-State Men — Further Correspondence — Arms Taken — Murder of Jones — Death of Stewart, ... 264

CHAPTER XXI.

SACKING OF LAWRENCE.

The Advanced Guard — Arrests — Reinforcements — Another Appeal — A Demand — A Surrender — Law and Order Speeches — The Allied Army enter Lawrence — Printing Offices Destroyed — Hotel Bombarded and Burned — Wholesale Plunder — Pro-slavery Version, ... 289

CHAPTER XXII.

GUERILLA WAR — THE DRAGOONS — LAW AND ORDER IN LEAVENWORTH.

Atchison passes through Lawrence — The Box Hoax — Pro-slavery Testimony — Guerilla War — "Burning" of Bernhardt — The Governor Victimized — Dragoons called out — Potawattomie Affairs — A Notice — Law and Order Arrests, ... 310

CHAPTER XXIII.

CAPT. WALKER — THE GOVERNOR ON SHARPE'S RIFLES.

Price on a Free-State Man's Head — The Alarm — The Muster — The Attack

—The Repulse — A Peace-Maker — The "Right of Search" — A "Law and Order" Governor — A Brave Little Girl— The Gallant Dragoons get in Trouble by Mistake — Another Alarm — A Capture — Prisoners Liberated, . 320

CHAPTER XXIV.

BATTLE OF BLACK JACK.

Capt. Pate's Expedition — Houses Burned and Prisoners Taken — Alliance between the Ruffians and Dragoons — Brutal Treatment of the Prisoners — Palmyra Plundered — A Preacher Outraged — Prisoners — Attack on Prairie City — Religion and War — A Boy Hero — The Reconnoitre — The Battle — The Surrender, ... 331

CHAPTER XXV.

BATTLE OF FRANKLIN.

State Prisoners — Franklin a Military Point — The Plan, or the Want of One — The Attack — Major Redpath — The "Music of the Spheres" — Evacuation of the Guard House — The Wakarusa Boys — The Retreat — Lawless Arrests — Indictments, ... 343

CHAPTER XXVI.

NIMROD WHITFIELD — DEATH OF CANTRAL — CAMPAIGNING IN THE WAR OF FREEDOM.

A New Proclamation — The Troops after Capt. Brown — Whitfield's Invasion — The Free-State Forces — The Young Guerillas — The March on Hickory Point — The Troops enter Brown's Camp — Pate and his Fellow-prisoners Released — The Border Ruffians Dispersed "upon their honor" — Cantral taken Prisoner — Reconnoitring — A Capture — The Dragoons — The Topeka Boys at Willow Springs — Death of Cantral, ... 356

CHAPTER XXVII.

SACKING OF OSAWATTOMIE.

An Appeal — A Visit to the Dragoons — What the Dragoons Did — Attack on Osawattomie — A Masterly Retreat — "Holding Out" against the Abolitionists, ... 370

CHAPTER XXVIII.

A CHAPTER OF OUTRAGES.

The Governor gets Alarmed — A Warning — Law and Order Operations on the Indians — A Letter of Invitation — Mr. Bailey's Statement — C. H. Barlow's Statement — Mr. Baldwin's Statement — A Fearful Letter — Missouri River Piracy, ... 377

CHAPTER XXIX.

DISPERSION OF THE LEGISLATURE.

Preparations for the Fourth — Federal Troops supersede the Ruffians — A Proclamation — Legislature Convenes — Military Correspondence — A Resolution — A String of Proclamations — Troops enter Topeka — Both Branches of the Legislature Dispersed — Troops Retire, ... 392

CHAPTER XXX.

CLOSING CHAPTER ON THE STATE OF CONQUERED KANSAS.

THE CONQUEST OF KANSAS.

INTRODUCTORY CHAPTER.

Little more than two years ago Kansas was closed to emigration. The remnants of numerous and powerful tribes were scattered over the eastern portion of the territory, on reserves given to them by government. These reserves embraced a considerable portion of the country adjacent to the Missouri river, and one hundred and fifty miles west of it. This is the richest and most available portion of the territory. Besides bordering on the Missouri, it includes the Kaw and its numerous tributaries; the head waters of the Osage and Arkansas rivers, and the many rivulets and streams which flow into them. It is prairie country, the timber being chiefly confined to the banks of the creeks and rivers. These are so abundant, that, in the portion to which I allude, the prairies are rarely more than four or five miles across. The soil is rich and deep; a black loam, for two or three feet, on a porous clay subsoil. The prairies are all rolling, and in some spots even hilly. The soil rests on a limestone basis. A coarse, gray, carboniferous limestone rock constitutes the upper strata. This dips out on the face and crests of the hills and prairie knolls, and the broken and detached fragments of rock mark them with a rocky belt at certain elevations. Beneath this limestone lies a blue sandstone, compact, even, and easily worked; beneath that, a finer quality of limestone. The western and southern parts of the country I am describing rest on beds of the yellow and red sandstone. On many of the rivers and small creeks coal has already been found; from the indications, it is probably abundant throughout the territory. The soil is loose and deep, and eminently calculated to sustain crops in dry weather. The climate resembles that of Southern Illinois and Indiana, only it is much more salubrious and dry. The breeze blows fresh from the mountains, meeting no obstructions on the plains. There is always a breeze, often high winds.

When the traveller is ascending the Missouri river, as he approaches the mouth of the Kaw, he is travelling west; at that point he first sees Kansas soil. The Kaw or Kansas river flows from the west. From its mouth the Missouri river takes a bend, and runs nearly due north for a considerable distance. From the mouth of the Kaw river, on the right bank, the boundary line between Kansas and Missouri runs directly south. The Kaw river thus runs diagonally through the eastern part of the territory. Immediately at the point of confluence between the Kaw and Missouri lies the Wyandot reserve. It is small, extending six miles from the mouth. It is densely timbered. The tribe is not numerous, but they are comparatively civilized. They have mostly good farms and good houses for the West. They are wealthy, many of them having intermarried with the whites.

Immediately above the Wyandot begins the Delaware reservation. The Wyandot was a purchase from the Delaware. The Delaware reserve is a large tract of country, chiefly prairie, but well timbered. It borders the Kaw on the north side, and runs up for forty miles. Ten miles wide of the northern part has been ceded, and will be sold to the highest bidder, under treaty. This is now covered with the settlements and claims of white men. Towns and future cities have been located upon it. The Delawares have been a powerful tribe, and several thousands of them are still on the reserve. They cultivate but little land. A few good farms are scattered along the military road, and a few patches and small farms may be seen elsewhere; but they are indolent, semi-barbarous, and depend chiefly on their annuities. They are unwilling to sell the remainder of their land. I do not think they can successfully mix with the whites. Their reserve is one of the most beautiful tracts of prairie and woodland, and lies in position to give it eminent commercial value. Immediately above the Delaware reserve is a strip of land belonging to the Kaw half-breeds. Above that, and on both sides of the Kaw, lies the Potawattomie reserve. It is a large, square tract, consisting of the finest land and timber, and the greater part of it lies, to all intents and purposes, a wilderness. A wilderness I fear it will remain, if the blossoms and fruit of civilization are to spring from the efforts of these Indians. They are like the Delawares, only "much more so." The Delawares are better familiarized with the whites, and possess in more eminent degree the marks of whiskey civilization. The Potawattomies, Kaws, Sacs, and Foxes, and several other lesser tribes, are of the Indians, Indianish. They are only one remove from the tomahawk and wigwam, and, take it all in all, I do not know if that remove is for the better.

The Kickapoo reserve lies between the Kaw and the Missouri. It is a tract of some ten by twenty miles. It touches the head-waters of the Grasshopper and the Stranger Creek. This is a fine prairie country, resembling in all essential points the Delaware reserve. The Kickapoos, unlike the "Rangers" of the same name, are comparatively civilized; but it is Indian civilization at best. Further north, and close to the Nebraska line, which is the base line of the surveys, there are a few small tribes scattered on petty reserves, some of them on the Missouri river, and some back of it.

To the south of the Kaw, and stretching upwards of thirty miles to the west from the Missouri frontier, lies the Shawnee reserve. The reserve borders the Kaw from a point near its mouth, and stretches far enough to the southward to be nearly square. This reserve consists mostly of high-rolling prairies. The timber is not so plentiful here as on some other parts, but those most familiar with it think there is enough. Limestone rocks on the prairie hills are very plenty, although confined, as in all such cases, to narrow strips and belts. These rocky belts are more common and striking on the prairie hills along the valley of the Kaw than in other parts of the territory. The Shawnee reserve is very fine land. I do not consider it the finest in the territory; but its contiguity to the richest and most thickly-settled part of Missouri gives it a value. The Shawnees are semi-civilized, and are, I think, more industrious than the majority of the Indians.

2

Many of them are farmers, and, in their houses, property, and management, resemble the poorer class of settlers in the West. They are half-educated, half-evangelized, half-labor*ized*, half-whiskeyfied, half-white man, and half-Indian. As no white man has been allowed to settle on these reserved lands, there are, of course, no legal preëmptions upon them; yet they have all been staked off. Scarcely a merchant or storekeeper's clerk — in fact, scarcely any one about Westport and Independence — but has a "claim staked out" thereabouts. These claims rest on a bowie-knife-and-revolver basis, and may prove good if the Indian and land agents are sufficiently rascally, and those who may incline to be contestants are sufficiently timid. These claims have mostly been taken during the various warlike and election raids on the free-state settlers; for the Shawnee reserve lies out from Westport, and is between the Missouri frontier and the New England settlements in the valley of the Kaw.

There is a great road, leading out from Independence and Westport into the territory, which has hitherto been an important thoroughfare. After it has entered the territory for a few miles it forks. One fork, bending up through the territory to the southwest, is the Santa Fe trail; the other, after crossing the Shawnee reserve, runs up between the Kaw and Wakarusa, crossing the former below Fort Riley, and leading out towards Fort Laramie. It is the California road. On the first of these roads the commerce with New Mexico has passed. Along the other, for years back, there has been a stream of human life pouring out from the States, carrying with it the elements for a new empire on the Pacific. Besides these roads, there are other two main roads or trails starting from Leavenworth, which, in business, are superseding the others; one a California road from Leavenworth to Laramie, the other by Fort Riley to Santa Fe. The travellers from every portion of the United States, who have passed over these roads for the last few years, have noted Eastern Kansas. As they crossed its streams, and looked down from the high prairie knolls upon the scene of fertility and beauty, marked the feathery outlines of timber which fringe the numerous streams, and observed the deep black prairie loam, not flat, but beautifully picturesque and rolling, they saw, in these indications of natural wealth and beauty, the seat of a future empire, a glorious state, lying at the feet of a Western commerce, long neglected, but great in the future. As they passed on through these rich valleys, and finally struck the coarse sandy soil, covered by a sparse buffalo-grass, they halted, ere they entered the regions of plain and barrenness, to fix on their memories a more definite picture to carry with them, and make this a future El Dorado to their wandering thoughts and wandering footsteps, which, in all their weary peregrinations, are never fated to press a rival of this "Italy of America and garden-spot of the world."

Many of these California emigrants are now in Kansas. Amongst others, Dr. Charles Robinson, while on his overland route some years ago, left the train, while the oxen and mules were picking their supper from the slopes that fall towards the Wakarusa, and took a stroll to look at the country, so new and full of interest. Amidst the tall prairie-grass, he traversed Mt. Oread. He stood on the spot where his house subsequently stood, and where its ashes now mark the footsteps of border ruffians, and looked down on the beautiful prairie knoll close to the river, sloping so gently in all directions. Before him was the site of the future Lawrence, then a beautiful wild, the tall trees on the left bank of the river throwing their dark shadows in the winding Kaw, which here murmured over a petty rapid.

Before the California emigration this territory was regarded as an Indian wild — a trackless and worthless waste. The frontier of Missouri was considered the outpost of civilization, and all beyond set down as a region of inhospitable barrenness, where the remnants of the once powerful Indian tribes could be gathered, and where they could be left until whiskey civilization, or the inexorable hand of fate, should effect their annihilation. Tribe after tribe was here located, and land set apart to them, with the promise that here they might permanently reside. A careful examination of this policy, and of the political record to trace the hands to which the country is indebted for it, will show that to the existence of the Missouri Compromise it must be attributed. By that restriction Kansas was shut to slavery. Western

Missouri is the seat of slavery in that state. It is chiefly confined to the few counties that border it. Western Missouri looked with an envious eye upon Kansas. It acted as if Kansas really belonged to it. Years before the American people heard a syllable about the repeal of the Missouri compromise, it was contemplated and discussed in Western Missouri. The propagandists, who, acting under the conviction that Kansas was lost to slavery, had tied it up with Indian treaties that would effectually prevent any attempted settlement, began to plan a double villany, a breach of faith with the aborigines, and a breach of the sacred compromise by which it had been hoped the vexed question was amicably settled. With covert and cunning movement the plot progressed; a plot that was not only to give Kansas to slavery, but to throw open the whole national territory to its embrace. But, even while Kansas was guaranteed to freedom, slavery was introduced. Nearly all of the Indian agents were slavery propagandists, and many of them owned slaves. The first slavery in the territory, however, was introduced by one who came professedly to preach the Gospel. Through all of the Indian tribes missionary stations and schools were scattered. These represented different denominations, some supported exclusively by the body that sent them, others in part by a per centage from the Indian payments, their chance for the latter being to some degree dependent on the esteem in which their "faith" and "practice" were held by the Indian agents.

Close to the frontier of Missouri, and within a few miles of Westport, stands one of the oldest missions in the territory, — the celebrated "Shawnee Mission," of the Methodist Church South. Three sections of the very finest land were granted by the Shawnees to this mission; besides which, no inconsiderable portion of government money and per centage on the Indian annuities have been expended in erecting three or four massive and extensive, but tasteless and filthy-looking, brick buildings, and in converting those three sections of fertile Indian land into a well-improved and beautiful farm, which I have heard estimated worth sixty thousand dollars. In the progress of events, and by a system of management which I cannot comprehend, much less explain, two sections of this farm, containing many of the best improvements, have fallen into the hands of the present head of the mission, the Rev. Tom Johnson.

Some twenty years ago, when this worthy came to Kansas, he was, as I have been emphatically told, "not worth a blanket." By "breaking the bread of life" to others, he seems haply to have acquired a reasonable portion of the baser, or "of the earth earthy," bread himself. The "laborer" was doubtless "worthy of his hire;" but whether it was hire for preaching the great Christian doctrine, "Whatsoever ye would that men should do unto you, do ye even so unto them," or in the vigorous inculcation of more critically orthodox doctrines on the relative duties of "servants" and "masters," is a point worth considering.

The Rev. Tom Johnson is a western man. Vulgar, illiterate, and coarse, I have heard his voice ring through the dingy brick wall of the Shawnee Mission in prayer, his style being characterized chiefly by extreme western provincialisms and very bad grammar. A violent pro-slavery partisan, he has been a useful tool in his way. His name may be found figuring in some of the most violent of the pro-slavery partisan meetings, and he was President of the Council of the Bogus Legislature which, within the walls of his mission, in the rooms dedicated to the service of Him who is the God of justice and truth, perpetrated one of the most flagrant outrages on right and justice recorded on the page of history. The Rev. Tom was elected in a district in which white men were not allowed to reside, with the exception of the few religious missions, and federal officers in the shape of Indian agents; his constituency coming chiefly from Westport, Mo. This worthy is said to have first introduced slavery into Kansas. He introduced and held slaves at the time when the existence of the restriction rendered it a violation of the spirit of the temporal law.

I conversed with one of the most intelligent of the Delaware chiefs on the political sentiments of his tribe. He told me they were nearly all free-state men, except a few on the south side of the reserve, close to the Shawnee country. On inquiry why these were pro-slavery, he shook his head, and said,

"There is no sense in it; for not one of them will ever be rich enough to own a nigger, or take care of him if they had him. It is these preachers who tamper with them. They believe everything they say."

Does not this out-Jesuit Jesuitism? I only mention these facts in this connection to show the means used to rob Kansas from freedom, and that the first step in the conquest was done under the shadow of the banner of the Prince of Peace. I would merely exhibit the point of all this by stating that when the treaties were arranged, a year and a half ago, the portion of the funds dedicated to religious uses fell into the hands of this Methodist Mission; the Quaker and Baptist Missions, in the same locality, which had also labored long in the field of Shawnee heathenism, were left out. Perhaps this was because it was conceived that the positions of these bodies would sustain the more republican theory of religious support, — on the *voluntary* principle; perhaps, because the agent was a pro-slavery man, and, in point of fact, a Missourian.

In the fall of 1853 the plot for the conquest of Kansas matured. In the struggle which ensued, the breach of faith with the Indians was comparatively lost sight of. It required no spirit of divination to foresee that, in opening the territory to a white population, the semi-barbarous occupancy of the finest lands by the Indians would inevitably terminate in some manner. I do not know whether the originators of the Kansas Nebraska Bill contemplated an amalgamation of the whites and Indians, to vindicate the faith of treaties and the progress of American civilization westward. If so, it was a blunder. Some few of the more intelligent and industrious Indians may be absorbed in the population of Kansas, but the great mass can neither use nor be used by civilization. There is no honorable escape from the dilemma in which the Kansas Bill places these matters. To leave the tribes on closely-guarded reserves would be a step eminently prejudicial to the best interests of a civilized community, and would be unjust and inhumane to the Indians themselves. To permit them to hold farms in individual occupancy, and thus merge and sink their tribe in the community, although the most just arrangement, would soon, in the progress of whiskey civilization, reduce them to a fraction of what they are, beggars and plagues to society. To deprive them of the power of selling these farms would only reduce them to the acute point of misery at an earlier date, and be a nuisance in the society they thus obstructed. A more humane policy would contemplate the extradition of the tribes — the less civilized portion — to wilds further west, where their nomadic and indolent habits would not expose them so surely to starvation, and where they would not be thrown in contact with a civilization with which they were not prepared to grapple.

Such are the Indian aspects of the Kansas question; grave and important considerations, which the din of political strife has caused to be too much overlooked, but which appeal to the intelligent statesman and the humane citizen.

That the design of the law organizing the Territory of Kansas was to make it a slave state, has since been conclusively shown by the agencies since set to work to remove the *unforeseen* obstacles which have arisen in the path of such a scheme. If further evidence were wanting, it could be obtained from the testimony of the actors themselves. Dr. Stringfellow, while under oath before the committee of Congress, stated that such "was the design of the Kansas Nebraska Bill;" and, when reminded of the political theories by which the northern supporters of that measure attempted to vindicate this position, rejoined, "That was all Buncombe — who believes that?" He stated that such were not only the objects of the organic law, but that the executive, and those who carried it through, so understood it, and added, that it was the expectation that the emigration from Western Missouri would quickly settle the question. He also states that it was the Eastern Emigrant Aid Societies that first threw doubt upon the success of this scheme, thereby causing trouble. But, to a question from Mr. Sherman, he admitted that the influx of any free-state settlers, sufficient to produce the same result, let them come in any way, would have caused trouble.

There is not the slightest doubt but such is the true state of the case. The two policies of the free and slave states are so opposite and hostile, and they could only triumph over each other to the so serious detriment of the defeated party, that the expedient of inviting them to settle their respective claims on the soil of a future empire, in dispute, is madness, and preëminently stupid. It is simply a reference of the case to fraud and violence; for intelligent and impartial popular voting can no more decide on the claims of these two interests, than they could decide on the claims of republicanism and absolute despotism, or decide for the delicate sentiment we call "religion of the heart."

The Kansas Nebraska Bill, or Organic Law of the territory, failed to define with sufficient clearness the rights of the settlers to the soil they were thus invited to occupy. It failed to secure the purity of the elective franchise. The federal courts it provided for referred the adjudication of cases involving the lives and dearest rights of the settlers to a set of men, the appointees of the executive, and the tools of the faction that used him. These and many other minor defects were designed, and have played an eminent part in the conquest of Kansas.

The startling feature of the organic law of the Territory of Kansas, and one the fierce discussion of which caused many of its other dangerous features to be overlooked, is contained in the following:

"That the constitution, and all laws of the United States not locally inapplicable, shall have the same force and effect within the Territory of Kansas as elsewhere within the United States, *except the* eighth section of the act preparatory to the admission of Missouri into the Union, approved March 6th, 1820, which, *being inconsistent with the principles of non-intervention by Congress with slavery* in the states AND TERRITORIES, as recognized by the legislation of 1850, commonly called the compromise measures, is hereby declared INOPERATIVE AND VOID, it being the true intent and meaning of the act not to legislate slavery into any state or *territory*, or exclude it therefrom; but to leave the *people* thereof perfectly *free* to form and regulate their *domestic institutions* in their own way, subject only to the constitution of the United States: Provided, that nothing herein contained shall be construed to revive or put in force any law or regulation which may have existed prior to the act of the 6th of March, 1820, either protecting, establishing, prohibiting, or abolishing slavery."

Such was the repealing clause. And in section nineteenth there occurs the following:

"And when admitted as a state or states, the said territory, or any portion of the same, shall be received into the Union *with* or without slavery, as their constitutions may prescribe at the time of their admission."

The organic law passed the houses of Congress after a protracted and memorable struggle. It filched northern votes from northern interests by means of a political theory styled "squatter sovereignty." It dealt a fearful blow at the prosperity of republican institutions everywhere, under the specious plea of "saving the Union." No sooner was it passed than the struggle began. The following is from the report of the committee of Congress founded on the testimony before them:

"Within a few days after the organic law passed, and as soon as its passage could be known on the border, leading citizens of Missouri crossed into the territory, held squatter meetings, and then returned to their homes. Among the resolutions are the following:

"That we will afford protection to no abolitionist as a settler of this territory.

"That we recognize the institution of slavery as already existing in this territory, and advise slaveholders to introduce their property as early as possible."

The leaders of the pro-slavery propaganda telegraphed to their friends in Missouri, who took steps at the earliest moment to secure many of the best locations, which they had looked out before. Treaties were secretly made with the Indians, the chiefs being taken to Washington for the purpose; and, as soon as certain tracts of land were ceded, the information was telegraphed by the slavery extensionists, who held the executive ear, to those in Missouri, who were prepared to take possession of the best localities before others could know that they were open to settlement. Other tracts of ceded land, which by terms of the treaty were not properly open to squatters, were taken possession of by Missourians, and the executive has winked at such infractions. The invasions of the Delaware lands were first made by Missourians; but settlers from other localities, seeing that this was done with impunity, and that the whole of the land would be secured and closed against them in this way, went on to these lands also; and, after they began to do so, went on in far greater numbers. I subjoin the protest of the Delaware chiefs:

"We, the chiefs, head men and counsellors of the Delaware nation, hereby notify our white brethren that all settlements on the lands ceded by the Delaware Indians, by treaty at Washington, dated 6th May, 1854, are in violation of said treaty; and that we in no wise give our will or consent to such settlement; and if persisted in by our white brethren, we shall appeal to our great father, the President of the United States, for protection."

The following are the outlines of the treaties made with the different tribes in Kansas, and the dates of such treaties. They indicate the amount still reserved for the use of the Indians:

On the 25th March, 1854, a treaty was concluded with the Otoes and Missourias, by which they ceded all their land in the territory, except a tract on the Big Blue, ten by twenty-five miles.

By treaty, dated March 25th, 1854, the Kickapoos ceded all their lands, except one hundred and fifty thousand acres, which were set apart for the western portion of their cession, and lie on the head waters of the Grasshopper, towards the Nebraska line.

On the 30th March, 1854, the Kaskaskias, Weasteorias, and Pinckashaws, ceded all their lands, except one hundred and sixty acres for each soul in their united tribes. The tribe to have ninety days for selection after the surveys are approved.

On the 6th May, 1854, the Delawares concluded a treaty, by which all their lands were ceded, except a strip along the north side of the Kansas river, ten miles wide, and running forty miles west. The ceded lands to be set up at auction after they were surveyed, and sold to the highest bidder, for behoof of the tribe; deducting the expense of survey and sale.

By treaty with the Shawnees, dated May 10th, 1854, all of their land was ceded, except two hundred thousand acres, to be selected between the Missouri state line and a parallel thirty miles west of it. The Shawnee families located throughout the reserve are to be allowed ninety days from the approval of the surveys to locate two hundred acres for each member. These locations to be deducted from the two hundred thousand acres.

By treaty, dated 18th May, 1854, the Sacs and Foxes ceded their lands, except fifty sections of six hundred and forty acres each. This is to be located in a suitable place, and in a body.

By these treaties many thousand acres of land were thrown open, or will be speedily thrown open, to settlement. Claims began to dot the surface of the country. In spite of a systematic and preconcerted effort on the part of Missouri to get possession of the territory, such was the enterprising character of citizens from other states, and the wide notice given of the opening of Kansas by the fierce discussion on the repeal of the Missouri Compromise, that ere long free-state settlers began to preponderate. Still, all the political influence, the federal offices and patronage, were thrown into the hands of the slavery extensionists. One or two mistakes in these appointments were made; but they were promptly and villanously remedied. The following editorial from the Washington *Union*, the executive organ, on this point, is deeply significant:

" A gentleman in Virginia calls our attention to the fact that the enemies of President Pierce in the South lay peculiar stress upon his appointment of Governor Reeder as proof of his willingness to favor free-soilers, and asks us whether, at the time of his appointment, Governor Reeder was regarded as a sound *national* Democrat. It is in our power to answer this question with entire confidence, and to say that down to the time that Governor Reeder went to Kansas to assume the duties of governor of the territory, there had not been, as far as we ever heard, or as far as the President ever heard, a breath of suspicion as to his entertaining free-soil sentiments. He was appointed under the strongest assurances that he was strictly and honestly a *national* man. We are able to state, further, on very reliable authority, that *whilst* Governor Reeder was in Washington, at the time of his appointment, he *conversed with Southern gentlemen on the subject of slavery*, and assured them that he had no more scruples in buying a slave than a horse, and he regretted that he had not money to purchase a number to carry with him to Kansas. We have understood that he repeated the same sentiments on his way to Kansas. We will repeat, what we have had occasion to say more than once heretofore — that no man has ever been appointed by President Pierce to office who was not at the time understood by him to be a faithful adherent of the Baltimore platform of 1852, on the subject of slavery. If any appointment were made contrary to this rule, it was done under a misapprehension as to the appointees. We may add that the evidences of Gov. Reeder's soundness were so strong that President Pierce was slower than many others to believe him a free-soiler after he had gone to Kansas. It is, therefore, the grossest injustice to refer to Gov. Reeder's appointment as proof of the President's willingness to favor free-soilers."

While such were the preparations, on the part of Missouri and the pro-slavery propagandists, to seize Kansas and make it a slave state, they were met by conflicting elements. It is a fact, which all subsequent developments will prove, that the free-state cause has, during the struggles, rested *mainly* on individual enterprises. Societies *have* been formed to settle the territory, and, while these had strictly no political cast, their tendencies were to send in a population favorable to a free-state policy. The following companies have been, and now are, in active operation.

American Settlement Company, New York City. This company founded the Council City settlement. The secretary is Theodore Dwight, 110 Broadway, New York.

The N. England Emigrant Aid Company, Massachusetts. This company has been more instrumental than all others in facilitating emigration, and in introducing capital and useful improvements into the territory. Near one half of the saw-mills in the territory were brought there by its capital. Towns have been laid off, and the process of settling a new country facilitated in an eminent degree. Never, until this and other kindred companies led the way, has capital gone ahead of labor, as a pioneer in the work of employing rich natural resources. It has also aided emigrants in getting to the territory, by carrying on emigration at "wholesale prices." On account of its activity, and the important results flowing from it, it has been intensely hated and misrepresented by the pro-slavery propagandists. It is conducted by Messrs. William B. Spooner, J. M. S. Williams, Eli Thayer, S. Cabot, Jr., M. D., R. P. Waters, Le Baron Russell, M. D., Charles J. Higginson, and E. E. Hale. Its secretary is Thomas H. Webb ; and its agents are Gen. S. C. Pomeroy and Gen. C. Robinson.

Then there were the VEGETARIAN SETTLEMENT COMPANY, the NEW YORK KANSAS LEAGUE, the OCTAGON SETTLEMENT COMPANY, and some other minor organizations to facilitate and unite emigration.

By these means more good blood has been poured into the "body politic" of Kansas than has ever flowed into any other new territory in its youth. Not only has capital preceded labor, but a high degree of intelligence and refinement has been introduced among the pioneers. The settlers from the Western States, also, have generally been of the better class. The coon-hunting, soft-soap-currency tribe of squatters, who have usually officiated as pioneers, have been superseded by a class who had to keep improvement on the gallop in order to retain their former habits.

The entrance of this class of settlers was regarded with the utmost jealousy and hatred by the Missouri slavery propagandists. They viewed it as an infraction of their rights, and, well knowing that this class of settlers were, and would be, hostile to slavery, considered their extradition from the territory essential to securing their ends. Early in July, 1854, about the time the first Eastern emigration came to the territory, the following resolutions were adopted at a meeting in Westport, Missouri. They fairly indicate a sentiment extensively prevalent in that state, and from which much of the disturbance has arisen.

"*Resolved,* That this association will, whenever called upon by any of the citizens of Kansas Territory, hold itself in readiness together to assist and remove any and all emigrants who go there under the auspices of the Northern Emigrant Aid Societies.

"*Resolved,* That we recommend to the citizens of other counties, particularly those bordering on Kansas Territory, to adopt regulations similar to those of this association, and to indicate their readiness to operate in the objects of this first resolution."

These were no Buncombe, effervescing resolutions; they were the fearful index of what has proved a fearful state of affairs. They were, also, prone to regard all settlers from Eastern or Northern States — in fact all who were not in favor of slavery — as "Emigrant Aid people." Nor have they treated free-state people, whom they have learned to have no connection with any society, a whit better than the others.

The amenities of life, the hospitality for which Southern people are justly reputed, were forgotten in the bitterness of the feud. When one stranger met another the question was where the other "came from," and his politics on the slavery question. Such was the aspect of affairs when the struggle began, and what we have been describing the preliminary steps. Then began the strife provoked by the repeal of the Missouri Compromise, and which left no alternative but a struggle or submission; — a warfare predicted by William H. Seward, in the United States Senate, in those memorable words:

"Come on, then, gentlemen of the slave states! Since there is no escaping your challenge, I accept it on the behalf of Freedom. We will engage in competition for the virgin soil of Kansas, and God give the victory to the side that is stronger in numbers, as it is in right."

CHAPTER II.

THE FIRST INVASION.

THE cabins of squatters had begun to dot the face of the country, and the music of the pioneer's axe was ringing amongst the timber that shaded the water-courses of Kansas. A code of "Squatter Laws" was adopted, which had application to the valley of the Kaw, and in which mutual assistance was pledged to sustain the "claims" taken, in the absence of other means of legalizing these inchoate titles.

It was in July, 1854, that the first company of Eastern emigrants arrived in Kansas. They were some thirty in number, and came under the guidance of Mr. Charles Branscomb. They located on the present site of Lawrence. It is a fine prairie knoll, close on the Kaw river, and the first point at which the prairie touches the river. It stands some six miles north of the mouth of the Wakarusa, which flows four miles behind Lawrence, directly to the south. Immediately behind Lawrence, about half a mile from the river, a bold hill, or prairie promontory, rises abruptly to the altitude of some eighty or a hundred feet. This is Mount Oread. When the first Eastern settlers reached Lawrence they found that some two or three Missourians laid claim to the spot. One of these had thrown a few logs together, but was living in Missouri. The settlers succeeded in "buying out" those who appeared to have any feasible claim. They pitched their tents on the knoll, close to the river, and the members of the party immediately scattered out, locating claims. In two weeks more they were joined by a second and larger company, numbering sixty or seventy, with whom came Dr. Charles Robinson and Mr. S. C. Pomeroy. It was at this time that the Lawrence Association was formed. Several Wyandot "floats" were located on the site, the city being laid out two miles square. These Wyandot floats are transferable rights, by which each of the Wyandot Indians could locate a section of land, six hundred and forty acres, on any unoccupied public land, and hold it in fee simple.

Immediately all claims near or adjoining Lawrence were taken. A saw-mill had been brought, but was still at Kansas city. Some of the emigrants, homesick, and unused to the privations of a pioneer life, returned after but a few days' experience. Several tents were scattered on the knoll that overlooks the Kaw, and a large tent was a public or general rendezvous. Preparations were made for more durable residence; but Lawrence was in this embryo stage of nomadic simplicity when the first border ruffian expedition came against it.

Rumors of "Yankee settlements" in the valley of the Kaw had been received along the border counties of Missouri, and had awakened a bloodthirsty wish to exterminate them. These Missourians regarded Kansas as delivered over to them by the Kansas-Nebraska bill; hence their fury against any interlopers who might jeopardize the chances of making it a slave state. The Yankees heard of the storm that was brewing, but had not travelled all the way to Kansas to be frightened off by a rumor.

Reader, did you ever see a border ruffian? A *bona fide*, Simon pure, unadulterated "Puke"?* After all, they are a good deal like the ordinary run of men, or rather like the ordinary run of "hard cases." What I mean is, they are neither one-eyed ogres nor "three-fingered Jacks." Still, they are decided characters. Most of them have been over the plains several times, — if they have not been over the plains, the probability is, they have served through the war in Mexico, or seen a "deal of trouble in Texas;" or, at least, run up and down the Missouri river often enough to catch imitative inspiration from the catfish aristocracy, and penetrate the sublime mysteries of euchre or poker. I have often wondered where all the hard customers on

* The *Puke* is the indignant term applied to the native of Missouri, as *Hoosier* belongs to Indiana, *Sucker* to Illinois, &c. &c.

the Missouri frontier come from. They seem to have congregated here by some law of gravity unexplainable. Perhaps the *easy* exercise of judicial authority in frontier countries may explain their fancy for them. Amongst these worthies a man is estimated by the amount of whiskey he can drink; and if he is so indiscreet as to admit he "drinks no liquor," he is set down as a dangerous character, and shunned accordingly. Imagine a fellow, tall, slim, but athletic, with yellow complexion, hairy faced, with a dirty flannel shirt, or red, or blue, or green, a pair of common-place, but dark-colored pants, tucked into an uncertain altitude by a leather belt, in which a dirty-handled bowie-knife is stuck rather ostentatiously, an eye slightly whiskey-red, and teeth the color of a walnut. Such is your border ruffian of the lowest type. His body might be a compound of gutta percha, Johnny-cake, and badly-smoked bacon; his spirit, the *refined* part, old Bourbon, "double rectified;" but there is every shade of the border ruffian.

Your judicial ruffian, for instance, is a gentleman; that is, as much of a gentleman as he can be without transgressing on his more purely legitimate character of border ruffian. He is of the Judge Leonard, or Colonel Woodson, or Hon. M. Oliver class. As "occasional imbibing" is not a sin, his character at home is irreproachable; and when he goes abroad into the territory, for instance, he does not *commit* any act of outrage, or vote himself, but, after "aiding and comforting" those who do, returns, feeling every inch a *gentleman.*

Then there is your less conservative border ruffian *gentleman*, of the Sheriff Jones, or Col. Boone, or Gen. Richardson type. They are not so nice in distinctions, and, so far from objecting, rather like to take a hand themselves; but they dress like gentlemen, and are so, after a fashion. Between these and the first-mentioned large class there is every shade and variety; but it takes the whole of them to make an effective brigade; and *then* it is not perfect without a barrel of whiskey. The two *gentlemanly* classes of ruffians are so for political effect, or because they fancy it is their interest. The lower class are pro-slavery ruffians, merely because it is the prevalent kind of rascality; the inference is, that they would engage in any other affair in which an equal amount of whiskey might be drunk, or as great an aggregate of rascality be perpetrated.

Such was the kind of customers who presented themselves to the astonished gaze of the early citizens of Lawrence, while it spread its tent-like, butterfly wings, just emerging from its chrysalis state, on the banks of the Kaw.

They came in wagons, and were truly an "army with banners." Every wagon appeared to be supplied with a piece of cloth, which was patched something to represent a star, or other more mysterious border ruffian symbols, and also a jug of whiskey. They had a fiddler or two with them, their nearest approximation to "martial music." They might be styled the shot-gun, or backwoods' rifle, brigade. In a representation of "The Forty Thieves" they would have been invaluable, with their grim visages, their tipsy expression, and, above all, their oaths and unapproachable swagger. As the first detachment only numbered eighty men, they took to the north side of the ravine, which runs through town, this being the Rubicon between them and the Yankees. When there they proceeded to swagger and drink, and shoot at marks, and swear by all that was good and bad that they would exterminate all the d—d Yankee abolitionists that dare come to Kansas. Towards the evening of the day they came a reinforcement of some twenty-five more arrived; but they either did not deem themselves strong enough yet, or had adopted some plan of operations requiring delay.

Night came on. The belligerents were within gunshot. The free-state settlers had watched the enemy with the utmost care, but had abstained from warlike demonstrations until they knew what these men intended to do. And yet it was with a feeling of deep anxiety that Dr. Robinson stood by the tent and looked across the ravine towards the camp-fires of the border ruffians. When these had first taken up their position across the ravine, three of the free-state settlers went over to request their business, and the meaning of the warlike demonstrations. To this a message was sent back that the "abolitionists" must take away their tents and leave the territory, or they would be "cleared out;" and that they might have until morning to do it *peaceably.*

There was no disguising the fact; the "tug of war" was before them.

All night long the sentries paced around the tents of young Lawrence. Sleepless and watchful, the leaders listened to every loud cricket-chirp, or watched each dancing fire-fly that flitted between them and the enemy. The brave indignantly watched, and carefully examined their guns, with clenched teeth, and cool determination. The timid and fearful shrank in horror from monstrous bowie-knife visions and dreams of gaping wounds; and a very few of the *conservatives*, who wished to be "right on the record," suggested that, "after all, *some* of the free-state men *did talk too freely*, and, upon the whole, it might be better to go back *till the thing was settled;*" but such counsels were, with few dissenting voices, voted down. Midnight came, and the noisy bivouac of the drunken ruffians was hushed. The sentinels paced their rounds. The stars twinkled away up in the heaven of God, like so many pure eyes looking down on this beautiful spot which the murderous hand of man threatened to disfigure with his brother's blood. Not a sound broke on the ear of the brave or timid listener, save the murmuring of the Kaw over its rocky rapid, or the buzz and hum of insects.

Day at last dawned on that weary summer's night. With the daylight the ruffians bestirred themselves, and, by the time they got breakfast, they were reinforced by another party, which increased their numbers to one hundred and fifty men. This last accession made their arrival with shrieks and yells, and the border ruffians being now in force, sent over a formal notification that, "the tent must be taken down, and all their effects gathered together, preparatory to leave by ten o'clock," and that the "abolitionists must leave the territory, never more to return to it;" all of which was of course "respectfully submitted," and just as respectfully and firmly declined.

As the Missourians had said they were coming over the ravine at ten o'clock, and as a general scrimmage about that time was to be expected, about sixty of the free-state men (the greater part of them), all who could get arms, formed into a military company, and were put on drill parade in front of the tent.

Ten o'clock came, but the enemy came not. About half an hour afterwards another *ultimatum* came. "They could have another half-hour to remove *that tent*, and get ready to leave." After that, if they refused to comply, they *were* coming, and every d—d one of them would be "put to the bowie-knife," or shot. "This was in earnest."

The half-hour passed away, and the free-state squatters kept going through their "drill" by the tent. Again the ruffians sent a message, but not until they had some fierce discussion amongst themselves. It was now when this "finality" was delivered. The border ruffians "would give them exactly till one o'clock to *take away that tent* and leave. Nothing but a *desire to prevent the effusion of blood* induced them to make this final proposition. If not complied with, they were coming over exactly at that hour—*they were*—and they would not hold themselves responsible for what might happen." Conscientious border ruffians!

The "wee short hour" went by. A summer's sun blazed down on the trodden grass, and the tents, and the squatter soldiers. The latter were beginning to appreciate the joke. The timid began to grow courageous. The hearty laugh of Dr. Robinson, as he said, "They are not going to come over, I will guarantee," acted as an additional sedative.

By half-past twelve the enemy had formed in martial array. They were drawn up in line over the ravine, in situations where the free-state men could *see* they were *all ready to march*. One o'clock came and passed, and again a messenger came over.

"Just ten minutes to move that tent."

He was received with a shout of laughter.

Meanwhile the border ruffians kept going through their evolutions. They paraded, and marched, and countermarched, and threatened, and swore. After noon they drank none, for their liquor was out; but how they did swear! "The army in Flanders" never swore "more terribly." They first d—d the "abolitionists" for cowards, and then for "fools, who did not know their *danger*."

At two o'clock P. M., one valiant man proposed that "we should have no more *mercy* on 'em; but go over and pitch into 'em." — "That 's the talk!" cried another; "give 'em h—l, d—m 'em!" "That 's it!" — "Put 'er through!" — "Let 'er rip!" came from many voices.

At three o'clock P. M., a man with a conservative aspect made a speech, and proposed that fresh negotiations and "*a little more time*" be sent over. This was denounced by a fire-eater, who "did not wish to make a fool of himself." Fierce debate raged between the ruffians, and, one or two of them having taken occasion to call some of the others "cowards," there was a prospect that there really would be a fight.

It was nearly sundown before this wrangle terminated, and it only did so when the party split, and some sixty of these bowie-knife and revolver heroes parted from the rest, and started back for Westport, swearing they would n't keep company with such a set of fellows. After the first party left, the remainder did not feel remarkably easy, as the "d—d abolitionists" did not appear to be a whit more willing to remove their tent. As twilight came on, they began to break up and go off in small parties, and the last lot went off in a hurry, shortly after dark, as if they fancied it was "devil take the hindmost." And thus gloriously retired the first invasion, emulating the King of France, who,

"With twenty thousand men,
Marched up the hill, and then marched down again."

Would that all the attacks on Lawrence had been thus managed, and thus terminated! It must not be supposed that these men were all cowards. There were, doubtless, amongst them many men who would have fought bravely, and made desperate enemies. Many of them, however, must have been cowards, and all were acting in a situation in which a man is not apt to be very brave. They had engaged thoughtlessly in an expedition, dictated by others, and when they encountered a firm nerve, and the stern aspect of deliberate attack in an unrighteous quarrel presented itself, they quailed before it. In such cases the danger is chiefly from an accidental collision that precipitates hostilities.

At this point I would mention another humorous incident that occurred a few days before what I have just narrated. It is rather on the other side. It happened with the first company of thirty, and before the second company arrived.

One of the company, Mr. T——, had some little doubt as to the courage and nerve of a few of his companions. He was desirous of trying them, and an opportunity offered. A rumor reached their camp that some slaves had run away from Missouri, — one of those tricks resorted to by the border ruffian leaders to exasperate their people. Although the story was without foundation, it afforded sufficient material for the project of our friend, who had heard it discussed in the company, and knew that most of them regarded this report started against them as a rather disagreeable bugbear.

Mr. T—— was out on a short journey, on horseback, when he met a half-breed Wyandot, — a very intelligent man, and so white that no one could detect the Indian blood in his veins. He was riding on a powerful mule, and might have passed very well for a border ruffian by more expert judges than the new-comers. Mr. T—— fell into conversation with him as they rode along, and, as they got on very good terms, our friend mentioned the joke he meant to play on some of his companions. He told the Wyandot the story about the runaway negroes, and asked him to go to the camp and represent himself as an officer from Missouri in search of them, and demand that assistance be rendered to make it, and see how many of them he could get. Our Wyandot, who appeared to have a fund of humor, readily agreed, and our friend T—— galloped ahead into camp to report that he had seen an *officer from Missouri*, who was "coming."

There was some little fluster when our man with the mule rode up. He appeared most consistently *stern*, and first demanded that the "niggers be given up." Several of the party undertook to explain to him that *they had not been there*. The man with the mule shook his head, and appeared dissatisfied.

"Look here," he said; "I don't want to be the means of bringing you folks into trouble; but I am an officer, and must do my duty. I hope you will meet the requirements of the law, and furnish me your aid to search for the niggers, who *I know* are here. If you refuse, I will have to go back and bring up a force *large enough* to make the search;" and the man on the mule looked sternly significant.

"Let me assure you, sir," began a very earnest and anxious-faced man, "let me assure you, upon my honor, that they are not here."

"Very likely, sir," was the dry response.

"I am positive — very positive."

"I don't dispute it," — sarcastically.

"But I pledge you solemnly that there are no niggers here; there *never* have been any here. We are not 'abolitionists,' sir. It is a vile libel we deny."

The man on the mule stroked his beard.

As it was evident that a majority present were inclined to pay no attention to his demands, the bogus officer rode out about two rods from the party, and, in a very impressive voice, said:

"Gentlemen, this is a very serious matter, and should be carefully weighed. I don't want to bring the Missourians upon you, who would only be glad of the opportunity to do so *legally*. I am anxious to prevent bloodshed and difficulty, and wish to know all those who are willing to vindicate the laws. Such of you as will assist me as a posse I desire to step over here, so that I may know them."

"Look here," said a conservative man to one of his companions; "had n't we better go, and save all trouble? There is no negro here, and it will show that we are not abolitionists!"

"No, d—n him!" responded the other; "he may hunt his niggers as long as he likes; that 's his business, not mine."

"O," said the other, angrily, "that incendiary way of talking won't do. It 's just fellows like you that get us in trouble."

One or two more were "conservative," and tried to persuade their comrades to fall in. "I 'll tell you what," said one, "I am as fond of standing up, when the right time comes, as any of you; but I want to make no bad steps. 'Let us keep right on the record,' and then we can maintain ourselves."

"Gentlemen," resumed the man on the mule, "let those who will sustain the law step this way."

About a half-dozen of the men, with an air of affected sternness, walked over, and one of them began telling the bogus negro-hunter that they were "law-abiding," and "no abolitionists;" to all of which Bogus manifested the utmost indifference.

A fresh and very impressive call for further volunteers having produced no effect, our friend T—— let the joke out, and Bogus, thanking the gentlemen for their kind assistance, and declining their further services, descended at once from his high-perched dignity and his mule, and laughed heartily while he chatted with the squatters. Those few who had been so anxious to keep "right on the record," got very sick of the joke, and I believe most of them left the territory.

CHAPTER III.

GOV. REEDER — THE FIRST ELECTION — THE BLUE LODGE.

The first officers appointed in the territory were A. H. Reeder, of Pennsylvania, Governor, — salary, $2,500; Daniel Woodson, of Arkansas, Secretary, — salary, $2,000. The officers of judiciary appointed were Samuel Dexter Lecompte, Chief Justice; Sanders N. Johnson and Rush Elmore, Associate Justices, with salaries of $2,000 each; Andrew J. Isaacs, Attorney, $250 and fees; and J. B. Donaldson, Marshal, — his salary being $300 and fees. These received their appointment for four years, commencing in 1854.

In October of the year 1854 Gov. Reeder arrived. As the connection this functionary has had with the affairs of the territory, first and last, is all-important, a slight sketch of him may be offered.

Andrew H. Reeder is a "Pennsylvania Dutchman,"— so reputed; but, beyond the mere fact of such extraction, he has no particular resemblance, except it be in rather a portly figure, slightly inclining to obesity. He is a gentleman of polish and considerable parts, and a most thorough lawyer. Rather past middle age, with hair inclining to gray, he yet stands as erect and firm as a grenadier. There is something in his goggle eyes at first repulsive; but you get familiarized to them, and to the curl of a magnificent gray moustache. He was always reputed a Democrat. When appointed, he was, and had been, a supporter of the organic act. He was an admirer of the "squatter sovereignty" feature, the ostensible democracy of which recommended the repeal of the Missouri Compromise to so many of the old Democrats. When he came to the territory he found that there was something more than abstract theory, or even fair popular voting, at work to settle the difficulties in Kansas. He came thoroughly impressed with the importance of sustaining the administration party, and would have sustained it to the end, if such course had been possible. Whether an honest indignation at the outrages Missouri was perpetrating on the territory, or a conviction of the impolicy and defeat of such a suicidal course, determined him, I know not. In any case, let him get credit for the position he took. Surrounded by party ties, liable to the charge of inconsistency, about which public men are generally too keenly sensible, almost every motive to induce him to compliance with the wishes of the slaveocracy existed, for whose behoof, and at whose instigation, the organic law was passed, and the officers appointed under it. A zealous advocate of that organic law and its theoretical apology, there was every motive to make him smooth over any difficulty, or oppose any movement, that would illustrate its fallacy. In these circumstances he was thrown into the struggle, and took the side of right and justice, even at the price of political ostracism. Gov. Reeder was too *strong* a man to make a good tool. What the border ruffians wanted was something pliant and docile, and Reeder had a will of his own; hence the jealousy, perhaps the beginning of the feud. No governor *could* conquer Kansas. The border ruffians knew it, and merely wanted to be permitted to do it themselves; but Reeder came to be governor, and governor he meant to be.

It has been falsely urged against him that he only took his position after his dismissal, and when he had no alternative. The following extract from one of the ablest border ruffian journals of Missouri, penned long before the March election, will indicate the prejudice with which the border ruffians regarded the governor:

"How little have our southern friends — impulsive, hospitable, and rash — understood the character of the Governor of Kansas! Many have often said, 'He will favor the South; his sympathies are with the South; but, coming from a free state, he dare not do it openly.' Upon what reasonable premises — upon what rational induction of the governor's acts and conduct — could such absurd hypothesis be predicated? 'We will yet make a proselyte of him,' said they. Such a proselyte as they would make of the shrewd, calculating, and far-sighted governor would be, to them, 'two-fold more the child of hell than he was before.' " [A remarkably candid admission, with a wide application. — AUTHOR.] "The developments that have already been made in the executive character are amply sufficient to found a sound conclusion in regard to his future course and intentions. Impulsive and unreflecting people! you have not scrutinized him closely. You have misread and mistranslated him. He has understood *your character* better than you have understood his. Affable and polite in outward manner, but cold, guarded, and designing within, — the external manner of a man wholly engrossed with self-aggrandizement and the steady accomplishment of his own private purposes. Possessing many qualities that go to make up a strong man, the executive character is yet deficient in one great essential. An infirmity of purpose, and a weak, nervous oscillation of mind, are idiosyncrasies with the Governor of Kansas. Governor he is, and would be senator hereafter! He is not without ambition — would play false — would wrongly win, and yet he fears to do it boldly like a man. He is a small nonpareil edition of Talleyrand and Metternich combined, without one spark or scintillation of the Jackson 'eternal!' in his whole composition.

"Isolated and alone upon the *frontier* he stood. In the midst of *gentlemen of high official character* and *talent*, the great 'non-committal' was distant and repulsive; for without the *encourage* of friends he *dared* not proclaim publicly that he was a free-soiler, and would do all, consistently with his official oath and dignity, to make Kansas a free state, as he had a right to say, and a right to do; for he knew not what evils the passions of an impulsive people, roused to their highest pitch in an exciting contest, might hurl around his devoted head. *No doubt*, in his midnight dreams, his Excellency saw his honor Judge *Lynch*, with his grave judicial aspect, sitting at the foot of his bed, remarking, with all the politeness of Richelieu to Baradas, that 'the court had taken his case in consideration, and decided that the *air* of Kansas did not agree with him.' "

There is something extremely refreshing in the closing portion of the article we quote. There is a candor in its admissions, only equalled by the coolness of its allusions to the "exciting contest" in which it admits Missouri to be engaged. We make no comments on the picture it draws, nor would we strike out one of its "lights or shadows."

When Reeder went to Kansas he was beset, not only by that class which generally dangle at the heels of governors, but by a more important class, representing both interests in the impending struggle. That he was, in those circumstances, "the great non-committal" — was "distant and repulsive," is probable. Gov. Reeder possessed no ordinary ability, and even a man of a higher order of talent would have found the circumstances perplexing. To these and his embarrassing political position we may attribute any errors or shortcomings which may have entailed trouble on Kansas. Perhaps the desire to appear impartial led him to tolerate certain evils which, however great, he would have had to travel a little out of his way to remedy.

In company with Gov. Reeder a Mr. Flenniken came to the territory. Mr. Flenniken was a candidate for delegate to Congress at the first election. He came in October, and the election was held in November. Some say he had admitted, on the way, that he was a candidate, and one witness before the committee testified to the fact.

Mr. Flenniken was a firm administration Democrat — a believer in squatter sovereignty, as "enunciated by the Kansas Nebraska bill." He came to Kansas full of ambition and political theories. As the accredited agent of a pure and unadulterated abstract Democracy, he came to uphold "squatter sovereignty," independent of abstractions. He was accused of being, first, pro-slavery, then non-committal, then free-soiler. In point of fact he was a genuine "squatter-sovereignty-as-enunciated" man. Fresh from the subtle theorizing on this position in the East, he fancied that the same seductive nonsense would hold good in Kansas and Missouri. In Kansas, however, he found it was "*slavery* as enunciated by the Kansas Nebraska bill." He made a great effort for a democratic impartiality on the question, and succeeded in being pretty generally suspected. His "*veni, vidi*" had no terminating "*vici*," for Mr. Whitfield had been nominated as the candidate of Platte County, and there they perfectly understood the matter.

Mr. Whitfield's position at that time was equivocal. Since then he has been candid and plain enough on the slavery question, in all conscience; but in that election he evaded the issue. Whatever might have been the understanding between him and the people of Platte, and Clay, and Jackson and Buchanan counties, he pretended that slavery was not the issue of the election in the territory. In this way he got many of the free-state men to vote for him. The people of the territory were not then conversant with *Kansas elections*. Mr. Whitfield looked like a gentleman, and he declared that he "was in favor of the people of the territory settling the question for themselves,"—the same specious theory; and upon it he got many votes, as some better, and, perhaps, a few worse men have done.

There was another candidate—Judge Wakefield. As a free-state man, the judge was unquestionable and reliable. He was a Western man, and no "abolitionist;" but, as he explained it in a speech we once heard him make, a "free-soiler up to the hub—hub and all." The judge is a character in his way. His public speeches and private conversation are characterized by a style and enunciation decidedly provincial, and his grammar sets up a standard somewhat independent of Lindley Murray; but he is sound and shrewd in his opinions and convictions, and honest to the core. The old gentleman is somewhat portly. He is a man with a presence, and had the choice been made, as Diedrich Knickerbocker tells us they elected magistrates in his time (by weight), the worthy judge would have distanced both of his competitors put together. Unfortunately the free-state men were divided, and had no great faith in either of their candidates. We honestly believe that the old judge was much the "smartest" of the three; the standard in neither case being very high. The worthy judge, moreover, was a specimen of that school, rapidly disappearing under the blows of young America, the "fine old gentlemen." With him the amenities of life were facts, and worth considering. Alas! the judge was doomed to be defeated, first by his friends and then by his enemies. In his own precinct

(Douglas), some four or five Missourians actually voted for him just to make game of him. They got him out to speak, and cheered him. They knew they were safe, and wanted to preface their career of despotism with a little malicious fun.

The following abstract exhibits the whole number of votes at this election for each candidate; the number of legal and illegal votes cast in each district; and the number of legal voters in each district in February following:

Abstract of Census, and Election of Nov. 29, 1854.

Districts, . .	Place of Voting.	Whitfield, . .	Wakefield, .	Flenniken, .	Scattering, .	Total, . . .	No. of Votes by Census,	Legal Votes,	Illegal Votes,
1	Lawrence, ...	46	188	51	15	300	369	300	—
2	Douglas, ...	235	20	6	—	261	199	35	226
3	Stinson's, ...	40	—	7	—	47	101	47	—
4	Dr. Chapman's, .	140	21	—	—	161	47	30	131
5	H. Sherman's, . .	63	4	15	—	82	442	30	52
6	Fort Scott, . . .	105	—	—	—	105	253	25	80
7	"110,"	597	—	7	—	604	53	20	584
8	Council Grove, . .	16	—	—	—	16	39	16	—
9	Reynolds', . . .	9	—	31	—	40	36	40	—
10	Big Blue Cross, .	2	6	29	—	37	63	37	—
11	Marysville, . . .	237	—	3	5	245	24	7	238
12	Warton's Store, .	31	9	—	1	41	78	41	—
13	Osawkie, ...	69	1	1	—	71	96	71	—
14	Harding's, . . .	130	—	23	—	153	334	103	50
15	Penseno, ...	267	—	39	—	306	308	100	206
16	Leavenworth, . .	232	—	80	—	312	385	150	162
17	Shawnee Agency,	49	—	13	—	62	50	62	—
18	———	—	—	—	—	28	—	—	—
	Total, ...	2268	249	305	21	2871	——	1114	1729

The following is the statement of the Congressional Committee in regard to this election:

"Thus your committee find that in this, the first election in the territory, a very large majority of the votes were cast by citizens of the State of Missouri, in violation of the organic law of the territory. Of the legal votes cast Gen. Whitfield received a plurality. The settlers took but little interest in the election, not one half of them voting. This may be accounted for from the fact that the settlements were scattered over a great extent, that the term of the delegate to be elected was short, and that the question of free and slave institutions was not generally regarded by them as distinctly at issue. Under these circumstances a systematic invasion, from an adjoining state, by which large numbers of illegal votes were cast in remote and sparse settlements for the avowed purpose of extending slavery into the territory, even though it did not change the result of the election, was a crime of great magnitude. Its immediate effect was to further excite the people of the Northern States, induce acts of retaliation, and exasperate the actual settlers against their neighbors in Missouri."

This was the second invasion, and in it upwards of seventeen hundred men marched from Missouri into the territory and voted. Whitfield, by deceiving the settlers as to his true position, succeeded in getting a majority of all the legal votes; but, as this had evidently not been expected, his vote from Missouri would have elected him by upwards of six hundred majority, if he had not got a vote from the territory.

This election was a systematic plot on the part of Missouri. Unable to realize Nimrod Whitfield's skill in getting free-soil votes on false pretences, they determined that it should, in any event, be successful. The leading men of the State of Missouri were at the bottom of it. Atchison, then United States senator, and ex-vice-president of the United States, took an active part. Witness the following speech he made in Platte County, Mo., a few weeks before the election :

"When you reside in one day's journey of the territory, and when your *peace*, your *quiet*, and your *property* depend upon your action, you can, without an exertion, *send* five hundred of your young men who will vote in favor of your institutions. Should each county in the State of Missouri only do its duty, the *question* will be decided *quietly* and peaceably at the ballot-box. If we are defeated, then Missouri and the other Southern States will have shown themselves recreant to their *interests*, and will deserve their fate."

Such was the tenor of his speech, which, throughout, violently inculcated the propriety of securing Kansas to slavery by the most reckless means.

In order to show how far Whitfield had imposed on the free-state men who voted for him, I quote from a subsequent speech of his, when the motive for dissembling was removed.

"We can recognize but two parties in the territory — the pro-slavery and the anti-slavery parties. If the citizens of Kansas want to live in this community at peace and feel at home, they *must* become pro-slavery men; but if they want to live with gangs of thieves and robbers they must go with the abolition party. There can be no third party — no more than two issues — slavery and no slavery, in Kansas Territory."

Such, indeed, was the true question, fairly stated, for such are, and have always been, the facts. The question was freedom and slavery, the parties were free-state and slave-state parties. They had been invited to try their respective claims on the virgin soil of Kansas, by the Kansas Nebraska bill, and the two parties thus created *in Congress* went fiercely to work. That slavery resorted to fraud and violence was certainly nothing new in its history. The idea of submitting it to an "honorable" and "moral" adjustment was absurd, and the pro-slavery propagandists *knew* it was, and took the field with the kind of weapons that would succeed.

At that election Judge Leonard from Buchanan County, and another judge from Cass County, led on and directed parties of these invaders. There is reason to believe that Atchison himself led one party. Colonel John Scott, the city attorney at St. Joseph, Mo., acted as judge of the election; and at all of the precincts, and with all of the parties, leading and influential men from Missouri, men who *ought* to have been respectable, figured pretty largely.

While policy led the chiefs, whiskey inspired the rank and file. The former had led the latter to do an act of reckless and unscrupulous wickedness, in which they villanously trampled under their feet the rights of their fellow American citizens, — rights which ought to be dear to every American heart, and sacred; for he who violently despoils a fellow-citizen of these rights hazards his own.

The invasion and voting resulted from the pro-slavery sentiment; its system, to a secret organization that was formed immediately after the passage of the Kansas-Nebraska bill. We have read with shuddering horror the history of the Assassins; and in the reckless and mysterious career of the secret order who obeyed the behests of the "Sheik el Jebal," we did not expect to find a prototype in a similar organization in Western Missouri, acting under the orders of a power far more potent, and not less corrupt, than was the "Old Man of the Mountain." In the secret tribunal of Westphalia we can recognize a dangerous and improper concentration of irresponsible power; still, in it we discern something like an object for good, perverted though it may have been. But in the Blue Lodge of Western Missouri we discover no redeeming trait, no mitigating circumstance. It was created to extend human slavery over soil hitherto uncursed by such a foe to good morals and republicanism. Its present and express object was to make Kansas a slave state, but it contemplated the introduction of slavery into all the national territory. It contemplated violence and the probable murder that would flow from it. At its secret meeting, men, not only in Kansas, but in Missouri, were "spotted," when their words or deeds rendered their position objectionable to these men. But the following extract from the report of the congressional committee explains its objects and character.

"It was known by different names, such as "Social Band," "Friends' Society," "Blue Lodge," "The Sons of the South." Its members were bound together by secret oaths, and they had passwords, signs, and grips, by which they were known to each other. Penalties were imposed for violating the rules and secrets of the order. Written minutes were kept of the proceedings of the lodges, and the different lodges were connected together by an effective organization. It embraced great numbers of the citizens of Missouri, and was extended into other slave states and into the territory. Its avowed purpose was not only to extend slavery into Kansas, but also into other territory of the United States, and to form a union of all the friends of that institution. Its plan of operating was to organize and send men to vote at the elections in the territory, to collect money to pay their expenses, and, if necessary, to protect them in voting. It also proposed to induce pro-slavery men to emigrate into the territory, to aid and sustain them while there, and to elect none to office but those friendly to their views. This dangerous society was controlled by men who avowed their purpose to extend slavery into the territory at all hazards, and was altogether the most effective instrument in organizing the subsequent armed invasions and forays. In its lodges in Missouri the affairs of Kansas were discussed, the force necessary to control the election was divided into bands, and leaders selected, means were collected, and signs and badges were agreed upon. While the great body of the actual settlers of the territory were relying upon the rights secured to them by the organic law, and had formed no organization or combination whatever, even of a party character, this conspiracy against their rights was gathering strength in a neighboring state, and would have been sufficient at their first election to have overpowered them, if they had been united to a man."

How reckless this power has been, how villanous and unscrupulous in waging war on the people of Kansas, this history will show. There is one phase of its despotism, however, which we are apt to overlook. It is a monstrous iniquity in Missouri. Although Missouri is a slave state, slavery is chiefly to be found in a few counties, and even there the large majority of the white men are not slave owners. They are men who have come from all states of the Union, some of them enterprising business men, who, in advancing their private interests, have still a reasonable pride in those liberties and privileges guaranteed to them by the constitution, and bought by the blood of the early patriots.

But freedom of speech is suppressed as thoroughly as ever it was in the despotic days of the Inquisition. Not only is the subject of slavery itself interdicted, but all opinions growing out of it, or that might haply endanger it, are forbidden. To such a strict rule as this, a money-making, conservative man might reconcile himself; and if his principles and impulses are properly under the control of his prudence and his pocket, this *suppressio veri* is, at least, not felt to be a burden. But this secret organization compels a more irksome service. Here the slave power requires not only passive obedience, but active support. An election is to be carried, and if there is not a sufficient number of rowdies to engage in it, from a natural love of mischief, and an acquired love of liquor, why, more respectable men must go. And if they do not go, they must at least pay the expenses of those who do.

How many worthy men do you suppose, dear reader, have been thus compelled to bolster a system they despise? Ah, that society has ruthlessly trampled on human rights in Missouri as well as in Kansas! Men who, in their "heart of hearts," regarded slavery as an evil and a corrupt political system, who deplored the existence of this corrupt secret society, and whose every instinct was against its lawless action, have been compelled to sustain it. Not a whisper must be breathed against this cruel taxation, or else the luckless wight, whose love of principle (or parsimony) made him object, would be subjected to a loss of caste, to which the condition of an Indian Pariah is a happy one.

The following speech, delivered by General Stringfellow, in St. Joseph, Missouri, at a public meeting where he was sustained and endorsed, will tell something of the story.

"I tell you to mark every scoundrel among you who is the least tainted with abolitionism or free-soilism, and exterminate him. Neither give nor take quarter from the d—d rascals. I propose to mark them in this house, and on the present occasion, so you may crush them out. To those who have qualms of conscience as to violating laws, state or national, the time has come when such impositions must be disregarded, as your rights and property are in danger. I advise you, one and all, to enter every election district in Kansas, in defiance of Reeder and his vile myrmidons, and vote at the point of the bowie-knife and revolver. Neither give nor take quarter, as the cause demands it. It is enough that the slave-holding interest wills it, from which there is no appeal."

We have been in Missouri often enough to learn that this is no empty threat. It is a rod held *in terrorem* over the heads of the suspected. Are you "sound on the Goose Question?" may be a query at which an Eastern or Northern man would smile, but it has had a fearful significance applied in Western Missouri.

Many an honorable mind has had to conceal and crush out an honest conviction thus. Did ever you feel a glow of indignation as you read of the slavery of opinion, of the press, and of speech, in France and Austria? I tell you the veriest tyrant in Europe *dare* not exercise so fearful and despotic control over opinion as the Blue Lodge of Missouri has done. If a man whose heart is good enough to condemn this violence and fraud is timid, as the majority of business men are, *and must be*, he dissembles. If he be positively cowardly, he affects to approve; and if to his cowardice he adds a little corruption and selfishness, he vindicates his own purity from such vile charges by denouncing others, and abusing "abolitionists" generally; with little knowledge, and not the slightest regard for what the term means. If a man in such circumstances be an aspirant for office, he is slavish in his submission, and makes himself the humblest tool of such rascality. He knows that those who entertain more liberal and nobler sentiments are easy and short-sighted, and will overlook such treason against their holiest interests; and he knows that the Blue Lodge and the slaveocracy, of which it is merely a weapon, *never forgives;* never overlooks its ruthless policy; never, in all its vileness, is false to itself. Therefore, every office-seeker in such circumstances is corrupted to be the tool of a thing so base as this. Instead of standing prominent amongst his fellow-men, as one with whom nobleness and true goodness would ever be sacred — a standard-bearer of pure republicanism and social morals — he is degraded into the abject servitude of this monstrous power.

The character of the Blue Lodge of Western Missouri may be illustrated by some of the testimony taken before the commission of Congress. Stringfellow, the Speaker of the Bogus Legislature, admitted enough to give a pretty clear indication of its character, although he refused to answer many of the most important questions, and labored to give a false color to the testimony.

Gen. Richardson, Major-General of the Kansas militia, when asked if he knew of the existence of a secret society, or Blue Lodge, replied,

"I decline to answer that question."

"Are you a member of such society?"

"I decline answering that question."

And so he answered to a series of questions propounded by Mr.

Sherman; only answering one of them, which was put so adroitly that he was afraid to reply as he had done to the other questions; so he admitted in that answer that he *did know of such society.* To the last question, "Do you know of any regulation of such society relative to testimony to be given or taken before this committee?" he replied,

"I also decline to answer that question. It could only have originated in a mind capable of such a mean act itself."

Not very direct as an answer, but exhibiting the fierceness and insolence of this organization, even towards the highest authority in the land.

By the testimony of a Mr. Davidson, all the particulars of this association were obtained; but the most interesting testimony was that of a young-man of the name of Prince.

He had removed from Missouri to the territory recently; and in his testimony told how he had been up with a party of some two hundred Missourians to the first election, who voted at a precinct in the south part of the territory.

He was a young man, not more than five or six and twenty. His face was ingenuous, and displayed a fair degree of intelligence. He was quiet and reserved, and when put on the witness stand had to be questioned on every point; although, when asked what he knew about any occurrence, told frankly all he knew in as plain and simple a manner as possible. He kept back nothing, dissembled nothing, took no pains to color his testimony, but volunteered nothing.

Mr. Howard asked him if he ever had been back to the territory to vote after that first time; and he replied "No," with an emphatic manner that clearly showed how he regarded it *now.*

"Witness," said the cold, inflexible Mr. Howard,—and he bent forward as he spoke, while his gray eye began to kindle till it animated the deep, stern lines of his face,—"Witness, do you know of a secret society, existing in Missouri or elsewhere, known as the Blue Lodge, or by any other name, that contemplates interference in the affairs of Kansas?"

The witness colored up over the temples, and then he grew pale and hung his head. The conflicting emotions of a mind possessing a fair share of sincerity, and some troubled visions on its mental retina of things past and wished-to-be-forgotten, were tracing themselves on that young man's face. Little did he think that one of the most skilful lawyers in the North-west was carefully reading it.

"Well, witness," resumed Howard, slowly and calmly, "you said that you had never gone into the territory but once; we want to know what induced you to go *that* time."

"Well, — the others were going — I — " and the young man raised his face as if to collect his ideas, but as he encountered that steady, penetrating glance, his eyes fell again.

"Witness, are you sure that some such society did not induce you thus to go into the territory? I gather from your language and your manner that you do not approve of it, — that you *know* it was a *wrong;* why did you do it? Those who ask have a right to know."

"Well," stammered the witness, "I have many friends in Missouri. I have some relatives there. Some of the best friends I have are there. I do not wish to say anything that would offend them. When I went into the territory to vote, I did not think much about it, — nearly everybody was going. I was asked by some of the best friends I had to go. Some of the most influential and *respectable* men in Cass County asked me to go."

"Witness," resumed Mr. Howard, and his eye, and the point of every feature in his thin, attenuated face, looked an inexorable judge, and the words "Thou surely wouldst not prevaricate" were written as plainly and legibly on every feature of that face as if they had been placed there in letters of gold, — "Witness, do you then mean to say that you were *not* influenced in your conduct by any such society as I have asked you about?"

The witness was deeply moved. I almost fancied I saw a tear glisten for a moment in the corner of his eye; but I must have been mistaken, for by an effort he raised his face, and, fixing it on Mr. Howard with an expression, at least as earnest and questioning, if not so profound, he said,

"There's one thing I want to know of you, and I hope you will tell me frankly, and just as you would if you were in my place. If you were here on oath, sworn to tell all you know, and the judge was to ask you to tell something that you have sworn solemnly on your honor *not to reveal*—how would you act? If,"—and the young man gained momentary courage, and warmed as he spoke,—"if you have to tell a lie, or forswear yourself either by answering or by not answering, might you not lie or forswear yourself as well one way as another?"

This was an intricate and delicate point in ethics; but neither the interrogatory of the young man, his earnestness, nor the dilemma, moved a muscle of the intellectually earnest but calm face before him. Howard spoke:

"I can readily comprehend the difficulty that presents itself to your mind; but, however sincere—and I do not doubt your sincerity—you suffer yourself to be misled. We understand that you have taken obligations that preclude, on your part, the performance of a duty which you, and every man, owes society. If—and we can only understand your embarrassment so—you have joined such an organization and been influenced by it, if you have taken oaths and obligations, it must have been at the hands of a person not qualified to administer an oath, and who, therefore, could not administer an oath, and did not really place you under the obligation which an oath is supposed to impose. It may be regarded that a promise is as sacred a thing as an oath; and in many senses it is and ought to be; but when a promise has been extorted by deception and conspiracy, when such a promise places an individual in a situation where he finds he cannot honorably stay, such a promise would have no binding effect to keep him there. If—as we suppose—you have belonged to such a society, and have thus unwittingly leagued yourself with a body of men, warring against the best interests of society, we presume you have been betrayed into the criminal connection, and that you have left it when you have ascertained its true character. I can understand why you would hesitate to reveal what you may have promised to keep secret, even there; but this does not excuse you from the solemn duty you owe society; nor can this committee excuse you. We have no disposition to be hard with you; but we are engaged in a serious duty, which we would rather that you should perceive and feel. We have already gained full particulars of this organization from those who have belonged to it; but it is necessary that we should also have the information we believe you to possess. If you have reluctance about mentioning the names of the officers or members of such organization, we will not insist on them; and should you feel you cannot give us the passwords and the signs, or reveal the secret means of communication, although we should desire that your state all fully and frankly, still we will not be hard on you even there; but the existence and general character of this organization, its action on society, and especially on the territory, with all of such a character as you may know, *we shall insist upon.*"

We enter into no discussion on the nice logical subtilties of this argument; suffice it to say, that the will of the strong man triumphed. The young man was broken and subdued. Not all at once, or prostrated by this single blow; but under it he began a revelation which had no backward course. Each step in the elaborate process threw him more completely into the hands of his skilful adversary, — for while the kindest feeling and confidence were expressed, it was an intellectual warfare. Step by step he revealed the character of that hideous system. To one or two of the hardest questions he demurred; and when Howard urged, he plead he "had *friends* in Missouri, and his business often *led him through it.*"

"Would your answer involve you in personal danger?"

"Well," — hesitating and faltering, — "it *might.*" He "had *friends* in Missouri, and must often pass through it."

Reader, when you peruse this, esteem his nice sense of honor and honesty, and thank Providence if you have no *friends* in Missouri.

CHAPTER IV.

SMART ELECTIONEERING — THE "INSTITUTION" ESTABLISHED — ITS ADVANTAGES — REEDER URGED TO CALL THE LEGISLATURE.

THERE was one clever electioneering trick at this election which is too good to be lost. Whitfield being an Indian agent, it was reported that he was going to muster a lot of the different tribes to vote for him; and, in point of fact, he did receive something of a "Native American" vote in this way. Under such circumstances, the Flennikenites felt very sore that they should be out-generaled after such a fashion. Had the "great unterrified," from whom they hailed, not been celebrated for good *management* in elections, from time immemorial? Should *they* not have a finger in such a pretty pie as this? Besides, were not the Indians, as a body, free-state men? and on the eve of the election Flenniken was a moderately good free-state man. As specimens, many of the Indians were certainly in a very *free* state, and, all in all, it was a very pretty opening.

So, at least, thought a zealous disciple of Flenniken, who revolved these matters over and over, and had come to the conclusion that "things was workin'." It was the eve before the election ere his thoughts matured and fructified. They were brought to the decisive point by observing that a majority of the free-soilers of Lawrence were going for Judge Wakefield; for, although many leading men had confidence in the position of Flenniken, still the larger number regarded his antecedents as suspicious, and his present position as at least equivocal.

As morning broke on that 29th of November, in the year of grace 'Fifty-four, this zealous politician, after a brief but anxious investigation of matters, determined that his services in the cause of abstract Democracy could be employed more serviceably in another field; so, mounting a horse, and crossing the Kaw at a ford, where his pony was so much submerged that he had to hold his feet higher than his principles, prepared to enter the Delaware reserve. He had learned that the Delawares were free-state men; and that they were favorably disposed towards other settlers than the Missourians, he had reason to believe. He had heard a specimen of these "brave Delawares" discoursing on the subject once before. This worthy, in addition to a semi-civilized costume, rejoiced in the possession of a scarlet blanket, a bead belt, and stolen honors of a white rooster's tail dangling at the back of a General Taylor hat; and expressed himself thus:

"Good man — heap — Yankee town. Missouri — slave-man, — bad — heap — heap! — d—n um!"

This was satisfactory.

Did you ever attempt to negotiate with an Indian? If you have not, don't. It is disagreeable, besides being of no use. When they take a notion to do anything, they generally do it; but as for persuading them — well, preaching moderation to border ruffians, or pig-driving, are, either of them, a joke to it. They have a very moderate faith in the disinterestedness of white men, and the more anxious a man is to persuade them to any course, they are more suspicious. As Mr. Weller would say, they take him for one of the "advice gratis" sort; and, in good sooth, they are not far from right.

Our friend, the politician, had some trouble in getting an auditory. The first Indian he met was riding over the prairie, and, hailing him, he gave chase. The Indian did not seem to relish this movement, for he could not comprehend the spontaneous and sudden growth of a politician's affection. He halted, however, and, staring suspiciously at our friend, replied to all of his interrogatories,

"Hu — umph!"

He had acquired a little English, it turned out, and, when closely questioned, disbursed his stock in trade, consisting of two words, in an objurgatory and interjectional way.

"Hell-fire! d—nation!"

> "'T was his only stock and store,
> Only that, and nothing more."

Talking politics with such a man was hopeless. Half the effort would soften all the "Hards," and harden all the "Softs." He rode on, and betimes met another. In the former case he had dived right into politics at once; but now he determined to use some policy. This individual was more accomplished. After the salutatory

"How! how?"

There was an interesting pause, broken by our friend asking the way to St. Leavenworth. This was plausible; but the Delaware shook his head.

"Miles — miles — many?" quoth our friend; and he held up the digits of one hand, and began, in dummy style, to count them with the forefinger of the other.

The Indian eyed the process with careful attention. He understood it, and grunted out,

"Hoondred."

He knew that he could not then be more than twenty-five from it, and the politician shook his head, and said,

"No, no; not so many."

The Indian again eyed him, and, in a true compromise spirit, gutturalized,

"Fifty."

Still our friend was dissatisfied, and shook his head.

The Delaware was accommodating. In imitation of his interrogator, he raised the digits of his own tawny hand, and said,

"Ten, may be."

This at least showed an obliging spirit; and, preliminaries being thus opened, our friend began a discourse on the propriety of the Indians voting in general, and Flenniken politics in particular. The Indian sat on his horse and listened with a stolid look. To the assurance that "Flenniken was a good man," he drawled out a

"Y-e-e-e-s,"

Though it was probable that he had never heard of him. To the query, "Would he vote?" he, after the question had been propounded a few times, responded,

"May be."

As he showed no disposition to reduce this compliance to effect, our politician left him in disgust. But the fates were more propitious. He next stumbled on an Indian house, where there were about a dozen Indians congregated. Some of the chiefs were there, and a few could talk English very well. It was a double, hewed log house, with a covered hall or opening between, and a porch running the whole length. Occasionally he could see a squaw diving in and out of the recesses of one of the buildings, and the pappooses with gravely antiquated faces, for such diminutive specimens, peered at him from under their straight, candle-wicky hair.

As our politician approached the group clustered in the porch, he felt that "now or never" was the time to gather "the noble sons of the forest," the brave "Aborigines of America," into the fold of the faithful Democracy.

Explanation was not difficult; they listened attentively, and seemed to approve. Several of those who could, expressed their full concurrence. He waxed eloquent. "The Indians ought to vote." "They had a *right* to vote." Their "party was the great Democratic party, and *recognized that right*." "In fact, this was one of the best chances the Indians ever would have to secure it." "By putting *them* in power, the thing would be as good as *done*." To all of which they grunted Yes, or in other ways expressed their full and hearty approval.

Having disposed of "general principles," our friend proceeded to details. "If it was right to vote, it was right to do it *now*." This was, indeed, "the appointed time." "They would be permitted to vote," and he had just come over to invite them, and wanted them to raise all they could, and go over with him that afternoon, and "he would see them through." The Indians got by themselves, and sat down to consult; an unnecessary precaution, by the by, for our friend was guiltless of "heathen tongue," and had experienced his ignorance of the language that day to his sorrow. The chief, or head man, who happened to be present, was a large, fat fellow, who "spoke English with a *slightly* Indian accent." Our friend watched the progress of the "talk" with profound interest. As a patriot, he felt that *he* had done *his* duty, and that, perchance, the fate of empires was big with his efforts.

Indians, as I have suggested, are not remarkably rapid in their operations. They have a moderation like Job's, and far distancing those who may be waiting on them. Our politician walked backward and forward impatiently, turning now and then an inquiring glance towards the deliberative group, pondered on passing time.

The day went on apace. Our politician knew that precious hours were passing by. He wanted to see these Indians scatter out, and, with a slogan cry, gather in the many hundred Delawares he had heard about; but he knew it must be, of necessity, a matter of time, and he was anxious to see them at work, so as to be in time to vote that evening.

The Indians kept muttering away in a guttural undertone, and it was impossible to ascertain the precise progress they had made. To vary the thing, an old Indian, with a handkerchief tied round his head, and rather an *outre* appearance, who appeared to be half stupid, and more than half drunk, interspersed the exercises with a song. He had not been permitted or had declined to take part in the "talk." His song was not exactly an electioneering song, and I am not sure that it was even patriotic. He leaned over, where he sat, and, swaying his body uneasily backwards and forwards, sung about as follows:

"He-ah haw-haw-haw, he-ah haw-haw-haw,
Ho-ah hee-hee-heeah, he-ah haw-haw-haw,
He-ah hum-hum-humah, he-ah hum-hum-hum,"—

"with variations."

Our politician lost patience, and intimated to the conclave that "time was up." This roused the venerable chief, who, after a few minutes more of hurried "talk," rose, and, standing before our expectant friend, pointed with the forefinger of his right hand into the palm of the left, moved it as he spoke, and tapped that palm with it in gesticulating precision, as he gave the result of their collective wisdom, thus:

"Tinkum four days — den vote heap — heapum! — sometime — may be."

Our friend broke in despair, and hurried back to be in time to vote himself. Should the reader know of a man in his neighborhood who is a public affliction on account of his electioneering propensities, get him to come out and electioneer amongst the Kaws and Kickapoos and Delawares. It is an infallible remedy.

I have said that slavery had been introduced to the territory even while the Missouri restriction prohibited it; it was also formally recognized some time before it was established by the Bogus Laws imposed on the territory by Missouri. The following is a resolution adopted by a meeting held in the territory, but composed chiefly of Missourians, which is contained in the testimony of the committee on the subject:

"*Resolved*, That the institution of slavery is known and recognized in this territory; that we repel the doctrine that it is a moral and political evil, and we hurl back with scorn upon its slanderous authors the charge of inhumanity; and we warn all persons not to come to our peaceful firesides to slander us, and sow the seeds of discord between the master and the servant; for, as much as we deprecate the necessity to which we may be driven, we cannot be responsible for the consequences."

A committee of vigilance of thirty men was appointed "to observe and report all such persons as shall * * * by the expression of abolition sentiments produce disturbance to the quiet of the citizens, or danger to their domestic relations; and all such persons, so offending, shall be notified, and made to leave the territory."

The meeting was "ably and eloquently addressed by Judge Lecompte, Col. J. N. Burns of Western Missouri, and others." Thus, the head of the judiciary in the territory not only assisted at a public and bitterly partisan meeting, whose direct tendency was to produce violence and disorder, but before any law is passed in the territory he prejudges the character of the domestic institutions, which the people of the territory were, by their organic law, "left perfectly free to form and regulate in their own way."

Another meeting, held about the same time, in Joseph, Missouri, formed a branch of the association formed in the western part of that state, to sustain and carry out in public the same thing that the Blue Lodge was working for in secret. The following are two of the series of resolutions adopted at that meeting:

"We do not regard slavery, as it exists in our country, as either a moral or political evil."

And also,

"We are in favor of the extension of negro slavery into Kansas Territory."

Thus was slavery admitted into the Territory of Kansas, — territory which had been sacredly guaranteed as free soil. One of the judges of the Supreme Court — Judge Elmore — took a considerable number of slaves with him into the territory, and has always been one of its strong and active champions, although he is a gentleman, and has not participated in any violent movement, merely laboring to secure and take advantage of the lawless efforts of more unscrupulous men.

Every effort was made in Missouri, and amongst the few pro-slavery men in the territory, to bolster this system. The Missouri press on the frontier devoted itself almost exclusively to the work. Fierce and incendiary resolutions, threats of lawless violence, and a wild denunciation of all who refused their aid to the work, characterized the press of Western Missouri.

But the most amusing thing connected with this literary warfare in the cause, was an elaborate and audacious apology, penned or claimed by Stringfellow. The annexed is one of the most atrocious portions of this singular and atrocious paper:

"Negro slavery has a further effect on the character of the white woman, which should commend the *institution* to all who love the white race more than they do the negro. It is a shield to the virtue of the white woman.

"So long as man is lewd, woman will be his victim. Those who are forced to occupy a menial position have ever been, will ever be, the most tempted, least protected. This is one of the evils of slavery. It attends all who are in that condition, from the beautiful Circassian to the sable daughter of Africa. While we admit the selfishness of the sentiment, we are free to declare we *love* the white woman *so much*, we would save her even at the sacrifice of the negro; would throw around her every shield to keep her out of the way of temptation."

It would seem almost incredible that a community could be so degraded as to issue and tolerate such monstrosity. It proves not only the low state into which society has sunk, but the reckless and unprincipled character of those engaged in this pro-slavery warfare. We do not know how the ladies of the slave states will regard this *excessive* consideration. They certainly must appreciate very highly a "love" so Platonic. This delicate sensibility is certainly the most chivalrous thing we ever heard of. Its safeguards to morality are of the most patent kind. It introduces a new school of morals, which it is a pity that the eminent philosophers of former days did not survive to contemplate. The only wonder is that the philosopher did not carry his deductions further. It certainly might be urged to be as great a remedy for matrimony. *Professor* Stringfellow has stopped short in the middle of his conclusions, although we incline to the opinion that his system, if carried into practical effect, would not.

The candid admission of "selfishness," in the second paragraph, is delightfully refreshing. Taken in connection with what precedes it, it certainly is the coolest piece of impudence of which we have ever heard.

A slight acquaintance with the characters of those with whom this doctrine is in favor, clearly explains its hidden meaning, and exposes the true intent and significance of this apology.

Shortly after the arrival of Gov. Reeder, he was waited upon by the pro-slavery men and Missourians, and urged to call an election for the territorial legislature at once. As this was evidently a movement to thrust forward matters of the greatest importance, Gov. Reeder declined to act on such suggestion. He saw very clearly from what quarter this effort to forestall action came, and, fearing that there was no power in the territory to secure a fair and impartial expression of popular sentiment, he put the threatened evil day afar off, in hopes that "something would turn up."

Lynchings and scenes of violence of various kinds were of frequent recurrence. A man dared not express himself as a free-state man in some communities, without subjecting himself to insult or violent assault. Every one who was not a slavery extensionist was styled an "abolitionist," and, in spite of the protest of many sensitive free-state men, this distinction was insisted on; and it was argued that all who were not for slavery and slavery-extension were against it, and *ergo* all who were against it were "abolitionists."

The distinction between establishing and abolishing slavery does not appear to be understood, or is at least ignored. Those who are engaged in the work of slavery extension have resorted to expedients a great deal worse than that.

The following morsel from the Atchison *Squatter Sovereign* will illustrate the manner in which these outrages were received, and the unblushing manner in which they are publicly chronicled. The "difficulty" alluded to was a gross assault on a man who had merely avowed free-state sentiments.

"Monday of last week a fight came off at Doniphan, K. T., in which bowie-knives were used freely. The difficulty arose out of a political discussion, the combatants being a pro-slavery man and a free-soiler. Both parties were badly cut, and *we are happy to state* that the free-soiler is in a fair way to 'peg out,' while the pro-slavery man is out and ready for another tilt. Kansas is a hard road for free-soilers to travel."

That such modes of justifying villany of this kind should be exposed by an intelligent and independent press, was to be expected. The manner in which such a course was vindicated from such attacks is equally characteristic. We clip again from the organ of pro-slavery and nullification:

"We can tell the impertinent scoundrels of the *Tribune* that they may exhaust an ocean of ink, their Emigrant Aid Societies

6

spend their millions and billions, their representatives in Congress spout their heretical theories till doomsday, and his Excellency Franklin Pierce appoint abolitionist after free-soiler as our governor, *yet we will continue to lynch and hang*, to tar and feather and drown every white-livered abolitionist who dares to pollute our soil."

CHAPTER V.

THE MARCH ELECTION.

FROM the day of the passage of the Nebraska Bill settlers had been hurrying into the territory. In spite of all the noise made about the "Yankees taking Kansas," the great bulk of the emigration came from the Western States. Missouri herself contributed more than an equal portion of settlers, as might be expected; and, what is noteworthy, more than half of those very settlers from Missouri were either free-state men when they came, or became so shortly afterwards. It is not remarkable that the poor people of the slave states should have little sympathy with slavery. Not only their interests, but their dignity and their civil rights, are compromised by it; and, although prejudice, and an habitual yielding to fear, may have made them pro-slavery men of some sort, as a general thing they have only to be removed from the influence of leading and wealthy slave-holding men to ignore the institution. Thus has it been in the territory. Where a slave-owner has settled, and formed a settlement or cluster round him chiefly of poor men from slave states, they have in most instances succeeded in retaining these men in the same subjection to their interests to which they have been compelled to submit in Missouri. What few pro-slavery towns there are in the territory have been made and sustained in this way. These are generally well supplied with whiskey-shops. The "treating" system always flourishes. It is the same degrading system that unhappily prevails in too many places in the South-west, and which degrades the manhood which ought to dignify a republican, be he ever so poor. Wherever the elective franchise is bought and sold with whiskey we need be at no loss to determine the exercise of the political power thus obtained. So important an element has whiskey been in the crusade of the slavery-propaganda against Kansas, that the scarcity and stoppage of supplies of this article have had the most fatal effect on several important expeditions against the territory. In this warfare it has, indeed, taken the precedence of other explosives. Of course, much of the deepest villany has been perpetrated by scoundrels of the lowest caste, many of whom had congregated on the border; but many men of a better class, or at least not so degraded, have, by a liberal distribution of whiskey, and a little palaver from some influential slaveholder, taken part in enterprises which, in their better moments, they would condemn and deplore.

Iowa sent many settlers into the territory; but these were all free-state men. Many came from Illinois, Indiana, Ohio, Wisconsin, and other states. There were, indeed, many New Englanders — more than ever came to settle a new territory. In some settlements they greatly preponderated; and these communities were generally characterized by a greater degree of intelligence and enterprise than has ever marked so young a settlement before.

Even the settlers from the Western States were of a better class than those who generally form the pioneers. In other Western States the pioneers were mostly of a peculiar sort. Good enough men in their way, of the Davy Crocket school; but, under favorable circumstances, it would take about three generations to bring them to a condition that Eastern people would pronounce "enlightened," and Western people "crotchety." The pioneers were usually men who could not stay in densely-settled countries. Like the bees, they kept hovering between the Indians and civilization. They had no "elbow-room" when settlers got within a mile of them. Deer-hunting was with them a science, coon-hunting a purely business affair; and the skins of these animals, and soft-soap, or hoop-poles, the usual currency, and a "legal tender." Schools with them were occasional, and very irregular; books and papers of small repute. Religion they "got" as they would the measles; and for the discussion of politics a bottle of whiskey was as essential as the speaker's mace in the British House of Commons.

These have haply "gone to Arkansas" or Texas, or located somewhere between the peaks of the Rocky Mountains and their western base. Certainly very few of them have come to Kansas. You can tell by the fences, and look of the houses, and by a thousand other things, that an industrious and calculating people are here. Everything is new and in a transition state. The old class of pioneers would have their farms and houses perfect in one or two years at furthest, the process being simple; but the class of settlers now in Kansas are going ahead, only beginning, and this transition stage will last forever.

"Conservative" people, or selfish politicians, who like to accuse other people of difficulties, for the blame of which they do not wish to be responsible themselves, say that the "agitation sent a class of fanatics to the territory." The truth is, the noise and argument — "agitation," if you like the word — sent a class of *thinkers* to the territory, who are, of all others, the worst to *manage*. Had the usual class of pioneers settled the country, the slave question could have been settled peaceably, with far less whiskey than it has taken to subdue it. The "agitation" has, therefore, been, in point of fact, "the cause of *trouble*."

By the Kansas Nebraska bill the people of the territories were to elect representatives for a territorial legislature. This is a feature which has crept into our territorial management, created by the very nature of the case, and conceded because the most sacred rights of a republican people would otherwise be all taken from them when they went into a territory. A territorial government is something contradictory in our history. It is unknown to our constitution, and foreign to the spirit of our institutions. The system has grown up and been tolerated by necessity. The theory of our government is simply that it shall be formed by the people among whom it obtains; shall be dependent on them, and thus express the popular sentiment. A territorial government is something very different from this, and it is so of necessity. The blunder, if there was any, lay in the acquirement of the territory at first. This *has* been done, however; and, judging from the popular feeling, it will be done again.

Those who have honestly been led away by the "squatter sovereignty" dodge, wished to apply this same feature to the territories. Douglas pretended this was the design of the bill; but Douglas knew better. Had he been sincere, he would not have dared to frame a bill by which the executive of the territory and the judiciary were simply the appointees of the President, and, it might be, the tools of a faction. Taking the position he pretended to take, he would have known that this was a gross imposition on men's rights. Having framed an organic law for the people of the territory,— one restricting even the legislature which *it allowed* to be created,— it then provides for the appointment of the officers to *execute* this law, and the judges and the courts to try offences under them, by a power outside of these people of the territory, foreign to them, and *not responsible to them;* for the people of a territory are not even allowed to vote for President, or send anything but a delegate to Congress, who cannot vote. It should require no logic to show that there was not much sovereignty of the people in this. The only feature — a small and restricted boon — was, that they could, under provisions laid down by the organic law, elect men to a legislature who could make local laws under certain restrictions. Even then they had no security that these would be enforced or carried out. As in this instance of Kansas, it has proved that the other features of the organic act, allowing the President to appoint corrupt officers, have prevented the people from having any means of remedy against the abuse of that power on them, except in revolution. The territorial executive ought to have been willing, and, when it undertook the trust, also *able*, to protect the territory from the invasion by which the people's rights were violently wrested from them. In failing to do this it incurred all the guilt of the most absolute despotism, since it prevented the people from defending themselves by assuming to be the government. If the "squatter sovereignty" feature is a true system, we ought not to be under the control of the federal officers. If the people who happen to be in and community are to govern it, it would be wrong — *despot-*

ism, in short — for any power outside of it to interfere with it. If "the people are to govern themselves," we have no business to govern even the Indians.

Governments are not theories, but facts. We *have* territories, — perhaps it is the better policy that we *should have*, — and having, it is our duty to preserve the rights of the people who are in those territories. We assume their government; having it, it is our duty to take care of them. Having introduced a feature foreign to our republican institutions, it is our duty, as the next best thing we can do, to make it conform to republicanism as much as possible. We would scarcely wish to allow some three or four irresponsible buccaneers to decide the future institutions and character of a great territory which was destined to form a component part of our great republic; and yet squatter sovereignty would compel us to do this. We cannot escape the dilemma by fixing any *number* of settlers as a point where principle interferes in favor of their rights. At what point of aggregation do men become capable of, and entitled to, self-government? We can neither escape the point nor its responsibility! In the good providence of God, we have got wide and fertile territories; as a nation *we own* them. A despotism — a clear and decided case of despotism — or "national sovereignty," or call it by any other name you like, that will express the requisite authority. Having this authority, it remains to be seen whether its exercise will prove us Tarquins or good rulers; whether our sway be that of

"Good Queen Bess,
Or Bloody Mary!"

The most zealous advocate of "squatter sovereignty" we have ever seen was not in favor of admitting any new state that had not a republican constitution. And why not? If people have a right to govern themselves in all cases, they certainly *have a right* to choose the *kind* of government. To deny them this overturns their authority at the outset. The Congress of the United States, which is the most direct and legitimate arm of the national power, has the right to say what kind of state shall be added to the confederacy. It has a right to see that no corrupt or injudicious feature is permitted to disturb the happiness or mar the prosperity of the whole. If it has a right to do this in *one* point, it has a right to do it in all that in any way concerns the confederacy.

Our general government is one of *conceded* rights; our state governments rest on *reserved* rights. The general government has no authority to go beyond the conceded, and the states none to go out of the reserved rights. If the national compact is worth anything, it is worth that much. But there is a difference between territories and states. A territory has conceded nothing and reserved nothing. It has no right to the advantage of a compact, for it is a party to no compact. A territory has no more right to organize itself into a civil body, and thrust itself into the Union with all the evils and impolicy of slavery, or polygamy, or cannibalism, than she has with Russian autocratism; even should the latter be a case of "general principles," and the former "local institutions." Neither would we be willing that she should set up independent of us. As a nation we claim to have authority over the national domain, and we suppose we mean to exercise it. We gained our authority over it, not by virtue of any principle, but by the sword; and, if we mistake not, it has been held by the same tenure. We have this authority, and can only lose it in two ways: it may be taken from us, or we may relinquish it. We presume no one would relish the idea of its being taken from us. We cannot relinquish it without some act of our own, and that act would have to be something very different from the Kansas Nebraska bill.

The most favorable view of our territorial government, as regards our republican institutions, that can be taken, is, that it is a part of the whole nation, and as the residents of the territory are a small minority, and the people of the states a large majority, therefore the majority should rule. This is a very pleasant view of the case, but it does not amount to anything, and has also the disadvantage of being false. We ignore the proposition of a great central government, and if what we described could amount to anything, it would amount to that. The people of the territory are no more sovereigns possessing state rights than the people of the states are residents of the territory. The people of the states have their clearly defined rights and powers; the people of the territory have their rights of preservation of life and property and happiness, which are guaranteed to United States citizens, wherever they are, throughout the world; but they have, necessarily, no political power but such as Congress concedes to them.

Of course, it is the true policy of the general government to respect the rights, *all* the *rights* claimed by American citizens, as far as it can. If the people in a territory, for instance, were to form a government for themselves, one that would make it a good member of the sisterhood of states, it would be the proper and true policy to admit her with that constitution, and allow the citizens of this independent state, thus created, the power to govern themselves, in compliance with the terms of the *conceded* compact. Nor does it appear to affect the case whether Congress shall or shall not have prescribed the mode of forming such a constitution. To insist on such a point would be a needless exercise of our despotic power. The moment that Congress is satisfied that a majority of these people have decided in favor of such an unobjectionable form of state government, it will be conceded, by every honorable and correct mind, that it is their duty to restore them to their rights as American citizens, — rights of which a fault, or fatality, in our history and policy, has deprived them; that is, give them the government, if they are capable of sustaining it. We will thereby release ourselves of a burden, and place them in a position they ought to occupy.

We have been thus particular in placing the matter in what we deem its true light, in order that what follows may be more clearly understood.

Governor Reeder caused a census to be taken, early in the season of 1855; the list being taken between the 20th of January and the close of February. That census exhibited a population of 8,501 souls (this being exclusive of Indians). There were 5,128 males, 3,373 females, and 3,469 minors. Of citizens of the United States there were 7,161; of foreign birth, 409. There were 242 slaves, and 151 free negroes. There were only 2,905 voters in the territory when the census was taken, but, as the election occurred on the 30th of March, that population had considerably increased.

Governor Reeder has been accused of favoring the Eastern emigration by waiting until that time. Had such a disposition existed on his part, it would have prompted him to defer the election at least a month later. By the 30th of March many spring emigrants from Missouri and the Western States could, and *did*, get into the territory, while but very little of the Eastern emigration got to the territory until later in the season.

The frauds of the November election had awakened more vigilance in the free-state party. It was organized, and had candidates in nearly all the precincts, and would have carried that election by a large majority, but for the invasion of a large army of armed voters. Not less than five thousand Missourians entered the territory. They began to come a few days before the election, and it was several days after before they went out. But the following facts, from the committee report, will convey the truth in a forcible light:

"By an organized movement, which extended from Andrew County in the north to Jasper County in the south, and as far eastward as Boone and Cole Counties, companies of men were arranged in regular parties, and sent *into every council district in the territory, and into every representative district* but one. The numbers were so distributed as to control the election in each district. They went to vote, and with the avowed design to make Kansas a slave state. They were generally armed and equipped, carried with them their own provisions and tents, and so marched into the territory. The details of this invasion, from the mass of the testimony taken by your committee, are so voluminous that we can here state but the leading facts elicited."

Not only did these men vote themselves, but they seized possession of the polls, and thus prevented the legitimate voters from exercising their privilege. This was done by threats and violence in some cases; but, in a good many of the precincts, when the legal voters came to the polls and found them in possession of a Missouri mob, who were desecrating them, they refused to vote, withdrew their candidates, and left the polls. Nor could they do otherwise, as the judges of election had either been ousted by violence, and Missourians appointed in their place, or they were intimidated into compliance with the wishes of the invaders. The following is the result of that election, as proved before the committee of Congress:

Abstract of Census and Returns of Election of March 30, 1855, by Election Districts.

No. of District.	Place of Voting.	Pro-Slavery Votes.	Free-State Voters.	Scattering.	Total.	Total of Legal Voters.	Total of Illegal Voters.	Census: No. of persons residents.	Census: No. of Voters.	C'cl.: No. of District.	C'cl.: No. of Members.	H'se.: No. of District.	H'se.: No. of Members.
1	Lawrence,	781	253	—	1034	232	802	962	369	1	2	2	3
2	Bloomington,	318	12	11	341	30	316	519	199	2	1	3	2
3	Stinson's or Tecumseh's,	366	4	2	372	32	338	252	101	3	1	4	
4	Dr. Chapman's,	78	2	—	80	15	65	177	47	1	—	1	1
5	Bull Creek,	377	9	—	386	13	380	—	—	—	—	—	—
	Potawattomie,	199	65	—	264	75	191	—	—	—	—	—	—
	Big Sugar Creek,	74	17	7	98	32	59	1407	442	4	2	7	4
	Little Sugar Creek,	34	70	—	104	104	—	—	—	—	—	—	—
6	Fort Scott,	315	35	—	350	100	250	810	253	5	1	6	2
7	Isaac R. Titus,	211	23	—	234	25	209	118	58	3	—	5	1
8	Council Grove,	17	17	3	37	37	—	83	39	3	—	5	
9	Pawnee,	23	52	—	75	75	—	86	36	6	1	8	1
10	Big Blue,	27	42	—	69	48	21	151	63	10	—	8	—
	Rock Creek,	2	21	—	23	23	—	—	—	8	—	8	—
11	Marysville,	328	—	—	328	7	321	36	24	9	—	9	1
12	St. Mary's,	4	7	—	11	11	—	—	—	10	—	9	—
	Silver Lake,	12	19	2	33	33	—	144	78	1	—	9	—
13	Hickory Point,	233	6	—	239	12	230	294	96	10	—	10	1
14	Doniphan,	313	30	3	346	—	—	—	—	7	—	11	—
	Wolf Creek,	57	15	6	78	200	530	1167	334	7	1	11	2
	Burr Oak, Hdgs,	256	2	48	306	—	—	—	—	8	—	12	2
15	Hayes,	412	—	5	417	80	337	873	203	9	1	13	2
16	Leavenworth,	899	60	5	964	150	814	1183	385	10	2	14	3
17	Gum Springs,	43	16	—	59	59	—	150	50	1	—	—	—
18	Moonestown,	48	14	—	62	17	45	99	28	7	1	—	—
	Total,	5427	791	92	6320	1310	4908	8501	2892	—	13	—	26

By this fraudulent election the following persons were reported to the governor by the judges of election, or self-styled judges of election. The Rev. Thomas Johnson, of the Shawnee Mission, who was elected president of the council. The other members of the council were Wm. Barker, A. M. Coffee, Dr. A. N. Grover, Richard R. Kees, H. J. Stricklar, C. Chapman, John W. Forman, A. McDonald, Wm. P. Richardson, M. H. Conway.

In the House of Representatives, Jos. C. Anderson, O. H. Browne, A. J. Johnson, M. W. McGee, Samuel Scott, Geo. W. Ward, Jas. Whitlock, H. W. Younger, Joel P. Blair, Wm. J. Matthias, A. P. Wade, A. Wilkinson, Jno. M. Banks, D. L. Crossdale, R. L. Kirk, H. D. M'Meekin, W. H. Tibbs, T. W. Waterson, S. A. Williams, F. J. Marshall, H. B. Harris, A. Payne, Jonah Weddle, Sam. D. Houston. Of this body Richard K. Rease, a member also, was elected president pro tem., and D. S. (Dr.) Stringfellow, member, was elected speaker. With the exception of two names, one in the council, Mr. Conway, and Mr. Houston in the house, all the members of either body were ultra pro-slavery men, and many of them then resided, and still reside, in the State of Missouri.

As the accuracy of these statements is a matter of importance, and as the limits of this work will prevent us going into details of this election, we subjoin the more striking portions of the report of the committee of Congress. The facts on which their testimony is based have been sworn to by a large number of witnesses, men of all politics, and residents of Missouri as well as Kansas.

"Your committee report the following facts, not shown by the tables:

"Of the twenty-nine hundred and five voters named in the census-rolls, eight hundred and thirty-one are found on the poll-books. Some of the settlers were prevented from attending the election by the distance of their homes from the polls, but the great majority were deterred by the open avowal that large bodies of armed Missourians would be at the polls to vote, and by the fact that they did so appear and control the election. The same causes deterred the free-state settlers from running candidates in several districts, and in others induced the candidates to withdraw.

"FIRST DISTRICT, MARCH 30, 1855. — LAWRENCE.

"The company of persons who marched into this district collected in Ray, Howard, Carroll, Boone, La Fayette, Randolph, Saline and Cass Counties, in the State of Missouri. Their expenses were paid, — those who could not come contributing provisions, wagons, etc. Provisions were deposited, for those who were expected to come to Lawrence, in the house of William Lykins, and were distributed among the Missourians after they arrived there. The evening before and the morning of the day of election about one thousand men from the above counties arrived at Lawrence, and camped in a ravine a short distance from town, near the place of voting. They came in wagons — of which there were over one hundred — and on horseback, under the command of Col. Samuel Young, of Boone County, Missouri, and Claiborne F. Jackson, of Missouri. They were armed with guns, rifles, pistols and bowie-knives, and had tents, music, and flags with them. They brought with them two pieces of artillery, loaded with musket balls. On their way to Lawrence some of them met Mr. N. B. Blanton, who had been appointed one of the judges of election by Governor Reeder, and, after learning from him that he considered it his duty to demand an oath from them as to their place of residence, first attempted to bribe, and then threatened him with hanging, in order to induce him to dispense with that oath. In consequence of these threats he did not appear at the polls the next morning to act as judge.

"The evening before the election, while in camp, the Missourians were called together at the tent of Captain Claiborne F. Jackson, and speeches were made to them by Colonel Young and others, calling for volunteers to go to other districts where there were not Missourians enough to control the election, while there were more at Lawrence than were needed there. Many volunteered to go, and the morning of the election several companies, from one hundred and fifty to two hundred men each, went off to Tecumseh, Hickory Point, Bloomington, and other places. On the morning of the election the Missourians came over to the place of voting from their camp, in bodies of one hundred at a time. Mr. Blanton not appearing, another judge was appointed in his place; Colonel Young claiming that, as the people of the territory had two judges, it was nothing more than right that the Missourians should have the other one to look after their interests; and Robert A. Cummins was elected in Blanton's stead, because he considered that every man had a right to vote if he had been in the territory but an hour. The Missourians brought their tickets with them, but, not having enough, they had three hundred more printed in Lawrence on the evening before and the day of election. They had white ribbons in their button-holes to distinguish themselves from the settlers.

"When the voting commenced, the question of the legality of the vote of a Mr. Page was raised. Before it was decided, Colonel Samuel Young stepped up to the window where the votes were received, and said he would settle the matter. The vote of Mr. Page was withdrawn, and Colonel Young offered to vote. He refused to take the oath prescribed by the governor, but swore he was a resident of the territory; upon which his vote was received. He told Mr. Abbott, one of the judges, when asked if he intended to make Kansas his future home, that it was none of his business; that if he were a resident then, he should ask no more. After his vote was received, Colonel Young got up in the window-sill, and announced to the crowd that he had been permitted to vote, and they could all come up and vote. He told the judges that there was no use in swearing the others, as they would all swear as he had done. After the other judges concluded to receive Colonel Young's vote, Mr. Abbott resigned as judge of election, and Mr. Benjamin was elected in his place.

"The polls were so much crowded until late in the evening that for a time, when the men had voted, they were obliged to get out by being hoisted up on the roof of the building where the election was being held, and pass out over the house. Afterward a passage-way through the crowd was made, by two lines of men being formed, through which the voters could get up to the polls. Colonel Young asked that the old men be allowed to go up first and vote, as they were tired with the travelling, and wanted to get back to camp.

"The Missourians sometimes came up to the polls in procession two by two, and voted.

"During the day the Missourians drove off the ground some of the citizens, — Mr. Stevens, Mr. Bond, and Mr. Willis. They threatened to shoot Mr. Bond, and a crowd rushed after him, threatening him, and as he ran from them some shots were fired at him, as he jumped off the bank of the river, and made his escape. The citizens of the town went over in a body, late in the afternoon, when the polls had become comparatively clear, and voted.

"One Missourian voted for himself, and then voted for his little son, but ten or eleven years old. Colonel Coffer, Henry Younger and Mr. Lykins, who were voted for and elected to the Legislature, were residents of Missouri at the time. Colonel Coffer subsequently married in the territory. After the polls were closed, the returns were made, and a man, claiming to be a magistrate, certified on them that he had sworn the judges of election before opening the polls. In the Potawattomie precinct the Missourians attended the election, and, after threatening Mr. Chesnut, the only judge present appointed by the governor, to induce him to resign, they proceeded to elect two other judges, one a Missourian and the other a resident of another precinct of that district. The polls were then opened, and all the Missourians were allowed to vote without being sworn.

"After the polls were closed, and the returns made out for the signature of the judges, Mr. Chesnut refused to sign them, as he did not consider them correct returns of legal voters.

"SECOND DISTRICT. — BLOOMINGTON.

"On the morning of the election the judges appointed by the governor appeared, and opened the polls. Their names were Harrison Burson, Nathaniel Ramsay, and Mr. Ellison. The Missourians began to come in early in the morning, some five or six hundred of them, in wagons and carriages and on horseback, under the lead of Samuel J. Jones, then postmaster of Westport, Missouri, Claiborne F. Jackson, and Mr. Steely, of Independence, Mo. They were armed with double-barreled guns, rifles, bowie-knives, and pistols, and had flags hoisted. They held a sort of informal election, off at one side, at first for Governor of Kansas, and shortly afterwards announced Thomas Johnson, of Shawnee Missions, elected governor. The polls had been opened but a short time when Mr. Jones marched with the crowd up to the window, and demanded that they should be allowed to vote without swearing as to their residence. After some noisy and threatening talk, Claiborne F. Jackson addressed the crowd, saying they had come here to vote; that they had a right to vote if they had been there but five minutes, and he was not willing to go home without voting; which was received with cheers. Jackson then called upon them to form into little bands of fifteen or twenty, which they did, and went to an ox-wagon filled with guns, which were distributed among them, and proceeded to load some of them on the ground. In pursuance of Jackson's request they tied white tape or ribbons in their button-holes, so as to distinguish them from the 'abolitionists.' They again demanded that the judges should resign, and, upon their refusing to do so, smashed in the window, sash and all, and presented their pistols and guns to them, threatening to shoot them. Some one on the outside cried out to them not to shoot, as there were pro-slavery men in the room with the judges. They then put a pry under the corner of the house, which was a log house, and lifted it up a few inches, and let it fall again, but desisted upon being told that there were pro-slavery men in the house. During this time the crowd repeatedly demanded to be allowed to vote without being sworn, and Mr. Ellison, one of the judges, expressed himself willing, but the other two judges refused; thereupon a body of men, headed by 'Sheriff Jones,' rushed into the judges' room, with cocked pistols and drawn bowie-knives in their hands, and approached Burson and Ramsay. Jones pulled out his watch, and said he would give them five minutes to resign in, or die. When the five minutes had expired, and the judges *did not* resign, Jones said he would give them another minute, and no more. Ellison told his associates that if they did not resign there would be one hundred shots fired in the room in less than fifteen minutes; and then, snatching up the ballot-box, ran out into the crowd, holding up the ballot-box, and hurraing for Missouri. About that time Burson and Ramsay were called out by their friends, and not suffered to return. As Mr. Burson went out he put the ballot poll-books in his pocket, and took them with him; and as he was going out Jones snatched some papers away from him, and shortly afterward came out himself, holding them up, crying, 'Hurrah for Missouri!' After he discovered that they were not the poll-books he took a party of men with him, and started off to take the poll-books from Burson. Mr. Burson saw them coming, and he gave the books to Mr. Umberger, and told him to start off in another direction, so as to mislead Jones and his party. Jones and his party caught Mr. Umberger, took the poll-books away from him, and Jones took him up behind him on a horse, and carried him back a prisoner. After Jones and his party had taken Umberger back they went to the house of Mr. Ramsay, and took Judge John A. Wakefield prisoner, and carried him to the place of election, and made him get upon a wagon and make them a speech; after which they put a white ribbon in his button-hole and let him go. They then chose two new judges, and proceeded with the election.

"They also threatened to kill the judges if they did not receive their votes without swearing them, or else resign. They said no man should vote who would submit to be sworn — that they would kill any one who would offer to do so — 'shoot him,' 'cut his guts out,' etc. They said no man should vote this day unless he voted an open ticket, and was 'all right on the goose,' and that, if they could not vote by fair means, they would by foul means. They said they had as much right to vote, if they had been in the territory two minutes, as if they had been there two years, and they would vote. Some of the citizens who were about the window, but had not voted when the crowd of Missourians marched up there, upon attempting to vote, were driven back by the mob, or driven off. One of them, Mr. J. M. Macey, was asked if he would take the oath; and, upon his replying that he would, if the judges required it, he was dragged through the crowd away from the polls, amid cries of 'Kill the d—d nigger thief!' 'Cut his throat!' 'Tear his heart out!' etc. After they got him to the outside of the crowd, they stood around him with cocked revolvers and drawn bowie-knives, one man putting a knife to his heart so that it touched him, another holding a cocked pistol to his ear, while another struck at him with a club. The Missourians said they had a right to vote if they had been in the territory but five minutes. Some said they had been hired to come there and vote, and get a dollar a day, and, 'by G—d, they would vote or die there.'

"They said the 30th day of March was an important day, as Kansas would be made a slave state on that day.

"SIXTEENTH DISTRICT.

"For some time previous to the election meetings were held and arrangements made in Missouri to get up companies to come over to the territory and vote. And the day before and on the day of election large bodies of Missourians from Platte, Clay, Ray, Chariton, Carrol, Clinton, and Saline Counties, Missouri, came into this district and encamped there. They were armed with pistols and bowie-knives, and some with guns and rifles, and had badges of hemp in their button-holes and elsewhere about their persons.

"On the morning of the election there were from one thousand to one thousand four hundred persons present on the ground. Previous to the election Missourians endeavored to persuade the two free-state judges to resign, by making threats of personal violence to them; one of whom resigned on the morning of election, and the crowd chose another to fill his place. But one of the judges, the free-state judge, would take the oath prescribed by the governor; the other two deciding that they had no right to swear any one who offered to vote, but that all on the ground were entitled to vote. The only voters refused were some Delaware Indians, some thirty Wyandot Indians being allowed to vote.

"One of the free-state candidates withdrew, in consequence of the presence of the Missourians, amid cheering and acclamations by the Missourians. During the day the steamboat New Lucy came down from Western Missouri, with a large number of Missourians on board, who voted, and then returned on the boat.

"The Missourians gave, as a reason for their coming over to vote, that the North had tried to force emigration into the territory, and they wanted to counteract that movement. Some of the candidates and many of the Missourians took the ground that, under the Kansas Nebraska act, all who were on the ground on the day of election were entitled to vote; and others, that laying out a town, staking a lot, or driving down stakes even on another man's claim, gave them a right to vote. And one of the members of the council, R. R. Kees, declared in his testimony that he who should put a different construction upon the law must be either a knave or a fool.

"The free-state men generally did not vote at that election; and no newly-arrived Eastern emigrants were there. The free-state judge of election refused to sign the returns until the words 'by lawful resident voters' were stricken out, which was done, and the returns made in that way. The election was contested, and a new election ordered by Governor Reeder for the twenty-second of May.

"The testimony is divided as to the relative strength of parties in this district. The whole number of voters in the district, according to the census returns, was three hundred and eighty-five; and, according to a very carefully prepared list of voters, prepared for the pro-slavery candidates and other pro-slavery men a few days previous to the election, there were three hundred and five voters in the district, including those who had claims but did not live on them. The whole number of votes cast was nine hundred and sixty-four. Of those named in the census one hundred and six voted. Your committee, upon careful examination, are satisfied that there were not over one hundred and fifty legal votes cast, leaving eight hundred and fourteen illegal votes.

"BURR OAK PRECINCT.

"Several hundred Missourians from Buchanan, Platte, and Andrew Counties, Missouri, including a great many of the prominent citizens of St. Joseph, came into this precinct the day before, and on the day of election, in wagons and on horse, and encamped there. Arrangements were made for them to cross the ferry at St. Joseph free of expense to themselves. They were armed with bowie-knives and pistols, guns and rifles. On the morning of the election the free-state candidates resigned in a body, on account of the presence of the large number of armed Missourians, at which the crowd cheered and hurraed. Gen. B. F. Stringfellow was present, and was prominent in promoting the election of the pro-slavery ticket, as were also the Hon. Willard P. Hall and others of the most prominent citizens of St. Joseph, Missouri. But one of the judges of election appointed by the governor served on that day, and the crowd chose two others to supply the vacancies.

"The Missourians said they came there to vote for and secure the election of Major William P. Richardson. Major Richardson, elected to the council, had had a farm in Missouri, where his wife and daughter lived with his son-in-law, Willard P. Hall; he himself generally going home to Missouri every Saturday night. The farm was generally known as the Richardson farm. He had a claim in the territory, upon which was a saw-mill, and where he generally remained during the week.

"Some of the Missourians gave as their reason for voting that they had heard that Eastern emigrants were to be at that election, though no Eastern emigrants were there. Others said they were going to vote for the purpose of making Kansas a slave state.

"Some claimed that they had a right to vote under the provisions of the Kansas Nebraska bill, from the fact that they were present on the ground on the day of election.

"The free-state men generally did not vote; and those who did vote voted generally for John H. Whitehead, pro-slavery, for council, against Major William P. Richardson, and did not vote at all for members of the lower house.

"The parties were pretty nearly equally divided in the district, some being of the opinion that the free-state party had a small majority, and others that the pro-slavery party had a small majority. After the election was over, and the polls were closed, the Missourians returned home. During the day they had provisions and liquor served out free of expense to all.

"THIRD DISTRICT — TECUMSEH.

"On the 28th of March, persons from Clay, Jackson, and Howard Counties, Missouri, began to come into Tecumseh, in wagons, carriages, and on horseback, armed with guns, bowie-knives, and revolvers; they encamped close by the town, and continued camping until the day of election. The night before the election two hundred men were sent for from the camp of Missourians at Lawrence. On the morning of the election, before the polls were opened, some three or four hundred Missourians and others were collected in the yard about the house of Thomas Stinson, where the election was to be held, armed with bowie-knives, revolvers and clubs. They said they came to vote, and whip the 'damned Yankees,' and would vote without being sworn. Some said they came to have a fight, and wanted one. Colonel Samuel H. Woodson, of Independence, Missouri, was in the room of the judges when they arrived, preparing poll-books and tally-lists, and remained there during their attempts to organize. The room of the judges was also filled by many of the strangers. The judges could not agree concerning the oath to be taken by themselves and the oath to be administered to the voters; Mr. Burgess desiring to administer the oath prescribed by the governor, and the other two judges opposing it. During this discussion between the judges, which lasted some time, the crowd outside became excited and noisy, threatening and cursing Mr. Burgess, the free-state judge. Persons were sent at different times by the crowd outside into the room where the judges were, with threatening messages, especially against Mr. Burgess; and at last ten minutes were given them to organize in, or leave; and, as the time passed, persons outside would call out the number of minutes left, with threats against Burgess if he did not agree to organize. At the end of that time the judges, not being able to organize, left the room, and the crowd proceeded to elect nine judges and carry on the election. The free-state men generally left the ground without voting, stating that there was no use in their voting there. The polls were so crowded during the first part of the day that the citizens could not get up to the window to vote. Threats were made against the free-state men. In the afternoon the Rev. Mr. Gilpatrick was attacked and driven off by the mob. A man, by some called 'Texas,' made a speech to the crowd, urging them to vote, and to remain on the ground until the polls were closed, for fear the abolitionists would come there in the afternoon and overpower them, and thus they would lose all their trouble.

"The Missourians began to leave on the afternoon of the day of election, though some did not go home until the next morning.

"In many cases, when a wagon-load had voted, they immediately started for home. On their way home they said if Governor Reeder did not sanction the election they would hang him."

The following is the closing part of this official report relative to this, and also to this election:

"This unlawful interference has been continued in every important event in the history of the territory. *Every election* has been controlled, not by the actual settlers, but by citizens of Missouri; and, as a consequence, every officer in the territory, from constables to legislators, except those appointed by the President, owe their positions to non-resident voters."

CHAPTER VI.

WHAT KANSAS AND MISSOURI THOUGHT OF IT.

As might be supposed, this outrageous violation of the right on which all our liberties and privileges rest awakened the utmost indignation throughout the territory and the country. The people of Kansas saw that it was the determination of Missouri and the slavery propagandists to secure Kansas to slavery by all means, and that violence must be met by violence, or every privilege they possessed would be taken from them, and their position and even their life endangered. It was almost immediately afterwards that military companies were formed amongst the settlers. But few of these were armed properly, and efforts were made by them to send for arms, and also many who were unable to purchase them appealed to their friends in the states to procure arms for them.

Indignation meetings were held, and protests issued against the election, and ignoring the authority of members elect under it. It was determined by the free-state settlers, who constituted at that time three fourths of the actual residents, that, as the whole thing was a violent usurpation and a fraud, no regard would be paid to any of their proceedings.

Nor were other remedies neglected. Protests and certificates of fraud were sent to the governor from meetings convened in the different precincts in the territory. It will ever be regretted that Gov. Reeder gave so little time in which to contest the elections. Protests had to be made and returned to the governor within four days. I need expend no time in showing that this was altogether inadequate. The territory was large, and the executive office on the edge of it. There were few roads at that time; besides, meetings had to be called, evidence obtained, and other preliminaries arranged. Again, many of the settlers were ignorant of the proper remedy for such emergency. The blow came on them so suddenly that it paralyzed, and, to some extent, intimidated them. The precious hours were thus permitted to pass in several of the precincts where the citizens were most indignant at the outrage, and anxious for some remedy. In other precincts the protests were too late to be in time; and thus, by unfortunate default, certificates were given to men whose names were returned with a certain number of votes, although no one doubted the fraudulent character of these returns.

While the organic act had failed to throw proper safeguards around the elective franchise, and while the territorial executive must be admitted to have occupied a critical situation, it cannot be denied that the action of Gov. Reeder at this time was not so bold or decided as the emergency required. True, he had to act on the nominal evidence before him; true, he might have rendered himself obnoxious to the charge of stepping behind the record, and being partial; true, he was jealously watched by the pro-slavery men, suspected by a pro-slavery administration, who appointed him, and anxious not only to *be*, but to appear, *impartial;* but, in spite of all this, he, the executive head of the territory, the only source of protection the outraged settlers had, ought to have spared no effort, and shrunk from no responsibility that could have saved these settlers from being injured by the color even of legality to such outrages upon them.

Protests having been received in time from six districts, and the frauds proved, the governor set aside the former elections, and called other special elections, with the following result:

Abstract of the Returns of Election of May 22, 1855.

No. of District.	Places of Voting.	Pro-Slavery Votes.	Free-State Votes.	Scattering.	Total.
1	Lawrence, . .	—	288	18	306
2	Douglas, . . .	—	127	—	127
3	Stinson's, . . .	—	148	1	149
7	"110," . . .	—	66	13	79
8	Council Grove,	—	33	—	33
16	Leavenworth, .	560	140	15	715
	Total, . .	560	802	47	1409

At this election it will be seen that upwards of eight hundred free-state votes were polled, and free-state candidates elected in all the districts save Leavenworth. In Leavenworth there was another invasion from Missouri. On this point there was a difference of opinion amongst the pro-slavery men. Most of the leaders declared that Reeder had no authority to call special elections under the Kansas Nebraska act for cases of fraud; and, as his proceedings were therefore irregular, it was only necessary to pay no attention to them. Some, on the other hand, were timorous, and thought it best to be sure. A writer in the Leavenworth *Herald*, after the special election was called, urged the pro-slavery men and their *friends* to vote in this election. Many of those in Leavenworth, and amongst them the pro-slavery men elected March 30th, were in favor of crushing this election directly by the same means. Consequently there was another invasion of voters from Missouri on that occasion at Leavenworth, and they voted for the same men previously elected. Of the pro-slavery votes polled there more than two thirds were fraudulent; and, owing to the violent seizure of the polls, many free-state settlers were kept from voting.

During this extraordinary state of affairs, the Missouri press made no attempt to conceal the facts. They publicly, in their columns, urged that such steps be taken as would secure the result. The Liberty (Clay County, Missouri) paper issued the following, with many similar articles, on the invasion of Kansas:

"The election in Kansas Territory is close at hand, and we embrace this, the last opportunity we will have before the event, of admonishing Missouri and southerners that it is the part of wisdom as well as prudence to employ every means of preparation necessary to a successful combat for the issue which is suspended upon it."

The Weston *Reporter* of March 29th (1855) says:

"Our minds are already made up as to the result of the election in Kansas to-morrow. The pro-slavery party will be triumphant, *we presume*, in nearly every precinct. Should the pro-slavery party fail in this contest, it will not be because Missouri has failed to do her duty to assist friends. It is a safe calculation that two thousand squatters have passed over into the promised land from this part of the state within four days."

After the election the Missouri papers were filled with jubilant expressions of victory. The Platte *Argus* says:

"It is to be admitted that they — the Missourians — have conquered Kansas. Our advice is, let them hold it or die in the attempt."

When the election was called in the first, second, third, seventh, eighth, and sixteenth districts, it was denounced after the following fashion by the border papers:

"We learn, just as we go to press, that Reeder has refused to give certificates to four of the councilmen and thirteen members of the house. He has ordered an election to fill their places on the 22d of May.

"This infernal scoundrel will have to be hemped yet." — *Brunswicker, Mo.*

At the same time violence was offered to those who dared to protest the March election. This was unquestionably the reason why protests were not made in some districts.

In Leavenworth the protest with an affidavit had been signed by a lawyer named William Phillips. A meeting was held in Leavenworth amongst the pro-slavery men, who denounced him as a "moral perjurer." He was notified to leave the territory. This he refused to do. On the 17th of May, just a few days before the special election, a band of pro-slavery men assembled. They convened in public meeting first, and passed resolutions of the most violent character. Free speech on the slavery question was denounced as a "disturbance of the peace and quiet of the community," and the action of the press in the same cause was denounced as "circulating incendiary documents." Free-state men were denounced as "Northern fanatics," and told to "go home and do your treason where you can find sympathy." Violence was recommended as necessary to the success of the pro-slavery party. Many of those who took a prominent part in that meeting, and the outrage that followed, have since been appointed to office under the Bogus Legislature, and also under the territorial courts and executive.

When the meeting was over, those composing it marched up the street to find Mr. Phillips. They were armed. Mr. Phillips was in company of some of his neighbors, who were erecting a building, when the pro-slavery band came upon them. As neither Mr. Phillips nor his friends were prepared for defence, none was made. He was taken prisoner and carried on board a skiff, and taken over the river and up to the town of Weston, some eight miles distant. Meanwhile his friends tried to get the authorities and the military to interfere and rescue him; but in vain. Fort Leavenworth, with a considerable military force, was only three miles off, and between Leavenworth city and Weston; but there was no remedy. When Mr. Phillips' captors got to Weston they stripped and tarred and feathered him. In this condition he was borne about the streets of Weston on a rail, subjected to the most grievous indignities and insults, and sold at auction by a negro. After suffering this they permitted him to escape, ordering him to leave the territory, with threats of death for non-compliance.

Subsequently, on the 25th of May, A.D. 1855, a public meeting was held, at which R. R. Kees, a member elect of the council, presided. The following resolutions, offered by Judge Payne, a member elect of the house, were unanimously adopted:

"*Resolved*, That we heartily endorse the action of the committee of citizens that shaved, tarred and feathered, rode on a rail, and had sold by a negro, William Phillips, the moral perjurer.

"*Resolved*, That we return our thanks to the committee for faithfully performing the trust enjoined upon them by the pro-slavery party.

"*Resolved*, That the committee be now discharged.

"*Resolved*, That we severely condemn those pro-slavery men who, from mercenary motives, are calling upon the pro-slavery party to submit without further action.

"*Resolved*, That, in order to secure peace and harmony to the community, we now solemnly declare that the pro-slavery party will stand firmly by and carry out the resolutions reported by the committee appointed for that purpose on the memorable 30th."

About the same time, or shortly before, another occurrence worthy of note took place. As the Missouri borderers were very much dissatisfied with Gov. Reeder, proposals to "elect a governor of their own" were freely made. That this would really have been done, if assurances had not been received from Washington that their wishes would be complied with, there is no question. As it was, the matter was widely discussed. At one of the election precincts, at the March election, votes were thrown for Rev. Tom Johnson, of the Shawnee Mission, to be governor. A meeting or convention was ordered, and the notices of it published in the Missouri papers, to be holden in Leavenworth, for the purpose of electing governor. Before this meeting was held the leading men in the border counties took the affair into consideration, and, under assurances that they would have a governor to suit them, interfered to prevent the action of the meeting. Another reason for this course might be the conduct of some of their tools. The Rev. Tom Johnson had received many evidences from the border ruffians of the esteem in which they held his pro-slavery services. Independent of pecuniary advantages, accruing through his "mission to the Indians," he had been elected member of the council by an almost exclusively Missouri vote. He was subsequently elected president of the council. But he was dissatisfied, and aspired to be governor. Absurd and unworthy as the most of these border ruffian appointments and elections have been, there was something so supremely ridiculous in the idea of making the Rev. Tom governor, that it disgusted even them. Hence they threw cold water on his ambitious projects.

Although it had been previously determined that the election for governor should be "nipped in the bud," still, many attended the meeting convened. The meeting having been adroitly turned from its legitimate object by the leaders, it proceeded to some deliberation on the "squatter laws" relative to claims in which all were more or less interested. A warm debate having arisen, and merged into a violent controversy, in which the lie was given, a pro-slavery man, named Malcom Clarke, raised a large piece of timber, or scantling, running at the person who had exchanged words with him — a free-state man named Cole McCrea — and struck him violently with it, and was raising it to strike him again, when McCrea drew a pistol and shot him dead. The friends of Clarke immediately pursued McCrea, and commenced firing on him with their pistols. He took refuge from their shots under the river bank, from which position he was released by his friends, who took him up to the fort for protection and examination. After having been subjected to a long imprisonment, he was tried before the territorial courts. At the first court before which he was brought the grand jury failed to bring a bill against him, deeming the case one of justifiable homicide. The court, Judge Lecompte, manifested a determination to convict the prisoner. The grand jury were adjourned to a subsequent term of the court. At that time the grand jury was packed, several of its members being those who acted or aided in lynching Phillips. A bill of indictment for murder was found, and the trial was slowly proceeded with, when the prisoner, fearing violence to his person even before conviction, made his escape.

If those in the territory who vindicated the rights of the settlers fared badly, those in the State of Missouri, who opposed these actions, fared no better. Shortly after the election, the *Brunswicker* (Mo.) found fault with a contemporary in the same state, who condemned the Missouri invasion of Kansas.

"The last Jefferson *Inquirer* is down on the citizens of Missouri who took steps to secure the election of pro-slavery men to the territorial Legislature of Kansas. This is in keeping with the *Inquirer's* past conduct. If the editor of that paper had been in Kansas on the day of election, he would have voted with the abolitionists. That he is a negro-stealer *at heart* we have no doubt."

Nor was the pulpit, even, sacred from these assaults. Some preachers, who had publicly or privately expressed disapprobation of such violence, or who were *supposed* to condemn it, were notified to leave, and mob violence was offered to them on more than one occasion.

Meetings were held in Platte, Jackson, Buchanan and Clay counties, Mo., to endorse the proceedings of the invaders, and denounce all those who dared to call them in question, or condemn them. The following resolutions, passed by a meeting in Clay County, in April, is a fair specimen of all the others:

"Those who, in our state, would give aid to the abolitionists by inducing or assisting them to settle in Kansas, or would throw obstacles in the way of our friends, by *false* and *slanderous* misrepresentations of the acts of those who took part in and contributed to the glorious result of the late election in that territory, should be driven from amongst us as traitors to their country.

"That we regard the efforts of the Northern division of the Methodist Episcopal Church to establish itself in our state as a violation of her *plighted faith*, and, pledged as its ministers must be to the anti-slavery principles of that church, we are forced to regard them as enemies to our institutions. We therefore fully concur with our friends in Platte County in resolving to permit no person belonging to the Northern Methodist Church to preach in our county.

"That all persons who are subscribers to papers in the least tinctured with free-soilism or abolitionism, are requested to discontinue them immediately."

But the most remarkable case of this kind was that of the Parkville (Platte Co.) *Luminary*. Immediately after the invasion that swept the March election, this paper contained an editorial, mildly condemning the invasion, and urging that the citizens of Kansas ought to be permitted to regulate their own affairs. For this it fell under the ban of the border ruffians. Mr. Park, proprietor of the paper, was one of the oldest citizens of Parkville, and had helped to build the town which bore his name. A large company was raised in Platte city, some ten miles distant, and, providing themselves with arms, marched to Parkville to destroy the press and lynch the editors. Mr. Park was absent. They broke his press, and threw it, with the whole of the material, in the Missouri river. They then seized the editor, who happened to be present (Mr. Patterson), and were about to lynch him. At this point his wife, a young and delicate woman, rushed into the crowd, and, throwing her arms around her husband, would not let him go. They ordered and threatened, and tried to drag her away; but she clung to him convulsively, and they were obliged to relinquish their attempt, and let him go, ordering him, however, to leave, under penalty of losing his life.

An account of this affair, and also of the efforts made to defray the expenses of the invasions, was given before the committee of

Congress, by a witness of Missouri, who lives near Parkville. This gentleman was a pro-slavery man, but, as he himself expressed it, was "down on all them fixin's." He was an oddity, a genius of the Davy Crockett stamp, and appeared, with all his peculiarities, to possess an honorable and upright mind. He had been over in Kansas, driving a lot of his cattle, in the spring of 1856, when the committee summoned him before it. An abstract of such a man's testimony, or an accurate official rendering of it, could no more convey all he swore to, than it could give the picture.

Mr. Thorpe was a tall, athletic man, in Western homespun, with a beard like a bottle-brush, and a face that looked as if it was as free from ablution as he said he was from "abolition." He had a great ox-whip, six feet long, with a lash much longer. This he grasped in his hand as he strode into the committee-rooms. The members of the commission were busy examining another witness; but our friend was not skilled in such niceties, so he walked up to the desk, and in a voice that might have been heard in the street, began:

"Well, gentlemen, I heered you was a wantin' me, an' so I jist cum down. You 've got my name there, I guess; that feller that cum after me had it. I 'm Tom Thorpe, myself."

Mr. Howard. "Ah, Mr. Thorpe," — bowing, — "we are engaged at present examining this witness. You will please take a seat until we are ready for you."

"Edzactly, of course. You see I 've ben a drovin' cattle over here on the Wakeruse — I 've got a fine lot on 'em, too — an' the boys tole me you 'd be after me and ketch me; an' I tole them that I did n't care a darn; an' so when the feller cum, I jist concluded I 'd step over an' see what you did want. Tom Thorpe an't afeer'd" —

"That is all perfectly right, Mr. Thorpe, and as soon as we are disengaged we shall be happy to examine you."

"Certainly — that 's all straight, anyhow. I 'm from Platte County, myself. I live" — Here the gentlemen of the commission conversed together, and, seeing it would be impossible to get rid of Mr. Thorpe, concluded that it would be cheapest to make the other witness, who was not in a hurry, stand aside until the ger tleman from Platte County could be disposed of.

"Mr. Thorpe," — to our friend who was still standing, whip i hand, — "you will be sworn."

"O, sartain. I 'm willin' to swar to all I 'm goin' to tel you. I tell the truth any way, myself, but swar away."

The oath being administered, Mr. Howard asked:

"Mr. Thorpe, you are a resident of Missouri; do you know o any parties coming from that state to vote in the territory?"

"Lord, yes; lots on 'em; but I suppose you 'd first want t know about that 'ere Parkville business. I was there, myself throwing the press in the river, I mean — an' seed all on it. guess that 's what you want to see me about, and that you wer arter me on that 'ere business — but, darn it, how do I know wha you want?" said Thomas Thorpe, straightening himself up, as i he recollected himself — "but, any how, I tole the boys that ' what I supposed you had me for, an' so" —

"Mr. Thorpe," interposed Mr. Howard, "the mobbing of th press at Parkville is a subject out of our jurisdiction; and it i neither our duty nor our wish to investigate the affair, howeve much we may condemn the outrage" —

"O, Lord, yes, it was a mighty mean thing; I was down on i myself. I tole 'em there, that day, I was *down* on it. I 'm prc slavery myself — there 's no abolitionism about me; but that ' cuttin' up a little too high. I 'm down on all them fixin's; an' just tole 'em" —

"Mr. Thorpe, you will please confine yourself to the subject o which we may question you. Did you reside in Missouri in th March of 1855?"

"Yes, sir, I 've ben in Platte County more 'n twenty year I 've" —

"Do you know of any Missourians going over from your neigh borhood into Kansas to vote at that time? — or who did sc vote?"

"Lots an' slivers on 'em, — but stop; let me get it right. Look-a-here, you chap," — motioning to Mr. Lord, clerk of the com mission, who was taking down his testimony, — "Look-a-here, I want to see that you keep that straight. What have you got there?"

Mr. Lord proceeded to read what he had taken, Mr. Thorpe expressing his approval until the last sentence, when he said, —

"Look-a-here, read that 'ere last piece again."

The clerk proceeded to read. "To Mr. Howard: — I have known lots of people who came over from Missouri into Kansas to vote."

"Well, now, Mr. Clerk, scratch that out. Tell you what it is, boys," turning to the members of the commission, "I 've got to keep mighty straight. I 've come from Platte County, myself, and I 've got to give an account o' this business to the boys when I go back. I an't afeerd. I tell you I 'm down on this thing of votin' over in the territory, as much as you dar be; but I can't swar to what I don't know. I wan't in the territory to see all they done. There 's no mistake about it, boys, *but they voted;* but you see I can't swar that."

"Only swear to what you know," said Mr. Howard. "You will please state if you knew of large parties going from the state, at the time of the territorial elections, into the territory, and whether such parties returned afterwards."

"Yes, sir, they did; any amount of 'em. They used to keep the roads busy, and the ferries, too, about them times. An' they used to raise companies to go; an' raise money for to keep 'em at it. They came to me to subscribe, but I tole 'em that I was down on this thing of votin' over in the territory, and that Tom Thorpe did n't subscribe to no such fixin's. They jawed me, too, about it — they did; but I guess they found that old Tom Thorpe could give as good as he got; for, says I" —

"Mr. Thorpe, you will please state at what time you observed these men thus coming and going. If you remember it, give us the date, or tell us at which of the territorial elections."

"O, they swarmed every time. They cum, an' they kep a-cumin'. It was jest the same thing. Whenever there was an election in the territory they were a fussin' roun', an' gittin' up companies to go, an' gittin' hosses, an' wagins, and all them fixin's. They used to ax me to go, but I tole 'em" —

"Witness, you will please state how many persons you hav seen going or coming in this way."

"They all cum; the whole *possitatus* of 'em. It was ginera kinder. It would be a heap easier for me to tell you who did n go over than who did."

"Can you give the names of any of them?"

"Well, yes;—there was Jem White, and Bill Bowers, an Bob Murphy, an' —"

"Stop!" cried the clerk, "not so fast."

"Well, look-a-here, I guess there an't no use in givin' all the names. I han't got a fust-rate memory myself to mind all o 'em, unless I was to git some time to study on it; but I tell yo what, there's lots on 'em—mor'n you'd want to put in tha book."

"Witness, do you know what induced these men to do this?"

"Well, I guess they felt like it. Some of the folks *did* pe suade the boys to go over and vote. They tole them they wante to make Kansas a slave state; an' they tole 'em the abolitionis war a-cummin' in; and that the Emigrant Aid Society Compan and Co. was pitchin' in, and they'd better too. You see, the took the boys over, and they got plenty liquor, and plenty to ea and they got over free ferry. They did say,—now I an't agoi to swar to this, 'cause I an't certain,—but they *did* say the gin some of them a dollar a day to go. Well, 't wan't a very bus time, and most o' them liked the joke, anyhow. You see ther was a heap of respectable folks went with 'em. There's D Tibbs, lives over in Platte, he used to go; an' you see the elected him. The boys tole me one time, when they cum back says they, 'We've elected Dr. Tibbs to the legislature;' and say I, 'Is it the legislature of the state or the territory?' an' say they, 'The territory.'"

"Says I, 'Boys, an't this a-puttin' it on too thick? It's a darne sight too mean enough to go over and vote for them fellers; but t put in a man that don't live there is all-fired outrageous.'"

"Is this Dr. Tibbs the W. H. Tibbs whose name is on the lis of territorial legislators?" asked Mr. Howard.

"Well, I don't know anything about that; but Dr. Tibbs, I d

know, was elected to the Kansas Legislature; an' was over makin' the laws, too. That was in July, ye see, an' our election cum on in August. For some of the boys wanted to run the Dr. for an office over there; but you see some on 'em thought it would n't work well for him to hold office both in the state and the territory, — though, for that part of the matter, he lived in the state."

"You say you knew this Tibbs to be a resident of Missouri?"

"Certain; he voted there at the August election, jist as he cum back from the legislature in the territory. I 've know'd him there ever since he cum to Platte County. He has a fine old woman, too;— she 's a mighty fine woman. She 's always ben there to home. But if you don't believe me, ax the Doctor himself. He 's an *honorable* man; he an't agoin' to deny it."

"Do you know whether these men, who thus went over, voted in the territory?"

"Well, I can't say that. They tole me, most on 'em did, as they went over, that they was agoin' to vote, and when they cum back that they had voted; but, I tell you what, I can't swar to it. Look-a-here, young man," broke off the witness, addressing the clerk, "read over that thing you 've got; I want to see you keep it straight."

"I will read it over when you get through."

"Well, I guess that 'll do. You see they sometimes used to have kind o' fusses. Some few o' the folks, like myself, did n't believe in it; an' that 's what led to this *Luminary* business at Parkville. They used to say that was an abolition paper, an' that it belonged to the Emigrant Aid Society Company & Co.; but I never seed no abolitionism in that paper; I tuck it too, an' got 'em yet. That Park, I used to think, was a pretty decent ole feller; no more an abolitionist than me, and I 'd like to see the man 'ud daar call me an abolitionist. You see I was in Parkville at the time the muss came off; an' I seed them smashing up things an' throwin' o' 'em into the river. I tell you, I could n't stand it. I jest stepped up and tole 'em that want the way to do. Says I, 'Boys, you might as well put my hoss or my ole woman's bureau into the river, as that ere press. That 's personal property,' says I. An' Dr. —— says to me, says he,

'Shut up! you 're a d——d old fool!' an' says I," — here Mr. Thorpe paused, and his eye turned over to the desk where the newspaper reporters were sitting, busily engaged, and, pointing over towards them, he leaned confidentially forward to Mr. Howard, and said, in what he intended for an undertone:

"Look-a-here, I did speak darned sharp to the Doctor, and I don't want to use any bad words afore them smart members o' Congress."

"O, never mind," said Mr. Howard, in his dry way, pointing with his hand to the reporters' bench, "these smart members o' Congress can hear what you have to say." To the clerk, "Don't put down any of this Parkville matter, of course."

"Well," resumed Thorpe, "I could n't think o' usin' such words afore them. The fact is, I spoke pretty sharp, an' he spoke back sharper, an' I hit him, an' he pitched into me, an' then we had it. It was right down by the river, an' the boys were busy pitchin' in them type, an' breakin' up them wooden dishes, an' when the Doctor an' I got to fightin', they screeched an' hollored an' went to bettin' on it; an' then some o' them separated us. Well, we 've ben good enough friends since. Doctor and myself had been drinkin'; fact is they were all a drinkin'."

"I suppose, then," said Mr. Howard, smiling, "it was merely the bad whiskey that did it."

"O, no, no; the liquor was good enough, that wan't it, but you see the boys had been cuttin' up so; an' says I, 'Boys, this is a breakin' down the rights of American citizens,' an' says I" —

"Mr. Thorpe, can you tell whether any of these men, who came into the territory to vote, were paid for doing so?"

"Well, now, that 's mighty hard to swar to. You see, I believe they really did pay a lot of the boys; some of them told me they did; but, you see, I can't swar to that. There 's my own nephew, — he came all the way up from Howard County, with a company to vote. He came over to see me and our folks as he went along. I says to him, says I, 'Jem Thorpe, han't you nothin' better to do than to come way up to vote in the territory?' Well, he told me that they wan't busy at home, an' that they got a dollar a day, an' their expenses an' liquor; an I says, 'Stop, Jem

Thorpe, that 's enough ; you can't stay in my house to-night, and nobody can that goes in for votin' in the territory. I tell ye what, boy, I 've always been down on that kind o' thing. I an't no abolitionist, neither. I tell you I 'm pro-slave. I 'm dyed in the wool, and can't make a free-soiler ; but, mind what I say, if the boys keep a cuttin' up so, I 'll come over to the territory and 'nitiate Betsey.' "

Here Mr. Thorpe made the " young man read the documents " to see if he had " got 'em straight." " Tell you what it is, boys," he said, " I 've got to give an account o' all this when I go back to the state. I 'm willin' to stand on the truth, but I 've got to have it mighty straight." Having got it " straight " enough to his notion, he wanted the clerk to sign for him, as he said, " You 're more used to that kind of a thing." When he had legalized the document with his own hand, he looked at it thoughtfully, and, laying his hand on it, sighed as he said solemnly :

" Well, boys, that 's all true, but it an't the tenth part of the truth."

CHAPTER VII.

THE BOGUS LEGISLATURE.

If the outrageous fraud by which the Missourians pretended to elect representatives for Kansas astonished the world, the proceedings of the conclave of vagabonds, assembled under this mob authority, were still more astonishing. Never did a less responsible body of men assemble under the pretence of making laws. The people of Kansas ignored them, and they appeared equally willing to ignore the people of Kansas; and, as for their Missouri constituency, it was merely a question as to "honor among thieves" as to how far they would comply with their wishes.

Before the March election the pro-slavery men were suspicious of Governor Reeder, and feared that he would, at least, not act with them. After the March election, and when Reeder refused certificates to those whose seats were contested, open war was declared against him. Nor did they intend to pay the least attention to the governor's authority in calling a special election. Instead of leaving the people of each district to attend to the legality of the election, which concerned them, a number of the leading pro-slavery men in the state and in the territory went to the governor to induce him, by persuasion and threat, to give certificates to all the pro-slavery men elected. Failing to do this, they held a meeting at the then seat of government, and passed the following resolutions:

"Shwnee Mission, *April 6th*, 1855.

"At a meeting of a portion of the citizens of Kansas Territory, held at the Shawnee Mission on the 6th inst., to take into consideration the course to be pursued by them in the event of a new election being called for the purpose of electing members to the Kansas Legislature, to fill the places of those who have been refused certificates of election by Governor Reeder, a committee was appointed for the purpose of presenting some plan for the consideration of the meeting. The committee retired, and, after short deliberation, presented the following resolutions, which were unanimously adopted:

"Whereas, there are elected, and to whom certificates have been granted, a majority of both houses; and whereas the right of ordering a new election is not delegated to Governor Reeder by the Kansas bill, except in case of a tie, or where a vacancy is caused by death or resignation; and whereas the right to decide all cases of contested elections, for the Legislature, is clearly recognized in the Kansas bill, and by the governor himself, as belonging to that body alone; therefore,

"*Resolved*, That, in the event a new election shall be ordered by the governor, in any district, we recommend to every law-abiding and order-loving citizen of Kansas Territory, not to attend said elections, but rely upon the returns already made to sustain the claims of those returned heretofore to their seats in each house.

"*Resolved*, That the secretary of this meeting have these proceedings published in all the public journals of this territory which advocate and defend the rights of the citizens of Kansas Territory against executive usurpation.

"The meeting then adjourned.

"J. W. FORMAN, *Chairman.*
"JOHN MARTIN, *Secretary.*"

In June, Governor Reeder had gone East. On his return, he was assailed by B. F. Stringfellow. Stringfellow called on the governor, then staying at Leavenworth, and took him to task about some speeches he had made in the East relative to the March election, and the share that Stringfellow had taken in it. After some words, Stringfellow, taking advantage of the reclining position of the governor, knocked him down and kicked him. The same spirit of violence characterized the proceedings of most of these border men.

The Legislature had been convened to assemble at Pawnee, a new town which had been laid off on the Kaw river, near Fort Riley. After being convened, the men elected by fraud at the first election being in majority, proceeded to turn out the members elected May 22d at the special election. It was on the 4th of July that this final outrage was performed, when the *only* legitimate representatives present were unceremoniously thrust out by these usurpers. Their places were given to the pro-slavery men whose election had been declared invalid. The ground taken was that the governor had no power to call a special election for alleged fraud, under the Kansas-Nebraska bill. Nor did they stop there. M. S. Conway had been declared elected to the council at the first election. He was a free-state man. His case was taken into consideration, and he was expelled, his pro-slavery competitor getting the seat. Just before his expulsion he sent his resignation to the governor. This only left one free-state man in the body, Mr. Houston, in the lower house. This gentleman there was not the slightest pretext for ousting. Finding himself thus surrounded by a group of invaders, who had no right to legislate for the territory, he resigned his seat, and withdrew from them.

Having thus got their body properly purified, they proceeded to take another step. They had assembled at Pawnee, which was more than a hundred miles from Missouri, on which they had to depend. As they intended to enact a code of laws for the territory which would violently outrage the people in it, they did not feel altogether safe so far into the territory they had invaded. When the Legislature passed the bill adjourning to the Shawnee Mission, the governor vetoed it. This measure was then passed over the veto by a two-third vote. The governor declared that, by the act of removing, the Legislature was dissolved. The position taken by him was that the Kansas-Nebraska bill vested this power in the governor; that the territorial officers under federal appointment must keep the seat of government where they were best able to attend to their duties and the wants of the territory. This adjournment would necessarily compel the federal officers to move, and the organic act had given the territorial Legislature no power over the federal officers. These were the arguments used;

but there is no question that the governor was heartily sick of the Legislature. Their fraudulent character was too palpable. Even the certificates they held from him could not cover up the monstrous iniquity; and doubtless these suggested that the evil was a great and radical one, which required and ought to have received promptly a great and radical cure.

The Bogus Legislature adjourned. During this short sojourn at Pawnee they indulged in the affectation of privation and want of accommodation. When they started from Missouri, as most of them did, they brought camping apparatus with them, and, although there was a hotel at Pawnee, they eschewed it, subjecting themselves to the great inconvenience of camping, in order to demonstrate the *necessity* for adjournment.

At the mission the Legislature were at home; that is, they were nearly so. It was only one mile from the Missouri line, and four miles from Westport. Hacks left the mission every evening, on the adjournment, taking the members to Westport, and brought them back next morning. And such splendid junketings and racketings these fellows had! A due supply of spirits was brought in bottles and jugs each morning, in order to keep the Legislature *in spirits* during the long summer days.

The amount of work this body pretended to do was certainly imposing. The code of Kansas laws forms a thick and ponderous law-book, the very size and thousand pages of which make the bare idea of reading it something fearful. On a moderate estimate it would have taken them the greater part of the time they were in session to have read through it once. The laws made by them were chiefly of a local character, all those they pretended to make being simply transcripts of the Missouri code. To make them conform to the organic act, they were in the habit of passing separate acts, defining the meaning of words. Thus, in taking up some Missouri law, they would pass a separate act, in which it set forth that in "said act" the word "state" was to be understood as meaning "territory." In this way the most of those acts, or laws, were gotten up, and were passed simply by reading the title of the bill.

So far as there is a difference between the Missouri and Kansas codes, the people of Kansas have the worst of it. So far as concerns the qualifications of electors, and members of the Legislature, official oaths of officers, attorneys and voters; the mode of selecting officers, their qualification, the qualifications of jurors, and the slave code, there is a material difference, not only between the code of Kansas and Missouri, but between Kansas and any other state, or, indeed, any country, where they are civilized enough to have a code of laws.

Of these enactments the committee of Congress testify:

"By the 'Kansas Statutes,' every officer in the territory, executive and judicial, was to be appointed by the Legislature, or by some officer appointed by it. These appointments were not merely to meet a temporary exigency, but were to hold over two regular elections, and until after the general election in October, 1857, at which the members of the new council were to be elected. The new Legislature is required to meet on the first Monday in January, 1858. Thus, by the terms of these 'laws,' the people have no control whatever over either the legislative, the executive, or the judicial departments of the territorial government, until a time before which, by the gradual progress of population, the territorial government will be superseded by a state government.

"No session of the Legislature is to be held during 1856, but the members of the house are to be elected in October of that year. A candidate, to be eligible at this election, must swear to support the fugitive slave law, and each judge of election, and voter, if challenged, must take the same oath. The same oath is required of every officer elected or appointed in the territory, and of every attorney admitted to practise in the courts.

"A portion of the militia is required to muster on the day of election. 'Every free white male citizen of the United States, and every free male Indian who is made a citizen by treaty or otherwise, and over the age of twenty-one years, and who shall be an *inhabitant* of the territory, and of the county and district in which he offers to vote, and shall have paid a territorial tax, shall be a qualified elector for all elective offices.' Two classes of persons were thus excluded, who, by the organic act, were allowed to vote, namely, those who would not swear to the oath required, and those of foreign birth, who had declared on oath their intention to become citizens. Any man of proper age, who was in the territory on the day of election, and who had paid one dollar as a tax to the sheriff, who was required to be at the polls to receive it, could vote as an 'inhabitant,' although he had breakfasted in Missouri and intended to return there for supper. There can be no doubt that this unusual and unconstitutional provision was inserted to prevent a full and fair expression of the popular will in the election of members of the house, or to control it by non-residents."

We subjoin copies of three of the most obnoxious laws. One relating to the election of all county and local officers by the Legislature directly, thus stripping the people of one of their most valuable privileges and means of security. Despotic and outrageous beyond all precedent though this proceeding is, it still was a necessary step. Without it, all their laws would have been a dead letter. They did not belong to the territory, and the people repudiated them, and would their works; hence the necessity on their part to reserve the appointing power in their own hands, so that none but their tools should be permitted to execute the law.

"AN ACT TO ESTABLISH A TRIBUNAL FOR THE TRANSACTION OF COUNTY BUSINESS, AND TO DEFINE ITS POWERS AND DUTIES.

"*Be it enacted by the Governor and Legislative Assembly of Kansas Territory.*

"SECT. 1. There shall, at the present session of the Legislative Assembly, be elected by joint ballot of the two houses, for the term of four years, a Board of County Commissioners for each county in the territory, consisting of three discreet and proper persons, actual residents of the county for which they are elected, of not less than twenty-one years of age; and the Legislative Assembly shall, every four years hereafter, proceed in the same manner to elect a Board of such Commissioners, and the President of the Council shall grant each person so elected a certificate of his election, signed by the President and attested by the chief Clerk of the Council, which certificate shall be by such commissioner deposited for record in the Recorder's office of the proper county.

* * * * * * *

"SECT. 6. The Board of Commissioners shall appoint all sheriffs, coroners, assessors, collectors, justices of the peace, constables, and all other officers, commissioners or agents, provided for by law, within their respective counties, except in such cases as other modes of appointment may be provided; and each officer commissioner, or agent, so appointed, shall receive a certificate of his appointment, as provided for in the appointment of Clerk of the Board of Commissioners aforesaid, and shall in like manner cause the same to be recorded."

The following two relate to the regulating of slavery in the territory, the suppression of free speech and free press. They need no comment.

"AN ACT TO PUNISH OFFENCES AGAINST SLAVE PROPERTY.

"SECT. 1. *Be it enacted by the Governor and Legislative Assembly of Kansas,* That every person, bond or free, who shall be convicted of raising a rebellion or insurrection of slaves, free negroes or mulattoes, in this territory, shall suffer DEATH.

"SECT. 2. Every free person, who shall aid or assist in any rebellion or insurrection of slaves, free negroes or mulattoes, or shall furnish arms, or do any other act in furtherance of such rebellion or insurrection, shall suffer DEATH.

"SECT. 3. If any free person shall, by speaking, writing, or printing, advise, persuade or induce any slaves to rebel, conspire against, or murder any citizen of the territory, or shall bring into print, write, publish, or circulate, or cause to be brought into, written, printed, published, or circulated, or shall, knowingly, aid or assist in the bringing into printing, writing, publishing, or circulating in the territory, any book, paper, magazine, pamphlet, or circular, for the purpose of exciting insurrection, rebellion, revolt, or conspiracy, on the part of the slaves, free negroes or mulattoes, against the citizens of the territory, or any part of them, such person shall suffer DEATH.

"SECT. 4. If any person shall entice, decoy, or carry away out of this territory any slave belonging to another, with the intent to deprive the owner thereof of the services of such slave, he shall be adjudged guilty of grand larceny, and, on conviction thereof, shall suffer DEATH, or be imprisoned at hard labor for not less than ten years.

"SECT. 5. If any person aid or assist in enticing, decoying, or persuading, or carrying away, or sending out of this territory, any slave belonging to another, with the intent to procure or effect the freedom of such slave, or deprive the owners thereof of the services of such slave, he shall be adjudged guilty of grand larceny, and, on conviction thereof, shall suffer DEATH, or be imprisoned at hard labor for not less than ten years.

"SECT. 6. If any person shall entice, decoy, or carry away, out of any state or other territory of the United States, any slave belonging to another, with intent to procure or effect the freedom of such slave, or to deprive the owner thereof of the services of such slave, and shall bring such slave into this territory, he shall be adjudged guilty of grand larceny, in the same manner as if such slave had been enticed, decoyed, or carried away out of this territory; and, in such case, the larceny may be charged to have been committed in any county of the territory, into or through which such slave shall have been brought by such person, and, on conviction thereof, the person offending, shall suffer death, or be imprisoned at hard labor for not less than ten years.

"SECT. 7. If any person shall entice, persuade, or induce any slave to escape from the service of his master or owner, in this territory, or shall aid or assist any slave in escaping from the service of his master or owner, or shall assist, harbor, or conceal any slave in escaping from the services of his master or owner, he shall be deemed guilty of a felony, and punished by imprisonment at hard labor for not less than ten years.

"SECT. 8. If any person in this territory shall aid or assist, harbor or conceal any slave who has escaped from the services of his master or owner, in another state or territory, such person shall be punished in like manner as if such slave had escaped from the service of his owner or master in this territory.

"SECT. 9. If any person shall resist any officer while attempting to arrest any slave that may have escaped from the service of his master or owner, or shall rescue such slave when in the custody of any officer, or other person, or shall entice, persuade, aid or assist such slave to escape from the custody of any officer or other person who may have such slave in custody, whether such slave may have escaped from the service of his master or owner in this territory, or in any other state or territory, the person so offending shall be guilty of felony, and punished by imprisonment at hard labor for a term of not less than two years.

"SECT. 10. If any marshal, sheriff, or constable, or the deputy of any such officers, shall, when required by any person, refuse to aid or assist in the arrest and capture of any slave that may have escaped from his master or owner, whether such slave shall have escaped from his master in this territory, or any state, or other territory, such officer shall be fined in a sum of not less than one hundred nor more than five hundred dollars.

"SECT. 11. If any person print, write, introduce into, or circulate, or cause to be brought into, written, printed, or circulated, or shall knowingly aid or assist in bringing into, printing, publishing or circulating within this territory, any book, paper, pamphlet, magazine, handbill, or circular containing any statements, arguments, opinions, sentiment, doctrine, advice, or innuendo, calculated to produce a disorderly, dangerous, or rebellious disaffection among the slaves of the territory, or to induce such slaves to escape from the service of their masters, or to resist their authority, he shall be guilty of felony, and be punished by imprisonment at hard labor for a term not less than five years.

"SECT. 12. If any free person, by speaking or writing, assert or maintain that persons have not the right to hold slaves in this territory, or shall introduce into this territory, print, publish, write, circulate, or cause to be introduced into the territory, written, printed, published, and circulated in this territory any book, paper, magazine, pamphlet, or circular, containing any denial of the right of persons to hold slaves in this territory, such person shall be deemed guilty of felony, and punished by imprisonment at hard labor for a term of not less than two years.

"SECT. 13. No person who is conscientiously opposed to holding slaves, or who does not admit the right to hold slaves in this territory, shall sit as a juror on the trial of any prosecution for any violation of any of the sections of this act.

"This act to take effect and be in force from and after the 15th day of September, A. D. 1855.

"J. H. STRINGFELLOW, *Speaker of the House.*

"Attest, J. M. LYLE, *Clerk.*

"THOMAS JOHNSON, *President of the Council.*

"Attest, J. A. HALDAMEN, *Clerk.*"

"AN ACT TO PUNISH PERSONS DECOYING SLAVES FROM THEIR MASTERS.

"*Be it enacted by the Governor and Legislative Assembly of Kansas Territory.*

"SECT. 1. If any person shall entice, decoy, or carry away out of this territory, any slave belonging to another, with intent to deprive the owner thereof of the services of such slave, or with intent to effect or procure the freedom of such slave, he shall be adjudged guilty of grand larceny, and on conviction thereof shall suffer death.

"SECT. 2. If any person shall aid or assist in enticing, decoying, or persuading, or carrying away, or sending out of this territory, any slave belonging to another, with intent to procure or effect the freedom of such slave, or with intent to deprive the owner thereof of the services of such slave, he shall be adjudged guilty of grand larceny, and on conviction thereof suffer death.

"SECT. 3. If any person shall entice, decoy, or carry away out of any state or other territory of the United States, any slave belonging to another, with intent to procure or effect the freedom of such slave, or to deprive the owner thereof of the services of such slave, and shall bring such slave into this territory, he shall be adjudged guilty of grand larceny, in the same manner as if such slave had been enticed, decoyed, or carried away out of this territory; and in such case the larceny may be charged to have been committed in any county of this territory, into or through which such slave shall have been brought by such person, and on conviction thereof the person offending shall suffer death."

Not satisfied with having usurped their seats, passed outrageous laws, setting the territorial executive at defiance, etc., they drew up a lengthy memorial, in which they prayed the President to remove Governor Reeder. We subjoin the two most noticeable paragraphs in the memorial:

"Already threats in advance have been made that no respect would be shown to any act passed by this Legislative Assembly, whensoever and wheresoever such act or acts may be passed. Several papers in the territory boldly advocate this position. A man, professing to have been elected to the Legislature (M. F. Conway), who afterwards tendered his resignation, advocates this doctrine of resistance. The governor is, and has been, on terms of intimacy with these very persons; and, with him as their leader, they may be led to the commission of acts which will inevitably result in wide-spread strife and bloodshed.

"In conclusion, we charge the governor, A. H. Reeder, with wilful neglect of the interests of the territory; with endeavoring, by all the means in his power, to subvert the ends and objects intended by the 'Kansas and Nebraska bill;' by neglecting the public interests, and making them subservient to private speculation; by aiding and encouraging persons in factious and treasonable opposition to the wishes of the majority of the citizens of the territory, and the laws of the United States in force in said territory; by encouraging persons to violate the laws of the United States, and set at defiance the commands of the general government; by inciting persons to resist the laws which may be passed by the present Legislative Assembly of this territory; and, finally, by a virtual dissolution of all connection with the present Legislative Assembly of this territory."

It was very natural that these Lycurguses should entertain doubts about the validity of their enactments. That these might have none was very obvious. Hence they resorted to a mode of ascertaining their validity in full keeping with their other proceedings. Instead of waiting until cases should arise under the law, they submitted some one or two of their acts to the Supreme Court of the territory. That court was organized at Shawnee, Missouri, at that time, doubtless, with some such an object. Overlooking the facts that there was no case before them, that they were prejudging any case that might arise under the statute, that the party who might be interested was thus condemned without a hearing, and that the whole proceeding was irregular and extra-judicial, the supreme judge, S. D. Lecompte, and one of his associates, Rush Elmore, decided in favor of these enactments, against the governor's veto, and bolstered up a lengthy and a confused legal opinion on the subject by the following superb piece of irony:

"In reaching this determination, they had been influenced in no small degree by their high appreciation of the constituent elements of your honorable bodies. Satisfied thoroughly that in the great requisites of intelligence and public virtue the Legislative Assembly of Kansas will compare favorably," etc., etc.

Nothing could be cooler than that; and yet we can fancy the sardonic grin of even these worthy justices when they penned it. An honorable body, many members of which lived in Missouri, and who violated their oath of office by usurping that office; who had then plundered the public of right and security by appointing their officers for them, and thus imposing a host of foreign petty tyrants on them; who were drunk every night in Westport, and often through the day at the mission. This *honorable* body, however, was filling a very important place in a great drama; a fearfully responsible transaction, in which some of the first officers of the nation were also implicated. It was, therefore, *necessary* to get up a little effervescence of this kind for circulation at a distance; for I do not suppose that either of those worthy judges expected that any one in Kansas or Missouri would do more than smile at it.

Judge Johnson, the other associate judge, dissented from the opinion; affirming that any attempt to decide these laws valid, as an abstract proposition, and before a case arose under them, was extra-judicial and irregular.

The attorney-general, a federal officer, also, *decided* along with

Lecompte and Elmore. This assumption of the powers of the bench by this officer was of a piece with the conduct of his compeers. He appended the following to this elaborate decision, immediately under their signatures:

"I fully concur in the foregoing opinion, and refrain from saying a word on a subject so well discussed. A. J. ISAACS."

These gentlemen did not neglect their pecuniary interests. They had the assurance to request Reeder's dismissal on account of alleged land-speculations, and yet immediately commenced similar or far more reprehensible ones. They created joint-stock companies, bestowing upon them extraordinary privileges; chartered prospective railroads, giving them unheard-of privileges; and these charters and corporate trusts they bestowed on their own members. Some few of the leading border ruffians, who had placed them in the position they held, received a share of such favors; but the worthy law-makers were accused by their indignant friends in Missouri of keeping everything to themselves.

They located the capital at Lecompton. This was a good speculation. A large sum of public money was to be expended there in building, and an immense plat of town lots was formed on the selected site. All of the present territorial Legislature, the territorial executive, and judiciary, are more or less interested in this scheme. It is generally believed that each of the members of the Legislature got a share in Lecompton for his vote.

Nor was this all the *special* legislation of this body. In creating the local county courts they appointed themselves to nearly everything. They created a major-general and three brigadier-generals of the "territorial militia" from their own number. William P. Richardson, a member of the council, and really a resident of Missouri, was elected to the supreme command, and L. J. Eastin, editor of the Leavenworth *Herald*, H. G. Stricklar, also a member of the council, who pretended to live in the territory, having a log shanty on a claim unclosed and unfinished, and William Barber, who is a sort of Captain Sutler, brigadier-generals. The two last are, in my opinion, also residents of Missouri.

In connection with the acquisitive faculty of this disinterested body, I append the following letter, sent by a gentleman in Independence to one in Lawrence, immediately after the adjournment of the Legislature. It is a precious morsel of awakened conscience and righteous indignation. As an explanation of it, I may state that many of the tools of the pro-slavery leaders were thoughtless, good-natured young men, who engaged in these enterprises through a love of adventure, and because it was fashionable in their neighborhood.

"INDEPENDENCE, MO., *Sept.* 1, 1855.

"SIR: Aware, as I am, that in the exposure now made of the contemptible mobocratic faction, with which I confess with shame I have hitherto acted on the Missouri frontier, I am placed in an unenviable situation, upon the maxim that 'the biggest rascal is the first to turn state's evidence;' still, I am actuated by the belief that the best reparation I can make for the injury I have done society, the principles of republicanism, and particularly the rights of the actual settlers of Kansas, is a full and fair exposition of the knavery and oppression of the banditti that has assumed, under color of law, to reduce them to the abject condition of slaves. And, first, it is true, as has been repeatedly asserted by free-soil presses, that the body of men lately assembled at the Shawnee Mission, in said territory, and which has just adjourned, was composed mainly of foreigners to the soil of Kansas, and whose actual residence was in the State of Missouri. In illustration I furnish you an anecdote of an occurrence at the mission, just on the eve of the adjournment of these political missionaries. An acquaintance of a member, who, when elected to represent the Fort Scott district, resided, if he does not still reside, at Lexington, Mo., appeared at the mission and inquired for his friend. He was asked 'if he wished to see the member from Fort Scott.' His reply was, 'Fort Hell!—I wish to see the member from Lafayette County, Mo.'

"Secondly, it is conceded here, as everywhere, that the election was a fraud on the actual inhabitants of the territory, and that this *legislative* body was elected by Missourians. Pardon another illustration. The Lawrence district was known to be free-soil; a body of from five to six hundred Missourians marched upon the town, armed with guns, pistols, bowie-knives, and two pieces of cannon. The ordnance was, however, left with the rear-guard at a convenient point some two miles from Lawrence. On their arrival they cast about for a suitable candidate, — one who, while subserving their schemes, would disgrace his *ostensible* constituents. This creature was called ———, formerly a waiter and hostler at the Union Hotel, in Kansas, Mo., from whence he was dismissed by the proprietor, a free-soiler, because of the incessant and ultra expression of his ultra and rabid abolition sentiments. It seems, however, that when this army appeared in sight a sudden change was effected in the gentleman's *views*. When within hailing distance, this chap, whose enunciatory apparatus is, by the by, somewhat irregular and defective, owing to the absence of a bridge between his nose and mouth, gave utterance to the following announcement:

"'Yente-eng! Inge 'ro-lavery, 'y 'od!'

"So the army elected him to represent Lawrence.

"As glaring, as odious, ay, infamous as his perfidy appears, I will show that his compeers were of equal turpitude. In the first place, if they concede the existence of a federal government, which would seem, from their legislation, matter of doubt, they have, to say the least, shown no manner of respect for its enactments.

"In the second place, they have perpetrated on the citizens of Kansas legislation the most invidiously partial, discriminating, and oppressive, and which the brief lucid intervals in their drunken debauchery failed to palliate or render sufferable in the judgment of all honorable men. But we, their Missouri constituents, might have pardoned these enormities, inasmuch as we were not the doomed objects of their vengeance, and only suffered in the good opinion of all right-thinking men from our relation to that body, — of which most of us are now heartily ashamed, — had *our* representatives remembered to whom they owed their 'little brief authority.' But, so far from it, every railroad company, joint-stock or town company, proposed to be incorporated, must embrace in its numbers a *majority of this Legislature.* But, worst of all, they have the modest delicacy to appoint themselves to nearly all the offices created by them during the session. In this closing act of treachery they have disappointed the just expectations of the veterans who served last March in the army of invasion, and whose unparalleled sufferings and servitude in upholding the principles of squatter sovereignty should have been appreciated and rewarded. But no. The judgeships, commissionerships, sheriffalties, etc., were all monopolized by *our servants;* and we who did the fighting, and the '*cavorting*,' and the swearing (when the judges of election required it, which was seldom), are left to starve at home, or enlist in any fillibustering enterprise that may offer.

"In conclusion, I regret to say that Atchison and Stringfellow are dead as herrings in Missouri, and that the conservative pro-slavery party is ashamed of them, and regard themselves *rowelled*, and repudiate their policy and tactics *in toto.*

"ONE OF THE ARMY OF INVASION.

"*Editor of Herald of Freedom.*"

CHAPTER VIII.

REMOVAL OF REEDER — GOV. SHANNON — THE BIG SPRING CONVENTION.

THE administration had determined to remove Reeder. Grea efforts were made to form a plausible pretext; for, habitually short sighted although the national executive had become, it had stil sufficient glimmerings of sense to know that it would never do t make the real motive the avowed one. The Missourians on th frontier were clamoring boisterously for his removal, and he wa removed accordingly. He was accused of having speculated i Kaw lands. Now he was merely one of a company that propose to purchase a portion of the Kaw half-breed lands, provided th general government would sanction such a purchase. The purchase in question was never made. It would naturally be inferred that Gov. Reeder was a large owner of real estate in the territory; such is very far from being the case. In fact, if the general government intend to dismiss governors of territories for land speculation, they may dismiss all the governors we have, or ever had. I have yet to learn that the governor of a territory should be the only man in it who is prohibited from speculating in land.

On Reeder's removal the office was tendered to Mr. Dawson, of Pennsylvania, but he prudently declined. It was then tendered to and accepted by Wilson Shannon, of Ohio.

Mr. Shannon is a man past middle age. His form is tall, but stoops forward, and is awkward and inelegant. His hair is gray, almost white. With acquirements not much above mediocrity, and abilities rather below it, it is difficult to comprehend how he could ever have been Governor of Ohio. Not only does his mind lack in weight, but in stability. Little confidence although the public have in the governor, he has still less in himself. His crimes, indeed, proceed not so much from his venom as from his weakness. He is a politician without being a statesman; not one of the cunning adepts at political chicanery, but a *working* politician, of the abject type, who permits himself to be moulded and used by others merely for what little honor or interest it may afford. His administration will ever be infamous, because it is one of the first attempts at subjugating the American people by corrupt and despotic rulers. He is also another evidence that the weakest man is often the greatest tyrant. He is no Nero, although like that tyrant he could have fiddled while Lawrence was in flames. Neither is he a Duke of Alva. He is one of those men who never look *in* to themselves for an abiding principle; habit, or an innate tendency that way, has made him look *out* for what others said and others would pay for.

I wish I could throw a few "lights" among these "shadows," in order to relieve the picture, and give it a look of patent impartiality in the eyes of those whose conservatism prevents them from taking anything like an extreme view of either men or things. He is, then, a good-natured, easy man, except in certain cases. A political habit has made him affable to all who are in the circle of his possible interests. This disposition has often misled some people as to his true position. In his company they would find that he professed regard for the interests and rights of all, and sometimes deplored or affected to deplore the unfortunate occurrences resulting from his bad management or corrupt intriguing with party. Many have thus been led to think and say that "he was not such a bad fellow," or that "he was going to do everything that was right *now;*" and only woke up to the delusion on the recurrence of some startling or outrageous act with which he was unquestionably connected.

I do not know that it is necessary to the veracity of an account that it should make the conduct of those it represents sensible or even rational. I wish, therefore, to appeal for the veracity of my description of him, and to urge that the apparent incongruities are incident to the subject. Had Governor Shannon been a good disciple of temperance, he would, in all probability, have been much better or a much worse governor. As it is, he is liable to follow an erratic course, and the opinion you form of him depends mainly at what particular stage of his potations you find him. While a member of Congress, Mr. Shannon often gave indication of these *symptoms;* but the care of an estimable and affectionate daughter saved him then from much of that depth into which he has since fallen. She watched him, guided him, kept him sober, and even, it is stated, wisely counselled him on his public course. Would that the administration had included her name in the territorial appointments! But he has always been a "*consistent Democrat;*" that is, according to the modern rendering of the term. His votes on that question (slavery extension) have always been thrown for the policy of the South. He has filled many important public offices, and has represented the United States abroad at more than one nation.

When Wilson Shannon received his appointment as Governor of Kansas he immediately set out for the territory. An effort had been made by the border men to secure the appointment of Secretary Woodson, who had always been true to them; but, though the administration yielded to them in everything else, it insisted on choosing the tool. While on his way up the river, Shannon met many of those leading Missourians who had taken an active part in invading the territory. With these he associated, and cordiality was exhibited in this intercourse, pregnant with promise for the future. At Westport, Mo., one of the most violent border towns, he was proffered and accepted a public reception. Besides convivialities, speeches were made, all relating to the policy to be pursued in regard to the territory. To have received such ovations, and have such interchange of sentiment on Kansas affairs with men who had been engaged in the most lawless and outrageous violation of the rights of the people of the territory, was certainly inconsistent with the dignity of the Governor of Kansas; but if a doubt of its impropriety could be entertained, it was dissipated by the speech he made on the occasion, of which the subjoined is the report of the able correspondent of the Missouri *Democrat*. Its accuracy has been vouched for by many who heard the governor.

"Gov. Shannon began his remarks by thanking the audience for their courteous reception. It gratified him, he said, not because it was personally flattering, but because it showed that they were not disposed to decide on his 'official career' in advance. It showed him that he might rely on 'YOUR AID' in endeavoring to overcome obstacles which he was aware existed, but hoped were not insurmountable.

"A voice — 'Yes, you shall have OUR aid.'

"He regretted to see, in certain portions of the territory, a disposition to nullify the laws which have been enacted by 'YOUR Legislature.' This was a revolutionary movement greatly to be deplored. He 'regretted,' he said, that he arrived too late to make the acquaintance of the members of the Legislature. He knew nothing of the laws passed by them; but, from the ability and patriotism of the gentlemen who composed it, he doubted not that they were wise and judicious. But, even if they were not wise and judicious, open resistance and nullification of them was not the proper way to defeat their provisions. If they were unconstitutional, there were courts to appeal to, which had been created for the purpose of deciding such questions.

"As to the Legislature that had recently adjourned at the Shawnee Mission, he regarded it as a legal assembly (cheers), and thought that the objections to its power, grounded on its removal from Pawnee, were puerile, as every Legislature enjoyed the right of removing the seat of government at pleasure. The executive and *judiciary* of the territory had acknowledged the Legislature as a legal body, and so would he! (Good.) He regarded the laws as binding on every citizen of the territory, and would use all his executive power and authority to carry them into effect. (Cheers.)

"He said it was not his intention to address them on the various questions that divided the parties in the territory; perhaps he did not understand them, and he had not expected to speak on this occasion.

"To one subject, however, he would allude — slavery. His official life and character were not unknown to a portion, at least, of the citizens of Kansas. He had no intention of changing h political faith. He thought, with reference to slavery, that, Missouri and Kansas were adjoining states, — as much of that im mense trade up the Missouri, which was already rivalling th commerce between the United States and some foreign countric must necessarily lead to a great trade and perpetual intercour between them, — it would be well if their *institutions* should *har monize;* otherwise there would be continual quarrels and bord feuds. *He was for slavery in Kansas.* (Loud cheers.)"

Gov. Shannon has, I believe, denied some of the positior reported in this speech; but, as his subsequent acts have mo than sustained the position taken, I deem all proof of its correc ness unnecessary.

As if the fact of having a public reception at Westport was nc enough, the governor rendered his position still more plain by de clining to visit or hold intercourse with some of the most promi nent towns in the territory. He took up his residence at Shawnc Mission, the seat of government chosen by the Missouri Kansa Legislature. On his first trip up into the territory he neglecte to visit Lawrence, then the most important town in it, going on t Lecompton, then merely a paper town without a house. Subse quently he had occasion to go through Lawrence, on his return t the mission. The people, who of course wished him for a friend if possible, called on him; he received them with coolness, hel himself aloof from the citizens of the place, and left as soon as h could, having declined any public reception, or to make an speech, or in any way to show sympathy with them. His pro ceedings at Westport, coupled with this, aroused the indignatio of many of the settlers. As he drove off from Lawrence, on th occasion referred to, a few boys evidenced the sentiment he ha awakened by groaning for him. This was suppressed by the dis creet and conservative, but was, unquestionably, an honest demon stration of the esteem in which he was regarded.

Such was the state of affairs in Kansas in the summer of 1855. An outside Legislature, inimical to their interests, and hostile to their persons and opinions, had made laws for them. A partisan judiciary had pronounced on the validity of those laws, without hearing a case. Gov. Reeder, who seemed inclined to do them justice, had been removed, and a man appointed who acted with their enemies, and who declared that these laws must be obeyed, before he entered the territory or had any means of knowing their true character, and by whom imposed. Under these circumstances there appeared to be but one remedy, and the experience of other territories suggested the remedy and supplied the precedent. The state movement is one that could have been made with propriety at any stage in the affairs of the territory, and which the present exigency promptly called for, as a remedy that would meet the case, and restore authority to govern themselves to the people of Kansas. In regard to this movement the committee of Congress affirms:

"While these enactments of the alleged Legislative Assembly were being made, a movement was instituted to form a state government and apply for admission into the Union as a state. The first step taken by the people of the territory, in consequence of the invasion of March 30, 1855, was the circulation for signature of a graphic and truthful memorial to Congress. Your committee find that every allegation in the memorial has been sustained by the testimony. No further step was taken, as it was hoped that some action by the general government would protect them in their rights. When the alleged Legislative Assembly proceeded to construct the series of enactments referred to, the settlers were of opinion that submission to them would result in depriving them of the rights secured to them by the organic law. Their political condition was freely discussed in the territory during the summer of 1855. Several meetings were held in reference to holding a convention to form a state government, and to apply for admission into the Union as a state."

Mass meetings and conventions were held, and the subject freely discussed. The following resolution, adopted at one of the primary mass meetings, will evidence the character of the movement:

"*Resolved*, That we, the people of Kansas Territory, in mass meeting assembled, irrespective of party distinctions, influenced by common necessity, and greatly desirous of promoting the common good, do hereby call upon and request all *bona fide* citizens of Kansas Territory, of whatever political views or predilections, to consult together in their respective election districts, and in mass convention or otherwise elect three delegates for each representative to which said election district is entitled in the House of Representatives of the Legislative Assembly, by proclamation of Governor Reeder, of date 19th of March, 1855; said delegates to assemble in convention at the town of Topeka on the 19th day of September, 1855, then and there to consider and determine upon all subjects of public interest, and particularly upon that having reference to the speedy formation of the state constitution, with an intention of immediate application to be admitted as a state into the Union of the United States of America."

The first convention was held at Big Springs on the 5th of September, 1855. It was numerously attended. One hundred delegates were present, and they represented every district and settlement in the territory. This convention had several objects. In the first place, it repudiated the laws and officers of the Missouri Kansas Legislature, and declared that body to be an illegal usurpation. They made a call for another delegate convention to be holden at Topeka on the 17th of that month, to determine whether a movement to organize Kansas as a state should be set on foot. But the most important act of this convention, and what made it the starting-point in these affairs, was the nomination of a candidate for delegate to Congress. Amongst their other acts the Bogus Legislature had made provision for an election to be held October 1st. As this act could no more be recognized than any other of a body declared illegal, and as the qualifications required of voters, in the shape of test oaths and tax, were irregular, in violation of their primary rights, oppressive, and illegal, they determined to hold an election on a different day. This election was to be regulated by the prescribed rules of the March election, excepting so far as appointing judges, etc., was concerned. As Governor Shannon was hostile to the movement, and recognized the validity of the Missouri Kansas Legislature, he, of course, was not going to appoint judges of election, or receive returns. Provisions were made for this by an "executive committee," which was created and endowed with provisional authority to assist in organizing a state government.

Subjoined are the most important of the proceedings of this body:

"Whereas, the constitution of the United States guarantees to the people of this republic the right of assembling together in a peaceable manner for their common good, to 'establish justice, ensure domestic tranquillity, provide for the common defence, promote the general welfare, and secure the blessings of liberty to themselves and their posterity;' and whereas the citizens of Kansas Territory were prevented from electing members of a Legislative Assembly, in pursuance of a proclamation of Gov. Reeder, on the 30th of March last, by invading forces from foreign states coming into the territory and forcing upon the people a Legislature of non-residents, and others inimical to the interests of the people of Kansas Territory, defeating the objects of the organic act, in consequence of which the territorial government became a perfect failure, and the people were left without any legal government, until their patience has become exhausted, and 'endurance ceases to be a virtue;' and they are compelled to resort to the only remedy left — that of forming a government for themselves. Therefore,

"*Resolved*, by the people of Kansas Territory, in delegate convention assembled, that an election shall be held, in the several election precincts of this territory, on the second Tuesday of October next, under the regulations and restrictions hereinafter imposed, for members of a convention to form a constitution, adopt a bill of rights for the people of Kansas, and take all needful measures for organizing a state-government, preparatory to the admission of Kansas into the Union as a state.

"*Resolved*, That a committee of seven be appointed by the chair, who shall organize by the appointment of a chairman and secretary. They shall keep a record of their proceedings, and shall have the general superintendence of the affairs of the territory, so far as regards the organization of a state government; which committee shall be styled 'THE EXECUTIVE COMMITTEE OF KANSAS TERRITORY.'

"*Resolved*, That we owe no allegiance or obedience to the tyrannous enactment of this spurious Legislature; that their laws have no validity or binding force upon the people of Kansas, and that every free man amongst us is at full liberty, consistently with our obligations as a citizen and a man, to defy and resist them, if he choose to do so.

"*Resolved*, That we will resist them primarily by every peaceable and legal means within our power, until we can elect our representatives, and sweep them from the statute-book; and that, as the majority of our Supreme Court have so far forgotten their official duty, have so far cast off the honor of the lawyer and the dignity of the judge, as to enter, clothed with the judicial ermine, into a partisan contest, and, by an extra-judicial decision, given opinions in violation of all propriety, have prejudged our case before we could be heard, and have pledged themselves to these outlaws in advance, to decide in their favor, we will, therefore, take measures to carry the question of the validity of these laws to a higher tribunal, where judges are unpledged and dispassionate; where the law will be administered in its purity, and where we can, at least, have the hearing before the decision.

"*Resolved*, That we will endure and submit to these laws no longer than the best interests of the territory require, as the least of two evils; and will resist them to a bloody issue as soon as we ascertain that peaceable remedies shall fail, and forcible resistance shall furnish any reasonable prospect of success; and that, in the mean time, we recommend to our friends throughout the territory the organization and discipline of volunteer companies, and the procurement and preparation of arms.

"*Resolved*, That we cannot, and will not, submit quietly to the surrender of our great 'American birthright,'— the elective franchise, which, first by violence, and then by chicanery, artifice, weak and wicked legislation, they have so effectually accomplished to deprive us of; and that we with scorn repudiate the 'Election Law,' so called, and will not meet with them on the day they have appointed for the election, but will, ourselves, fix upon a day for the purpose of electing a delegate to Congress."

In pursuance of this latter resolution steps were taken to hold a popular election for delegates to Congress on the second Tuesday of October, 1855. The convention put the name of A. H. Reeder in nomination. Governor Reeder accepted his nomination in a speech of more than usual fervor.

"As he paused, there was, for an instant, a deep silence, as when a question of life or death is being considered; every man drew a long breath, but the next instant the air was rent with cries, 'Yes, we will strike!' 'White men never can be slaves!' 'Reeder!' 'Reeder!' 'Nine cheers for Reeder and right!' During his speech he had been constantly interrupted by shouts and shaking of hands; but now the enthusiasm was ungovernable, the crowd gathered around him with the warmest greetings."

A platform was chosen, at this convention, for a free-state party, and the effort made to organize all under it in a movement to secure the admission of Kansas as a free state. Below is a preamble, and a synopsis of the resolutions:

"Whereas, the free-state party of the Territory of Kansas is about to originate an organization for concert of political action in electing our own officers and moulding our institutions; and whereas it is expedient and necessary that a platform of principles be adopted and proclaimed, to make known the character of our organization, and to test the qualifications of candidates and the fidelity of members; and whereas we find ourselves in an unparalleled and critical condition, deprived by superior force of the rights guaranteed by the Declaration of Independence, the Constitution of the United States, and the Kansas Bill; and whereas the great and overshadowing question, whether Kansas shall become a free or slave state, must inevitably absorb all other issues, except those inseparably connected with it; and whereas the crisis demands the concert and harmonious action of all those who, from principle or interest, prefer free to slave labor, as well as of those who value the preservation of the Union, and the guarantees of republican institutions by the constitution."

The first resolution invites men of all parties to join in the movement. The second resolution denounces non-resident voters, no matter where from. The third declares it the policy that Kansas must be a free state. The fourth expresses a determination to make "reasonable provision" for slaves now in the territory. The fifth resolution, that no negro, bond or free, shall be permitted to come to the territory (this being the celebrated black-law feature). The sixth repudiates the charge of "abolitionism," as affixed to the free-state party. The seventh asserts the doctrine of state rights, and discountenances any interference with the constitutional rights of the state to regulate their domestic affairs.

Sundry other resolutions and reports were adopted.

CHAPTER IX.

DELEGATE ELECTION — TOPEKA CONVENTION.

There were two Topeka conventions. The first, a primary one, decided that the territory should be organized into a state, and provided the means. Relative to the proceedings of this body, the committee of Congress report:

"They met at Topeka, on the 19th day of September, 1855. By their resolutions they provided for the appointment of an executive committee, consisting of seven persons, who were required to 'keep a record of their proceedings, and shall have a general superintendence of the affairs of the territory, so far as regards the organization of the state government.' They were required to take steps for an election to be held on the second Tuesday of the October following, under regulations imposed by that committee, 'for members of a convention to form a constitution, adopt a bill of rights for the people of Kansas, and take all needful measures for organizing a state government, preparatory to the admission of Kansas into the Union as a state.' The rules prescribed were such as usually govern elections in most of the states of the Union, and in most respects were similar to those contained in the proclamation of Governor Reeder for the election of March 30, 1855."

The election for delegates to the constitutional convention was held at the same time that the free-state settlers voted for delegate to Congress. The pro-slavery residents of the territory refused to act with them, the existing state of affairs being exactly suited to their policy. On the 1st of October, Whitfield received some three thousand votes for delegate, at the election fixed by the Bogus Legislature, and received a certificate from Governor Shannon. There is no question but what over two thousand of

11*

the votes given were illegal votes. By the report of the committee upwards of eight hundred of these have been proved to be illegal; but the committee did not institute a very thorough search into this election, deeming it more important to investigate the March election. In the different precincts the people voted for delegate, throwing twenty-eight hundred and sixteen votes for Reeder. In some of the precincts, such as Atchison, Kickapoo, Shawnee, Church, and one or two other pro-slavery points, no vote was allowed to be taken.

About this time there was a rather humorous illustration of border ruffian interference. The Bogus Legislature, amongst its other business, divided the territory into counties. Either by accident, or on account of the multiplicity of business before them, they neglected to locate all the county seats. In most of the counties this was a matter of no consequence, as the settlers paid no more attention to the location of counties than to the other action of that body. In the case of Leavenworth, however, there was an interesting contest. The city of Leavenworth, although it contains a majority of free-state men, so far recognizes the Bogus Legislature as to accept a city charter under it. In doing this, and in much of the subsequent conduct of the people there, they were influenced partly by business considerations, and partly by timidity. Although the resident pro-slavery population was smaller than that of the free-state, still it was numerous. Again, it is situated just over the river from Platte County, — a convenience which has its drawbacks as well as its advantages. The business men of both parties in Leavenworth were not so wrapt up in politics as to overlook money-making. An election was held in Leavenworth County to locate the county seat. This occurred early in October. Three points contended for the honor. Leavenworth, the largest, and now the largest city in the territory, felt sure of it; so sure that no very *special* effort was made. Kickapoo was another contestant. Kickapoo is a river town, being some ten miles up the Missouri river from Leavenworth. It is a cotton-wood town of the "great futurity" school, and does a heavy business in the whiskey-retailing line. The other point, Delaware, is also a river town, eight miles below. This latter place has an admirable *faculty* for making a great place, there being scarcely anything of it now.

As Delaware and Kickapoo, added together and multiplied by two, would not make Leavenworth, it was clearly evident to both modern Kickapoo and Delaware that it was a hopeless case unless "something was to turn up." Previous elections had taught them a lesson, and furnished a valuable precedent. Western Missouri is just over the river from Kickapoo, and many of the citizens of the former place have an interest in the latter. So it is with Delaware; many of the most deeply interested speculators in this yet-to-be Babylon live in Clay and Platte Counties, Missouri. Under these circumstances it is not wonderful that it was not difficult to arouse an interest in this election in Missouri. Another thing against Leavenworth — it was reputed to be an "abolition hole." The election came off. Leavenworth polled some five or six hundred votes, which I suppose the town and county adjacent could do at that time. Between Kickapoo and Weston the steam-ferry ran free all day. Missourians poured over as they had done at former elections, being naturalized in the ferry-boat by a ceremony in which whiskey, bread and cheese, figured extensively. Kickapoo, which might have been able to poll one hundred and fifty votes, rolled up eight hundred for the county seat.

At Delaware, also, they attended to their interests. A steamer was chartered to run between Delaware and any point on the other side where there were voters. *Public sentiment* was aroused by a band of music, free whiskey, and other edibles, and *kept aroused* by objurgations on the "d—d abolitionists of Leavenworth!" Delaware struck out a new feature in electioneering. Instead of being satisfied with one day's voting, they kept their polls open and the boat running until they had time to ascertain how many votes had been polled at Kickapoo, and also as much longer as it required to make up a larger vote. By the evening of the third day they had obtained nearly nine hundred (they could not have thrown more than fifty legal votes); so the polls closed in triumph. The first authority, to whom these election returns were made, declared in favor of Kickapoo; deciding that keeping polls open for three days was an "unheard of irregularity." Kickapoo was jubilant. Leavenworth felt sore. Her pro-slavery men were grievously indignant. So long as this kind of operation had been directed against the "abolitioners," it was fun; but now *they* began to realize a touch of "squatter sovereignty, as enunciated in the Kansas-Nebraska bill." The Leavenworth *Herald*, whose pro-slavery editor had been a member of the Bogus Council of the Shawnee Mission, began to print moral lessons and homilies on the "tendencies of these things." All of the respectable, which means the property-holding, pro-slavery men about Leavenworth, looked solemn; so much so that their friends were seriously apprehensive that they would "ketch religion."

The Kickapoo *Pioneer*, a fire-eating, pro-slavery paper, taunted Mr. Easton, of the Leavenworth *Herald*, about his sudden conversion to the "purify-the-polls" doctrine; and finished a somewhat sarcastic article by asking, "Who elected *you* to the Legislature?" This was severe, but fair. In the dilemma, the *Herald* got off the following interesting morsel, being part of a "grievous article" two columns long:

"Much has been said by the abolition presses throughout the country about 'armed invasions of Kansas by the border ruffians of Missouri;' but, as we then asserted, and still assert, they were acting solely in self-defence; and history will tell of the purity of their purposes, and of the justice of the *cause they vindicated.* They came here actuated by the noblest of human sentiments, determined to ward off a blow which was aimed against their institutions, and against their peace. As such, with open arms we welcome them; and, when victory crowned our common efforts, and the black flag of abolitionism was trailed in the dust, how grateful were the feelings which we experienced to those who had rallied with us to a hand-to-hand encounter with the aggressive foes!

"But, did any pro-slavery man in or out of Kansas for a moment imagine that, by reason of such elections, Kansas had surrendered unconditionally, and that Missouri had made the conquest of the territory for the sole use and benefit of Platte County upon her border? and, worse than this, to be made the plaything and puppet of a few demagogues and hucksters in Weston and Platte city? The idea is simply absurd."

Absurd though it might be, it still was a "fixed fact." Even Kickapoo had to bite the dust before the sovereign will of "majority." The election was referred to a *court*, which decided in favor of Delaware. This was, at least, consistent; for, as all the pro-slavery courts, which means all the courts in the territory, had decided in favor of bogus authority, it was not going to do to establish so dangerous a precedent as setting an election aside on account of any irregularity.

The Constitutional Convention assembled at Topeka on the twenty-third of October, 1855. It was by far the most respectable body of men, in point of talent, that ever convened in Kansas; indeed, it would have compared favorably with legislative bodies anywhere. Talent and the weak vanity which apes it were there; true virtue and a more plastic school of morality; patriotism and number-one-ism; "outside influence" and a lobby; sober, staid, business habits, brandy, temperance, whiskey, prayers by the chaplain, profanity, and oyster-suppers. It lacked in none of the great essentials.

It was composed of three distinct classes in, I should suppose, nearly equal proportions. First, there were the stern men of unyielding principles, who realized the full responsibility of the struggle in Kansas; and, in doing so, felt the necessity of making the interests of the cause the only consideration until a happier state of things could be brought about. Then there was a class, mostly young, who, while deeply sensible of the interests of Kansas, were not entirely oblivious to their own. These were true citizens and first-rate free-state men. They were determined to do their duty by the country, and that Kansas should go ahead as a free state, and that they should go ahead with it. They were not anxious about any present emolument, as the facilities for obtaining it were moderate, very; but, aware that Kansas had to cut her future greatness out of her present "raw material," were anxious to be manufactured into the great men aforesaid. The third class was one more difficult to describe. It consisted of politicians who were — no, not broken down, as that they only would have been if they had stayed at home; but, in short, of "men who had seen some little of their country's service." Some of these gentlemen came to Kansas without any ostensible occupation, but all of them had "served their time" at working in *wire*. As manœuvring is an essential part of legislation, now-a-days, they were highly useful. They were determined not to let the press of more important business permit them to neglect the *proper* formation of parties in the territory. As this was merely a philanthropic desire to prevent the spread of political unorthodoxy, they were, of course, highly commendable. That they electioneered with the young members was natural; they electioneered with everybody. As soon as such characters see a man they approach him by the irresistible force of political gravitation. They grapple him by the button-hole, and, with head anxiously bent towards their victim, they explain "the meaning of all this." It may be that they were eloquent on the excellence of some party, which was perfect, immutable, and eternal; or the formation of a "state ticket" as soon as Kansas should "come into our glorious Union." If the latter, the victim was assured that *he* "must be a candidate for something;" "the public cannot afford to lose his services." And, if the victim blush, or hesitate, or say something about "not caring for office, only will let my *friends* do as they please," the politician goes off in a wrapt study for a moment, and then, as if inspired by an idea, releases the button-hole, and, slapping the victim on the shoulder, exclaims, "Look here, I have it — I'll attend to this! The fact is we must act together. Union is strength, you know." Our politicians are adepts at that trick. Like Satan, they make free to offer "all the kingdom in the world" to those who will "fall down and worship them."

I do not say that such was the particular convention at Topeka, in order to show it was a corrupt body. I believe, take it all in all, it was as honorable and devoted as any representative body ever is in these times. Their self-denying position was a guarantee for their sincerity. I only mention it to show that, in all the great requisites for modern law-making, it was "nothing lacking." One feature there was not in the convention, that is, a pro-slavery delegate. There were men from the South, however.

Most of the states in the Union were represented. The close-calculating man from "way down east," in Maine or New Hampshire, the impulsive and proud South Carolinian, the astute and earnest thinker from Massachusetts, the hospitable and frank member from Kentucky or Tennessee, a politician from New York, an old hunker or fossiliferous Whig from Pennsylvania, or an Ohio man who had "left that state because he was growing fanatical." Then there was a fair sprinkling from the Western States, — Suckers, Wolverines, Hoosiers, with some who had been to Iowa or Wisconsin. The "Old Dominion" had a couple of representatives who dated from the pine-girt hills of Roanoke. There was an English clergyman; a Baptist preacher from Missouri, of what particular "shell" I cannot say, for he kept his religion within it while at Topeka. A son of the "Emerald Isle" was also there. He had lived in Indiana, in Tennessee, — but I tire the reader.

The business of the convention progressed with considerable expedition. There was, of course, the usual amount of speechifying; but no more than was requisite for the "*political* economy" of the body. The majority of the members worked night and day, — by day in the hall, at night in the committee-rooms. Each man who could get a copy of the constitution of the state he came from, did so, and when anything varying from that standard was offered, rose to explain that such a feature "was not in the constitution" of "Indiany," or "Pennsylvany." By dint of the friction a constitution was produced, — as good a specimen of organic law as can be found in the West, with rather less of a statutory character than is usually placed in such documents.

By this constitution it was decided that "slavery shall not exist in the state;" although, by express provision, those slaves now in the territory are permitted to be held in it until July 4th, 1857. The boundaries are those laid down in the Kansas-Nebraska bill; although a definition of the boundaries to include only two hundred miles of the north-eastern portion was strongly advocated. Married women, under this constitution, are to be secured their right to property obtained either before or after marriage, and an equal right to control or educate their children. In all prosecutions for libel, the truth, as alleged, is to be given in evidence, and received as a justification. A state university and normal schools are to be established. The judiciary is to be elective. Civilized and friendly Indians are to be admitted to citizenship. An amusing discussion occurred on this measure, relative to the words in the report, when drafted, "shall conform to the habits of the whites;" it being believed that some of the "habits of the whites" would make a rather singular basis for the elective franchise, or political power generally. It was suggested that the capacity to drink a pint of raw whiskey be deemed an evidence of "conforming to the habits of the whites." Topeka was selected as the temporary seat of government; the location of a permanent seat being left with the Legislature. Some little time was consumed by a venerable Whig from "the Commonwealth of Pennsylvania," who wished that Kansas be not called a state, but the "Commonwealth of Kansas." The proposition was not adopted.

To this constitution there were two addenda. One of these was a provision for a free banking system. The other was a resolution of instructions to the first Legislature, requiring them to frame a law to exclude free blacks from settling in the territory. These two were to be submitted to the people as separate articles. The article relative to the exclusion of free negroes, called the "black-law," created considerable discussion. Many wished to include it in the constitution. This resolution was one of the humbugs, or tests, which decide nothing, while they create a party. In deciding upon its merits neither Legislature nor people took a true or comprehensive view of the question. To have a community of white people only is certainly desirable; but, instead of discussing this in connection with its comparative justice and humanity, the whole issue turned thus. An advocate of the measure would get a man by the button-hole, and say:

"Look here,—this black-law is a great thing. They accuse us Kansas folks of being abolitionists. Now we an't abolitionists, are we?"

"No, SIR!"

"No, sir-ee—I know we an't; so the thing is to vote for the 'black-law,' and that will prove we an't 'abolitionists.'"

So Kansas voted for the "black-law" to demonstrate that she was not an "abolitionist."

It was on a Saturday night when the convention drew its labor to a close. For some days back the revising committee had been working night and day. At last the organic law was finished, and the members of that convention clustered round to sign it. Their names stand recorded in the order I take them.

Robert Klotz. — Major Klotz was a Pennsylvania Democrat, of the days when there was a Democracy in Pennsylvania; but he eschews the "national" kind. He was an officer in Mexico, and served gallantly at the National Bridge. He has reddish hair and whiskers, which circle his good-humored face like a flame of fire; and he has a happy faculty for laughing himself, which generally spreads like contagion whenever he gets on his feet to speak. He did not indulge in long speeches; but would occasionally rise with a sharp or sarcastic question "for information," and spoke whenever he fancied anything wrong was about to occur.

Marcus J. Parrott. — Mr. Parrott is a lawyer, — a South Carolinian by birth, but who came from Ohio to Kansas. He is a young man of dark complexion and Southern temperament. He was an administration Democrat when he came to Kansas; but I scarcely feel safe in laying down dates for the opinions of this class of politicians after they have experienced "squatter sovereignty as enunciated under the Kansas Nebraska bill." Of thorough acquirements and profound thought, he was yet paralyzed by a listless indolence truly Southern.

Mark W. Delahay is a character, — a Democrat of the "majority" kind. He came to Kansas a worshipper of "squatter sovereignty as enunciated," etc.; and regarded Stephen A. Douglas as the "greatest moral hero of the age." Mr. Delahay spoke often. In person he is tall and dignified; for his face, take a portrait of the Czar Nicholas, and add a little saturnine expression. When he speaks, he has a habit of leaning forward and poking out his arm, with his hand and forefinger stretched as if he had got an idea on the end of it, and was anxious to send it home. He said in the convention that he "would as soon buy a nigger as buy a mule;" which I believe; and, indeed, think he would rather, if he got it for the same money. He was the laborious advocate throughout the session of a resolution to endorse, save and redeem Douglas and his Kansas Nebraska bill. As a politician he is earnest, as a free-state man *conservative*, as a gentleman bland and serene. He is not a Maine-Law fanatic.

W. R. Griffith I do not clearly remember. The ghost of something like a quiet figure, rising once or twice to a point of explanation, comes occasionally and vaguely on my mental retina, and makes me think I have seen him; but I will not be positive.

G. S. Hillier. — Mr. Hillier is a Western man. I think he was a Whig, but has been a Republican in Kansas. He is tall, pleasant-looking, and, I think, a family man, from his appearance. He spoke often briefly, but never made a formal speech, and seemed to think it more important to "watch" than to pray.

Wm. Hicks was a quiet member, who, in remembering he was a free-state man, seemed to sink most of his other political views. He voted quietly and consistently.

S. N. Latta. — Judge Latta has been a conservative Whig; sympathized with the conservative national men, and finally grew into a conservative Republican. He is a very useful man withal. Never made a speech of any length, but spoke when he had something to say. He is a tall man, of uncertain age, and a bachelor.

John Landis looks like a border ruffian; but he is not. A right stanch, good free-state man he has been. I am not positive about his politics, but I think he is some kind of a Democrat.

C. W. Stewart, H. Burson, J. M. Arthur, and J. L. Sayle. — These are very fair specimens of the quiet members of the convention. They spoke occasionally, but never inflicted speeches. They are Western men, or have been for some time in the West.

Caleb May is a character; a Missourian, tall, dark-visaged and stern. He is one of those men you would not like to meet for an enemy. He was a free-state man, of the black-law school, but had a remembrance that he had been a Democrat. He was a good and true man, however, but rigid and stern.

Samuel Mewhinny spoke seldom in the convention, but was listened to respectfully when he did.

A. Curtis. — Mr. Curtis spoke often, but never long. He was ealous on the black-law.

Almon Hunting is one of those dark-garmented, white neck-othed, estimable gentlemen, whom you can no more convert nto a Western man by bringing him West, than you can cultivate an Osage orange into a dahlia. He is an elderly gentleman. He was a working man, and kept a close watch of business. I think he is a Republican.

R. Knight. — The Rev. Richard Knight was an Englishman and a clergyman. A man of ability, he was fully conscious of its possession. As chairman of the Committee on Education, he devoted much of his attention to that department. An ultra anti-slavery man, he carried his opinions to an extreme which prevented him from having sufficient respect for those who differed from him. le was tall, and striking in figure, but not handsome. Cold, self-possessed, and selfish, he walked through the convention not loved, but respected.

O. C. Brown. — Mr. Brown, like the other members of the great family of Brown, was a person of some consequence, and rather a prominent member.

W. Graham. — Dr. Graham is a son of the Emerald Isle, although you would scarcely recognize him as one. He has been in Tennessee and Indiana, and, I believe, some other states, and has become westernized. He is a short, chunky man; was a Democrat till his party went off and left him.

Morris Hunt. — Philosophers who find a resemblance between sound and sense will trace a pleasant instance in our friend Morris Hunt! How pleasant and euphonious the name! and just so the pleasant-faced, blue-eyed down-easter. Judge Hunt, besides one labored speech, made a great many less ambitious efforts. He had been a Whig; may be one yet, for aught I know.

J. H. Nesbitt. — Mr. Nesbitt might have set for Rembrandt's "Jew;" dark-visaged, and dark-bearded. He took a fair share in the proceedings, and was of the Democrats.

C. K. Holliday. — Mr. Holliday is a Pennsylvanian, a lawyer, and a man of ability. He was often out of the hall, but held a respectable position when in it.

David Dodge. — Mr. Dodge came from Iowa to Kansas, and I forgot where he was from formerly. He was a lawyer, a bachelor, and a Democrat; the two latter phases he may change, as he is young yet. He is one of those fine young men, whom I can conscientiously recommend to all mothers of marriageable daughters. He introduced quite a creditable proposition about the location of the capital. It was a theory, however, and theory now-a-days never locates capitals.

J. A. Wakefield. — I have already given some account of the judge, and must not trespass on the reader's patience; but to dismiss the venerable gentleman in this way would not do. What should we have done at that Topeka Convention without those speeches of Judge Wakefield's? There was something delicious in them, which broke the dull monotony of egotism and politics. The judge is an old man. He is a Western man; a Virginian to begin with. He has been in Kentucky, "Eelenoy," Iowa, and was one of the first settlers in Kansas. The judge, amongst his other accomplishments, has a faculty for quoting Latin. He has "ben a judge whar there was thirty lawyers a practisin';" has filled a prominent sphere in politics. He fills a large sphere anywhere.

W. Y. Roberts. — Mr. Roberts came from the State of Pennsylvania. He has been in the Legislature of that state, a fact of which he informed the convention repeatedly during the session. Tall, rigid, slim, and attenuated, he looked like a mummy which had undergone the process of resuscitation. Upon parliamentary usage he was *au fait*. It was delightful to contemplate him as he rose to correct some juvenile members for a breach of rules, or to explain considerately to the unenlightened how such and such things ought to be. On these occasions his small eye glistened with all the enthusiasm of a man who feels how much of a blessing it is for the world to enjoy his services, and he pointed his long, bony finger, as if both Cushing's and Jefferson's manuals were condensed at the end of it. He was the living impersonation of a Pennsylvania Hunker Democrat.

G. W. Smith. — When I first saw the portly and venerable figure of Judge Smith I regarded him as the "tallest man" in the convention. He was a Pennsylvania Whig, slightly old fogyish. The judge has seen some little public service in his time, and is, upon the whole, a sensible man. He made good speeches, but rather lost caste on account of some voting, which the critical did not choose to regard as consistent. He is an open and frank personage.

J. A. Thompson I have been trying to remember. I have a favorable impression of him, though my memory will not carry me into the particulars.

G. A. Cutler. — The doctor is a young Kentuckian, and a pretty good fellow. He spoke often, and made one rather affecting effort in favor of the "black-law." He is a republican, but has a holy horror of "niggers" and "abolitionists."

J. K. Goodin, of Blanton's Bridge, north end, is an expatriated Buckeye, having been all his life a "consistent Democrat." He got into disgrace by not knowing how to vote on the "Delahay resolution," endorsing Douglas. He begged to be excused. The convention would not excuse. "Well, you *must* excuse me — I cannot vote," said Joel, in the most lamentable tone; but the convention was inexorable.

J. M. Tuton. — The Rev. J. M. Tuton has been a Missourian, but not of the border ruffian caste. Although a "divine," he has some faith in temporal weapons, for I have seen him flourish a long Western rifle in circumstances where there might have been a chance for him to use it. He spoke often on the current business. He had sometimes trouble to catch the speaker's eye, and I have seen him stand for five minutes at a time in hopes of filling a vacancy. He was a "black-law man," and was generally "down on" everything he was pleased to consider "abolitionism." He was, singularly enough, opposed to allowing slave-owners more than one year to take their slaves from the territory, declaring,

"I kem to Kansas to live in a free-state, an' I don't want niggers a' trampin' over my grave."

Thomas Bell has not left an impression on my memory strong enough to put on paper.

R. H. Crosby. — Mr. Crosby was the youngest member of the convention. He came from "'way down in Maine," but has recently been in Wisconsin. A republican, young, earnest, and enthusiastic, he received some sharp twitting from the older and more experienced politicians.

P. C. SCHUYLER. — Judge Schuyler was by far the most dignified-looking member of the convention. An old man, of large figure, and gray hair, unusually dignified and urbane. He spoke often, is a republican in politics, and took an active part.

J. S. EMERY. — Mr. Emery was an active member. A young New Yorker, a Democrat (not national), ambitious, and nervous; he held a respectable place.

I have been thus particular in drawing these pictures, for this was an important body in Kansas history, and all its phases are worth remembering.

Two of the most important characters who figure in the convention I have not spoken of yet, and they have been the two most prominent men in the territory. I mean, J. H. LANE, who was president of the convention, and CHARLES ROBINSON.

I will not attempt a portraiture of either of these, as my feelings might mislead me. I subjoin an article on them both, penned by one of the ablest writers who ever wrote about Kansas, and who was well qualified to write about these men. I will merely state, Colonel Lane, the president of the convention, was also the Democratic leader of the convention. Robinson was the leader of the Republicans. Lane, with all his faults, was not without many good qualities. He was indefatigable, restless, warm-hearted, and brave; as a politician, he was "of the politicians." Robinson was the very reverse of Lane. To strangers reserved, and almost cold; he never courted popularity by seeking favors with all. He has many of the elements out of which great men are made; but I leave the picture to the writer of the annexed extracts:

"Kansas has more great men, *perhaps*, than any other country of its size and age on the globe. If any one doubts this, we need only refer to our Atchisons and Stringfellows, our Smiths and Lanes, our Pomeroys and Robinsons, to vindicate triumphantly our position. Deferring, until a future occasion, particular mention of all others, we proceed to speak of two — Governor Robinson and General Lane — whose names have been associated more intimately, perhaps, with our political affairs, than any others. We shall

> 'Speak of them as they are —
> Nothing extenuate or set down aught in malice.'

Robinson is cool-headed, cautious, and calculating; just the man to plan and direct. Lane is hot-headed, rash, regardless of consequences, but not wanting in bravery; just the man to carry out the plans and directions. Robinson looks ahead, counts the cost of everything, weighs every consideration, no matter how trifling, and comes to an unchangeable conclusion. Lane looks only to the present, acts only for to-day, never gives a thought about how his acts will appear in history, and considers a 'bird in the hand worth two in the bush.' Whilst Robinson thinks communities, like children, must have time to grow and mature, Lane would move further West in search of a faster people, if Kansas did n't get to be a well-formed, full-grown state at a jump. Robinson is an Eastern man; Lane is a cross between a Western mountaineer and a Broadway dandy. One never was known as a politician; the other, until lately, was never known as anything else. Neither are finished speakers. Robinson is a good thinker, and, we should judge, writes better than he speaks. Lane can't sit still long enough to write anything, if he can write at all. He has always been used to mounting a stump, whenever an idea struck him as worthy of notice, and 'letting off' extemporaneously. He is a capital stump orator; his style is not Ciceronian, nor Websterian; it is not copied from the classic masters; it is peculiarly Laneish. Here 's a portraiture, drawn from life. Time and place, night and a crowded meeting; a tall, wiry, Hoosierish-looking fellow mounts the stand; both hands in his breeches' pockets; both eyes shut; mouth full of tobacco. Somebody in a remote corner of the hall commences stamping; others take it up, and the applause becomes general. Quiet restored, the fellow on the stand straightens his face and legs, and commences: 'The American flag still waves — STILL WAVES! Beneath its stars and stripes, we will oppose any and all attempts, come from whatever source, to trample upon our rights as American citizens — AS AMERICAN CITIZENS!' &c. As he warms with his subject, he makes fewer repetitions and more gestures, letting fall unique sayings and good hits in chunks. If a ludicrous idea strikes him while soaring aloft spread-eagle fashion, he sputters it out, even if it spoils what he has just said. 'It 's worth as much to hear Colonel Lane speak, when he lets himself loose, as it is to go to the Theatre,' is a common remark with Young America. In short, as Micawber would observe, Lane is great on 'turning up,' — is here, there, and everywhere at the same time — to-day at the bottom, to-morrow at the top of the heap; always on the strongest side; a great lover of excitement, and will have it; a great lover of office, and will have it; will always be a favorite with the people, and will be true to them — so long as they are true to him."

Such were the component parts of the Topeka convention, and such the result of their labors. Saturday night was lost in Sunday morning when those labors were completed; but there, in that hall in Topeka, in the darkness of the midnight, these men, as the representatives of the people of Kansas, pledged themselves to sustain the movement thus given to the world. When they had finished their work, three long and loud cheers were given for the "Constitution of the State of Kansas," and the echoes of that cheer broke the stillness around the slumbering Topeka, and echoed far up the valley of the Kaw.

CHAPTER X.

PAT LAUGHLIN — PARDEE BUTLER — LAW AND ORDER CONVENTION.

Early in the summer of 1855, a young Irishman, named Patrick Laughlin, who lived in the territory near Doniphan, became an active participant in the free-state movement. He had been reputed a pro-slavery man at first, but affected to be impressed in favor of free-state principles out of sympathy with the free-state men, and condemnation of the conduct of Missouri. After the March election meetings were held in the neighborhood of Doniphan, as they were held in all parts of the territory, to discuss the state of affairs and devise a remedy. Into these meetings Laughlin intruded himself under pretence of being a convert to the cause. Mr. Laughlin is a young man under thirty. He has resided in Kentucky, in which state I believe he kept a grocery for a short time. His person is rather under middle height, and thickset. His head is large, face rather flabby, red and pimpled. He exhibited some little ability, had received a good common education, would speak passably well, and was possessed of an unusual amount of cunning. In the free-state meetings he pretended to have been converted from the pro-slavery faith by the outrages of the Missourians, and was, under the circumstances, willing to work to make Kansas a free state. During the summer he was elected one of the delegates from Doniphan precinct to the Big Springs Convention.

At this time the necessity of arming the people of the territory, and putting them, if possible, in the shape of an available military force, was keenly felt. It was by violence and force of arms that the rights of the citizens of Kansas had been wrested from them, and it was only by resistance that the recurrence of such outrages could be prevented. Different opinions prevailed as to how this should be done. The timidly conservative, afraid to do anythin that might draw the attention of their enemies, and perhaps pre cipitate an attack, offered objections to nearly every scheme pro posed, and steadily refused their assent to all efficacious means. The great masses, however, were willing to have an organized popular militia, to act openly and devote such time as could be spared. The difficulty in the way of this was the time it would consume. The settlers were all hurried with their buildings, their business, or their farms, and could only be induced to desert these to drill or wield arms when the danger became so imminent as to bring the moment of action; nevertheless, independent military companies were formed in many localities, and an effort made to secure arms, of which the settlers were deficient. Besides these organizations several secret military organizations were formed. The most important of these was the Kansas Legion. Its object was to enroll men to be ready at any moment for the defence of the territory. It also had signs and passwords, by which one member could appeal to others for assistance in case he was attacked by the common enemy. They were bound by an obligation to secrecy. This organization, which has acquired some celebrity, never held the position in the territory which it is often supposed to have held. It was short in its duration, and, while most flourishing, was limited in extent as regards the territory. Many of those who enrolled in it disapproved of its unnecessary secrecy, got tired of its useless requirements and formality, and, while they saw nothing really improper in its character or objects, contended that these would be better served with independent companies. Besides, its secrecy and mode of operating gave an opportunity of filling important places in it to men who had not the confidence of their respective communities. It was, to some extent, an imitation of the Blue Lodge of Missouri, although, unlike that body, it did not propose to interfere with the rights of others, but only to defend its own. From the secret character of the organization, and the causes I have enumerated, it fell into disrepute a few months after it was organized.

Into this Kansas Legion Pat Laughlin was admitted, and succeeded so far in gaining confidence that he was chosen to form several new encampments, and did so. At the Big Springs Convention he made most zealous declarations in favor of free-state principles, and was placed on some of the most important committees. Returning to Doniphan, Laughlin formed an encampment or branch of the Kansas Legion, and administered the oath of secrecy to a considerable number of the citizens of that place, whom the necessity for defence and the novelty of the mode proposed induced to join it. Amongst those thus initiated was a Mr. Collins, who had a saw-mill in Doniphan. Mr. Collins was a Western man, a prominent free-state man in that locality, and became an officer in the Legion referred to.

At what particular moment Pat Laughlin concluded to desert the cause in which he was thus actively engaged, or whether he had been all along a spy and a traitor, is and must remain a mystery. His own statements, about an awakened conscientiousness and sudden opening of his eyes to the evils of this organization, are clearly incredible. His neighbors in Doniphan do not hesitate to state that he was bought up, and even specify, amongst other articles received, "a cow." Whether such purely mercenary motives prevailed with him, or if he felt that he could, in the position and with the power entrusted to him, make more by going back to the pro-slavery men than by remaining, is a matter of no consequence. He began to covenant with the pro-slavery leaders, not only about Doniphan but in Atchison and over in Missouri, and after due deliberation published his *exposé*, which obtained some little notoriety at the time, from the fact that the pro-slavery press were anxious to publish anything that would, or might, militate against the free-state men. In this publication Laughlin not only distorted the facts, but made many misstatements; still a perusal of his *exposé* offers nothing particularly remarkable.

Had Laughlin remained content with making the *exposé*, it probably would have elicited nothing more than the hearty contempt of all with whom he had been acting. He was taken by th hand, patronized by the pro-slavery leaders, who doubtless in tended to turn his peculiar qualities to account. While thus a ing with these men he was secretly intriguing with the enemies o the free-state men about Doniphan, and fomenting in the bosoms o the violent borderers hostility to these men, thus endangering their personal safety. It was at this stage of affairs that Mr. Collins chanced to meet Laughlin in the office of a physician. A was natural, violent words passed between them, and there woul probably have been violence of some kind but for the interferenc of the bystanders.

It was on the ensuing morning, the 25th of October, that th unhappy rencontre took place. Laughlin's pro-slavery friend assert that Collins was armed and seeking Laughlin when th affair happened; but the fact of its occurrence close to the saw mill of Mr. Collins, where the latter gentleman and his sons wer employed, and the fact that Laughlin and three or four other pro slavery men were there, armed, makes it certain that they cam there armed. That Collins was also armed and prepared for conflict is likely. After they had come together, and warm word had passed between them, it is probable that they might hav parted peaceably had not Laughlin thrown an insulting remar towards Collins. The latter instantly turned on him. A pro slavery man, who stood thirty yards off, fired at Collins, and it i supposed hit him. Collins discharged his gun without effect, an as Laughlin drew a pistol and pointed it at Collins, the latte grasped his gun by the barrel and advanced on him, when Laugh lin fired. Collins fell dead, and his sons and nephews fled, bu not till there had been some more firing and fighting with bowie knives, in which several were wounded on both sides. Laughli was seriously wounded with a knife early in the scuffle.

This occurrence did not, of course, do much towards allayin popular excitement. Meanwhile, Laughlin was taken to the tow of Atchison, where, after he had recovered, he was employed as salesman in a pro-slavery man's store.

It was only a short time before this that occurrences of an out rageous nature took place in Atchison. Atchison is close to th

Missouri river. It is a small place, and most of its citizens are violent pro-slavery men. It has generally been regarded as unsafe for free-state men to be about it.

In July, or early in August, a female slave belonging to a man in Doniphan had been so abused by her master that she committed suicide by throwing herself in the Missouri river. Anxious to secure themselves from the consequences of their own villany, and at the same time make a little political capital out of their crimes, those responsible for the sad fate of the unhappy creature had the assurance to charge her suicide to the "abolitionists." To have charged anti-slavery men with aiding the escape of negroes might have been a probable story; and, true or false, would have gained credit. To suppose, however, that even the most ultra anti-slavery man would have recommended the poor woman to kill herself, — much less that any human being, no matter how degraded, would calmly listen to and act on such advice, — is simply preposterous. In Atchison, at that time, there was a Mr. J. W. B. Kelley. This man would certainly not have been regarded as an "abolitionist" anywhere but in the town of Atchison. He was a free-state man, however, and the pro-slavery men were determined that none such should be permitted to remain in Atchison. He was seized by a mob, beaten and abused, and then, to the detriment of his pecuniary interests, driven from the place.

It was in the month of August that the Rev. Pardee Butler fell into their hands. The Atchison *Squatter Sovereign* thus describes it:

"On Thursday last one Pardee Butler arrived in town with a view of starting for the East, probably for the purpose of geting a fresh supply of free-soilers from the penitentiaries and pest-holes of the Northern States. Finding it inconvenient to depart before morning, he took lodgings at the hotel, and proceeded to visit numerous portions of our town, everywhere avowing himself a free-soiler, and preaching the foulest of abolition heresies. He declared the recent action of our citizens in regard to J. W. B. Kelley, the infamous and unlawful proceedings of a mob; at the same time stating that many persons in Atchison, who were free-soilers at heart, had been intimidated thereby, and feared to avow their true sentiments; but that he (Butler) would express his views in defiance of the whole community.

"On the ensuing morning our townsmen assembled en masse, and, deeming the presence of such persons highly detrimental to the safety of our slave property, appointed a committee of two to wait on Mr. Butler and request his signature to the resolutions passed at the late pro-slavery meeting in Atchison. After perusing the said resolutions, Mr. B. positively declined signing them, and was instantly arrested by the committee.

"After the various plans for his disposal had been considered, it was finally decided to place him on a raft composed of two logs firmly lashed together; that his baggage and a loaf of bread be given him; and, having attached a flag to his primitive bark, emblazoned with mottoes indicative of our contempt for such characters, Mr. Butler was set adrift on the great Missouri, with the letter R legibly painted on his forehead.

"He was escorted some distance down the river by several of our citizens, who, seeing him pass several rack-heaps in quite a skilful manner, bade him adieu and returned to Atchison.

"Such treatment may be expected by all scoundrels visiting our town for the purpose of interfering with our time-honored institutions, and the same punishment we will be happy to award all free-soilers, abolitionists, and their emissaries."

The Rev. Pardee Butler held some property in Missouri, opposite Atchison. He had a claim in the territory, with a house and improvements upon it. There he and his family reside. He is a tall man, but slim and delicate, and has a good deal the look of a Western preacher. I do not think there is much of the "abolitionist," as the term is employed in the East, about him.

He gave an account of his own experience, mentioning that one of the editors of the pro-slavery paper published there was an active member of the mob, and that he played the part of an artist in painting his face, and that he also towed out his strange craft into the stream. While many of the mob were reckless characters, they were led on by those who claimed to be the "respectable" people of the place. When he was thus turned adrift to the mercy of the stream, the facetious ruffians affixed a flag to his strange craft, with the following inscriptions:

"Eastern Emigrant Aid Express. The Rev. Mr. Butler, Agent for the Underground Railroad." "The way they are served in Kansas." "For Boston." "Cargo Insured, — unavoidable danger of the Missourians and the Missouri River excepted." "Let future Emissaries from the North beware. Our hemp crop is sufficient to reward all such scoundrels."

This was wickedly clever, but evidently intended for outside effect, as they well knew that their victim had probably never seen Boston, and knew, probably, as little of the hated Emigrant Aid Society as they did themselves. After he was painted and otherwise tricked out by these *articles*, they ventured to quiz him on his appearance, and recommended him to go East and lecture, telling him ironically that he would "make a fine speculation of this."

The progress of the state movement in Kansas had from the first alarmed the border ruffians. When they had carried all the elections, — succeeded in getting pro-slavery tools appointed to all the territorial offices under the executive, — had made laws for Kansas under which it would be impossible for Kansas to come in as a free state, and even appointed the local officers to enforce them, — they thought they had most certainly succeeded in the struggle, and were inclined to resent and crush out violently all counter-movements which might interfere with such arrangements. The fact is, there was a large population in Kansas who were opposed to slavery. Many of them, when they came to the territory, cared little about the question; but, being free-state men, and thus suffering from slavery-extension aggression, they soon learned to hate, not only the oppressors, but the system of slavery, from the violent extension of which they suffered. The pro-slavery men residing in the territory, and especially the border Missourians, felt particularly aggrieved at the existence of free-state settlers in the territory. This emigration of men from free states they have always regarded as peculiarly aggravating. Well did they know that the institution of slavery would never be apt to flourish in Kansas while such a population was on its soil. To get rid of them, therefore, became a fixed object in their minds, was publicly discussed, and resolved on in a most bitter spirit.

For months after the Bogus Legislature had gone through its farce of legislation no attempt had been made to enforce its edicts. There was no power in the territory to enforce them, and Missouri could not be always in Kansas. Under these circumstances, and with the object of overthrowing the state movement, a Law and Order Convention was held in Leavenworth on the 14th of November. This meeting, or convention, was called by notices signed by some fourteen pro-slavery men; but it was well known throughout the territory that Gov. Shannon, and others of the territorial officials, had an active hand in it, and that the whole thing was concocted by the border Missourians and these together.

This convention was the origin, or starting-point, of "law and order" in Kansas. Here it was that the pro-slavery party, both in Missouri and the territory, claimed the title "law and order party." They knew that the territorial law was their creature, and that in enforcing it their policy was safe. Hence they, with a coolness that was preposterous following their numerous outrages, declared themselves the orderly, law-loving party, and banded thus together to sustain each other by mutual pledges that the "law" would be enforced.

In spite of its importance this convention was not very numerously attended. Outside of the citizens of Leavenworth there were not more than eighty persons present, and by far the larger portion of these were from Missouri. The leading men on the Missouri border were there. The Stringfellows were officers of the convention, and several of the vice-presidents and secretaries were residents of Missouri. It may look a little strange that the governor of the territory should take an active part in a popular meeting of this kind, the avowed object of which was the execution of the laws by popular force. Still more singular is it that Gov. Shannon should take an active part in an assemblage where the violent Missouri borderers had the sway, and where its character as a simple pro-slavery convention was so apparent. The governor, in doing this, conclusively showed that he was the tool of the Missouri borderers, and blindly obedient in their scheme of subduing Kansas to slavery.

Governor Shannon reported himself to that convention as a delegate from Douglas County, where Lawrence is situated, in which he did not then reside; nor do I suppose there were three men in that county, or anywhere else, who knew they had the honor to be represented by the governor. Governor Shannon was elected president of the convention. The chairman first elected was Major Richardson, a Missourian, one of the leaders of the Missouri invaders, a man of violent temper, and reckless character, who had been a member of the Bogus Council, and, while legislating for Kansas, got himself elected by that body as major-general of the Kansas militia. Into the chair just vacated by this person Governor Shannon entered, and made an indiscreet partisan speech, in which he declared that he would enforce obedience to the laws enacted at the Shawnee Mission; and he called upon those by whom he was surrounded to aid him in enforcing the laws. He took occasion to denounce the constitutional movement at Topeka; declared it treasonable, and expressed his determination that such a state of affairs must not be permitted. In this speech he also alluded, in disrespectful terms, to the majority in Congress, and said that, in the next presidential election, the party with which he then acted would carry everything before them.

There were only two prominent speakers before that convention, Governor Shannon and Mr. John Calhoun, Surveyor General of the territories of Nebraska and Kansas. The border ruffians, pleased to get federal dignitaries thus to fiddle for them, kindly permitted these gentlemen to lay down the "law," and cheered them in encouragement of this official error.

If Shannon's speech was improper and indefensible, that of Calhoun was bitterly partisan and violent. He denounced free-state men as "vile abolitionists," and there was no epithet too mean to hurl at this class, — the large majority of Kansas citizens. He said they "were so vile they would lick the slime off the meanest penitentiary in the land;" and, progressing in his violent and profane tirade, declared, "they would bow down and

13*

worship the devil if he would only help them to steal a nigger." It would be needless to add that a public officer, who could evince such partisan vulgarity, did not scruple to lend himself to all the violence for which this meeting was convened.

A platform of resolutions was adopted to send out to the world. These had nothing necessarily to do with the objects of the convention, and, as they were merely intended for outside effect, were placed in the hands of a revising committee, who kept remodelling them until they could not have been recognized. Several other speakers addressed this convention. These were of the border ruffian class, and their speeches were denunciations of the state movement, and threats to enforce the bogus laws, until the "Missouri river should run red with blood."

Mr. Parrot, a free-state man, who had been an associate Democrat with Governor Shannon in this, tried to speak, but was not permitted to do so. Shannon, as president of the convention, refused to notice him, and Stringfellow told him that "the convention did not want to hear a free-state man."

Before this convention adjourned it pledged itself to sustain the governor whenever he should call on them to enforce the law.

CHAPTER XI.

THE RESCUE OF BRANSON.

WHILE the political sentiment arising from the slavery question has been the moving cause of all the difficulty in Kansas Territory, quarrels about claims have often been the means of precipitating them. The inefficiency of the authorities to preserve the rights of the settlers, the scarcity of courts or judicial officers, and the little confidence felt in what there was of these, prevented the people from securing their rights to their claims, or obtaining redress for any grievance upon them. In some localities the settlers of both shades of political faith commenced a struggle for the possession of a desired spot. One of these contested places was Hickory Point, a heavy body of timber lying some miles south of the Wakarusa, on the Santa Fe road. As this was a valuable piece of timber land, in the midst of the richest prairies, the earliest settlers flocked into it.

The first settlers of that region were free-state men from Indiana. Other free-state men, from the Western States generally, and some of them from Missouri, also settled there. After the grove had been mostly taken by the settlers, some pro-slavery men came in, took claims, and some of them jumped claims already taken. In some of the cases where these claims were invaded the persons holding them had forfeited their right to them by their absence; but in several other instances the seizure was violent and fraudulent. In the same vicinity, at the lower end of the grove, on the Santa Fe road, a town called Palmyra had been laid off, and early in the summer of 1855, a party of men from Missouri came up and ordered the settlers in the place to leave it, or they would be driven away; and serious apprehensions of violence and bloodshed were entertained. The settlers mostly kept their ground. It was with much the same spirit that the pro-slavery men who came and settled in the grove were animated. One of these men, Franklin Coleman, not only took violent possession of several claims, but stole the building materials, which had been prepared by a free-state man, from another claim, and built a house for himself with them.

A might be expected, the free-state and pro-slavery settlers had many angry bickerings, and probably nothing but the numbers of the free-state men prevented the earlier effusion of blood. One cause of ill-will was the aid the free-state men rendered each other. So much was this the case that even Coleman, in his own statement of the transaction afterwards, could not refrain from saying,

"This he did" — alluding to Branson — "by encouraging free-state men to settle about him, giving them timber from his land, and informing them of vacant claims. In pursuance of this, he and his friends invited a man named Dow, an Ohioan and an abolitionist, to occupy a claim adjoining my own; a claim that belonged rightly to Wm. White, of Westport, Mo."

I thus quote Coleman's own statement, in order to show the true cause of the quarrel. On this claim of Dow's (for the reader will understand the nature of a claim of a man living in Westport), this man, Coleman, with several of his pro-slavery neighbors, cut timber, burnt a lime-kiln, and otherwise invaded his rights, for the obvious purpose of causing difficulty. Having already burned one lime-kiln, they proceeded to cut timber for another, when they had plenty of timber on their own claims. Dow determined to put a stop to this, and notified them that they must not attempt anything further of the kind. Just before this, Mr. Branson had received an anonymous letter, ordering him to leave. This, beyond all doubt, came from his pro-slavery neighbors, and was a rich document, between bad chirography, inflammable threats, and questionable grammar. These pro-slavery men had worked themselves into a passion, and had threatened to kill and drive off all the free-state settlers in the grove. That this was not a mere empty threat was unhappily proved.

On the 21st of November, Mr. W. Dow left the house of Mr. Branson, where he boarded, as he was an unmarried man, and, as it was close to his claim, and, taking with him a small wagon-skein, which had been broken, went up the Santa Fe road, towards a blacksmith's shop, to have it repaired. As he went to the blacksmith's shop he passed in sight of the houses of Coleman, Hargus, and Buckley, the two latter pro-slavery neighbors of Coleman. Shortly after Dow got to the shop, he was followed by these three men, who came armed with guns. Seeing their threatening aspect, Dow avoided a discussion at first, but they commenced abusing him, and denounced him, saying they would cut timber from the claim in question. During the discussion, one of these men, Harrison Buckley, raised his gun, cocked it, and presented it at Dow, who, looking at him steadily, said,

"You would not shoot me, Buckley?"

The villain's hand had not nerve enough for the murder he had contemplated, and he dropped his gun. Apprehensive of further violence, Dow left the shop and started back. Coleman followed him, and soon overtook him, and the two men were seen by several thus going down the Santa Fe road. Buckley and Hargus followed, but at a distance near enough to see what happened. When Dow and Coleman got opposite Coleman's house, which was some yards from the road, they parted, and Coleman went to his house, and, standing on his door-step, cocked and presented his gun at Dow's back, who was going from him down the road, pulled the trigger, but the cap burst, and it did not go off.

The bursting of the cap startled Dow, who turned round and looked at Coleman. They were about twenty-five yards apart, when Coleman, who had put on a fresh cap, presented the piece at his victim. Dow threw up his hand, as if to implore him to desist, but the appeal fell on an inhuman heart. The next moment Coleman fired, and a portion of the contents, a heavy load of slugs and buckshot, from a shot-gun, entered the heart of the unhappy Dow. He fell where he stood, and his head lay in the wheel-track of the Santa Fe road, while the blood coursed amongst the dust from the wounds in the breast and neck of the young man.

It was a November noon when the deed was done, and, although several saw the occurrence, the body lay unheeded where it fell. Hargus and Buckley soon came up to Coleman, and they talked together, at first fiercely and boastingly; but that silent figure lying dead — dead! — full in their sight, would have smitten the most remorseless with a guilty fear, if not a pang of conscience. It was now feared that the free-state settlers would revenge the death of their friend, and Coleman, taking his family and household effects in a wagon, started back to Missouri. One of his guilty associates and another pro-slavery man, who lived close by, and saw the affair, also left with their effects and families for Missouri.

Through the whole afternoon the body of that young man lay neglected where he had fallen. About evening, Mr. Branson, having heard something of the affair, went up and brought the dead body of his friend home. Whether he had died as he had fallen, or had lived in expiring agony, without a drop of water or a friend to raise him, will never be known.

By the 26th of the month no action had been taken by the authorities, and, as the inference was that the murderers would go unpunished, a meeting of the settlers was called at Hickory Point, and assembled on the day in question. The action of the meeting was marked by no violence; they merely passed resolutions deploring and condemning the murder, and appointed a committee, whose duty it should be to take steps to bring the murderers to justice. As some of the more indignant of the settlers were in favor of burning the houses of the murderers, a resolution was passed, condemning and deprecating such an act, even against these men.

Meanwhile the fearful murderer had fled to Westport. There he met Sheriff Jones, then postmaster of that place, and, after counselling with him and others of the Westport border ruffians, it was concluded that Coleman must go through the farce of giving himself up. It is stated — and I have no doubt of its truth — that he had received assurances that he would be protected.

Coleman, therefore, went to the Shawnee Mission, and, after going through the farce of surrendering himself to Governor Shannon, started up into the territory with Jones, for the ostensible purpose of going to Lecompton to be examined. But a deep and villanous plot had been laid, and it was desired to use what could be made of this incident to further that design. The law and order convention had declared that the bogus officers should be sustained; and now all that was wanted was an opportunity.

Jones and his quondam prisoner stopped at Franklin, where they began to contemplate the state of affairs. There they were joined by Buckley and Hargus, one of whom had also been in Missouri, but had returned to "see the fun." Here these gentry concocted their scheme, which was nothing less than to arrest Mr. Branson, carry him to Lawrence, where it was presumed he would be, under such circumstances, rescued; and then that there would be a very pretty *casus belli*.

The manner in which they had to proceed about this showed the character of the whole affair. Jones had got a commission for a justice of the peace all filled but the name; and found a man named Cameron, a recreant free-state man, of low repute, who, vain man, for the title "justice of the peace" was willing to sell what little he had of principle.

Before this patent justice Buckley came; and, swearing that he was afraid of his life for threats made by Jacob Branson, this *Esquire* Cameron issued a peace-warrant for the arrest of said Branson, doing so at the same time he received his commission from Jones. The next thing was to secure a posse. Coleman, it was decided, should not go; but he was unloading the pistols and guns, and making other preparations for the expedition. Before long a party of fifteen men, including Jones, Hargus, and Buckley, were ready for the expedition. It was night when they left Franklin; and they proceeded up along the sloping bottom of the Wakarusa until they reached Blanton's Bridge. There they refreshed their "inner man," many of them being about half-intoxicated, and proceeded onwards toward Hickory Point. There they made some accessions to their force from the pro-slavery residents, until they numbered somewhere between twenty and twenty-five.

At the time these men passed Blanton's Bridge they were seen by a young free-state man from Lawrence, Mr. S. P. Tappan, who was returning thither from the meeting that day at Hickory Point. He rode in amongst Jones' posse before he knew who or what they were. They at first took him for one of their friends coming to assist them; and some of them were indiscreet enough to let drop a few hints about their mission before they suspected that their visitor might be on the other side. After they had started off towards Hickory Point, Mr. Tappan learned enough to know the motives of their visit, and hurried back to warn his friends.

It was between nine and ten o'clock at night. Old Jacob Branson was in bed asleep, his family asleep around him, when he was awakened by a stir around the house. Just at that moment there was a knock at his door.

"Who is there?" inquired Branson.

"Friends," was the answer.

"Come in."

But scarcely had he uttered the word, when the frail door was burst open, and a band of armed men rushed into the apartment. The foremost man was Jones. Drawing a pistol, and pointing it at Branson, who had got out of bed, and was standing before him, he said:

"You 're my prisoner!"

"What for — and what authority?" stammered Branson.

"I 'm the sheriff of Douglas County," said Jones. But he showed no writ. As Branson seemed to hesitate, Jones resumed:

"Look sharp — you must go with us."

"You would n't hurry me. If I have to go, I shall go when I get ready."

"God d—n you!" said Jones. "I 'll blow you to h—ll if you don't get ready directly!"

Thus pressed, Mr. Branson dressed and got ready to go with them; while his family, frightened and distressed, feared that the bloody fate of Dow was about to befall the head of their family. Two of the murderers of Dow they saw with the party, and several other of their violent pro-slavery neighbors.

Branson was taken out and placed on a mule, and the posse and their prisoner rode off. As soon as they had done so, a young lad, who had been staying at Branson's, started to alarm the neighbors.

It was as beautiful a moonlight night as ever smiled on the prairies of Kansas. The moon was about the full, and the sky was clear, and the air mild, for November. Jones and his band did not proceed direct for Lawrence. They rode backwards and forwards in the point, between the houses of the pro-slavery men, drinking, whenever they could get anything to drink, and passing profane and obscene jokes. At length the volunteers they had picked up in the point left them, and Jones, with his prisoner and fourteen of the posse, rode down the road that leads from the prairie highlands near Hickory Point, towards Blanton's Bridge.

As Branson felt somewhat uneasy as to what would be the sequel of this nocturnal adventure, he addressed a man who was riding near him, inquiring what he was taken for.

"Dun-no," replied the man, curtly.

A little further on Branson addressed another, who he thought looked more decent, and, to his inquiries, this person replied:

"O, well, I believe it 's a peace-warrant only."

"Where are we going?"

"Lawrence, I believe."

Branson breathed a little more freely when he heard of his probable destination; although he doubted if they would venture to take him there.

About this time Jones rode up to him, and, fancying he might be more communicative, asked:

"There was a meeting in the grove, to-day, near your house, of at least a hundred men, was there not?"

"There was a meeting. The neighbors round held a meeting where Dow was murdered, to see if the murderers could not be brought to justice."

For a moment this threw a disagreeable damper, but Jones resumed:

"They were Yankees, mostly, with Sharpe's rifles, were they not?"

"There might have been Yankees there, but not very many. It was mostly the neighbors. They did not attend the meeting armed."

"That's a d—d lie!" exclaimed several.

"I wish, boys," said Jones, "that we had got there before those hundred Yankee abolitionists got off. We have had no fun."

"D—n 'em!—we would have given 'em h—ll!" cried several voices. "We'd a show'd 'em how to pass resolutions." And, with these and sundry other valiant threats about what they would have done if they could *only* have met "those hundred abolitionists," they rode on.

Now the intention was to have Branson rescued in Lawrence; a plot which I believe would have worked to a charm, only *something* interfered to prevent it. Mr. Tappan and the young man who had left Branson's had both been busy; and about fourteen of the neighbors were gathered near Mr. Abbott's house, near which Jones' posse had to pass on their way to Blanton's Bridge. So quickly had they gathered, and so dilatory was the posse in its perambulations, that the little party at Abbott's began to think they had taken another road, when the man on guard gave the alarm, and, rushing out into the road, they saw Jones and his men rapidly advancing. Jones and his party, in spite of their anxiety to find the "hundred abolitionists," evidently felt that "discretion was the better part of valor," and, turning their horses off the road into the prairie, attempted to shy past the party. On this the free-state men immediately spread out as if to intercept them. Jones then turned into the road with his party, when the others also folded in and formed in the road before them. The posse halted, and Jones cried,

"What's up?"

"That's what we want to know," said one of the free-state men. And several of his party asked Jones, in return,

"What's up?"

There was a pause, which Branson broke by saying,

"They have got me prisoner here."

"Is that you, Branson?"

"Yes."

"Well, come this way," said Mr. Abbott.

"If you move," said several of the posse, "we will shoot you."

"I am going," said Branson to Jones.

"I will shoot you if you do," was the response.

"Come ahead!" cried S. N. Wood; "D—n them, if they shoot, *we* will."

Jacob Branson, who was in the midst of his captors, rode through them and joined his friends. Not a gun was fired.

"Whose mule is that?" asked several.

"Belongs to them," said Branson.

"Then get off, and drive it back."

Branson dismounted, and was sent into the house. The mule was turned towards its owners, but hesitated as if in the uncertainty between "serving two masters." At this juncture Mr. S. N. Wood stepped up to it, and expedited its departure for the pro-slavery ranks by a couple of kicks.

"Gentlemen," said Jones, "if you don't give Branson up we will fire!"

"We have nothing to do with it," was the response.

At this moment the pro-slavery men raised their guns, and were heard cocking them. At this interesting moment the rescuers raised their pieces, and the sharp click of more than one Sharpe's rifle was heard.

And here let me state, in explanation, that the "forty abolitionists" in buckram, about whom Sheriff Jones prepared an affidavit that found its way to the President, nevertheless, were neither more nor less than fifteen persons. Of these, eight were armed with Sharpe's rifles, one had got a shot-gun, a few had revolvers, and one man, whose anxiety to be there hurried him too much to make preparation, had actually nothing in the shape of arms. Thus the parties were equal numerically. It was soon evident, however, that the border ruffians felt it was not their mission to *shoot* on that occasion; a conclusion precipitated, no doubt, by a humane desire to "prevent the effusion of blood."

Jones got off his horse, and tried everything in his power, from threats to coaxing, from curses to "soft sawder," to induce them to give up Branson; but his efforts only seemed to amuse the men he talked to.

"I 'm the Sheriff of Douglas County," he said; but this was received with jeers. He then went on to threaten that he should have five thousand men to come up and "wipe out Lawrence and all of them." This threat had no effect. He then took several members of the rescuing party aside, and tried to persuade them into the propriety of letting him take Branson. Amongst others whom he thus took aside, was Mr. Samuel C. Smith, of Lawrence. Jones said, confidentially:

"I 'm sorry to see a person of your appearance here, sir; but I hope you will use your influence with these men to prevent them from doing this."

"My appearance, sir, is very much at your service," was the dry response.

"My name is Jones; I 'm the Sheriff of Douglas County, and I 'm United States Marshal. What is your name, sir?"

Mr. Smith hesitated; but, remembering that he had a patronimic that could not be sworn to, replied:

"My name is Smith."

Smith—Jones. The bogus sheriff looked incredulous, but continued:

"If Branson is given up I will say nothing about this; but if not, I will bring up five thousand men, and then it will be an affair not to be trifled with. Let Branson go with me. I will pledge *my word of honor* that he will not be hurt."

"Mr. Jones, Branson can't go with you to-night." This Mr. Smith enunciated in his dry, deliberate way. The bogus sheriff fared no better with the others, or, rather, he fared worse; for there were not lacking those who cursed the Bogus Legislature in general, and all the bogus officers in particular; and very especially Esquire Cameron, under whose newly-fledged dignity this outrage had occurred, as they learned from Jones, who now stated that he had a writ for the arrest, issued by "Esquire Cameron."

Finding that it was utterly impossible to do anything in the way of coaxing or threatening, and not being willing to fight, the valiant border ruffian chief, who had led more than one band up into the territory, on voting and warlike deeds intent, was obliged to face about, and make the best of his way, by a circuitous route, to Franklin.

Shortly after the rescue was effected, several other men from the neighborhood of Hickory came to Abbott's. The party remained there for a short time, and then, considering it unsafe to disperse and go back to their homes, those connected with the rescue took up their line of march for Lawrence. It was after midnight before they started, and that little body of men might have been seen winding along the low grounds of the Wakarusa, under the clear moonlight. That moon was far in the west, and its beams were paler and the night darker, as they entered Lawrence. It might be an hour before day when the "beat of the alarming drum" roused up the half-slumbering citizens. Apparently unimportant although this affair was, those who comprehended the state of political matters in the territory well knew its significance. The threat of Sheriff Jones, that five thousand men would soon be in Lawrence, was felt to be too likely a thing to be trifled with. The "resolutions," so often passed at meetings and conventions, to the effect that "the bogus laws and the bogus officers would be resisted," had been realized, and that, too, under circumstances most favorable to the rescuers; for the arrest of Branson was so violent and irregular, and the circumstances so aggravated, that scarcely a legal officer in the community could have sustained himself in such arrest.

CHAPTER XII.

THE WAKARUSA WAR.

When Sheriff Jones returned to Franklin he felt very sore. The design was to have Branson rescued in the hated Lawrence. In this he had failed; besides he had been worsted by a hastily-gathered party of Branson's neighbors, and had yielded to a force, to say the most of it, equal to his own. How could the bully, who had vomited out threats of annihilation against "hundreds of abolitionists," appear before his confreres, after being so humiliatingly worsted? Under this state of feeling he wrote a note to Col. Boone, of Westport, his business partner, and as active a border ruffian as himself. What this despatch was we can only guess, for I have never seen a copy; but its contents may be guessed from the remarks of Jones at the time to those around him when he sent the messenger with the despatch.

"That man is taking my despatch to Missouri, and, by G–d, I will have revenge before I see Missouri!"

Amongst those present, when this despatch was sent off, was a pro-slavery man, who had come to Kansas from a free state, — Iowa. Impressed by the recklessly irregular course pursued by Jones, he interposed, and said:

"There 's a right way and a wrong way of doing things. We 're the 'law and order' party, and having got right, want to keep right. You ought to have sent your despatch to the governor, and asked him to give you the men."

"D—n the governor!" — Jones, with all his faults, is remarkably candid; and if he ever goes into a manœuvre that could be called a "dodge," it is only on the suggestion of others. Thus, when his "law and order" friend urged that "the governor could call out the militia," he responded:

"Where 's the militia?"

"Well, the force that comes to help, you know, ought to be militia."

"That 's their business; — they 'll see Shannon, I guess."

"Yes; but the governor has pledged himself to support the laws, and he is the person to apply to."

After further cogitation the following despatch was penned, and sent by Hargus to the governor; he starting only half an hour after the first messenger:

"DOUGLAS COUNTY, K. T., *Nov.* 27, 1855.

"SIR: Last night I, with a *posse* of ten men, arrested one Jacob Branson, by virtue of a peace-warrant regularly issued, who, on our return, was rescued by a party of *forty* armed men, who rushed on us suddenly from behind a house, upon the roadside, all armed to the teeth with Sharpe's rifles.

"You may consider an open rebellion as having already commenced; and I call upon you for THREE THOUSAND MEN, to carry out the laws. Mr. Hargus (the bearer of the letter) will give you more particularly the circumstances.

"Most respectfully,

"SAMUEL J. JONES,

"*Sheriff of Douglas County.*

"To his Excellency,

"WILSON SHANNON,

"*Governor of Kansas Territory.*"

Now the governor, as well as Sam. J. Jones, was perfectly aware that the "militia of Kansas Territory" was a myth; a thing impalpable and unsubstantial. True, the Bogus Legislature had conferred upon those of its own members who were ambitious of military distinction, such titles as major-general or brigadier-general. A very fair sprinkling of these *military* gentlemen were residents of Missouri, and the rank and file were purely imaginative characters; "law and order" goblins, conjured up by an act of the Bogus Legislature, but without a local "habitation or a name." Gov. Shannon, speaking on the subject says:

"And it may be stated here that the militia of Kansas were at this time (and still are) totally unorganized. The Legislature had, it is true, elected two major-generals in the southern, and one in the northern division, as well as some brigadiers; but, so far as the rank and file are concerned, the organization was not even commenced."

To make a demand for three thousand "militia," under such circumstances, was certainly a very cool thing in Jones, but not half so cool as it was for the governor to issue the following despatch:

"HEAD QUARTERS, SHAWNEE MISS., K. T.,
Nov. 27, 1855.

"MAJ. GEN. WM. P. RICHARDSON—

"SIR: Reliable information has reached me that an armed military force is now in Lawrence and that vicinity, in open rebellion against the laws of this territory, and that they have determined that no process in the hands of the sheriff of that county shall be executed. I have received a letter from S. J. Jones, Sheriff of Douglas County, informing me that he had arrested a man under a warrant placed in his hands, and, while conveying him to Lecompton, he was met by an armed force of some forty men, and that the prisoner was taken out of his custody, and defiance bid to the laws. I am also duly advised that an armed band of men have burnt a number of houses, destroyed personal property, and turned whole families out of doors in Douglas County. Warrants will be issued against those men, and placed in the hands of the Sheriff of Douglas County for execution. He has written to me, demanding *three thousand men* to aid him in the execution of the process of the law.

"You are, therefore, hereby ordered to collect together as large a force as you can in your division, and repair without delay to Lecompton, and report yourself to S. J. Jones, Sheriff of Douglas County, together with the number of your forces, and render him all the aid and assistance in your power in the execution of any legal process in his hands. The forces under your command are to be used for the sole purpose of aiding the sheriff in executing the law, and for no other purpose.

"I have the honor to be your obedient servant,

"WILSON SHANNON."

"HEAD QUARTERS, SHAWNEE MISSION, K. T.,
Nov. 27, 1855.

"GEN. H. J. STRICKLAR—

"SIR: I am this moment advised by letter from S. J. Jones, Sheriff of Douglas County, that while conveying a prisoner to Lecompton, whom he had arrested by a virtue of a peace-warrant, he was met by a band of armed men, who took said prisoner forcibly out of his possession, and bid open defiance to the execution of law in this territory. He has demanded of me three thousand men to aid him in carrying out the legal process in his hands. As the southern division of the militia of this territory is not yet organized, I can only *request* you to collect together as large a force as you can, and at as early a day as practicable, and report yourself, with the men you may raise, to S. J. Jones, Sheriff of Douglas County, to whom you will give every assistance in your power towards the execution of the legal process in his hands. *Whatever forces* you may bring to his aid are to be used for the sole purpose of aiding the said sheriff in the execution of the law, and no other.

"It is expected that every good citizen will aid and assist the lawful authorities in the execution of the laws of the territory and the preservation of good order.

"Your ob't serv't,

"WILSON SHANNON.

"To GEN. STRICKLAR."

It will be seen that Gov. Shannon dates his epistle from "head quarters." The military spirit was no doubt uppermost in his mind, and as commander-in-chief he goes to work in a style which would have been ridiculous, if he had not known that the deficiencies of Kansas "militia" would be amply made up in Missouri.

To show that the governor did *more* than merely *know* this, I subjoin the following "extra," published at Independence, over the names of two citizens of repute in that quarter:

"INDEPENDENCE, MO., *Dec.* 2.

"An express, in at ten o'clock last night, says all the volunteers, ammunition, &c., that can be raised will be needed. The express was forwarded by Gov. Shannon to Col. Woodson, and by Woodson to this place, to be transmitted to various parts of the county. Call a meeting, and do everything you can.

"DRS. MCMURRY AND HENRY."

This was circulated widely in Missouri, the Col. Woodson referred to being an eminent border ruffian of Independence, who had invaded the territory before.

While Gov. Shannon, under Jones' instruction, was thus busy, Col. Boone, of Westport, who had received the other despatch from Jones, was not idle. He issued a violent war despatch, containing assertions that the free-state men of Kansas had not only rescued Branson from Jones, but were committing unheard-of atrocities, burning houses, killing people, and driving pro-slavery men away. This kindled the first flame, and many proceeded to the territory, in obedience to it, or the dictates of the secret Blue Lodge rather, in which all of these matters were discussed and settled. In order to create effect, Col. Woodson, of Independence, Mo. (who had been actively at work before he wrote), and Dr. McMurry, of the same place, wrote to Col. Boone relative to the authenticity of his despatch. This called out the following reply, which was extensively circulated:

"SHAWNEE MISSION, *Nov.* 30, 5 *A. M.*

"TO DR. MCMURRY AND COL. SAM'L WOODSON:

"Your favor was received. I thought I was too well known in the community to be thought capable of practising a hoax. The marshal has a requisition from the governor to arrest forty-two men in Lawrence, and they refuse to give them up, and he calls for volunteers, and if the citizens refuse to aid him, I cannot help it. They also say publicly that they will take Coleman and Jones, and hang them both.

"They are drilling in the open prairie every day, and have five fine pieces of artillery, and openly bid defiance to the laws.

"A large number of them were seen crossing from Delaware and Leavenworth yesterday, going to Lawrence.

"A member of the Legislature was from there yesterday morning for guns. We can only send twenty. Jones also sends for a wagon-load of ammunition and cannon.

"Now act, or not, as you please; if you will send the cannon here, I will take it there myself. In haste,

"A. G. BOONE."

Similar despatches and inflammable circulars were spread throughout the towns of Western Missouri, and soon all these towns, and indeed the whole of Western Missouri, was disturbed, and large numbers sprang to arms. By regulations adopted in the blue lodges at that time, those who could not go were mulcted in a certain sum of money to sustain those who did. Besides this forced levy, voluntary contributions were resorted to, and large sums raised and expended; for only those who have some little experience in the commissariat of an army can form an estimate of the expense of keeping over one thousand men in the field. Besides other stores, several wealthy and respectable friends of the cause subscribed a barrel of whiskey each. The Mayor of Kansas city gave one barrel, nor did he stop there. The following despatch was sent from Kansas city to encourage the "ruffians" of Platte:

"KANSAS CITY, MO., *Dec.* 3, 8 P. M.

"Mr. Payne, the mayor of this city, went to Liberty to-day, and succeeded in raising two hundred men and one thousand dollars for the assistance of Jones."

In order to show the object they had in view, I give the following despatch, sent back to Missouri by those who first went up. It was published as an extra, in flaming characters:

"INDEPENDENCE, *Dec.* 3, 8 P. M.

"Jones will not make a move until there is sufficient force in the field to ensure success. We have not more than three hundred men in the territory. You will, therefore, urge all who are interested in the matter to start immediately for the seat of war. *There is no doubt in regard to having a fight, and we all know that a great many have complained because they were disappointed heretofore in regard to a fight. Say to them, now is the time to show game, and, if we are defeated this time, the territory is lost to the South.*

"Signed by T. J. Shaw, H. T. Chiles, E. C. Chiles, J. C. Irwin, E. C. Renick."

The signers of this paper belong to a class considered respectable in their own localities, and, I have no doubt, influential.

Governor Shannon, having issued orders to call out the "militia," on the 27th of November, and having taken the initiatory steps to have the whole border ruffian force of Missouri poured into the territory to murder the settlers, happened to think, about two days afterwards, that the proper course would have been to issue a proclamation, and proceeded to do so on the 29th, as follows:

"PROCLAMATION.

"THE GOVERNOR OF KANSAS TERRITORY.

"Whereas, reliable information has been received that a numerous association of lawless men, armed with deadly weapons, and supplied with all the implements of war, combined and confederated together for the avowed purpose of opposing, by force and violence, the execution of the laws of this territory, did, at the County of Douglas, on or about the 26th of this month, make a violent assault on the sheriff of said county, with deadly weapons, and did overcome said officer, and did rescue from his custody, by force and violence, a person arrested by virtue of a peace-warrant, and then and there a prisoner, holden by the said sheriff, and other scandalous outrages did commit in violation of law:

"And whereas, also, information has been received that this confederated band of lawless men did, about the same time, set fire to and burn down a number of houses of peaceable and unoffending citizens, and did destroy a considerable amount of personal property, and have repeatedly proclaimed that they would regard no law of this territory, resist by force of arms all officers, and those aiding and assisting them in the execution of the laws, or any process issued in pursuance thereof:

"And whereas, also, I have received satisfactory information that this armed organization of lawless men have proclaimed their determination to attack the said Sheriff of Douglas County, and rescue from his custody a prisoner, for the avowed purpose of executing him without a judicial trial, and, at the same time, threatened the life of the said sheriff and other citizens: Now, therefore, to the end that the authority of the laws may be maintained, and those concerned in violating them, brought to immediate and condign punishment, and that the said Sheriff of Douglas County may be protected from lawless violence in the execution of the lawful warrants and other process in his hands, I, Wilson Shannon, governor of said territory, have issued this my proclamation, calling on all well-disposed citizens of this territory to rally to the support of the laws of their country, and requiring and commanding all officers civil and military, and all other citizens of this territory, who shall be found within the vicinity of these outrages, to be aiding and assisting, by all means in their power, in quelling this armed organization, and assisting the said sheriff and his deputies in recapturing the above-named prisoner, and aiding and assisting him in the execution of all legal processes in his hands. And I do further command that the district-attorney, for the district in which these outrages took place, and all other persons concerned in the administration or execution of the laws, cause the above offenders, and all such as aided or assisted them, to be immediately arrested and proceeded with according to law.

"Given under my hand and the seal of this territory, this 29th day of November, in the year of our Lord eighteen hundred and fifty-five.

"[L. S.] WILSON SHANNON.

"By the Governor: D. WOODSON, *Sec'y of the Territory.*"

Whether the authorship of this document belongs to Governor Shannon or Secretary Woodson is doubtful; but from what little I know of the facts, I incline to believe that it was concocted by both of them at Shawnee Mission, and penned by Woodson at Lecompton on the 30th. That gentleman went up from Shawnee Mission to Lecompton on the 30th. The proclamation was received and printed at Leavenworth on the first of December.

General Eastin, the editor, bogus councilman, brigadier of "militia," &c., gave publicity to the pronunciamento, and also to the following documents, which were issued on the same handbill, and circulated freely in Platte, Buchanan, and Clay Counties, Mo., although I never heard of but one having been seen in the territory:

"Head-quarters of Second Brigade of Northern Division of Kansas Militia, LEAVENWORTH CITY, *Nov.* 28, 1855.

"*To the Militia of the Second Brigade:*

"Information has been received by me that a state of open rebellion is now in existence in Douglas County, Kansas Territory. This is, therefore, to command the militia of my brigade of the Northern Division to meet at Leavenworth city, on Saturday, 1st day of December, 1855, at 11 o'clock, A. M., armed and equipped according to law, and to hold themselves in readiness, subject to the order of Major-General W. P. Richardson.

"Bring your arms and ammunition along.

"LUCIAN J. EASTIN,

"*Brig. Gen. of 2d Brigade, Northern Division Kansas Militia.*"

"TO ARMS! TO ARMS!

"It is expected that every lover of law and order will rally at Leavenworth on Saturday, December 1st, 1855, prepared to march at once to the scene of rebellion, to put down the outlaws of Douglas County, who are committing depredations upon persons and property, burning down houses, and declaring open hostility and resistance to the laws, and have forcibly rescued a prisoner from the sheriff. Come one, come all! The laws must be executed. The outlaws, it is said, are armed to the teeth, and number one thousand men. Every man should bring his rifle, ammunition, and it would be well to bring two or three days' provisions. Let the call be promptly obeyed. Every man to his post, and do his duty.

"MANY CITIZENS."

About the same time the following document was read before a meeting in Platte city, Mo. It was addressed to a certain general in Leavenworth, and handed by that accommodating individual to the proper parties:

"DEAR GENERAL: The governor having called out the militia, this is to inform you to order out your division, and proceed forthwith to Lecompton. The governor not having the power, you can call on the Platte Rifle Company, as our neighbors are always ready to help us. Do not implicate the governor, whatever you do."

This copy I obtained from a gentleman, who copied it from hearing it read several times. He also appended a signature, reported to have been attached to the letter; but, as a certain high territorial officer under the national executive has sworn and subscribed to an affidavit, in which it is certified that he did not send such a letter, I, therefore, append no name, not wishing, of course, to implicate any one else, and let the reader conclude that it *must* have been one of the *base fabrications* of the border ruffians, got up for effect.

As the report has been circulated that the *bona fide* inhabitants of the territory were first called, and that, failing to realize a sufficient force thus, the Missourians volunteered, and were received; I will state, that so far from this being the case, the first, and *only men in camp against Lawrence for several days*, came from Missouri. The first company, consisting of about fifty persons, from the neighborhood of Independence and Westport, came up on the 29th of November, and halted and camped at Franklin. Immediately on their arrival I rode down from Lawrence to see them. They had six wagons, a buggy, and spring-wagon, which were drawn up in a semi-circle, in an opening near the centre of the village. They were a motley crew. A considerable number of them were shooting at a mark; all had been drinking, and many were staggering about tipsy. From their appearance I should judge that they were the scum and riff-raff of the two places mentioned, and had doubtless been easiest started, from the fact of having no occupation. They were the pioneer party, and had no territorial functionaries, bogus or otherwise, with them, or near them, when I saw them. They freely admitted that they were from Missouri.

They were not yet under military orders, and did not keep a very strict camp. They were loud in denunciation of the "abolitionists," and profuse in threats about "drawing a bead on a blue-bellied Yankee," and "running the d—d abolitionists out of the territory." About the avowed *casus belli,* the rescue of Branson, they seemed to know or care nothing.

I append the following extracts from statements made by Governor Shannon, which ought to be authority as to the persons that composed the invading army :

"I can thus account for the intense excitement which was generated among the pro-slavery men of the Missouri frontier, and which finally resulted in their flocking to the aid of the upholders of *territorial law* in Kansas.

"Missouri has fifty thousand slaves in that portion of her territory which borders upon the frontiers of Kansas. By estimating the average value of each of these slaves at six hundred dollars (a low rate), we have a total of $30,000,000. Now, should Kansas become a free state, it would be ruinous to the slave-holding interests of Missouri."

While I venture to take exceptions to the governor's conclusions, still there is, unquestionably, a great deal of truth in his premises. It is also certain that something of the feeling to which the governor alludes existed; but whether it arose solely from the cause which he mentions, or from desire to extend slavery into the territory, hatred to all that was inimical to slavery extension, or from a desire to secure political power to nationalize the institution, is a point on which men may differ.

The governor further says:

"Missouri sent not only her young men, but her gray-headed citizens were there; the man of seventy winters stood shoulder to shoulder with the youth of sixteen."

If this were true it would only show that the mischief was deeply seated, when the experienced and influential should thus readily engage in an outrage in a neighboring territory.

These men from the first, and all through the campaign, claimed to be acting as territorial "militia," and that they were acting under orders from the governor. How true this was may be judged from the following apologetic statement from Shannon:

"These men came to the Wakarusa camp to fight; they did not ask peace; it was war — *war to the knife.* They *would* come; it was impossible to prevent them. What, then, was my policy? Certainly this; to mitigate an evil, which it was impossible to suppress, by bringing under military control these irregular and excited forces. This was only to be accomplished by permitting the continuance of the course which *had already been adopted,* without my knowledge, by Generals Richardson and Stricklar; that is, to have the volunteers incorporated, as they came in, into the already organized command. A portion of these men, who were mostly from Jackson County, Mo., reported themselves to Sheriff Jones, by giving in a list of their names, as willing to serve in their *posse;* and he, after taking legal advice upon the question, determined to receive them. They were accordingly enrolled."

It would be useless to follow the governor through the fallacies of the above statement. Its sophistry is too glaring, and the assigned reason altogether inconsistent. If the two generals disobeyed him in thus enrolling militia, it was certainly an odd "policy" on his part to endorse it. That it was the hope of thereby preventing their attack, will be proved false in the sequel. The fact is that all of these apologies were only thought of, and set forth, at a much later date, when the consequences of his imprudence became apparent.

CHAPTER XIII.

WAKARUSA WAR — ITS INCIDENTS.

The morning after the rescue of Branson there was a meeting held in Lawrence. Mr. S. N. Wood, one of the rescuers, was called to the chair, and took it with a sword belted to his waist. The chairman gave an account of the rescue, and stated his participation in it. Mr. Branson was called on, and in simple style related the occurrence. He spoke, also, of his murdered friend Dow. In conclusion, he appealed to them for support; but said if they wished it he would go home, and, if necessary, die there.

His address was received with acclamations, and the hastily gathered meeting declared that he should be protected. They also passed resolutions declaring that no officer under that Bogus Legislature should be allowed to make arrests. Several prudent voices dissented from any public action on this, but the majority were determined. In doing so there is no question but they were merely carrying out the expressed wish of the meetings and conventions held in the territory. The position taken called for resistance to these bogus officers. And when this rescue had been considered, with all the aggravating circumstances connected with the arrest, it indeed presented a true issue of the point in dispute. So thought and so said the first meeting held in Lawrence.

But there was another view of the question, and that the more thoughtful were not slow to take; in fact, Dr. Robinson took it from the first. It was that Lawrence must not assume anything for which it was not responsible, be the quarrel just or unjust. It was well known that a pretext was sought to destroy Lawrence, and it was determined that the ruffians should have no apology for their attack, if it was to be made. In the afternoon session of the same day, it was therefore decided that Lawrence had and would have nothing to do with the matter, leaving the position to be taken by any of its citizens, with regard to the bogus laws, for their own individual action at such times as the pretended officers might assail them. This position, when taken, was not supposed to concede anything. All united in regarding the laws and officers, imposed by the body of men who assembled at the Shawnee Mission, as having no power or effect, and that the action of any of these would-be officers was simply a case of assault on any one on whom they might pretend to operate. But those who managed the defence of Lawrence reasoned that they could not organize a force contemplating resistance to any body of men simply because these men pretended to be legislators or officers. In doing so they would refer their rights to the arbitration of violence, which they were not inclined to do.

A war kindled thus might have been most disastrous in its consequences, and have furthered the schemes of the Southern nullifiers. It was a love of the Union, and a patriotic desire to save it from the flames of civil discord, that induced the prudent and high-minded men entrusted with the defence to forbear raising a warlike issue themselves on this. It was hoped that Congress, just then about to assemble, would, the moment the case was presented, take steps to secure the rights of the settlers, without resorting to civil war. But they had not even then fully realized the inveterate purpose of their enemy, or the weakness of the government to aid them.

In consideration of the threatening aspect of affairs, a committee of safety, composed of ten persons, was formed for the protection of the town. These selected Dr. Robinson, one of their number, as commander-in-chief of the defence; and that gentleman, with their consent, authorized Col. Lane, who had distinguished himself in the Mexican war, to take immediate charge of the field force. Other officers of experience were there to assist in defence, if necessary.

While these steps were taken, and some two hundred men were mustered into service, it was concluded to keep everything as quiet as possible, to make as few warlike demonstrations as was compatible with safety, and not send to other portions of the territory until assistance was imperatively demanded. While Gen. Robinson and the committee were thus at work, meetings were held every night, and also in the day-time. The state of affairs was freely and warmly discussed, and whenever the leaders saw that the popular excitement ran too high they adroitly diverted it by letting it off in resolutions.

The rescue happened on the 26th, and it was the 29th before the first company of Missourians came up and encamped at Franklin, as stated in last chapter. All of this time Jones had never been heard from, and his movements could only be inferred from the thousand rumors constantly afloat. All of the rescuers returned to Hickory Point, where they lived, except Messrs. S. N. Wood, S. F. Tappan, and S. C. Smith, who lived in Lawrence; Branson also remained. Shortly after the Committee of Safety organized, and as soon as reliable information that a hostile force was beginning to assemble had reached them, they determined that the issue must be placed in its legitimate shape. It was known that the armed force was really gathering to attack and destroy Lawrence, and as Lawrence was not connected with the rescue, they deemed it proper that she should not be compromised by it. Branson was, therefore, requested to remove himself to some other part of the territory, where he could be safe. The three persons connected with the rescue, who lived in Lawrence, were also requested to leave, as the town was unwilling to organize a force for the defence of their persons against the threatening force; although Gen. Robinson, the committee, and the people of Lawrence were willing, and would be prepared to defend the town and citizens against any and all attacks from a hostile force.

The reader will doubtless think that this was avoiding the issue, and such refusal to sustain such men publicly in an honorable act, for which they respected them in their hearts, was undignified, inconsistent, and timorous policy. To such I would merely say that diplomacy in time of war, and indeed at all other times, is a science.

All day on the 29th of November, Missourians had been drilling and shooting at a mark in Franklin. The first company thus up, was, as I have stated, fifty men. A rumor came into Lawrence, at dusk on that evening, that a reinforcement of seven hundred men had arrived, and that Lawrence was to be attacked that night. I went out into the streets of Lawrence that night, and, though all was quiet enough, found here and there a guard pacing the streets with a Sharpe's rifle on his arm; and a few other silent indications I noted told that those who had assumed the responsibility of defence "slumbered not, nor slept." The moon was not up, and the stars shone but dimly through a haze of smoky air, the prairie grass being in a flame in several directions. Some teams, that had come in from Westport at dusk, had reported having met armed horsemen, and men in wagons, with arms, ammunition, and provisions, coming up from Missouri. One man said there was a company drilling at Franklin in the afternoon. I also learned that a meeting had been convened at Westport the day after the rescue of Branson, and that runners were sent to seven counties to raise men; later still, that they were enrolling men at Independence, and mulcting those who would not go, in five dollars, to defray expenses. Under these circumstances it is not surprising that there should be a good deal of uneasiness; indeed, I was only surprised that there should not have been more. Groups were assembled here and there. Hearty bursts of laughter occasionally told that some few discredited the danger, or despised it; but serious whisperings, and talk about the "seven hundred men at Franklin," showed that others were not so easy. Indeed, all knew that if Lawrence was not attacked that night it was only because its enemies could not raise force enough to venture.

About eight o'clock two men came in, and reported themselves as just up from Franklin, and that the seven hundred men were really there. I entered the chamber where the Committee of Safety was deliberating, and found by their anxious looks and preparations that the report was credited. Having been in Franklin that day, I, for several reasons, doubted its truth, and urged the propriety of such a fact being positively known if it was true. In company with Mr. Wm. Hutchinson, a member of the committee, I walked down to Franklin that night. When we entered Franklin we found all silent, and the place where the camp had been was deserted. The town appeared to be wrapped in sleep, and not a noise was heard but the creaking of the swinging sign in front of the tavern, and the sound of our footsteps as we walked through. Being anxious to know where these men had got to, and whether they had received the reported reinforcements, we went on. Immediately below Franklin the ground breaks, and there are one or two miles of flat bottom between that point and the Wakarusa. Just as we were leaving Franklin we saw a couple of sentries, with their guns, pacing in front of us. As we approached they walked up, as if they wished to interrogate; but we passed them with a blunt "Good-night," and they did not venture to molest. We had only gone about eighty yards when first the one and then the other discharged their pieces. We knew that they had not fired at us, and kept a sharp look-out, well knowing that it was a signal to those below. The Missourians had moved their camp down into the timber of the Wakarusa, and pitched it a quarter of a mile below the ford on the California road. This became the celebrated Wakarusa camp. They had received some reinforcements that evening, but they were light, and they had not force enough to make the attack. Having ascertained enough to know this, we returned.

Next day I again went down to their camp. A portion of them had moved up to Franklin for the convenience of the groceries, and were drinking and swearing, and shooting at a mark. They had several wagons there, from which banners with all kinds of mysterious devices were fluttering. When I got to the camp in the bottom, I learned that there were about one hundred and fifty men there. Riding on down the road, I saw four men stationed as guard near the ford. They were reclining on the ground when I first saw them, with long rifles in their hands. As I approached they sprang up to their feet and eyed me closely; but I rode on without paying any attention to them, and they did not molest me. While going down the road I met several teams and horsemen coming up. They were all armed; I conversed with most of them, and learned they were from Missouri. Indeed, as they were coming up the Westport road, which leads through Indian reserve to the state, this was apparent. One lot of these invaders particularly struck me. The party was composed of five men. They had two ox-teams. They were dressed in homespun, and looked like Western farmers of the poorer class. Three of them were young, one of these quite a lad. A middle-aged man, with a forbidding look, and a face like a bottle-brush, sat in the first wagon; an old man of sixty, his hair gray, beside him. As they approached, I reined up my pony, and saluted them. They returned my salutation, and stopped their wagons.

"Are there many more of the boys on the road?" I asked.

"Yes, lots of 'em," responded one of the young men.

"Where are you from?"

"We 're from the neighborhood of Independence."

"Are there many more coming from that quarter?"

"Yes; we started ahead of the company; we 're three days out. How many are in camp?"

"O, well, not quite two hundred."

"By G—d! is that all?" exclaimed two of them, in a breath; and one asked, "How many Yankees are there in Lawrence?"

"I cannot say exactly; a good many of them."

"Look here," said one of these youngsters, who evidently felt a little uneasy, "where is our camp? How far is it from Lawrence?"

"O, it 's just across the creek at the ford. It is six miles from Lawrence."

While this was passing, the old man, who had not yet said a word, got out of the wagon, and, coming over to me, laid his great rugged hands on my horse's mane, and looked up at me from a sharp gray eye that time had not dimmed much. There was a whole volume of interrogation in that keen, scrutinizing look; and as I looked down in his hard wrinkled face with as bland a smile as possible, I could read his suspicions in every lineament of those wrinkled features.

"An't you a Yankee?" he at length asked.

"O, no; I 'm a Sucker."

"D—n it! I knew he was all right," said the half-tipsy man. The old gentleman was evidently not reässured; but appeared to be at a loss how to continue his inquiries. One of the young men broke in here.

"Look here, stranger, did you ever see any of them Sharpe's rifles?"

"Yes, I have seen them."

"What sort o' fixin' are they?"

"Terrible gun."

"Say they kin load 'em ten times a minute — 's that so?"

"Expect it is."

"Well, how 'n thunder can they do it?"

"It 's done by machinery," we rejoined very mysteriously.

"Is it a revolvin' fixin'?" asked the youngest of the lot.

"Not exactly."

"Well, how fur kin they carry?"

"O, well, I do not believe all the stories they tell of them. Indeed, I am confident that they cannot carry a ball with any degree of accuracy much more than a mile; that is, to do close shooting." I said this with as much coolness as possible, and it required an effort to repress a smile as I saw the anxious faces of the inquirers.

"Have they got any cannons, them Yankees?"

"They say that they have plenty of them, and any quantity of grapeshot and bomb-shells, and every other infernal machine; but I don't believe it."

My avowed scepticism did not appear to relieve them, and they drove on, looking very anxious.

Shortly after I left them, I galloped off the road towards the east, and, after a desperate ride through bushes, and a somewhat unsafe and disagreeable fording of the Wakarusa, at a place below which looked shallow, but where there was no road, I came up to the Wakarusa camp from the other side, and, tying up my horse, went in amongst them. I found most of them anxious and rather despondent. They had expected that two or three thousand men would have been in their camp before this; and, as they had heard terrible stories about a "thousand men in Lawrence," they sagaciously concluded that they were not very safe. How they cursed those who were coming for their dilatoriness; d—d the leaders for their bad management, and swore at the "big bugs" who had got them into it, and thus left them, and the pro-slavery men in the territory for not helping them!

"Look here," said one pretty determined-looking chap, in buckskin breeches, and a red flannel shirt; "look here, if them infernal Yankees should take it into their head to come down here we would be in a darned nice scrape!"

"Pshaw!" said another; "we could use up a nation o' them white-livered Yankees."

"Not so fast, Tom," said a third. "If a thousand o' them fellows were to come to town with them infernal guns o' theirn, they 'd make this here patch pretty hot, I tell you."

Before I left the camp, another reinforcement of five wagons and a lot of horsemen arrived from Clay County, Mo. They had some of the stolen public arms with them, and one cannon. Over one of the wagons a large flag floated. In the centre of it there was a large purple star. These men were received with yells and enthusiasm; the camp resounded with shouts and wild screams. In the midst of these the strange flag was hoisted on a tree in the centre of the camp. I rode off unperceived, as it went up amidst the wildest shrieks and yells, and, as I looked back, and saw the fillibusters' flag floating over them, felt thankful that they had not disgraced the flag of our common country.

It was late in the afternoon as I returned through Franklin. The revellers were still there. Most of them were tipsy, and a few were stretched out on the sward hopelessly drunk. One of their number, a swarthy-looking disciple of Paganini, in home-spun pants, and dirty blue shirt, was perched on a log, playing on the fiddle, while a group of wild-looking, tipsy men were dancing round him, and cutting all kinds of capers. Another half-tipsy crowd were trying to prop up the back of a little log grocery, while they sung,

"We 've camped in the wilderness
For a few days, for a few days;
We 've camped in the wilderness,
And then we 're going home.
I 've a right up yonder," &c.

When a copy of the governor's message reached Lawrence,

which it did two days after its date, — a copy being brought from the frontier of Missouri, — it aroused the liveliest indignation. A committee of the citizens was appointed to report on it, which they did as follows :

"That the allegations contained in the proclamation aforesaid are false in whole, and in part; that no such state of facts exists in this community; that if such representations were ever made to Governor Shannon, the person or persons who made them have grossly deceived him. That no association of lawless men, armed with deadly weapons, has ever been formed in this community for the purpose of resisting the laws of the country, trampling upon the authority of its officers, destroying the property of peaceable citizens, or molesting any person in this territory, or elsewhere, in the enjoyment of their rights."

A day or two afterwards a memorial to Congress was framed, and numerously signed. When it was drawn up, the Missouri "posse," or "militia," had commenced their depredations, and it alludes to this:

"*To the Honorable the United States Senate and House of Representatives in Congress assembled:*

"Your memorialists, citizens of the United States, and residents of Kansas Territory, respectfully represent unto your honorable body that, without any justifiable cause whatever, Governor Shannon has caused to be issued a proclamation, and under it military orders have been issued, calling upon the militia of Kansas and Missouri to meet at certain points within the territory, armed and equipped, and to march against certain portions of our people and territory. Copies of such proclamation, military orders, and a letter from Daniel Woodson, Secretary of the Territory, to Lucien J. Eastin, editor of the *Kansas Herald*, are herewith inclosed; from which it will be seen that your memorialists are exposed to the authorized march of a military force from Missouri, who are arresting our citizens, and committing depredations on persons and property only known in cases of war between hostile countries. Devoted as we are to the Constitution and the Union, and estimating neither as secondary to slavery, we earnestly invoke the interposition of Congress so far as to send for persons and papers to substantiate the truth of our statements herewith inclosed."

That it was no part of Jones' object to make peaceable arrests is clear from the fact that he came into Lawrence on the first of December, and went about the streets without any one paying the slightest attention to him, — that is, to molest him. Mr. S. N. Wood, who, at first refused to leave town, and said they could arrest him, accosted Jones, and invited him to dinner. Jones never said a word about having writs against him. He was evidently in town merely on a military reconnoisance.

The invaders began to get very uneasy about this time. Both officers and men were apprehensive of an attack; hence General Eastin sent the following letter to Governor Shannon:

"LEAVENWORTH, K. T., *Nov. 30th*, 1855.

"GOVERNOR SHANNON: Information has been received here direct from Lawrence, which I consider reliable, that the outlaws of Douglas County are well fortified at Lawrence with cannon and Sharpe's rifles, and number *at least* one thousand men. It will, therefore, be difficult to dispossess them.

"The 'militia' in this portion of the state are entirely unorganized, and without arms.

"I suggest the propriety of calling upon the military at Fort Leavenworth. If you had the power to call out the government troops, I think it would be best to do so at once. It might overawe these outlaws, and prevent bloodshed.

"L. J. EASTIN,
"*Brig. Gen. Northern Brigade, K. T.*"

This humane desire of the general to prevent the "effusion of blood" is, under such circumstances, pretty good. The governor immediately complied with its request, and sent a despatch to Colonel Sumner, at Fort Leavenworth, to ask the aid of the troops. Colonel Sumner sent back the following prudent missive:

"HEAD QUARTERS, 1ST CAVALRY,
FORT LEAVENWORTH, *Dec.* 1*st*, 1855.

"GOVERNOR: I have just received your letter of this day. I do not feel that it would be right in me to act in this important matter until orders are received from the government. I shall be ready to move instantly whenever I receive them. I would respectfully suggest that you make your application for aid to the government extensively known at once, and I would countermand any orders that may have been given to the movement of the militia until you receive the answer. I write this in haste.

"With much respect, your obedient servant,

"E. V. SUMNER,
"*Colonel First Cavalry.*

"His Excellency, GOVERNOR SHANNON."

This is a very fair indication of what Sumner thought of the "militia" movement. In compliance with the suggestion of Col. Sumner, the governor telegraphed to the President, asking the aid of the troops. That this movement was extremely objectionable to the Missourians, and the border ruffian leaders generally, is certain. It was unquestionably an indiscretion on the part of Eastin, as a member of that party; for, although the threatening aspect of the case seemed to require it, the leaders well knew that the troops would only be in their way, and would probably prevent the destruction of Lawrence. They did not despair of getting men enough; although the fact that ten days of active exertion only succeeded in getting up some fifteen hundred men, showed that the Missourians were more ready in volunteering to vote than to fight. With regard to the number of the invading force, I subjoin the following statement of Shannon's:

"The pro-slavery forces thus collected, including the militia, amounted on the 1st or 2d of December, 1855, as it was then stated to me at the Shawnee Mission, to about fifteen hundred men; and it was also reported that an equal number of free-state men had collected in Lawrence."

On Saturday and Sunday the camp on the Wakarusa increased rapidly, and a camp was formed at Lecompton. In the camp at

Lecompton there were, perhaps, fifty pro-slavery residents of the territory, including the Kickapoo Rangers. At no time during the war were there more than seventy-five or eighty pro-slavery residents under arms. The camp at Lecompton was mostly made up from Platte and Buchanan Counties, Missouri. As they began to get stronger they grew proportionably bold. On the second of December strict orders were issued to both camps. Lawrence was placed under surveillance; the roads were guarded; travellers were stopped, searched and disarmed, and sometimes taken prisoners; wagons were stopped, and, under the pretence of search for arms and stores, they were plundered. Besides this, scouting parties went over the country, plundering many of the settlers.

As it was feared by the ruffian leaders that the attempt to make arrests would not make a sufficient *casus belli*, General Richardson sent the following letter to the governor:

"LECOMPTON, K. T., *Dec. 3d*, 1855.

"HIS EXCELLENCY, GOVERNOR WILSON SHANNON —

"DEAR SIR: I believe it to be essential to the peace and tranquillity of the territory that the outlaws at Lawrence and elsewhere should be required to surrender their Sharpe's rifles. There can be no security for the future safety of the lives and property of law-abiding citizens unless these unprincipled men are (at least) deprived of the arms, which, we all know, have been furnished them for the purpose of resisting the law. In fact, peaceable citizens will be obliged to leave the territory unless those who are now threatening them are compelled to surrender their rifles and artillery, if they have any.

"I do not, however, feel authorized, by the instructions which you have given me, to make this demand. Should you concur with me in my opinion, please let me know by express, at once.

"A fresh rider had better be sent up in lieu of this, as he will be fatigued. I am diligently *using every precaution to prevent the effusion of blood*, and preserve the peace of the territory. As the Sharpe's rifles may be regarded as private property *by some*, I can give a *receipt* for them, stating that they will be returned to the owners at the discretion of the governor.

"Very respectfully, your obedient servant,

"WILLIAM P. RICHARDSON,

"*Major-General, commanding Kansas Territorial Militia.*"

When the report of the burning of the shanties of Hargus and Coleman reached Lawrence it excited a feeling of regret and anger.

There is but little doubt that these shanties were burned by the men who had endeavored to arrest Branson, or some of them, and was a deep-laid part of the same scheme which was evidently designed to precipitate the quarrel. I have not seen a free-state man who does not deprecate the transaction; few of these believe that any free-state man did it; and when it was supposed at first that some foolish free-state man had done so in the excitement, there was a general wish to ferret it out and have him punished. An examination of the facts shows that the guilt in all probability lies at the doors of those who wish to make capital out of it. At the meeting held at Hickory Point, to investigate the murder of Dow, a resolution was introduced, and unanimously sustained, which deprecates reprisals of that kind, as likely to bring reproach upon the free-state men, no matter what the provocation. It is also known that all the free-state men in the immediate vicinity were engaged in the rescue of Branson, and came on with him to Lawrence. Buckley had been seen in the direction of his own house by some women about the time it was burned. The houses destroyed were only shanties, worth little, and had nothing in them, as the owners had left them a day or two before.

CHAPTER XIV.

ADVENTURES WITH THE BORDER RUFFIANS.

For miles around Lawrence the country was in a state of warlike preparation and excitement. Armed companies of citizens from different parts of the surrounding county and territory began to arrive in Lawrence. The town was invested by the enemy, although to the south people were still coming and going. Such was the state of affairs when, on Monday morning, I started to go down once more to reconnoitre the camp on the Wakarusa, and, if I could get through, to go down and see the governor.

Passing through Franklin, I observed that there was now no regular camp in the village; but there were some fifty or sixty idlers from the camp below, drinking and loafing around the place, for lack of something better, or worse, to do. They had no regular guard; but two or three of them, with arms in their hands, marched up to me as I was riding along, and ordered me to halt.

"Where are you going?"

"Down below," said I.

"You can't do it."

"Why not?"

"Orders are given to let no one pass."

"There is no guard here."

"D—n it, we're the guard! Where are you from?"

"I am staying in the territory."

"Have you any business down there?"

"Yes."

"I believe he's from Lawrence," said one of the number; "he's been down here every day."

Reader, did you ever happen to be in the centre of a group of some twenty ruffianly fellows, half-tipsy, armed to the teeth, vowing murder on their enemies, of whom they suspect you to be one? If so, you can realize my sentiments as I regarded the group by which I was surrounded.

"By G—d, sir," said one man, "if you go down there, you will wish you was back again! They 'll take you."

"If I once get to the camp where the officers are I am not afraid of being taken." And I said this with an assumed coolness and as much assurance as I could muster. It seemed to have the desired effect, for they gave way, and one of them said:

"Well, let him go; if he an't all right, he 's safe enough."

I rode on as rapidly as possible. Immediately below Franklin the upland prairie breaks, and a broad, flat bottom, covered with a very luxuriant grass, stretches between the slope and the timber that skirts the Wakarusa. As I descended the slope I saw a horseman before me. Numerous other parties were galloping across the plain in every direction, but he was travelling alone and at a moderate pace. I overtook and saluted him. He was mounted on a powerful gray horse, had a long rifle thrown across the saddle before him, and a couple of pistol-holsters. In appearance he was a cross between the gentleman and border ruffian; only a slightly sinister expression gave the latter the preponderance. He was a strongly-built man, and well equipped for travel. It was Marshal Jones.

Riding to the sunny side of him, I addressed him as blandly as possible. He returned the salutation, but looked at me suspiciously; and, as I rode alongside of him, he said:

"May I ask where you are going, sir?"

"I am going down below."

"How did you get through the guard at Franklin?"

"Guard! They do not stop people on the highway, they?"

"Certainly. The whole country is in a state of war."

"War! Who declared it?"

"Which way did you come?" said he, abruptly.

"I came from above."

"Well, I mean in what part of the territory do you live?"

"I have not located yet. I have been all over it."

"What state are you from, stranger? And may I ask what is your business?"

"I am an Illinoisan, an editor, and a lawyer. May I inquire your name and place of residence?" I said, thinking it time to have some questions from the other side.

"My name is Jones — Marshal Jones. I live in Westport."

He said this with an evident disinclination to be questioned. He continued:

"Look here, sir. I don't see where you could have come from, or how you could have travelled, not to have heard about the war before this, or have been taken."

"I *did* hear about the difficulties, but did not suppose war had been declared, or that any one could declare it as matters are."

"Where did you hear of them?"

"In Lawrence."

He eyed me very sharply when I said this. I rode on, looking as indifferent and careless as possible.

"Well, sir, let me tell you," he resumed, "you 're well out of Lawrence. That place will be wiped out one of these days. By G—d, sir, they are all traitors, there, and d——d abolitionists! We 've got to wipe them out. There will be no peace in the territory till it 's done; and we 'd better do it before they get any stronger."

"But such an attack on the place would lead to a war."

"Well, d—n it, that 's what we want."

"But, if war begins this way, where will it end? Might it not endanger the peace of the whole country, and even the Union?"

"D—n the Union!" he said. "We have gone in for peace long enough. We have got to fight some time or other, and may as well do it now. We have got the law and the authorities on our side, and we will take that town. It 's no use talking; we have got to fight. We have seven hundred men in the camp down there; there is a large reinforcement coming on, that will arrive to-night or to-morrow, and the Platte County people will be here.

All of these troops, sir, are enrolled, and accepted by the governor. They are here to enforce the laws; and, by G—d, they 'll do it! We have got the law with us, and all this matter has been arranged by long heads, who know what they are about. We shall insist that the people of Lawrence give up those fifteen men to us and also that they give up their Sharpe's rifles, and other arms and we will destroy the big hotel."

"But you cannot expect compliance with those requisitions. Those men are not in Lawrence. The guns they will not give up especially when they are menaced."

"Well, d—n them, we 'll make them!"

"Well, I cannot hope and pray for your success."

"What!" and his eyes lighted up more fiercely; "do you mean that you will hope and pray for the other side?"

And, as he spoke, he lifted his rifle a little on his arm; it might have been merely for a change of position, it might have been a menace. I, merely by chance, loosed the button of my overcoat, inside of which was my revolver, and, changing the subject, I pointed to the plain we were traversing, and said:

"This is a very rich bottom — it would make a fine meadow or would it not suit for the production of hemp? I am not much acquainted with its culture."

I avoided his eye, for I felt I could not look into it pacifically enough. I saw he looked fierce; but my indifference disarmed him, although he did not respond to my remark very cheerfully I continued to inquire about the soil, and other commonplaces which seemed to annoy him, although he tried to answer as politely as he could.

We soon entered the timber, and in a few minutes more reached the fresh-beaten path that led off the road into the camp. He halted his horse at that point, as did I. For a moment he appeared to be wrapped in thought; then he said:

"This is our camp, in here, sir, and you can't go in; at least you had better not."

"Why?"

"Why, because they will take you prisoner, and I don't know that I should let you pass. But I believe you don't mean any harm, although you talk too freely for these times. Where are you going?"

"I am going down below."

"Well," he said, as if he had made up his mind to a magnanimous thing, "well, I'll see you safe through the guards at the ford."

"What is the ford guarded for? By whose orders?"

"By orders of the governor. All of these men are regular militia of the territory. Had you gone there alone they would have taken you prisoner in about five minutes."

He rode down to the ford with me. As we approached it I saw a wagon in the bed of the creek; it appeared to be loaded with merchandise, doubtless designed for some unfortunate merchant in the interior. Three or four armed men were rummaging and searching it with great zeal. The bed of the Wakarusa is nearly dry at the ford, and very wide. At the opposite side from Lawrence the road goes through a narrow cut in the bank; and here the sentries were posted, armed with long rifles and revolvers. As I had no intention of giving up my arms, and knew that was part of the ceremony, I merely waited until my obliging companion had got ready, and our horses had drank, when we rode up to the guard, and my companion said:

"This man is travelling — going down below — let him go through."

I was riding on, when the person in charge of the guard said:

"Stop, we must examine you; our orders are positive — come back, sir."

Now no chieftain amongst the border ruffians likes to have his authority called in question. Marshal Jones fancied himself of sufficient importance to act; and, as he had told me "he would see me through," with an air of perfect security in his power to do so, he felt piqued, and his reputation was at stake. He said to the captain of the guard:

"I will endorse this man. He's all right. He's going below. I will see to it."

"Marshal Jones," said the captain of the guard, respectfully, "that may all be; but we've got orders from General Stricklar, and they come from the governor, and we can let no one pass whatever without taking their arms, and if they are not all right we take them prisoners." As he said this they approached me, and two of the cut-throat looking individuals were just about to put their hands on my overcoat to feel for arms, when, not approving of such familiarity, I struck my pony with my heel, and trotted out from them.

"Stop! stop!" cried the sentry in command, advancing towards me, and pointing a revolver. "Stop! stop!" cried the other sentries, lowering their rifles; and I saw the sunlight gleam on the long barrels as they were brought down. "Stop! for God's sake, stop!" cried Jones, riding up.

I had ridden through them, and about eight yards up the bank. My intention was to ride on; for I did not think they would dare to shoot a traveller under such circumstances. But when I heard them shout to me I looked round, and as my eye wandered over the long gun-barrels pointing towards me, and I saw a wild devil in the men's eyes, I halted.

"You must give up your arms!"

"I am travelling; I may need them; I do not want to lose my property."

"I will guarantee its safety," said Jones.

I had an excellent six-shooter in my belt, and a small four-barrelled French revolver in my pocket. I took out the latter and handed it to Jones, saying I should hold him responsible for it.

"You see, gentlemen," said Jones, "he has given up his arms."

"Well," was the surly response, — for the guard would rather have had my pistol themselves, — "he must go back to the camp and be examined." Such was the next demand. My first determination was to resist it; but, reflecting that this would be the only chance to go into camp now, I turned my horse around, trotted across the creek again, and rode down into camp, Jones at my side, and an ill-favored looking scoundrel behind us.

The camp had received considerable additions since I had last seen it. Wagons and carriages were scattered here and there in all directions. I saw several dirty-looking tents, and the smoke of the camp-fires curled up among the oaks and elms; and around these the idle adventurers were lying in groups, many of them evidently in liquor. There were two or three banners flying, with different devices, but the large flag, with the lone star on it, was over the centre of the camp, being the symbol of the great secret Blue Lodge of Western Missouri, of which Atchison and Stringfellow are the leaders, and these fierce and half-civilized men the disciples.

A crowd gathered round us. The captain of the guard was sent for, and some of the fellows commented on my presence, and the fact of my having been there often enough before. I also learned that they had a man confined in the camp, and concluded from their remarks that my chance of keeping him company was very fair. However, after some detention, I succeeded in getting away, Jones returning me my little French revolver, and another escort seeing me over the creek. Even then the sentries were very unwilling I should pass, and were for again questioning me, but I rode on.

While in the camp I had instituted as close an examination as I could as to the state of affairs there. When I had ridden on a mile or two I stopped at Fish's "Shawnee Hotel." I knew the proprietor to be a good free-state man. While there I saw a young Vermonter, fresh in the territory, and just on his way up. I told him he could not get through the guard. He "guessed he could if I could." Finding, on a little more conversation, that he was a person of some information, and of a bold and fearless disposition, I told him exactly how he would find the enemy's camp, and what difficulties he would have to encounter. He thought he could get through. I then wrote a note to Gen. Robinson, stating the precise condition in which the enemy's camp, their artillery, arms, etc., then were, and also informing him that the attack would not be made before Thursday at the soonest (a fact which I had ascertained). I also recommended them to have no uneasiness about my absence. Having got my despatches ready, and the young man having expressed his willingness to carry them, I gave them to him. He very coolly deposited them between the leather on the top of his boot, closing up the place so adroitly that a cobbler would never have suspected there were treasonable despatches or anything else there. He said he would be in Lawrence that night, and would deliver them to the general; and off he went; and he got safe through, as only a Yankee could.

He rode up to the guard at the ford, and before they had time to challenge him he gave the military salute, which might be mistaken in a hurry for the travelling sign of the border ruffians, and in a sharp voice said:

"Why don't you demand the countersign?"

"Go on," said the officer of the guard, fancying he was all right. Reinforcements were indeed arriving every few moments from the direction in which he came. Having got in, he contrived to get out pretty much in the same way; having managed it, as he told me afterwards, by "coming the Yankee over them."

I started on my way to Shawnee Mission. I knew the governor had been a good deal in the hands of the pro-slavery men, and that he was weak and vacillating. I intended to make a true representation of the facts to him, and urge him to defer the enforcement of the few obnoxious laws until Congress met; or, if he must enforce them, to do it by officers really belonging to the territory, or by the United States courts.

It was thirty-five long and weary miles off, and it was now noon; but I started at a brisk trot, walking up all the steep hills to rest my pony. The road was thronged with teams of invading border ruffians, and, during the afternoon's ride, I met some half a dozen buggies and carriages. In these there were generally a couple of gentlemen, armed almost invariably with double-barrelled shotguns, — titular dignitaries, colonels and majors, the politicians of Western Missouri. The rank and file of the marauding host were less intelligent and more noisy, often shrieking and yelling so that you could hear them afar off. Their equipment was simple and uniform, — a box full of corn and other feed, a box of provisions, some guns and other articles scattered in the bottom of the wagons, and generally two or three men within, and several horsemen accompanying the wagon. Dressed as the rougher backwoodsmen dress, with faces unwashed, and hair and whiskers unkempt, they appeared in full keeping with their lawless occupation. Most of them had been drinking.

Night set in when I was still several miles from the mission. Arrived there, weary and travel-worn, I learned that the governor was in Westport. I rode on to Westport, which is some four miles distant. Not knowing where the governor stayed, I went to several houses, which appeared to be hotels, and inquired; but when at last I found where he had been, I learned that he had started for the Mission; so I despaired of seeing him that night.

The hotels and other places of entertainment were crowded, and several camps of the border ruffians, on their way to Kansas, were around the town. As I was in several of the public places, I heard much of the discussion that was going on. I ascertained that Gov. Shannon had got despatches that night from the President. What these were I could not learn authentically, but inferred it from the exclamation that, as "they had now got the authority of the government, they could go ahead safely." Whatever may have been said of outrages elsewhere, I heard little mention of them here. The remarks were of a congratulatory kind. "Now was just the time." "The river navigation was just closed, and there could be no reinforcements or supplies sent to the abolitionists" (the term they apply to the free-state men indiscriminately). "These fellows must be cleaned out of Kansas some time, and it would be easier to do it now than a year hence;" that "there were only about three thousand five hundred free-state men in the territory," and that "a large number of these were dough-faces, and would not fight, and that men enough could be got in Missouri to 'clean them all out.'"

They unfolded their plans, which were, to demand that Lawrence should deliver up all concerned in the rescue, and that the free-state men surrender their arms; that Lawrence be demolished, the leaders of the free-state party lynched, and the others warned to leave the territory. There was also a great deal of bullying and bragging about being "able to draw a 'bead' on a blue-bellied Yankee," together with a good many other threats and suggestions too elegant and pithy to enumerate.

I walked round town for some time. Camp-fires were gleaming

in every direction. Indeed, the appearance of Westport that night was one of the most alarming indications of the amount of force to be brought against us that I had seen. It was about ten o'clock, but I determined to go on to Kansas city, three miles further, that night.

My horse was so completely tired that, after riding a short distance, I got off and led him. I met one or two parties of border ruffians, who had come out of Clay County, Missouri; but they did not molest me.

I had travelled about half way to Kansas when, having occasion to cross a small stream, I mounted my pony, and almost immediately heard horses galloping behind. I rode on at about the same steady gait (perhaps a mile an hour), and in a few minutes a couple of horsemen dashed up to me, and passed, one on either side, reining in their horses about eight yards ahead. They whispered together, and I saw one of them pass something, which I took for a pistol in the dark, and then they dropped back alongside of me. I heard the rest of the party coming up behind.

"Now may all the saints in the calendar take care of me this time!" thought I. Whether my friend the Vermonter had been taken, and my despatches found in his boots, or whether some knowledge of my position on the staff of the *Tribune* had leaked out, were subjects that chased each other through my brain; but they did not keep me long in suspense.

"Did you see a man going along the road?" asked one of them.

"No."

"Well, there was a man rode down this way, and if you have not seen him we will hold you responsible."

"That is rather singular."

"You must go back with us."

"I believe not; my horse is tired, and I am going on to Kansas."

"That is nothing; we arrest you."

"Have you a warrant? has any crime been committed? or what do you want me for? Has any one been stealing a horse?"

"No, not for that," said one of them; "but there is trouble in the territory, and we have orders to let no one pass. You came out of the territory, did you not?"

"Yes, sir."

"What part of it?"

"Up above."

Now my friend Marshal Jones was not at all inquisitive about the locality of "down below," and "up above," but these gentry appeared to be more captious.

"Up where?—what part of the territory do you live in?"

"I have not located in any point yet."

"What point did you leave this morning?"

Now my first impression was to answer no more of their impertinent questions. Then a little devil whispered that I should suggest "the south part of the territory;" but I voted down the lying whisper mentally, and said, with something like dogged determination, I suspect,

"Lawrence."

Then some of them gave a whistle.

"How did you get through?" asked the captain, who had been the chief spokesman.

"I rode down."

"Pish!" said the captain.

By this time there were a dozen of them about me, and they halted their horses. As I had no wish to stop, I kicked and switched at my pony, but he was immovable, and too glad for an excuse to stop to mind my kicking.

"Do you know Gen. Pomeroy?" asked one.

"No, not personally; I have heard of him."

"Are you not carrying despatches from Lawrence to him?"

"No," I replied; "I am travelling on the highway, and do not want to be molested."

"Well, we have reason to *know* that you are carrying despatches," said the captain.

"Who are you, sir?" I asked.

"My name is Jones."

"Jones—Jones?" thought I. Sheriff Jones—Marshal Jones—Captain Jones!—the Joneses were as plenty as blackberries.

Were all the border ruffians of the Jones family? "And your name?" said I to the fellow on my left elbow.

"Brown."

Brown — I would as soon have thought of hunting for a needle in a hay-stack as finding out a man called "Brown." "And yours?" said I to a third.

"I don't see that it makes a d—d bit of difference to you what my name is," said he.

"You must go back to Westport," said Jones.

"My horse is tired, — I cannot go; — besides, I have no business there."

"We'll find some for you!" growled the surly man without a name.

"I cannot go if you have not a warrant."

"We have authority for what we do."

"What is your authority?"

"The governor."

"What governor?"

"Gov. Shannon."

"You forget, gentlemen, that we are in Missouri."

This seemed rather to nonplus them, but they continued:

"You must go back."

"I will not."

"We will take you."

"Very good."

Here the party came to a halt. My horse was so tired that he stopped too, and would not budge; and there I was in the midst of these scoundrels. As they were fingering their weapons, I also laid my hand on mine; but I was very loth to shoot, for I knew that my chances would be slim in such a case. They looked at me, and I looked at them; and there was one of those distressing pauses which are liable to occur when some one of a dozen men is expected to do something, yet no one feels exactly like assuming the responsibility. I feel confident they thought I was going to shoot the first man that laid a finger on me.

"Look here," said Capt. Jones, "we don't want any bloodshed.

This don't amount to anything serious, I expect. Go back with us, and if we find all right you won't be molested."

"I can't go, gentlemen. How do I know but you may be highwaymen? And if you want to do me any mischief, you might as well do it here."

"What state are you from?"

I gave Capt. Jones an account of my antecedents, which was true as far as it went.

"O, well," said he, "you 're a Western man."

Finding that I would not go back, they urged me to withdraw to a house not far off, and wait until the rest of their company came up, when, they said, we would all go to Kansas together, and, if I was found "all right," I could go my way. Fearing that the scoundrels would forcibly seize me, and that the affair would end in bloodshed, and having a promise, on their honor, that I should not be molested in the house to which we were going, I went with them. The expected reinforcement did not come up, however. I learned subsequently that their intention was to go to the American Hotel and take out Pomeroy and lynch him; but as they had expected fifty men to take a hand in it, and as they were only about fifteen, they did not attempt it. As I stood in front of the fire warming myself, and wondering what they were going to do with me, I heard them talk freely about what they had already been doing and intended to do. They spoke of the capture of Judge Johnson and others. They were drinking pretty freely, and the owner of the house where we went seemed to act as one of them. They drank once or twice without asking me to participate; and then one of them, more *humane* than the rest, said,

"Well, I 'm darned if this arn't too bad! — Stranger," said he, approaching me with a jug, "take something to drink."

"Thank you, I never drink."

"Never drink!" exclaimed two or three, with gaping eyes; and then one of them said,

"That 's just it! This thing o' temperance, and abolitionism, and the Emigrant Aid Society, are all the same kind o' thing."

I found I had fallen still more in repute, if possible. But I cannot detail all the incidents of that eventful night. I was subjected to the indignity of an examination for despatches, which I was supposed to have, and had only the remedy (which I was not inclined to apply) of shooting one of these lawless scoundrels through the head. The search was instituted with some degree of courtesy, and only by two of them, who invited me into another room for the purpose.

While I was in the hands of these men I heard them lay a plot for lynching Pomeroy, and express a fear that he would get out of the territory before they could catch him. The majority were for hanging him at once; but one more conservative than the rest said he "did not approve of that sort of thing." He thought he ought to be only tarred and feathered, after a good beating, and sent adrift on the river. Another offered an amendment to this proposition by suggesting that he should be rubbed with oil, and carefully blackened, so that the color would not come off, and then be set adrift on the river. These moderate sentiments appeared to be overruled — the majority declaring that he must be hung. They also determined that the American Hotel should be torn down.

I went immediately to Kansas, learned that the wires were down, and that I could not get a despatch off; and then sought out Gen. Pomeroy, got an introduction to him, and warned him of his danger. Several others in Kansas had also apprised him of it. He had made up his mind to start for Lawrence after dinner. I had intended to return to the Mission to see the governor, but fearing he would have started for Lecompton, and that I should again miss him, and being requested by some gentlemen to accompany Pomeroy through the Delaware reserve, as they feared the scouting parties would pick him up, I concluded to go back to Lawrence with him.

We crossed the Kaw river at the Wyandot ferry. There were two sentries there, but they did not venture to accost us. The moment the ferry-boat had fairly started over the river they hastily took the direction for Kansas city, and I have learned since that a party crossed after us in about an hour and a half. They would have to be true scouts to find us. We took every crossroad we came to, zigzagging; and after nightfall reached the Baptist Mission, and were kindly received by the Rev. Mr. Pratt. He secured an Indian guide for us, and, after resting and feeding our horses, we set out on a journey of twenty-six miles, starting at nearly ten o'clock.

Our taciturn guide led the way by Indian trails, and through the whole of that long, weary night we travelled. It was so dark that the guide finally lost his way; and, after wandering about for a while, dismounted and lay down on the grass, saying, in rather unsatisfactory English, "Well, I believe we are altogether lost." Having induced him to resume his march, we at length, after some miles of very rough riding, found the way. About three miles from Lawrence we came to a camp-fire; but those who had been there had left. The Indian overheard me tell Pomeroy that I was in favor of forcing our way through any picket we should meet, for I had decided objections to going again into the camp at the Wakarusa. So he got off his horse and lay down, and we could not induce him to go further. Having discharged him, we resumed our way, and reached the river opposite Lawrence, a short time after, without encountering interruption.

At the river bank I wanted my companion to lead the way, as I was not acquainted with the ford. He did not know it, either, and wished me to go in first; and, as he was an older man, I plunged in, although I inwardly wished I could exchange my little pony for his large horse. By mistake in the dark I took the river at the ferry crossing instead of the ford, which I learned after was a hundred yards above. As I went in it got deeper and deeper, and still through the darkness I could see the broad river before me. The current is very strong, and the bottom a quicksand; when I had got half way over, it became so deep that it was up to my saddle; and then the strength of the current and the false bottom carried us down, and immediately I was in deep water. My pony could scarcely swim, and tumbled over and floundered with me at a dreadful rate. I dismounted, and attempted to swim the rest of the way across, but a heavy overcoat and a load of other clothes, together with a couple of pistols, and such miscellaneous matter, proved too much for me. I found I could not struggle against the current, — that I could scarcely sustain myself, — and for a few moments sincerely thought *The Tribune* would require another Kansas correspondent. Making a great effort, I swam to my horse again, and, grasping the pommel of the saddle, spoke to him, and guided him. He was completely bewildered. We kept going round and round, and for a few moments I almost felt like "giving up the ship." But no! To escape scathless from the border ruffians, and die in the muddy waters of the Kansas, would never do. I made another effort with my pony. Finding it impossible to get him over, I guided him to the shore we had started from, where Pomeroy, who had not come in so far, still remained. Half dead with fatigue, I clambered up the bank. We had to halloo nearly an hour before we could get the ferryman, and would have relinquished all efforts to get over, but I was freezing. The slumbering Charon was at length aroused, and with the gray of a chilly December morning we entered the beleaguered city of Lawrence.

CHAPTER XV.

WAKARUSA WAR — DEATH OF BARBER.

During the last week of the siege Lawrence was a stirring sight. Besides the citizens of the town there were nearly five hundred men under arms from different parts of the territory. The Free-State Hotel, still unfinished, but sufficiently comfortable to inhabit, was the head-quarters. Two chambers in the third story, in the south-east corner of the building, were the council-room and the general's quarters. Many of the companies had their quarters in the hotel. Below, the dining-hall was used as a general place of reception for the soldiers. Two sentinels guarded the door, to let none in but those who had business or had the password.

But the soldiers were not confined to the hotel. Every house in town was converted into a barrack for the time being, and the expense incurred not only in the public but the private barracks, and, indeed, the whole expense of this siege, forms a fearful-looking sum of money (on paper), and conveys an impressive moral about the cost of war.

Three large circular earth-works, a hundred feet in diameter, were thrown up so as to defend the place from an attack made on the north-west, south, and south-east. These defences were not commenced until the last week of the siege, when the size of the force to be brought against them, and the fact of the enemy being all well mounted, led to a defence suited to the kind of attack expected. It was a stirring sight to see the men working in the trenches, and even at night they could be found plying the spade and mattock, officers guiding the progress of the work, and holding lanterns.

In the afternoon of each day there was a drill-parade. The band would commence playing martial music in the street, and the star-spangled banner might be seen waving over Fort Smith, at the foot of Massachusetts-street. The star-spangled banner also flew from the Free-State Hotel and several other buildings. Then the volunteer troops were mustered on parade, while Col. Lane, now Brigadier-General Lane, walked beside the companies, in an easy, swinging military gait, and gave the orders in his sharp, shrill voice when on the parade-ground. On such occasions, after parade and drill, Lane would sometimes make a speech; and if General Robinson and staff went out to the parade, he was invariably called upon, and sometimes spoke. On such occasions Lane was fiery, and his remarks calculated to rouse up the men to the fighting point. Robinson, on the other hand, restrained them. He urged them to avoid making any attack, and, when they might be sent with patrol or scouting party, not to be intimidated or induced into a skirmish. To "suffer and be strong" was his motto.

If Lawrence was a scene of interest through the day, it was not less so at night. So closely was the town guarded that all egress or ingress was precluded. A horse patrol of a dozen mounted men would go round the outer line of posts once or twice in the night, and would proceed to the point where the Lawrence road forked from the California, about half way to Franklin. This was a disputed point, and the general impression was that a skirmish between the enemy's patrol and ours would occur. Horse patrols from the camp on the Wakarusa would come up every night to that point, and remain there for some time, as if to hold it. One night, when the free-state patrol approached the forks of the road, where they were ordered to go, they saw the enemy's patrol, about twenty strong, halted close to the forks of the road. One or two officers of the general's staff had volunteered that night with the patrol, Adjutant-General Dietzler having the command. As we approached, the leader of the enemy's company shouted,

"Halt! — Who goes there? — Give the countersign."

"D—n you, we 've no countersign for you! We 're the Lawrence guard," said Dietzler.

"The Lawrence guard will please file to the left," said the border ruffian chief, and his own command drew off the road, but remained close to it on one side, while we defiled past them. The two companies thus passed each other, there being little more than the road between them. It was an interesting moment, each party watching the other closely, so that, if fighting was to be done, one party would not get the advantage of the other. Gen. Robinson's orders, however, were to avoid a collision, and in no case to fire till the last extremity, and whatever the orders of the border ruffians were, they seemed to have no particular wish to commence. Many an oath was uttered by those in the patrol, who swore, as they rode back, at the non-resistant orders. It would have made a very pretty skirmish, for though their party had the advantage in numbers, ours had in arms, and in the fact of their being picked men.

Similar incidents happened frequently. Besides that, the enemy made it a point to send out small parties of well-mounted horsemen, who would gallop up to within one or two hundred yards of our foot sentries, and fire on them. This was done every night for a week, and sometimes at half a dozen different points in one night. The only wonder is that they did not shoot somebody; but bullets in the dark are uncertain things. One sentry had a bullet put through his hat, which would have finished him had he been an inch or two inches taller; another man, who had ridden out to see one of the guards, had his horse shot; but he had no business there. The guards had orders not to return fire on any such irregular shooting, and in no case to use arms but when an attack was made with evident intention to take or kill the sentries.

Gen. Robinson was of opinion that this conduct was designed to precipitate the quarrel, and give the enemy an excuse to attack the place, and that if our men were to fire it would be construed into an attack on peaceable travellers. Still it was a trying thing to stand guard, and have even random shots fired, without having the satisfaction of firing back on the rascals. The conduct, vigilance, and coolness of those men who stood guard round Lawrence during the siege, is worthy of all praise.

The guard one night came across Sheriff Jones, and, in spite of the indignation of that worthy, kept him prisoner until the officer of the guard was called, and the case reported, when the bogus sheriff was permitted to go without further molestation. Several of the Missourians, while skulking about our lines at night, were taken and lodged in the guard-house till morning. One spy, who had contrived to make his way to one of the rifle-pits before he was taken, was brought in. Next morning General Lane went to him, and took him with him and showed him the rifle-pits, forts, and other earth-works; took him in, and showed him a twelve-pounder (brass howitzer), the only piece we had, although Lane showed it with an air as if there had been fifty more. He showed him the quarters of two of the regiments, and then, taking the frightened border ruffian out, gave him in charge of an officer, with directions that he be seen safe through the lines, General Lane bidding him adieu thus:

"Go back now, sir, and report yourself, and tell what you have seen."

Of course, the town was under martial law to some extent; but in day-time people came in and went out freely. Sheriff Jones came in several times, evidently to spy, as he neither spoke of nor tried to make arrests. Several of the captains from the camp below would drive in, and, on several occasions, remained in Lawrence all night, and left without being interfered with. Two gentlemen from Independence, Missouri, attended a meeting in Lawrence, and heard a speech from the Vermonter who brought up my despatches, and several other speeches, and not only reported the proceedings in their camp, but published them in one of the papers at Lexington. It was certainly unfortunate that this free access to the town by the enemy was unavoidable; but it was considered as improper for Lawrence to assume the right to take and hold prisoners, as this would at once have precipitated the crisis.

On the 6th of December the influential men of the Delaware and Shawnee nations came to General Robinson, and volunteered the services of the warriors of their respective tribes to aid in repelling the invaders. General Robinson treated these chiefs with great respect and attention; thanking them for their offer, and telling them he would avail himself of it as soon as the right time came. He did not want a force of several hundred armed Indians in town, until he saw that war was unavoidable, as this would have been an apology for hostilities.

It was during that last week of the siege that the twelve-pound howitzer was brought in. It was known to be boxed up in Kansas city, where it had been for some time. Two men named Buffum and a young Yankee, whose name I have forgotten, started down after it with a train. It was known that we could not send a force strong enough to go to Kansas city and take it, and so it was resolved to have it smuggled through by stratagem. When the men, who had gone to Kansas city after it, got there, they found the commission merchant to whom it had been consigned cross and unaccommodating, which conduct was the more contemptible as he had had a lucrative business with the free-state settlers. They inquired for certain boxes, described by them. The merchant refused to deliver them up without a written order from the man in Lawrence to whom they were consigned. This was an unusual thing, and had neither been foreseen nor provided for; but one of the party said they had an order, but he had forgotten it, in his overcoat, up at the hotel. Up to the hotel he went accordingly, and forged one, knowing that the proper parties would sustain him in doing so in the emergency. Still the old fellow was captious and wanted to know what was in the boxes, when Mr. R. Buffum, or Bob Buffum, took an axe and knocked a hole in one of the boxes, having told the merchant that he believed it was a carriage. Part of one of the wheels being then exposed to view, the old fellow was at last satisfied, although he must have been very verdant to mistake the small thick wheel of a howitzer for a carriage wheel. The party crossed the Kaw river at the Wyandot, intending to go through the Delaware reserve. They professed to be going to Leavenworth with "store goods." The bluff of the Wyandot village is very steep, and as the gun, together with several cases of canister, grape, shell, and round shot, was very heavy, they were "stuck." In this situation they were met by a company of the border ruffians, who stopped to question them. They told these they were going to Leavenworth, which, for the direction they were taking, was more likely than that they were going to Lawrence. Bob Buffum feigned to be tipsy, and, his being half so, in point of fact, helped him to sustain the character. His buffoonery was very well received by the ruffians, who were at length persuaded to dismount, and put their shoulders to the wagon-wheel, and thus extract the artillery of their enemy. By rapid driving they got over the reserve, until they reached the enemy's lines, a few miles from Lawrence. Scouts having brought intelligence of their approach, a patrol of twenty well armed and mounted men went out and brought the gun safely through the enemy's lines to Lawrence. The cavalcade was received with great enthusiasm.

It was about the same time that two of the ladies of Lawrence performed an equally bold and successful feat. It was feared that the supply of powder and other ammunition would run short in case of much fighting; and, as there was a lot of powder, caps for Sharpe's rifles, and other ammunition, over at the house of a free-state man near the Santa Fe road, two ladies volunteered to go through the lines and bring it in. This they did successfully. They got out of town without molestation. Arriving at the place where the ammunition was, they stowed away the greater part of two kegs of gunpowder, a lot of caps for Sharpe's rifles, and lead, in those mysterious conveniences, so amply provided for by the dress of a lady in modern times, and succeeded in conveying it into Lawrence. They were stopped by a patrol of the border ruffians; but the ruffians, to do them justice, are a gallant set — very. They were so very reserved as to keep several rods off, for fear of frightening the ladies, and thus the "latest fashions passed inspection," eliciting nothing further than the profound admiration of which the ruffians are capable.

The camp on the Wakarusa had many fearful visions of the "terrible explosions" in Lawrence. Little did they think that we had bombshells manufactured in so fine a model.

The two ladies, who so successfully engaged in this really intrepid affair, were Mrs. Wood, wife of Mr. S. N. Wood, formerly of Ohio, and Mrs. Brown, wife of the editor of the *Herald of Freedom*, formerly of Pennsylvania. Besides these, others, indeed nearly all of the ladies of Lawrence were engaged in making cartridges, and it is even reported that there was a secret company of these women enrolled, under lady officers, ready to defend their houses, if necessary; but this was purely an affair of their own.

Governor Shannon, having had complaints made to him relative to the armed force, and the fraudulent representations made to him in regard to the difficulties, and having (which was the true secret of his awakening reflection) found that the men now threatening Lawrence set his authority at defiance, even after he had enrolled them and legalized their outrageous conduct, sent a despatch to Jones, requesting that the *posse* be kept from doing anything till he got up, and also that he would send him the names, and a copy of the papers he had got for making the arrests he proposed. It was rather late in the day for such a movement, and the following was Jones' answer:

"CAMP OF WAKARUSA, *Dec. 4th*, 1855.

"HIS EXCELLENCY GOVERNOR WILSON SHANNON —

"SIR: In reply to your communication of yesterday, I have to inform you that the volunteer forces, now at this place and at Lecompton, are getting weary of inaction. They will, I presume, remain idle but a very short time longer, unless a demand for the prisoners is made. I think I shall have a sufficient force to protect me by to-morrow morning. The force at Lawrence is not half so strong as reported. I have this from a reliable source. If I am to wait for the government troops, more than two thirds of the men here will go away very much dissatisfied. They are leaving hourly as it is. I do not, by any means, wish to violate your orders, but I really believe that, if I have sufficient force, it would be better to make the demand.

"It is reported that the people of Lawrence have run off these offenders from that town, and, indeed, it is said that they are now all out of the way. I have writs for sixteen persons of the party that rescued my prisoner; S. N. Wood, P. R. Brooks, and Samuel Tappan, are of Lawrence, the balance from the country round. Warrants *will* be placed in my hands for the arrest of G. W. Brown, and probably others in Lecompton. They say that they are willing to obey the laws, but no confidence can be placed in any statement they may make.

"No *evidence* sufficient to cause a warrant to issue has, as yet, been brought against any as the lawless men who fired the houses.

"I would give you the names of the defendants, but the writs are in my office at Lecompton.

"Most respectfully, yours,

"SAMUEL J. JONES,

"*Sheriff of Douglas County.*"

The manner in which Jones evades the request for the names of the persons to be arrested is characteristic. His information about "warrants *about* to be placed in his hands," is significant as to how such processes were obtained and served.

The following letter was written about the same time by Mr. Anderson, a resident of Lexington, Mo., and member of the Bogus Legislature. He is quite a young man, and would be calle rather a good fellow for a border ruffian. His request that th Governor of Kansas would protect them, in the arms they had stolen from a public arsenal, against the United States troops, is refreshing. The letter was addressed to

"MAJOR-GENERAL WILLIAM P. RICHARDSON —

"SIR: I have reason to believe, from rumors in camp, that before to-morrow morning, the *black flag* will be hoisted, when nine out of ten will rally round it, and march without orders upon Lawrence. The forces of the Lecompton camp fully understan the plot, and will fight under the same banner.

"If Governor Shannon will pledge himself not to allow any United States officers to interfere with the arms belonging to the United States, now in their possession, and, in case there is no battle, order the United States forces off at once, and retain the militia, provided any force is retained, all will be well, and all will obey to the end, and commit no depredation upon *private* property in Lawrence.

"I fear a collision between the United States soldiers and the volunteers, which would be dreadful.

"Speedy measures should be taken. Let the men *know at once* — to-night — and I fear that it will even then be *too late to stay the rashness of our people.*

"Respectfully your obedient servant, J. C. ANDERSON."

Not far from this time the most tragic occurrence of the war ook place.

It was about noon of the 6th of December when Mr. Thomas V. Barber, with his brother Robert, and another relative, Mr. ierson, left Lawrence to return home. They lived in a north-esterly direction from Lawrence, about seven miles off. At this ime, while the Missourians had invested Lawrence, they found it ifficult to keep it closely guarded to the south and west. There as a distance of twenty miles between the camp at Lecompton nd Wakarusa. General Atchison had a force on the north side f the Kaw river, opposite Lawrence; but, while it was guarded us on three sides, the only means of preventing people from aving Lawrence for the south of the territory was by horse atrols, which scoured the country. Up to this time the citizens f Lawrence had been guilty of no aggressive act; neither had ey resorted to violence in their defence when attacked.

When Mr. Barber and his friends left Lawrence they went up he ravine that penetrates Mount Oread, and got on the California ad. While riding up this road, and when four miles from town, hey observed a party of horsemen, fourteen in number, riding to e right of the road. This party was led by Major-General ichardson, and, besides others of less note, there was in that atrol Judge Cato, one of the federal judges appointed by the resident for the territory, Judge Wood, a local bogus judge formerly a free-state man, and physician in Lawrence, now a raitor and informer), Major Clarke, a government Indian agent, nd Colonel Burns, a merchant of Westport, Mo.

The party has since stated that they were not patrolling, but ere merely going down from Lecompton to the camp on the Vakarusa. Give them the advantage of this statement, and how oes their conduct look? A pretended senator and officer for ansas orders men to be taken prisoners, and shot on the highway, and a judge of the Supreme Court, a federal officer, aids and abets, and stands by and sees it done, and helps to screen the murderers; — a man, too, who had just been patching up indictments and warrants for innocent people in Lawrence, which were designed as the ground-work of a quarrel. But I digress.

When Barber and his friends saw the party in question, they left the road and took a path to the left. This they did because the road was shorter, and because they desired to avoid the other party. Mr. Barber was totally unarmed, having not even a knife; his two friends had each a pistol.

As soon as General Richardson's party saw the others leave the road, two of their number, Major Clarke and Colonel Burns, were detailed to stop them, or bring them in prisoners, the remainder of the company halting. As this party was ahead of Mr. Barber and his friends, Clarke and Burns had merely to ride into the prairie to the right in order to intercept them. The Barbers, when they saw they were to be attacked, neither attempted to run, nor did they hasten their gait beyond a walk, when the others rode up and halted before them. Richardson, Cato, and the others, were in full sight, and within gunshot.

The two Barbers were riding first, Thomas to the right. Pierson was behind them. Major Clarke gave the order to "halt;" at which all of the party stopped.

"Where are you going?" demanded Clarke.

"We are going home," said Thomas Barber.

"Where are you from?"

"We are from Lawrence."

"What is going on in Lawrence, just now?"

"Well, nothing in particular."

"Nothing in particular, hey?" said Clarke, who then added, "We have orders from the governor to see the laws executed in this territory. We arrest you."

"What laws have we broken or disobeyed?" asked Mr. Barber. "Or what laws have the people of Lawrence broken?"

Clarke here raised his hand, and, pointing to the horsemen upon the California road, said:

"Turn your horses' heads, and go with us."

"We won't do it," said Barber.

At this Clarke spurred his horse, and rode to the right of Thomas Barber, who partly turned his horse and looked at Clarke as if he scarcely knew what Clarke was going to do. The latter, having got in the position referred to, pulled out his revolver, and saying, "You won't, won't you?"—fired. At the same instant Colonel Burns, who had also drawn his revolver, fired. Robert Barber pulled out his pistol, and fired three shots at them, but without hitting either of them. They rode a few yards off. Clarke said something to Burns, and then they started back for their comrades. Mr. Pierson had been unable to get his pistol out of the holster in time to fire. As Clarke and Burns rode off, Thomas Barber said to his friend, "Let us be off;" and they started at the gallop.

As they rode along, Thomas Barber turned to his brother with a sickly smile, and, pressing his hand on his side, said:

"That fellow shot me."

"Where—where are you shot?" asked Robert.

"Here," said Barber, still pressing his hand upon his side. And he gave another sad smile.

"It is not possible, Thomas!"

The wounded man shook his head and said, "It is;" then he dropped the reins and rode unsteadily. He would have fallen had not his brother caught him. At this time General Richardson's full party were in pursuit of them. It was a terrible ride of life and death; for Robert Barber held the body of his dying brother until the nerves began to relax, and the brain to reel. Then the corpse fell, the brother holding it and clinging to it until it reached the ground.

Robert Barber dismounted, and stopped both horses. He stooped over the body of his brother, and found him dead—dead! They saw the enemy approach, and, as they could do nothing more for the deceased, got on their horses, and galloped off. The murderers came only near enough to see their work, and then wheeled and galloped off to Franklin.

It was not long before intelligence of the occurrence reached Lawrence. The soldiers had been on parade. After parade the volunteers were addressed by Colonel Lane in an inspiring manner; and General Robinson, being called on, made one of his prudent, cautious speeches, in which he urged them not to allow the daily outrages to drive them to commence hostilities.

It was just then that a son of Judge Wakefield, and two or three others, drove rapidly into town, and announced the murder. At first Robinson gave orders to keep it secret, for fear the men would do something rash; but before half an hour it was in every mouth, the public having got it before the officers. Many were for marching immediately on the Wakarusa and driving out the villains camped there. Indeed, it was with the utmost difficulty that Generals Robinson and Lane restrained them.

A carriage was sent out for the body, which was guarded in by a company of horsemen. The dead body was laid in an apartment in the Free-State Hotel; and deep and fervent were the denunciations of those who thus saw an estimable citizen stricken down.

A scene of the most distressing character occurred next morning. The wife of the murdered man came in. She had not heard of her bereavement till then, and the agony she evidently felt was heart-rending.

The following is the account given by the pro-slavery men of the same transaction. They had seen Barber's party when they turned aside from the road. They state that their party were merely on their way from Lecompton to Franklin:

"Colonel Burns and Major Clarke were detailed and rode to overtake the free-state men. This they did; and, after halting them, a conversation ensued, in which the free-state men not only declared that there was no law nor order in the territory, but declined to surrender themselves in compliance with the demands of Clarke and his companions. Upon this both parties commenced drawing their arms, with the exception of one of the free-state men (who was most probably the man killed); this person sat on his horse a little apart from his companions. He had a switch in his hand, but drew no arms, nor did he appear to have any Both parties 'squared to each other,' and fired pistols, being the only weapons used. On the part of the pro-slavery men, Clarke was armed with a small five-inch Colt's revolver, while Colonel Burns had a navy revolver, which is heavier, and carries a much larger ball. After exchanging shots, the free-state men galloped off. Burns proposed to send a long-shot after them with his rifle; but Clarke objected, saying, 'Let them go.' Burns is said to have admitted that he thought he hit the man he fired at, as he saw him press his hand to his side, or, as others state it, 'saw the fur fly from his old coat.'"

CHAPTER XVI.

THE "PEACE-MAKERS."

Two gentlemen, Messrs. Lowry and Babcock, members of the Committee of Safety, were despatched on the fifth to the Shawnee Mission, to see the governor. At Franklin they were stopped by a party of the invaders, who demanded the countersign. Mr. Lowry handed them a bottle of whiskey, which, he said, "was all the countersign he had got." After the ruffians had drank they allowed them to pass, declaring they were "sound on the goose." They had further detention below; but succeeded, by the intervention of the officers, in getting down to the executive office. The governor wrote a long and ambiguous epistle, in which he talked a good deal about "enforcing the law," without specifying what law, against whom it was to be enforced, or who was to enforce it. He, however, promised to come up next day and try to have the matter settled peaceably, if possible.

On the sixth the governor got to Franklin. There he found that his "militia" and Jones' "posse" were altogether unmanageable, and threatening blood and murder generally. He found that they were stealing from everybody, only giving orders on him to the Indians and pro-slavery residents. Terrified at the startling aspect of affairs, and alive to the punishment that might be meted to his official follies and crimes, he sent a despatch to Sumner. Before he had left the Shawnee Mission he had written to Sumner, informing him that he had received despatches from the President, authorizing him to use the troops, and that instructions to that effect would be sent from the war department. Meanwhile he had urged Colonel Sumner to meet him with his regiment at the Delaware crossing of the Kaw.

In reply, Colonel Sumner wrote as follows:

"HEAD QUARTERS, FIRST CAVALRY,
December 5th, 1855.

"GOVERNOR: I have just received your letter of yesterday, with the telegraphic despatch of the President. I will march with my regiment in a few hours, and will meet you at the Delaware crossing of the Kansas *this evening*.

"With high respect, your ob't servant,
"E. V. SUMNER,
"*Col. First Cavalry.*"

The colonel, however, after sober second thought, sent this other despatch a few hours later than the first:

"HEAD QUARTERS, FIRST CAVALRY, FORT LEAVENWORTH,
December 5th, 1855. *Afternoon.*

"GOVERNOR: On more mature reflection, I think it will not be proper for me to move before I receive the orders of the government. I shall be all ready whenever I get them. This decision will not delay our reaching the scene of difficulties; for I can move from this place to Lawrence as quickly (or nearly so) as I could from the Delaware crossing; and we could not, of course, go beyond that place without definite orders.

"With high respect, your ob't servant,
"E. V. SUMNER,
"*Col. First Cavalry.*"

Thus it stood when the governor got up to the camp on the Wakarusa, when, as I have said, terrified at the aspect of affairs, and in hopes of restoring his waning authority with the force he had thus been instrumental in bringing into the field, he sent off the following:

"WAKARUSA, *December 6th*, 1855.

"COL. SUMNER, FIRST CAVALRY, U. S. A.—

"SIR: I send you this special despatch to ask you to come to Lawrence as soon as you possibly can. My object is to secure the citizens of that place, as well as all others, from a warfare which, if once commenced, there is no saying where it will end.

I doubt not that you have received orders from Washington; but if you have not, the absolute pressure of this crisis is such as to justify you, with the President and the world, in moving with your force to the scene of difficulties.

"It is hard to restrain the men here (they are beyond my power, or at least soon will be) from making an attack on Lawrence, which, if once made, there is no telling where it may terminate. The presence of a portion of the United States troops at Lawrence would prevent an attack, save bloodshed, and enable us to get matters arranged in a satisfactory way, and, at the same time, secure the execution of the laws. *It is peace, not war*, that we want, and you have the power to secure peace. Time is precious. Fear not but you will be sustained.

"With great respect,

"WILSON SHANNON.

"N. B. Be pleased to send me a despatch."

The border ruffians, who were aware of what the governor was about, and who did not want the troops there, for fear they might interfere with their murderous intentions, laid a plot to intercept the governor's messenger; but one of the chiefs, to curry favor with him, betrayed it, and the bearer of the despatch was got off by another route. Sumner, however, still refused to move, until he had express orders from the department himself. He was, doubtless, afraid of using his command under the orders of a man who had shown himself so reckless and stupid as Governor Shannon. On Friday the governor sent up a messenger to Lawrence informing General Robinson that he had arrived at Franklin, and was ready to come up.

A deputation of ten men was despatched by General Robinson to escort the governor. That dignitary arrived with his escort, and three very gentlemanly-looking companions, Colonel Boone, of Westport, Colonel Kearney, of Independence, and Colonel Strickland, also a Missourian. These were fine-looking Southerners; but I certainly would rather have seen the governor of the territory come to his people in other company. Perhaps these were the only men who could have influence with the violent armed force below, and it might thus be the best policy to have them here during the pending of negotiations; but if there *was* such a necessity, and I doubt it not, what an exemplification of the pitiful depth to which the governor had fallen!

They entered the Free-State Hotel, and as they went up stairs a little incident occurred. In the room at the head of the first flight of stairs the dead body of Barber was laid out, in all the frightful rigidity of death. The door was open, and it was almost impossible to go up stairs without seeing it. As the cortegé went up, the governor alongside of General Robinson, the eye of Shannon happened to wander into that room. There was a start. I could see the weak, vacillating, guilty governor tremble as his first glance fell on that silent figure. He *had heard* of the occurrence, but he proceeded to inquire of General Robinson the particulars of the case, which the general calmly told him. The next on the stairs were General Lane and Colonel Kearney. The Colonel expressed surprise, and asked the "meaning of this," of Lane.

"O," said the latter, "it is our yesterday's losses!"

Colonel Boone expressed surprise and regret, and begged that no one should mention the name of any gentleman as having been of the party that fired, until it could be proved.

The conference lasted for an hour, when General Robinson took the governor and his party home to dinner. The matter was then finally adjusted, and it was pronounced that the parties had "not understood each other." What a fearful misunderstanding!

The difficulty did not so much lie in actual difference to adjust, as in putting a stop to the warlike invasion, and preventing them from executing their bloody threats. The governor had got into a bad scrape by his folly and wickedness. He had hoped that the troops would enable him to retain his authority, hold the ruffians in check, and still crush the free-state men beneath his feet. The troops would not come to his aid, and the border ruffians, now that he had clothed them with authority, despised him, and determined to carry out their bloody purpose independent of his authority. He had no resource left but the free-state settlers, whom he had abused, and still desired to abuse and crush. But he was not prepared for the border ruffian measures, neither was he willing to shoulder the responsibility he was likely to incur. The free-state men merely desired to use the governor in the way he had been used by others. They wished him to authorize them to defend themselves, and to strip the ruffians below of their cloak of legal authority. Such were the motives of General Robinson and the free-state leaders. The governor engaged in treaty-making, for the purpose of gaining time, as he still was in hopes of the arrival of the troops. According to his own language, he desired "that all parties should be placed right in the eyes of the world." With these sentiments the "high contracting parties" went to work, and a liberal supply of wines and liquors, supplied by the shrewd negotiators, kept the thirsty governor in temper during the proceedings.

Negotiations were pending on Friday and Saturday, and all of that time the enemy were momentarily expected. A large force posted themselves on the opposite river bank, in sight; these had two objects in view: first, to cut off all supplies from town; and, second, to throw themselves in the rear of the town whenever an attack should be made in front. On Saturday night negotiations were brought to a close, and the anxious and expectant people clustered around the doors of the great hotel to learn the result.

The governor, having been called on, stood at the door of the hotel, and addressed the people assembled in Lawrence. He had been speaking for a few minutes when I got there, and continued in substance as follows:

"There was a part of the people of this territory who denied the validity of the laws of the territorial Legislature. He was not there to urge that validity, but these laws should be submitted to until a legal tribunal had set them aside. He did not see how there was any other course but such submission to them, and it certainly was not his part, as an executive officer, to set them aside or disregard them. He was happy to announce that, after having an interview with the officers of their committee of safety, he had found them induced thus far to respect those laws, they being willing to see them enforced, provided they had the reserved right of testing and escaping from them legally. He was happy to announce that all difficulties were settled. (Faint cheers.) There was a perfect understanding between the executive and the committee. The difficulties had arisen from misunderstanding. He would go down and disband the sheriff's posse. He would dismiss the officers of the territorial militia, Generals Richardson and Stricklar, but would order that their forces be not disbanded until they were taken to Leavenworth, or the neighborhood of Westport. All the difficulties were adjusted, and he was willing and anxious to do all in his power to prevent a collision and the shedding of blood. He hoped that the men now in the territory and in camp below would be got out of the territory without hostilities intervening. He would do all in his power to influence them. He would urge upon the people of Lawrence to be moderate, to pursue a wise course to avoid a collision. 'Don't be too belligerent.' (Here a jackass across the street brayed vociferously.) He wanted them to consult their judgment and their reason, not their feelings and their passions. One advantage they would now have if they had to fight, — the fight would now be between them and a mob. Of course, he could not condemn them for defending themselves. They were right, and he would do all in his power to sustain them; but he hoped the men encamped would now be induced to leave, and that there would be no effusion of blood. He wanted it understood that he had called on no one but the people of the territory in his proclamations. If there were Missourians here, they were here of their own accord.

"He hoped and believed that the people of Lawrence and vicinity were law-abiding people. Indeed, he had learned that he had misunderstood them, and that they were estimable and orderly people; but houses, it was said, had been burned, and other outrages had been charged upon the free-state men. They must remember this when they judge of these things. They were, perhaps, innocent, but he hoped they would abide a judicial tribunal. He hoped now to preserve order, and to get these men out of the territory. If he could serve the people of Kansas, as a governor or as a private citizen, he would always be happy to do so. (Faint cheers.)"

Colonel Lane was called, and spoke briefly. "If we fight now," he said, "we fight a mob. Any man who would desert Lawrence, until the invaders below had left the territory, was a coward." Lane was cheered heartily, and the applause he received, as well as the enthusiastic cheers that greeted General Robinson when called, was a striking commentary on the cool feeling that was still entertained toward the governor. General Robinson said he had "nothing to say; they had taken an honorable position."

There was an evident suspicion among the people that the negotiations had been closed too easily, and that their leaders had conceded something.

Captain Brown got up to address the people, but a desire was manifested to prevent his speaking. Amidst some little disturbance, he demanded to know what the terms were. If he understood Governor Shannon's speech, something had been conceded, and he conveyed the idea that the territorial laws were to be observed. Those laws they denounced and spit upon, and would never obey — no! Here the speaker was interrupted by the almost universal cry, "No! No! Down with the bogus laws! — lead us down to fight first!" Seeing a young revolution on the tapis, the influential men assured the people that there had been no concession. They had yielded nothing. They had surrendered nothing to the usurping Legislature. With these assurances the people were satisfied and withdrew. At that time it was determined to keep the treaty secret, but before many days it was sufficiently public.

"ARTICLES OF NEGOTIATION AND ADJUSTMENT.

"Whereas, there is a misunderstanding between the people of Kansas, or a portion of them, and the governor thereof, arising out of the rescue, near Hickory Point, of a citizen under arrest, and some other matters; and whereas a strong apprehension exists that said misunderstanding may lead to civil strife and bloodshed; and whereas it is desired by both Governor Shannon and the people of Lawrence and vicinity, to avert a calamity so disastrous to the interests of the territory and the Union, and to place all parties in a correct position before the world:

"Now, therefore, it is agreed by the said Governor Shannon,

and the undersigned people of Lawrence, now assembled, that the matters in dispute be settled as follows, to wit:

"We, the said citizens of said territory, protest that the said rescue was made without our knowledge or consent; but, if any of our citizens were engaged, we pledge ourselves to aid in the execution of any legal process against them; that we have no knowledge of the previous, present, or prospective existence of any organization in said territory for the resistance of the laws, and that we have not designed, and do not design, to resist the legal service of any criminal process therein, but pledge ourselves to aid in the execution of the laws, when called on by proper authority, in the town or vicinity of Lawrence, and that we will use all our influence in preserving order therein; and we declare that we are now, as we ever have been, ready at any time to aid the governor in securing a posse for the execution of such process. Provided, that any person thus arrested in Lawrence or vicinity, while a foreign force shall remain in the territory, shall be duly examined before a United States district judge, of said territory, in said town, and admitted to bail; and provided further, that Governor Shannon agrees to use his influence to secure to the citizens of Kansas Territory remuneration for any damages sustained, or unlawful depredation, if any such have been committed by the sheriff's posse in Douglas County. And, further, that Governor Shannon states that he has not called upon persons, residents of any other states, to aid in the execution of the laws, and such as are here in this territory are here of their own choice; and that he has not any authority or legal power to do so, nor will he exercise any such power, and that he will not call on any citizen of another state, who may be here. That we wish it understood that we do not herein express any opinion as to the validity of the enactments of the territorial Legislature.

"WILSON SHANNON,
"(Signed,) "C. ROBINSON,
"J. H. LANE."

It will be at once seen that this ill-starred paper is full of inconsistencies. It is liable to be interpreted in a variety of ways.

Each party flattered itself that it had duped the other. In the first place, the parties had no right to treat at all, unless Shannon had concluded to go to war with his people merely to compel them to *say* they would obey certain laws. Laws are only to be enforced against those whom the proper authorities decide have broken them; and in the United States people can *say* what they please about the laws, or about what respect they will give them. They are only amenable to the law when they break it by an overt act, and then, only to the extent of the punishment affixed, under the process prescribed, and by the proper officers.

The people of Lawrence "protested that the said rescue was made without their knowledge or consent;" but they had no intention of saying that they disapproved of it, or conceded that, under similar circumstances, they would have no right to do so. The other party understood them to do this. When the people of Lawrence pledged themselves to "aid in the execution of any *legal* process," they did not intend to include any of the bogus authority as *legal* authority; — their opponents thought they did; although Shannon was well aware that such was the construction placed upon it by those with whom he treated, the matter having been discussed. The parties should have taken issue for or against the bogus laws, and fought about it; but for Shannon to bring up an army to fight on such an issue would have been intensely ridiculous; and the free-state party had too much sense to go to fighting about an abstraction, especially with those who had no right to catechize them on it. It was the governor's business, when he found the true state of the case, and when he found he had no legal pretext for fighting Lawrence, to disband the army he had concentrated against it, and send them home; but the governor ought to have known all about this before he engaged in the affair, and above all he *could not* disband them. Being willing to do nearly fair with the free-state settlers, in the strait to which he was reduced, they, on the other hand, were willing to get him out of the scrape as easily as they could. The treaty was merely got up to cover a retreat, and Shannon knew it.

The statement made by Shannon, that he "had not called on any resident of another state to aid in the execution of the laws," is manifestly false, in the face of his non-admissions as to enrolling them as militia. Relative to this attack on Lawrence, the committee of Congress, with the evidence before them, report:

"Among the many acts of lawless violence which it has been the duty of your committee to investigate, this invasion of Lawrence is the most defenceless. A comparison of the facts proven, with the official statements of the officers of the government, will show how groundless were the pretexts which gave rise to it. A community, in which no crime had been committed by any of its members, against none of whom had a warrant been issued or a complaint made, who had resisted no process in the hands of a real or pretended officer, was threatened with destruction in the name of 'law and order,' and that, too, by men who marched from a neighboring state with arms obtained by force, and who, in every stage of their progress, violated many laws, and among others the Constitution of the United States."

Immediately after he had spoken the governor drove down to Franklin, whither Generals Robinson and Lane accompanied him. They had there to meet a deputation of thirteen captains from the Missouri camp, and the farce of negotiation had again to be gone through. Here there was even less prospect of unanimity; and after a stormy time, in which they were likely to effect nothing, Shannon declared that there was no cause of attack on Lawrence, and he ordered the militia to disband. The following order to Richardson is a fac-simile of those to Strickland and Jones:

"CAMP WAKARUSA, *Dec. 8th*, 1855.

"SIR: Being fully satisfied that there will be no further resistance to the laws of the territory, or to the service of any legal process in the County of Douglas, you are hereby ordered to cross the Kansas river, to the north side, as near Lecompton as you may find it practicable, with your command, and disband the same at such time and place, and in such numbers, as you may deem most convenient. "Yours with great respect,

"WILSON SHANNON.

"Major-Gen. RICHARDSON."

Not to negotiation alone was the country indebted for peace. Many were really terrified at the idea of attacking Lawrence when they supposed the people there were going to fight, and had slipped on, glad to get home. Then the supply of whiskey was exhausted; and on that eventful Saturday night the elements warred with peculiar bitterness against the border ruffians in camp. Night set in; it was as dark as Erebus. The wind had blown from the south all day, and threatened rain; at dusk it wheeled to the north, and came down with icy keenness, and driving a snowy sleet. It was a fearful night. The wind blew almost a hurricane, as it knows how to blow in Kansas. I had passed through the inner line of guards, and had given the countersign "Pitch in," which had been issued by the gallant Adjutant-General Dietzler in the temporary absence of Gen. Robinson. I passed through the outer line of guards, having given the word, and occasionally saw patrols of horsemen going here and there like shades in the gloom, or shivering at their post in that bitter and inclement night. So wildly swept the wind and the driving sleet that I had often to stop while I held my hat with both hands, and swayed in the blast. Away over the plain the lights of Lawrence were twinkling in the gloom, from windows, or the lanterns of the citizen soldiery who watched the earth-works during that inclement night, lest they might fall into the hands of the enemy.

But Lawrence was a tame sight, that night, compared with the Missouri camp on the Wakarusa. In the bitter cold the adventurers stood around their camp-fires, or tried to nestle under the wagon-covers that flapped in, or were overthrown by, the furious wind. Logs were piled high on the camp-fires, and the wild gale swept the flames and sparks up through the gnarled limbs of the old oaks and walnuts in the Wakarusa bottom. Shots were being fired in all directions, and incessantly in the camp,—the wild noise being suited to the taste of those border crusaders, and being partly intended at that time, I suspect, as a sort of intimidation to the "Yankees," as some fears were entertained that the free-state men would attack their camp, now that they were stripped of all legal authority.

Cold and more bitter grew the night, and the wind was so high that many of the fires had to be put out, as the furious flames were blown about so as to endanger all of those near them. No guard was kept by these men, that night; or, at least, I saw none. Every man appeared to shrink, chilly and helpless, from the pitiless storm. In the early part of the night there had been speechifying. Some wanted to go up to Lawrence, and were bent on going. Others, — and amongst them ex-Senator Atchison, — urged that no attack should now be made, as they were stripped of their authority. But, had that been a mild and pleasant summer's night, there would have been an attack, and as likely a severe defeat of the border ruffians. As it was, a night of suffering brought a morning of repentance; or, rather, it froze out the little hostile spirit. In the morning, too, many left, and the remainder, thus weakened and dispirited, began to fear an attack in turn. On Sunday there was a pretty general scattering. A few parties remained until Tuesday, bent on mischief; but, finding themselves too weak to do anything, reluctantly went home, cursing Shannon and the "cunning abolitionists." Stringfellow, in the camp at Lecompton, made a speech, in which he said, "Shannon has played us false; the Yankees have tricked us; the Governor of Kansas has disgraced himself and the whole pro-slavery party."

On Sunday Governor Shannon, with Jones and Stricklar, came into Lawrence. The governor was all kindness and attention to the citizens. He was introduced to many of the ladies of Lawrence, and expressed himself much at home. He talked of coming to live at Lawrence, and at that time it looked a little as if he would not be safe anywhere else. Gen. Robinson offered him chambers, and both he and Lane offered to *protect* him.

In consideration of the troubled state of the territory, the governor commissioned Generals Robinson and Lane to defend the territory. The following authority, addressed on the outside to "Generals Chas. Robinson and J. H. Lane," was the important document:

"To Charles Robinson and J. H. Lane:

"You are hereby authorized and directed to take such measures, and use the enrolled force under your command in such manner, for the preservation of the peace and protection of the persons and property of the people of Lawrence and vicinity, as in your judgment shall best secure that end.

"(Signed), WILSON SHANNON.

"LAWRENCE, *Dec.* 9, 1855."

So far from this having been obtained by fraudulent representations, it agreed with the assurances he had given, of the people's right to defend themselves, both on Friday and Saturday. More than that, when asked, he promised to review the free-state troops, and would have done so that day; but, as it was Sunday, the thing would not have looked well in Lawrence.

On that eventful Sunday, if governors ever get drunk, his supreme highness, Wilson the First, got superlatively tipsy. Even Jones had been imbibing rather freely; but Jones had sense enough to hold his tongue under such circumstances, which is more than can be said for the governor.

After as jolly a Sunday as ever was spent in Lawrence, the governor left the free-state head-quarters, and wound his devious way across the street to the Cincinnati Hotel, in company with Jones and an escort of honor. The governor was conversing on the merits of "Governor Shannon."

"Now, ge—entlemen, you — hic — you don't understand me. You all abuse me, but — hic — but it's be—because you don't know me. Get to know me right — hic — well, and you'll — hic — you'll find I'm a — hic — I'm a h–ll of a fellow!"

And thus terminated the Wakarusa war.

CHAPTER XVII.

MOBBING THE BALLOT-BOXES.

If there were time, a very interesting chapter could be written about the arrest and detention of a number of those who fell into the hands of the border ruffians during the Wakarusa war. It is quite romantic to read about prisoners of war, and interesting, should any of these unfortunates have a faculty for imitating Baron Trenck by making their escape. The ruffians made quite a haul of prisoners. They got as many as they wanted, and rather more than they were able to take care of. Besides a promiscuous picking up of travellers, they succeeded in capturing several small parties of three or four, or half a dozen, who were hastening to the rescue of the besieged. But a small number volunteered to come from Leavenworth city, and those were nearly all taken. Mr. Parrot was taken with a companion and his carriage, and compelled to ride across the Kaw at a deep ford, where he got wet, and in this condition he spent that fearful night of the 8th of December. Mr. Pomeroy, while attempting to pass through the Delaware reserve, was taken. He attempted to palm himself off as a Baptist preacher; but the ruffians, believing that he had not yet been "dipped," led him through the same Kaw river to their camp on the Wakarusa, where they kept him till peace was declared. While there, it is probable that the interposition of some of the officers alone saved him. One Dutch squatter was taken prisoner because he was unable to show these gentry a ford at the Kaw river, and was detained as a prisoner, as an "abolitionist," although he assured them there was no "abolitionist" in the county he came from. Several of the Topeka men were taken. A few of these unfortunates had a lot of the newly-printed state constitutions, and the possession of such incendiary documents was very near having a bad effect on their physical constitutions. One gentleman, with a rope round his neck, made a compromise speech, in which he assured them that he was a "conservative free-state man;" whereupon they spared his life, as "conservative" free-state men are not dangerous. Dr. Cutler and Mr. Warren were arrested, in the neighborhood of Atchison, by a mob from Weston, Mo. After going through the farce of a trial for "high treason" before a bogus justice of the peace, they were taken sixty miles to the camp of Lecompton. There they suffered from abuse and the inclement weather, the doctor being sick. They were cooped up in a little crib of a log cabin, nearly all the conveniences of which were monopolized by Sheriff Jones and another border ruffian, who were playing poker. One night Jones lost twenty dollars in this way, and amused himself and vented his spleen on little Warren, by asking him to inform them all about the state-affairs in Lawrence, and adding, when Warren declined, that he must "tell or swing." Some of the prisoners at Lecompton camp were compelled to cook for the ruffians, and do other menial services, but escaped this duty very adroitly by hinting something about poison. Two other unfortunate youths, on the stormy night of the eighth, were compelled to hold up a blanket in the camp, so as to shelter a lot of the rowdies whom the war of the elements had not deterred from playing "euchre." These fellows played upon a stone close to one of the fires. As the fingers of the free-state men began to freeze, or as they relaxed from fatigue, away would go the blanket, and, whisk, off went the cards before the wind, followed by a torrent of oaths.

"G—d d——n your abolition souls to h—ll! Hold up that blanket!"

When peace was declared the prisoners were released; the pro-slavery men in camp having as much as they could do to take care of themselves. On Sunday morning (the 9th) many Missourians hurried up to Lawrence, shivering and half-frozen, in search of liquors. They expressed themselves anxious to drink to the "union of the free-state and pro-slavery parties," and as they rode up, with blue nose and chattering teeth, looked as if they were fully sensible there was "a North."

Those who think that this affair caused needless alarm, and did not and could not amount to anything, had better think again, for they are wrong. Near two thousand men were drawn up in battle array against each other, inspired with mutual animosity. One spark would have touched this mass of combustible into flame, and, once kindled, when would it have been extinguished or burnt out? Great praise is due Gen. Robinson, and also the other members of the Committee of Safety, for their great prudence and wisdom.

And, yet, the exemption from the horrors of civil war was purchased at a price. Those who consider that diplomacy must be above evasion will regard the treaty as a mutual concession to mutual fears. The treaty was a mere piece of moonshine to save the governor, but under that moonshine was apparent concession. The acts of the false Legislature are still like the "stumbling-blocks which caused Israel to sin."

Lawrence was now a fortified city. Four large earth-works or forts, and several lines of ditches and intrenchments, attest the industry of the besieged, and will remain for some time a memorial of these transactions, or may haply be required for a similar occurrence. Dow lies in his narrow bed, — the hope of bringing his murderers to punishment almost lost in the occurrence of other transactions. Barber, a martyr to the cause of freedom, is also mouldering beneath the sod. Business of every kind has been suspended in the territory. The settler, who had his house to close from the storms of winter, or his farm to open, and the merchant and man of business, were alike paralyzed by the danger that threatened, and the effort to defend themselves from invasion. The expense in sustaining the people in the vicinity of Lawrence, though considerable, is only a tithe of the loss. The burning of houses and hay-stacks, the stealing and killing of cattle, and abstraction of convenient and desirable articles, are mere trifles, and only exhibit an honest desire on the part of the besiegers to take something if they could not take Lawrence.

The pro-slavery invaders also lost something. They hazarded, if not lost, their reputation for courage; — reputation for anything else, I believe, they never had. They carried back three dead bodies with them. One of these was shot by one of their own guard, who mistook him in the dark for a free-soil spy; another was killed in a drunken row among themselves, and the third shot himself by accident while playing with his gun. The wounded man shot himself through the foot in the same blundering way; and if to these I add the man shot and wounded by Gen. Clark, we have a large if not "respectable" chapter of accidents.

On Monday night after the treaty there was a peace-banquet in the Free-State Hotel. It was largely attended, — so largely that it was a perfect jam. It was a commingling of pleasure and politics; soldiers, weary and begrimmed, from the trenches or the piquet guard; officers who wanted to coin their brilliant services into the largest amount of future popularity; ladies, dancing, and flirtation.

On the next day the volunteers were disbanded. Each soldier got a discharge, showing that he had served "gallantly and faithfully" so many days, etc. These documents the happy recipients felt confident would entitle them to pay (as soon as any one could be found willing to pay) and to a quarter-section of land; and, certainly, many a volunteer has got his quarter-section for less.

On the 15th of December the state constitution, framed at Topeka, was to be submitted to the people. Circulars, giving notice of the election, had been posted up throughout the territory. Copies of the constitution had been freely circulated. All had been invited to vote for or against the constitution. It had been the design to have speakers sent to every part of Kansas Territory, to arouse the people to a sense of the importance of voting at this election, but, owing to the Wakarusa war, this had been impossible. That war was one cause of the light vote polled. People had been away from their farms to the war, and when they hurried back, in the cold, rainy and wintry weather that set in, every man was struggling, if possible, to get his house closed tight enough to exclude the storm. The importance of voting on the constitution was not realized by many. But the chief cause of the vote being cut short was violence. In Atchison the circulars calling the election were torn down, the men who brought them driven violently from the town, and the election not permitted. At Kickapoo the houses of two men, appointed judges of election, were burned down, and although the polls were opened by the judges at a place close to the town, but few knew of it, and the vote was consequently light. At all the towns on the Missouri river, near which there are many large settlements polling a heavy free-state vote, there

Abstract of the Election on the Adoption of the State Constitution, Dec. 15, 1855.

Districts.	Precincts.	Constitution. Yes.	No.	General Banking Law. Yes.	No.	Exclusion of Negroes and Mulattoes. Yes.	No.	No. votes cast.
1	Lawrence,	348	1	225	83	133	223	356
	Blanton,	72	2	59	14	48	20	76
	Palmyra,	11	1	9	3	12	—	12
	Franklin	48	4	31	15	48	2	53
2	Bloomington,	137	—	122	11	113	15	137
	East Douglas,	18	—	13	4	14	4	18
3	Topeka,	135	—	125	9	69	64	136
	Washington,	42	—	41	1	42	—	42
	Brownsville,	24	—	22	2	22	2	24
	Tecumseh,	35	—	23	11	36	—	35
4	Prairie City,	72	—	39	33	69	3	72
5	Little Osage,	21	7	16	12	23	7	31
	Big Sugar,	18	2	5	16	20	—	21
	Neosho,	12	—	6	6	12	—	12
	Potawattomie,	39	3	21	19	25	18	43
	Little Sugar,	42	18	33	13	42	2	60
	Stanton,	32	—	4	33	33	5	37
	Osawottamie,	56	1	33	20	38	17	59
7	Titus,	39	5	32	7	25	15	44
	Juniata,	30	—	23	6	10	19	31
8	Ohio City,	21	—	16	5	20	1	21
	Mill Creek,	20	—	—	20	20	—	20
	St. Mary's,	14	—	—	14	14	—	14
	Waubaunsee,	19	—	17	1	7	11	19
9	Pawnee,	45	—	16	29	40	5	45
	Grasshopper Falls,	54	—	19	34	50	3	54
10	Doniphan,	22	—	5	14	21	—	22
	Burr Oak,	23	—	7	16	22	1	23
	Jesse Padur's,	12	—	1	11	12	—	12
11	Ocena,	28	—	8	20	28	—	28
	Kickapoo,	20	—	7	13	16	4	20
13	Pleasant Hill,	47	—	37	6	45	1	47
	Indianola,	19	—	—	18	19	—	19
	Whitfield,	7	—	3	4	6	—	7
14	Wolf River,	23	—	11	12	18	6	24
	St. Joseph's Bottom,	15	—	4	9	14	1	15
15	Mt. Pleasant,	32	—	32	1	30	2	33
16	Easton,	71	2	53	19	71	—	73
17	Mission,	7	—	3	—	1	2	7
	Total,	1731	46	1120	564	1287	453	1778

N. B.— The Poll-book at Leavenworth was destroyed.

was either no election allowed to be held, or the election was stopped, or the voters at least intimidated from voting by the presence of a mob from Missouri. The election returns are on the preceding page, and, in spite of the causes I enumerate, they show a heavier list of votes than there was of pro-slavery voters in the territory at that time.

The *Nota Bene* here requires an explanation. I was present at Leavenworth, and, as I saw the whole transaction, will endeavor to depict it. The election was held on a Saturday. For several days previous it had been raining. I had feared very much that the rain would keep the voters away, but, on Saturday afternoon, it cleared away cold and sharp, but with sunlight and fair weather. The voters came in, not so numerous as on other occasions, but by noon there were nearly three hundred votes polled; and, as the voting had only commenced at ten o'clock, it was supposed that there would be at least six or seven hundred votes counted. My attention was first attracted by large boat-loads of people coming over the river. The ferry-boat was a large, wide, flat boat, capable of holding several wagons or many horsemen.

I had strolled down to the river about nine o'clock in the morning, and then I observed this extraordinary emigration. Opposite to Leavenworth there is an island, behind which there is a dry slough, or old channel of the river. The island in question seemed as if by magic to swarm with life.

They commenced crossing in parties of ten or a dozen early in the afternoon; but about twelve o'clock they came over in whole boat-loads. About noon I learned from a person who came down the river side that they were also crossing at the horse-ferry at Fort Leavenworth, three miles above, and were coming down by land. As the Missourians have never voted at these elections, pronouncing them "illegal," and have merely attempted to intimidate, I naturally concluded that all of these Platte County scoundrels were not coming over for any good. On inquiry, I learned that Brigadier-General Easton, of the territorial militia, had stated in his paper and had proclaimed that his "brigade" should be disbanded in Leavenworth that day; and as these fellows had been out in the "law and order" campaign against the "abolitionists" of Lawrence, they were over to-day to get "an *honorable* discharge," which should entitle them to the gratitude of Uncle Sam to the tune of two dollars fifty cents a day. Bad as this version of the story looked, I suspected that it only explained part of the truth. That the disbanding should have been postponed for five days might have been accounted for on a mathematical calculation to the effect that these five days would amount to twelve dollars and fifty cents extra per man; but that it should have fallen exactly on the day that the new constitution framed at Topeka was to be submitted to the people looked a little like a calculation on the part of the gallant General Easton, or whoever had been at the bottom of it.

I do not think I ever before saw so many cut-throat-looking villains in one crowd. The groceries were thronged, and the spirit of evil commenced its work. Hard-featured, unkempt and unshaved, they evidently belonged to "the great unwashed and unterrified." With red blankets and blue blankets and dirty white blankets and no blankets at all, with "garments dyed in mud," and of a homespun look, and many of them with long Western rifles, they swaggered about, cursing the "abolitionists" generally, and a few persons about Leavenworth in particular.

I had learned that the parade and disbanding were to come off at two, and fancied that nothing would happen before that time; but I was mistaken. The clerks and judges of elections had been closing the polls to go to dinner; all of them had left the voting-room but three.

Soon amongst that motley crowd the tall figure of Mr. Payne was visible in an attitude of command. Payne is a Virginian, but such another Virginian I never saw! He must have come from the mountain districts, where they all belong to the "unterrified." He went with an easy swagger, and from the tip of his slouched hat to the point of his toes he looked an unmistakable member of the "first family" of ruffians. He had been a member of the Bogus Legislature, a judge of the County of Leavenworth, under appointment of the body of which he was a member, and now claimed to be a colonel of the "militia" who lately distinguished themselves before Lawrence.

There was another prominent person at the polls that day. His name is Dunn. He distinguished himself in this part of the world, and acquired an *influence* by keeping a grocery; and those only who know can comprehend the immense importance of a grocery-keeper in Border Ruffiandom.

The voting had been done at a window, and to this the crowd I have been describing made a rush. They were led on by Payne and Dunn. The movement was thoroughly understood before it was made, and around the house, and in the streets adjoining, the crowd was dense. There were several hundred of them. The window was driven in, glass, sash, frame and all. Dunn exclaimed,

"In the name of 'law and order' I demand that ballot-box!"

"No d—d parleying!" cried Payne, cocking a six-shooter and presenting it at the clerks. "Take the box, G—d d—n it, take the box!"

Two of the three persons in the room at the time it was attacked got off without injury, having arms; the third, a man named Wetherill, one of the clerks of election, and who was unarmed, tried to take away the ballot-box, and make his escape by a door opening on another street. Closely pressed, he threw the box under a counter, and as he emerged into the muddy street was knocked down by clubs. Not less than thirty men were around him and jumping on him. One man had an axe raised to strike him, if he could have done so for the crowd. It was the work of an instant, and immediately some few of the free-state men, who had not been frightened off, interfered. The first who interposed was a pro-slavery man, who seemed to have a trifle of the Samaritan in him; but a young man from York State, named Anthony, and a Captain Brown, both good and tried free-state men, cocked their pistols, and rushed forward, as did some others. Wetherill was raised and carried home.

The mob, having got possession of the ballot-box and poll-books, paraded them off in triumph. The streets resounded with shrieks and yells, and it was evident that the half-tipsy invaders were ripe for further mischief.

A panic had seized the free-state men, or rather they wanted some bold and active leaders. The polls had been violated while most of the people were at dinner; but the border ruffians kept possession of the quarter of the town where the voting had been held, and but few free-state men were to be seen venturing among them. Perhaps the apology for this timid spirit lay in the fact that the men of Leavenworth were unarmed, or but indifferently armed, and that they had no volunteer or military organization, the known members and officers of which could be relied on. It was with a feeling of shame and bitterness that I saw these invading, lawless villains thus violate the dearest and most sacred rights of American freemen.

The mob was swaying uneasily to and fro, and was evidently animated by some new work of mischief. The words "abolition papers," "Delahay," "D—n it! burn the whole infernal thing up!" "Throw it in the river!" showed that mischief to Colonel Delahay's office, the *Territorial Register*, was contemplated.

In this emergency the city mayor, who was elected on the free-state ticket, sent off to the fort for the troops. He might as well have sent to Jericho for the horns that blew the walls down. The commandant had other business. The *Register* office was locked up. Its owner, who had refused to go to the aid of Lawrence during the siege, might have been found, peering down from a back street on the mob who threatened his press, and in a state of trepidation which showed he was not very anxious for political martyrdom just at that moment. A couple of his hands ventured to remain in the office.

Delahay's office was not mobbed. There is not the slightest doubt that putting it in the river on Saturday was part of the programme; but two things saved it. In the first place, a person who does not subscribe to the non-resistant creed informed the friends of the pro-slavery paper here that if the Missourians put the *Register* office in the river, the *Herald* office would be placed snugly beside it as soon as they left town. I do not endorse such a sentiment, of course, but I think it had a salutary effect. The other reason was, a hesitation on a part of a few of the more conservative of the pro-slavery men here, who, like Davy Atchison at the Wakarusa, were afraid that too much of a good thing "might injure the democratic party." An effort was made to satisfy the victorious heroes of the ballot-box with their laurels for the day, and the disbanding of the "militia" afforded the means of diverting the current.

The men were marshalled out to an open space toward the back of the town, and then came off the second edition of the "law and order" humbug.

Judge Payne, who now figured as Colonel Payne, called the meeting to order,—that is, he tried to do so,—and also introduced the gallant General Eastin to the men whom he was about to disband; and this he did in quite a handsome manner.

General Eastin congratulated them on their good and orderly conduct, on which their recent occupation was an excellent commentary. He also complimented them on their appearance, which was quite diverting. But by far the most important part of his speech was a proposition that these men should immediately enroll themselves into regular volunteer companies as soon as they were disbanded. He said there were three thousand stand of arms due the territory from the United States, and that if they took the proper steps they could get them. Atrocious as this proposal may look, I have investigated the matter as far as possible, and am satisfied it was really the intention thus to get the arms designed for the defence of the territory into the hands of those who are to invade it. A part of the force thus to be armed would be pro-slavery men, residents of the territory; but the great bulk of these arms would thus find their way into the hands of the border ruffians.

As there were evidently a dozen more orators to immortalize themselves, I left. Returning to the river's edge, I saw another large party of the Missourians on the island, who wanted to get over even at that late hour, but the ice had begun to run thick, and the ferry-boat was stopped for the time being. There were about forty on horseback who had come down to the sands opposite, and were evidently very anxious to get over. On the island I should judge there were not less than a hundred men.

Night set in, and with it the renewed fears of the inhabitants. There had been no attempt made to get new poll-books, and commence voting again. I heard it asserted by the border ruffians, in the most emphatic manner, that no such election should be hereafter permitted.

After dark it was learned that the attack on the *Register* office and on several other houses was yet to be made. A party of Missourians had gone out and encamped in a hollow above town. Some of them had left altogether, and some still remained.

A few of those whose anxiety for their bones, or to "keep right on the record," had not interfered too much with their willingness to fight, assembled at different points of the town to prepare for defence if an attack was made. There were not more than eighty men in all, thus bearing arms, and many of these were armed with old rusty muskets and shot-guns, only fit for a museum, and which it would have been as safe to stand before as behind.

Night went on, and the foe came not. Hours went by, and weary watching began to extinguish the military order.

There was no attack that night, and next morning all of the border ruffians who had not gone back were struggling towards home, their "blushing honors thick upon them."

CHAPTER XVIII.

SKIRMISH AT EASTON.

The winter of 1855–6 was unusually severe throughout the Northern and Western States, and it was particularly so in Kansas. By Christmas the deep drifting snow covered the prairies, and those who had been deprived of the opportunity to get their houses made comfortable, by the necessity of defence, or harassing persecution, suffered severely. Thus it was in Kansas, — snowy, cold, with biting winds, — when the people were called upon to vote for those officers who should form the government of the prospective state.

In Leavenworth city a free-state mayor had been elected in the fall of 1855; but, after the disastrous election on the 15th of December, Mr. Slocum, intimidated by the threatening conduct of the border ruffians, or feeling that the people were dissatisfied with him for not venturing more in the defence of the place, resigned. Taking advantage of this opportunity, the pro-slavery men, by fraud and violence, elected one of their tools. Under his dispensation it was ordered that no election be held in Leavenworth city; and, as it was well known that any number of ruffians could be got from the adjoining state to enforce that order, it was not attempted. Some of the leading free-state men determined that an election should be held in the Leavenworth district, and it having thus failed on the 15th of January, the day appointed, the judges of election adjourned the polls until the 17th, when they were to be opened at Easton, or near it, at the house of a Mr. Minard. Easton is some twelve miles distant from Leavenworth city, and by this arrangement it would be needless to add that comparatively few could go to the polls through a deep snow in such severe weather, well knowing, as they did, that the chances for a fight even there were pretty good. In fact, while Leavenworth could have polled upwards of five hundred free-state votes, little more than a hundred were polled at Easton.

So quietly had this been managed that the enemy were not sufficiently aware of what was going on to make sufficient provision against it. On the morning of the 17th of January, 1855, the polls were opened according to the adjournment, and voting began. In a very short time the pro-slavery men became aware of what was going on, and began to rally. The evening before, a small number of pro-slavery men, who had known that an election was to be held at Mr. Minard's, attempted to get possession of the place so as to prevent it, but were driven off. Many of the free-state men who went to the polls took guns with them. A small party of these, while going through Easton on their way to the polls, were attacked by a larger number of persons, who had congregated in the store of a pro-slavery man named Dawson. By these men the free-state voters in question were disarmed and driven back in a different direction from the polls.

During the day parties of pro-slavery men, who were congregating about Easton, went over to the place where the voting was going on, and threatened to attack the house. Seeing that the free-state men were ready to defend themselves, they did not attack. These threatening visits were made several times during the day, and on each occasion the most violent threats were made; but they dared not attack. During the day voters going to or coming from the polls were molested, and disarmed or driven back.

As it was well known that the ballot-box would be taken and destroyed, as had been threatened, it became an object of some interest to save this record of the popular will. Many of the voters had left; but there were still some eighteen or twenty who remained to guard the ballot-box.

In the early part of the night an attack was expected, and the free-state men were prepared for it. They knew that messengers had gone to Kickapoo for the Kickapoo Rangers, and an attack was looked for whenever they arrived. Late that night, and when the danger of attack was supposed to be past for the present,

Mr. Stephen Sparks, with his son and nephew, started for home. Their route lay through Easton. When close to Easton they were attacked by a dozen of armed men, who had been watching at one of the groceries, and swarmed out on them. Mr. Sparks and his son retreated into the fence corner, where they drew their revolvers and kept their enemies at bay. The nephew, who had been some distance behind, wheeled about and went back full speed for help.

It was a trying moment for the two men in the fence corner. Their enemies clustered only a few yards off, pouring out against them a torrent of bitter imprecations. They ordered them to surrender; but the two men in the fence corner, well knowing the danger of surrendering to such characters, maintained their trying position. A struggle so unequal could not last long. The pro-slavery men seemed to think that the first who made the assault would pay the forfeit with his life. They began to gather closer and get more excited; but before their rage could rise above their cowardice, Capt. E. P. Brown, with fifteen mounted men, dashed up to the rescue. The pro-slavery men immediately retreated as they saw the others advance.

It was just about this time that the Kickapoo Rangers approached the scene of action. Capt. Brown, with his men and those they had rescued, were riding off, when a party of about thirty mounted and armed men appeared coming over the ridge. All of the parties were close to Easton. The captain of the Rangers ordered Brown's company to halt and to surrender. This was refused. Brown drew up his men in line. At this moment the Rangers commenced firing on the free-state men. Capt. Brown immediately ordered his men to fire, and a volley was poured back.

There was only one Sharpe's rifle in the company; and, as the guns loaded at the muzzle, the process was slow. After two or three volleys, the Kickapoo Rangers dismounted and retreated into some empty houses thereabouts, from which they kept up a brisk fire. Finding his men exposed, Capt. Brown threw them into some empty houses close by. The young man with the Sharpe's rifle lay down at the back of a snow-bank and fired at the

houses, where the enemy was, so long as he had ammunition. The others of Brown's men loaded their pieces, and fired them as often as they could see anything to shoot at.

This irregular and uncertain fight lasted for two or three hours, when the pro-slavery men ceased firing. As Capt. Brown knew his force was too weak to make an assault on the enemy for the purpose of dislodging them, and as it was evident nothing further could be accomplished then, they returned to Mr. Minard's.

In this engagement Mr. Sparks received two wounds, but they were not dangerous; and another free-state man was also wounded, but slightly. On the other side a pro-slavery man named Cook was killed, and one or two others hit, but not badly hurt. It is wonderful that more of them were not killed; but in the darkness and amidst the excitement the chance of taking aim was not very good. After the parties took to the houses, which were some little distance apart (a long range for such guns), there was little mischief done.

As it was impossible for any number of men to remain at Minard's, the ballot-box was sent off to what was considered a place of greater safety, and the parties started home. Capt. Brown, with seven others who lived in the neighborhood of Leavenworth or Salt Creek, started home, some of them in a buggy, and some in a horse-wagon. They had proceeded some distance when they saw a wagon full of men approaching them. The free-state men drove past the wagon. Not a word was spoken on either side, although the parties eyed each other intently. Scarcely had they passed the wagon when a bend of the road revealed two wagons more and some horsemen. They were the Kickapoo Rangers.

Thus fairly trapped, Capt. Brown jumped out of the buggy, and, taking his gun, told the others to defend themselves. As the chances were desperate, Mr. Adams and Mr. Green urged that they should surrender, and Mr. Brown reluctantly complied. Having obtained possession of the arms of the free-state men, some of the most violent of the Rangers proceeded to abuse them. They had given a promise that their persons should be safe if they would surrender their arms; but the moment this was complied with, the terms were violated, the leaders of the pro-slavery men being unable to control some of the more desperate characters they were leading on. One young man was knocked down, and a man was going to cut him with his hatchet (the Kickapoo Rangers carry hatchets), when he was prevented by the friends of the young man, and Captain Martin of the Rangers.

At length the prisoners were taken back to Easton and put into Mr. Dawson's store, or grocery. Shortly after they were taken there, Captain Brown was separated from them, and put in an adjoining building. A rope was purchased at the store, and was shown to the prisoners, with the intimation that they should be hanged with it.

It is but justice to say that there were a few men amongst this pro-slavery party who were unwilling that violence should be done the prisoners. Captain Martin exerted himself to save them. It was fiercely discussed for hours what should be done with them; and meanwhile liquor was drank pretty freely, and they who were brutal enough without anything to make them more so, became ungovernably fierce. Seeing the threatening aspect of affairs, and being unwilling that all of these men should thus be murdered, Captain Martin allowed the prisoners in the store of Dawson to escape. As nearly all of the pro-slavery ruffians were engaged in taunting and insulting Brown, the others succeeded in getting off, although they were perceived before they had gone far, and some of them were pursued.

Mr. Adams hastened to Fort Leavenworth in hopes of getting some troops to go and rescue Brown; but it was a vain attempt. Such protection was refused, and even then it would have been too late.

Then followed a scene of atrocity and horror. If there is one reader who thinks my language towards the border ruffians is disrespectful, let him look at this scene, and say if the term "ruffian" is not mild.

Captain Brown had surrendered his arms, and was helpless. His enemies, who dared not face him the night before, though they had a superior force, now crowded round him. When they began to strike him he rose to his feet, and asked to be permitted to fight any one of them. He challenged them to pit him against their best man, — he would fight for his life; but not one of the cowards dared thus to give the prisoner a chance. Then he volunteered to fight two, and then three; but it was in vain. Capt. Martin tried to save him; but it was a vain effort to stay the torrent of blood-thirsty vindictiveness. Seeing his task hopeless, sick of the prospect, he left.

It would be needless to dwell on the sickening spectacle. These men, or rather demons, rushed around Brown, and literally hacked him to death with their hatchets. One of the Rangers, a large, coarse-looking wretch, named Gibson, inflicted the fatal blow, — a large hatchet-gash in the side of the head, which penetrated the skull and brain many inches. The gallant Brown fell, and his remorseless enemies jumped on him, while thus prostrate, and kicked him. Desperately wounded though he was, he still lived; and, as they kicked him, he said:

"Don't abuse me — it is useless — I am dying!"

It was a vain appeal. One of the wretches, who has since disgraced the office of United States Deputy Marshal, stooped over the prostrate man, and, with a refinement of cruelty exceeding the rudest savage, spit tobacco-juice in his eyes!

Satiated brutality at last went back to its carousals, and it was then that a few of their number, whom a little spark of conscience, or a fear of punishment, had animated, raised the dying man, still groaning, and, placing him in a wagon, his gaping wounds but poorly sheltered from the bitter cold of that winter's day, drove him to the grocery of Charles Dunn, on Salt Creek. Dunn was of their number. There they went through the farce of dressing his wounds; but, seeing the hopelessness of his case, took him home to his wife. So far, struggling nature, and a vigorous constitution, had refused to sink; but, as he was borne in to his startled and agonized wife, the pulse of life was ebbing out. She asked him what was the matter, and how he came thus.

"I have been murdered by a gang of cowards, in cold blood, without any cause!" he said. And, as the poor wife stooped over the body of her gallant husband, he expired.

Thus died Captain E. P. Brown, a true martyr to the cause of freedom. It was his fearless independence that signalled him out and aroused the venom of the corrupt tools of the slave power. Then "cracked a noble heart." I knew him well, and have seen how he demeaned himself in the hour of stern danger more than once, and know that he was brave and true.

He is buried on the top of Pilot Knob, which overlooks the valley of the Missouri. He left a wife and one orphan child. As I stood on his lonely grave I felt like exclaiming:

> "Were I Brutus,
> And Brutus Antony — there were an Antony
> Would ruffle up your spirits, and put a tongue
> In every wound of Cæsar's, that should move
> The stones of Rome to rise and mutiny."

Precisely one week after the election in December there was a party-caucus held in Lawrence to nominate a free-state ticket for state officers under the Topeka Constitution. As in all similar bodies, there was, of course, some wire-working and manœuvring; but, as this chiefly concerns the people of Kansas alone, I need not occupy space with the particulars.

The most important nomination was that of General Robinson for governor. This was not only justice to his abilities, but, in the circumstances of the territory, was an indispensable step. General Robinson is a man of calm, dignified, yet fearless character. Few men could have been found anywhere better qualified for the position he was called to fill. Possessing integrity, which unfortunately was scarce in the territory, a thorough judge of human nature, and willing to act in circumstances the most dangerous and responsible; temperate in his habits to abstemiousness, chaste in his language, and possessing all the qualities which dignify the character of a gentleman, he is a man you can honor for his ability without feeling ashamed of his character.

Next to him, as the person meriting the confidence of the people, General Lane unquestionably stands. With all his faults he has a heart; is a brave man, active and indefatigable, and may be eminently useful. He is thoroughly a Western man, with a Western man's peculiarities. At times I have admired him, and again shrank from him with the conviction that the public interests could never be safely entrusted with him. And yet, after all, on a fair estimate, there are worse fellows than "Jim Lane." It would never do to try him by the same standard as Robinson; but he fills a standard of his own in a no less prominent and useful way.

W. Y. Roberts is a much smaller man than either. With him politics is a science, and himself its professor. He was nominated and elected lieutenant-governor, but was made candidate for governor on a bolting ticket got up in opposition to the regular free-state ticket. When questioned as to whether he endorsed the position of the men who thus nominated him, he declared that it was without his consent; but a reference to the election-returns will show that the bolting ticket, which had few votes anywhere, received twenty-nine out of thirty votes in Roberts' own precinct.

I am particular in speaking of the convention, for it had something important to do with the future of the territory. Besides the candidates for governor and lieutenant-governor, whose names I have mentioned, Judge P. C. Schuyler was nominated for secretary of state, Dr. G. A. Cutler, auditor, J. A. Wakefield for treasurer, H. Miles More, Esq., attorney-general, Messrs. M. F. Conway, S. N. Latta, and M. Hunt, for judges of Supreme Court; Mr. C. B. Thurston for reporter of Supreme Court, Mr. B. Floyd, clerk of the same; Mr. John Speer, printer. All of these were elected.

The Leavenworth vote was polled at Easton. At several other points, where the pro-slavery men had the power, or where the voting-place bordered on Missouri, no voting was allowed. It is justice to add that Judge Johnson and Mr. Parrot were on the bolting ticket against their will.

By these steps was the state government ready to be put in motion. At the Topeka Convention it was urged that the government in question begin in January; but it was decided that no attempt to organize should be made till the first of March, 1856, by which time it was expected that Congress would act on the application for admission.

CHAPTER XIX.

STATE LEGISLATURE — THE DRAGOONS — SHERIFF JONES SHOT.

During the month of February, 1856, threats of fresh invasion were common. It was believed that Missouri would pour out another horde of law-and-order heroes, to "wipe out" the state Legislature in blood. Not satisfied with wresting from the people the only show of political power they had, and of holding in violent usurpation the government of Kansas, they were determined that there should be no revolt from under their rule. No provision was made, under the constitution, to sustain civil power by hireling soldiery under the orders of the government, because it was at once conceded that, when a government could not sustain itself amongst the people, it ought to fall. But now there was a mighty change in the political history of the country. Newspapers in the pay of the government, or its employés, and calling themselves "*democratic*," began to talk about "treason," as if the rights of a republican people had merged into submission to some recognized written law, or official power. Officers, high in public trust, did not fear to give official sanction to this innovation on popular rights. The people asserted their most sacred political right, and "Treason! Treason!" was the cry of *democratic* journals. Reckless politicians who, under the pretext of "popular sovereignty," had wrested from the people their most sacred rights, the moment the people attempted to recover what was thus filched from them, echoed the cry, "Treason! — Treason!"

As the appearance of affairs, judging from past experience, indicated fresh troubles, a memorial was framed by the people of Kansas, asking protection from armed invasion, and to be secured in their rights. As a reply, the President issued a proclamation, in which, amidst an unmeaning denunciation against "invasion," he declared substantially that all the usurpations of the Bogus Legislature, — its men selected from Missourians and elected by them, — who imposed the Missouri code on Kansas, and infamous laws destructive of popular liberty; — who stole from the people the right to elect their public officers, and thrust its tools upon them; — a despotism, which could not have had a day's vitality in the territory without Missouri bravos, or federal bayonets, — that these usurpations would be sustained "by the whole force of the government."

As an admirable offset to the few sophisticated parts of the proclamation, are the following preamble and resolutions, adopted by a meeting called in Independence, Missouri, to *consider* the President's proclamation:

"Whereas, information having been received through the public papers that the President of the United States had received information that armed organizations had been raised in the Territory of Kansas, and without the territory in the neighboring states, for the purpose of 'resisting the laws of the territory,' clearly implying that the border counties of the State of Missouri contemplated such armed resistance, and has issued a proclamation based thereon."

Here follow a string of resolutions, denying that Missouri got up armed resistance to the "laws of the territory." This resolution was also offered:

"*Resolved*, That we offer to the President *our assistance* in suppressing any armed resistance to the laws of Kansas Territory, whether it be from the North or South."

Admirably cool! They comprehended the President's proclamation. *They* had offered "no resistance to the *laws of the territory*." Why should they? — they made them. And this view of the case was no joke; it has been since fearfully realized. Missouri, so far from resisting the "laws of the territory," volunteers to help Franklin Pierce enforce them; *and she has done it;* — ay, and done it unrebuked. As a border ruffian told me during the Wakarusa war, when I had pointed out the propriety of

Missouri enforcing the bogus laws, if they were to be enforced at all,

"We made them — Missouri made them, sir, and she has *a right* to enforce them; and if she don't, who will?"

As an evidence of what Missouri meant by "suppressing armed resistance, etc.," from the "South," I quote resolutions adopted first at Lexington, Mo., and then at Independence, Mo., some of the same men being officers of the meeting adopting them. They were offered on the occasion of the arrival of Col. Buford's armed regiment from Alabama and Carolina, who came for the avowed and sole purpose of aiding Missouri in the conquest of Kansas:

"*Resolved*, That we hail with delight the interest now being manifested in the Southern States in regard to the settlement of Kansas, with her pro-slavery and law-abiding citizens; and that we welcome with open arms those gallant sons of Alabama and of other Southern States, now on their way to their new homes in Kansas Territory, as well as those who have preceded them on their way, as men with whom the South can trust her dearest rights under the constitution; and we hereby pledge ourselves to them, and *each to the other*, that we will aid and assist them in every *proper* way, and, should emergencies require, we will march shoulder to shoulder with them to the *last* struggle for Southern rights.

"*Resolved*, That we shall ever cordially welcome to the soil of *Missouri* our friends of the South, who have forsaken their homes and firesides *to join us* in the contest now going on in Kansas, and that we assure them that our homes shall be theirs, our *hopes* theirs, our fortunes theirs, and, *in fine*, *Missouri* grasps the hand of the South, and trusts that the future State of Kansas will be another tie to cement *us* in a common brotherhood."

Nor was the "aid and comfort" confined to resolutions. Large sums of money were raised for their equipment and support, and finally, a property tax was levied for their support, so that lukewarm men, or "abolitionists at heart," would be compelled to sustain the expense of conquest.

On the first of March the State Legislature assembled at Topeka, with the officers of the prospective governments. The House of Representatives was called to order by the Chairman of the Executive Committee of Kansas Territory; the oath of office administered, and the roll was called by the Secretary pro tem. Thirty-two members responded as their names were called. A quorum being present, they proceeded to elect a Speaker, and T. Minard, of Easton, was declared duly elected. On taking the chair, he made a few appropriate remarks. Joel K. Goodin, of Blanton, was elected clerk, and Samuel Tappan, of Lawrence, assistant clerk, J. Snodgrass and G. F. Gordon, transcribing clerks, and J. Mitchell, sergeant-at-arms. After the election of doorkeepers, etc., a message was received from the Senate, that they had organized, and proposed to go into joint session to witness an inauguration of the state officers. Governor Charles Robinson took the oath of office, which was administered by the President of the Senate. He then delivered his inaugural address.

The bodies thus convened proceeded to memorialize Congress for the admission of Kansas as a state under the Constitution. A committee from each legislative branch was appointed to frame a code of laws for the future state, during the recess or adjournment of the Legislature. Other steps were taken, but all of a preparatory nature. Nothing was done which would bring the territorial government and the new state government in conflict. The Senate and House, in joint session, proceeded to elect the United States Senators for Kansas, who should be prepared to take their seats on the admission of the state into the Union. The persons thus elected were Andrew H. Reeder and J. H. Lane. Having taken these steps, the Legislature adjourned until the 4th of July, 1856. During the sitting of the Legislature, S. J. Jones, who claimed to be Sheriff of Douglas County, went to Topeka, which is in another of the counties made by the Bogus Legislature, and attended the sittings of the State General Assembly. He did not attempt to molest any one, but busied himself in "taking notes," writing the names of the members and officers in his memorandum book.

And now came a new era in Kansas history, and one prefigured in the President's proclamation. The national House of Representatives had sent a committee of three of its members, Messrs. Howard of Michigan, Sherman of Ohio, and Oliver of Missouri, to Kansas, to investigate the alleged election frauds and outrages on the people, and collect testimony to be submitted to that body. This was an all-important step, and faithfully did the majority of the committee perform their duty. Their colleague, Mr. Oliver, was placed in a critical situation. As the representative not only of the slave power but of border ruffianism, he was expected to make a report sustaining these interests, and that in the face of testimony so overwhelming, that the effort could only make him ridiculous. Had he possessed the magnanimity of a great statesman he might have abjured party and all perverting influences, and joined with the majority in condemning outrages which it was hopeless to conceal or defend. But for such a cause the slave power would never have forgiven him. Even had he been noble enough to rise above this threatened political ostracism, there was a forbidding spectre between him and this honorable position. Amongst the testimony taken before the committee is evidence that Mr. Oliver came over from Missouri to the territory with a number of Missourians, and made speeches to them at the March election.

While this committee were in session it became all-important to the border ruffians that the investigation should, if possible, be broken up, and that its sittings should at least be attended with trouble. For this purpose Sheriff Jones again commenced his legal persecution. The old ghost of the rescue of Branson, which had been neglected for some time, was now revived. Captain Abbott, who lived on the Wakarusa, was persecuted, hunted like a beast, evidently in hopes that, by taking him, another rescue would be made, which would be the foundation for more capital; but the captain eluded them.

While the committee were in Lawrence an attempt was made to arrest S. N. Wood. The sheriff, indeed, got possession of his person, but a few men who happened to be present stepped up and interfered, saying that "they could not have any fighting in town; they must not quarrel," etc. Jones tried to pull out his revolver, when one of the parties adroitly took it away from him. Baffled and enraged, Jones left. On the following Sunday Jones returned. This time he had a well-matured design in view. As it was the Sabbath many of the citizens were going to places of public worship. Jones interrupted these people, addressing himself to some of the most influential and respectable persons in town, amongst them one preacher. These men he summoned to act as his posse, to help him to make arrests he said he wanted to make. As might be expected, they did not pay the slightest attention to him. His object was gained. He returned and made a demand on Governor Shannon for the federal troops (all of which was arranged beforehand, of course.) The governor sent for the troops in question. Instructions had been forwarded to Colonel Sumner, by the Secretary of War, to furnish federal troops for the purpose of sustaining the bogus laws and bogus officers, and Colonel Sumner, of course, complied with Shannon's requisition, and a small detachment was sent. These were placed subject to the orders of the ruffian Jones, who trooped about the country with them at his heels. At the same time, Colonel Sumner sent over the following letter to Lawrence:

"HEAD QUARTERS, FIRST CAVALRY,
FORT LEAVENWORTH, *April* 22, 1856.

"SIR: A small detachment proceeds to Lecompton this morning, on the requisition of the governor, under the orders of the President, to assist the Sheriff of Douglas County in executing several writs, in which he says he has been resisted. I know nothing of the merits of the case, and have nothing to do with them. But I would respectfully impress upon you and others in authority the necessity of yielding obedience to the proclamation and orders of the general government. Ours is, emphatically, a government of laws, and if they are set at naught there is an end of all order. I feel assured that, on reflection, you will not compel me to resort to violence in carrying out the orders of the government. I am, sir, very respectfully,

"Your obd't serv't,

"E. V. SUMNER,

"*Col. First Cav. Com.*

"To the Mayor of Lawrence."

However much they deprecated the action of the general government, the people had not made up their minds to resist. Indeed, a loyal sentiment to federal authority was universal. The steps taken to organize a state government were considered in full accordance with the national constitution, and the only precedents the case offered. It was, therefore, determined by the citizens of Lawrence that no resistance should be offered, at the present time, to federal authority, no matter how despotic; or even to Jones, when he came thus clothed with the federal authority.

Thus it was that Jones was permitted to enter the town with the troops and arrest several of the most respectable citizens. The persons he took were those whom he had asked to be his posse the Sunday previous, and who were thus arrested on a writ of contempt. Trivial and aggravating as this cause of arrest was, it did not save the parties from the rudest treatment and indignity; one of this number had his clothes torn by Jones in the rough handling he got. These prisoners were cooped up in a tent, and treated as if they had been the most infamous felons, as their offence (admitting the official existence of Sheriff Jones) was a trivial one, and bailable. These men were thus kept in Lawrence, the design being, beyond all question, to provoke the people of the town to a rescue, when there would be another excuse for attacking the place, and, in the disturbance, destroying the testimony taken, if not killing the commissioners.

Such was the state of affairs when an unlooked-for event occurred. The people of Lawrence, with few exceptions, had calmly made up their minds to submit to this outrage for the time being, in hopes that they would have some remedy, the use of which would not place them in antagonism to the United States authority. But, while this was the resolution of the staid and conservative, there were a few bolder spirits who were prepared to go greater lengths; men who did not stop to reason on nice subtleties, which timid minds will balance and set forth, in order to exonerate themselves from the charge of inaction. They remembered that Jones' official presence was an outrage and an insult in itself, and that his mode of acting as an officer was violent, irregular, and insulting. But even these were so far under restraint that they submitted to the desire of the majority that there should be no resistance, and they would only have acted with a body and publicly.

There was one spirit, fearless, wild, and reckless, who took another view of the subject. A young man, almost a boy, with warm impulsive nature, he cared little for the subtle distinctions of political theorists. Of the world he knew but little, although he was far from illiterate, but he regarded men and things as facts, not fancies; and when he recognized an enemy his instinct was to crush him. The youth regarded the distinctions about territorial authority and federal troops as merely the apologies by which the fearful endeavored to cover up their cowardice or shrinking from responsibility.

It was the night of the 23d of April. Lawrence was quiet. The dragoons were in their tents; there also were the prisoners, and Sheriff Jones was in one of the tents. A fire was burning in front, and there was a light in it. Jones rose and went to the opening of the tent and looked out.

Quietly and stealthily, but resolutely, that young man had entered Lawrence, and now he stood some forty yards from the military tent. The guard was pacing his rounds with his carbine in his arm. Jones was standing in the door of the tent. Slowly that young man raised his pistol, till he thought it covered his enemy. Was there no fluttering pulse in that young heart? Was there nothing that whispered that it might be fairer to meet his enemy face to face? Was there not even the timorous, trembling fear, that measures guilt by its probable punishment? A sharp report rang out; the ball missed Jones, and the report merely arrested his attention. He stepped out, thinking, no doubt, it was a random shot. Again there was a report. Jones stooped down; the ball had cut his foot and grazed his leg. "That was intended for me," he muttered, and he went into the tent. The guard had halted in his rounds, and was listening and looking intently through the night, and the clicking of his gun-lock might have been heard in the stillness. Daring to rashness, fired by the determination to accomplish that for which he aimed, the young man stepped lightly several paces nearer the tent; he saw the figure of Jones

by the light in it, and once more raising his pistol he fired. Jones fell, and the boy assassin fled.

Then there was hurrying and bustling with alarm. The town was alive with people, and lights were going to and fro. "Jones is shot!" went from mouth to mouth. The honorable and high-minded were displeased that this should have been done, and felt that it might give envious enemies a right to say that there were midnight assassins in Lawrence. The timorous and cowardly were loud in their denunciations of the unknown assassin, and strove by their noisy declaration of "the atrocity," to clear their skirts from the charge of guilt in the eyes of those who might be suspicious. The wounded man was taken into the Free-State Hotel, and every attention was offered to him. Dr. Stringfellow was in attendance with other physicians. Next day his friends sent back to his home in Missouri to bring up his wife, and the citizens of Lawrence strove, by their attention to him, to show that they did not sympathize in the attempt.

Then another view of the affair seized the minds of the suspicious and abused people of Lawrence. It was a trick; the wild Blue Lodge, which scruples at nothing, had determined that one of their men should go to the length of shooting Jones, in order to involve the people of Lawrence in his guilt. Others thought that some of Jones' pro-slavery enemies — and a man of his character has no scarcity of enemies anywhere — had taken the opportunity thus to shoot him when Lawrence would be accused of the crime, and thus a double purpose served. Such were the conflicting opinions in Lawrence on this mysterious subject, and as Dr. Stringfellow was his physician, there were not lacking those who believed the whole thing a hoax, — that the firing was done for effect, and that Jones was not shot at all.

Next day after the shooting an indignation meeting was held. Ex-Governor Reeder, Governor Robinson, and others, made speeches denouncing the act, and resolutions of the same character were adopted almost unanimously; although there were a few who thought, if the "assassin" was to be indicted at all, it should be for taking such poor aim.

If any one feels like striving to serve an oppressed people after

the manner of Charlotte Corday, in such a community as Lawrence, let him read and ponder over these resolutions. Nor are they a humbug. There were free-state men who would have handed that youth over to justice (bogus justice). Whether they would have done so from a moral sensibility of the great guilt, or a selfish desire to eschew all risk or culpability, I am not prepared to say.

At the earnest request of many influential free-state men, Gov. Robinson offered five hundred dollars reward for the apprehension and conviction, in the United States Court, of the person or persons who made the assault.

It was at this time that Col. Sumner, whose conscientiousness so far interfered with strict official duty that he could counsel the free-state men to *submission*, wrote:

"HEAD QUARTERS, FIRST CAVALRY,
CAMP NEAR LAWRENCE, *April* 27, 1856.

"SIR: As there are no municipal officers in the town of Lawrence, I think proper to address you before returning to my post. The recent attempt made upon the life of Sheriff Jones will produce great excitement throughout the territory, and on the Missouri frontier, and I consider it of the utmost importance that every effort should be made by your people to ferret out and bring to justice the cowardly assassin. It is not too much to say that the peace of the country may depend upon it, for if he is not arrested the act will be charged by the opposite party upon your whole community. This affair has been reported at Washington, and whatever orders may be received will be instantly carried into effect. The proclamation, which requires obedience to the laws of the territory, as they now stand, until legally abrogated, will certainly be maintained, and it is very unsafe to give heed to people at a distance who counsel resistance. If they were here to participate in the danger, they would probably take a different view of this matter.

"I am, sir, very respectfully, your obedient servant,

"E. V. SUMNER, *Col.* 1*st Cavalry Commanding*.

"To Mr. CHARLES ROBINSON."

By the officer who brought this the following reply was forwarded to Col. Sumner:

"LAWRENCE, K. T., *April* 27, 1856.

"SIR: Your note of this morning is received, and in answer permit me to say that the cowardly attack upon Mr. Jones receives no countenance whatever from the citizens of Lawrence, but, on the contrary, meets with universal condemnation, and if the guilty party can be found, he will most certainly be given over to justice. It is and has been the policy of the people of Lawrence to yield prompt obedience to the laws and officers of the federal government, and as Mr. Jones was acting with the authority of that government on the day of the assault, the guilty party was an enemy to the citizens of Lawrence, no less than a violator of the laws. The people of Lawrence are without any organized municipal government, and, consequently, no person or persons can speak or act officially for them; but, from what I know of their feelings and disposition, I have no hesitation in saying that they will ever be found loyal citizens of the government, and ready to do all in their power to maintain the laws of their country.

"As an evidence of the public sentiment of this community, I inclose a copy of the proceedings of a public meeting held on the morning after the unfortunate affair occurred.

"Very respectfully, your ob't servant,

"CHARLES ROBINSON.

"COL. E. V. SUMNER."

How prompt was President Pierce in securing justice to the wounded Missouri bully who was shot while trampling on the rights of a free people!

Not so was it when Mr. Mace was shot at the same time. Mr. Mace had given testimony before the committee, and that night he was attacked and wounded at his house by pro-slavery men, who thought they had killed him. But there is no "report" sent to Washington about this, nor about the outrage perpetrated much nearer the dragoon head-quarters, on the person of Rev. Pardee Butler. It was the second time that this last-named gentleman was outraged, and the scene is described by himself thus:

"April 30th I returned to Kansas and crossed the Missouri at Atchison. I spoke to no one in town save two merchants of the place, with whom I had business transactions since my first arrival in the territory. Having remained only a few minutes, I went to my buggy to resume my journey, when I was assaulted by Robert S. Kelly, junior editor of the *Squatter Sovereign*, and others, was dragged into a grocery, and there surrounded by a company of South Carolinians, who are reported to have been sent out by a Southern Emigrant Aid Society.

"In this last mob, I noticed only two were citizens of Atchison or engaged in the former mob.

"It is reported that these emigrants from the Palmetto State do not seek out a claim and make for themselves a home; neither do they enter into any legitimate business. They very expressively describe themselves as having 'come out to see Kansas through.'

"They yelled, 'Kill him! kill him! Hang the d——d abolitionist!'

"One of their number bustled up to me and demanded,

"'Have you a revolver?'

"I replied, 'No.'

"He handed me a pistol, saying, 'There, take that, and stand off ten steps, and, G—d d——n you, I will blow you through in an instant!'

"I replied, 'I have no use for your weapon.'

"I afterward heard them congratulating themselves, in reference to this, that they had been honorable with me. The fellow was furious; but his companions dissuaded him from shooting me, saying they were going to hang me.

"If I can picture to myself the look of a Cuban bloodhound, just ready with open jaws to seize a panting slave in a Florida swamp, then I imagine we have a correct daguerreotype of the expression worn by these emigrant representatives of the manly sentiment, high-toned courage, and magnanimous feelings, of the South Carolina chivalry, when first they scented, in their own imagination, the blood of a live 'abolitionist.'

"'Hang him!' they yelled, 'hang him! hang the d——d abolitionist!'

"They pinioned my arms behind me, obtained a rope, but were interrupted by the entrance of a stranger, a gentleman from Missouri, since ascertained to be General Tut, a lawyer of Buchanan County. He said,

"'My friends, hear me. I am an old man, and it is right you should hear me. I was born in Virginia, and have lived many years in Missouri. I am a slaveholder, and desire Kansas to be made a slave state, if it can be done by honorable means. But you will destroy the cause you are seeking to build up. You have taken this man, who was peaceably passing through your streets and along the highway, doing no person any harm. We profess to be law and order men, and should be the last to commit violence. If this man has violated the law, let him be punished according to law; but for the sake of Missouri, for the sake of Kansas, for the sake of the pro-slavery cause, do not act in this way.'

"They dragged me into another grocery, and appointed a moderator. Kelly told his story.

"I rose to my feet, and calmly and in respectful language began to tell mine. I was repeatedly jerked to my seat, and so roughly handled that I was compelled to desist.

"My friend from Missouri again earnestly besought them to set me at liberty.

"Kelly turned short on him and said, 'Do you belong to Kansas?'

"He replied, 'No; but I expect to live here in Atchison next fall; and in this matter the interests of Missouri and Kansas are identical.'

"Mr. Lamb, a lawyer in Atchison, and Mr. Dickson, a merchant of the same place, both pro-slavery men, also united with Gen. Tut in pleading that I might be set at liberty.

"While these gentlemen were thus speaking, I heard my keepers mutter, 'D——n you, if you don't hush up, we'll tar and feather you!'

"When Kelly saw how matters stood, he came forward and said, 'He did not take Butler to have him hanged, only tarred and feathered.' Yet in the other grocery they had said to the mob that 'they should do as they pleased!' He dared not take the responsibility of taking my life; but when these unfortunate men, whose one-idea-ism on the subject of slavery and Southern rights has become insanity, when these irresponsible South Carolinians, sent out to be bull-dogs and blood-hounds for Atchison and Stringfellow — when they could be used as tools to take my life, he was ready to do it.

"Our gunpowder moderator cut the discussion short by saying, 'It is moved that Butler be tarred and feathered, and receive thirty-nine lashes.'

"A majority said 'Ay,' though a number of voices said 'No.' The moderator said, 'The affirmative has it.'

"There was a good deal of whispering about the house. I saw dark, ominous, and threatening looks in the crowd.

"The moderator again came forward, and in an altered voice said,

"'It is moved that the last part of the sentence be rescinded!'

"It was rescinded.

"I was given into the hands of my South Carolina overseers to be tarred and feathered. They muttered and growled at this issue of the matter. 'Bey ——,' said they, 'if we had known it would have come out in this way, we would have let —— —— shoot Butler at the first. He would have done it quicker than a flash.'

"One little sharp-visaged, dark-featured, black-eyed South Carolinian, as smart as a cricket, who seemed to be the leader of the gang, was particularly displeased.

"'D——n you,' said he, 'if I came all the way from South Carolina, and spent so much money, to do things up in such milk-and-water style as this!'

"They stripped me naked to the waist, covered my body with tar, and then, for the want of feathers, applied cotton-wool. Having appointed a committee of three to certainly hang me the next time I should come to Atchison, they tossed my clothes into my buggy, put me therein, accompanied me to the suburbs of the town, and sent me naked out upon the prairie.

"I adjusted my attire about me as best I could, and hastened to rejoin my wife and two little ones, on the banks of the Stranger Creek. It was rather a sorrowful meeting after so long a parting. Still, we were very thankful that, under the blessing of a good Providence, it had fared no worse with us all.

"The first mob that sent me down the Missouri river on a raft — always excepting Robert S. Kelly — were courteous gentlemen compared with this last one. When I was towed out into the middle of the stream, I do not remember to have heard a word spoken by the men on shore. This last mob, when they left me on the border of the town, shrieked and yelled like a pack of New Zealand cannibals. The first mob did not attempt to abridge my right of speech. In reply to all the hard and bitter things they said against me they patiently heard me to the end. But these men, who have come to introduce into Kansas that order of things that now exists in South Carolina, savagely gagged me into silence by rapping my face, choking me, pulling my beard, jerking me violently to my seat, and exclaiming, 'D——n you, hold your tongue!' All this was done while my arms were pinioned behind me.

"Many will ask now, as they have asked already, what is the true and proper cause of all these troubles which I have had in Atchison. 'The head and front of my offending hath this extent, no more': I had spoken among my neighbors favorably for making Kansas a free state, and said in the office of the *Squatter Sovereign*, I am a free-soiler, and intend to vote for Kansas to be a free state. It is true that Kelly, by an after-thought, has added two new counts to his bill of indictment against me. The first is that I went to the town of Atchison last August, talking abolitionism. I have not the honor of being an abolitionist. And, second, that I spoke, somehow or other, improperly in the presence of slaves. All this is not only utterly false, but the charges are ex-post facts; for not a word was said of this the day they put me on the raft."

Jones recovered. To recover thus, after being "shot in the spine," as reported, was a feat of medical and surgical skill almost miraculous, and which should immortalize Dr. Stringfellow, if he were not already sufficiently celebrated. The Missouri papers could not afford to let him recover, however, and the "tributes to his memory" were numerous and affecting. The following I clipped from a border-ruffian sheet, and it will exhibit the amount of "law and order" capital that was to be made out of this event:

"Kansas is once more in commotion. The traitors of Lawrence have again set the laws of the territory at defiance, and this time have added murder to their crime. Sheriff Jones, of Douglass County, than whom a braver man never lived, has been murdered while in the performance of his official duties — shot down by the thieving paupers of the North, who are shipped to Kansas to infringe upon the rights of Southern settlers, murder them when opportunity offers, steal their property, and, if possible, to raise a storm that will cease only with the Union itself.

"The excitement in this city, during the past week, has been very great. Rumors of various kinds have reached us, and although we believed a difficulty had occurred, we were not prepared to hear of such lamentable news, — the death of the patriot Jones. His death must be avenged, his murder shall be avenged, if at the sacrifice of every abolitionist in the territory. If the pro-slavery party will quietly sit still and see our friends, one by one, murdered by these assassins, without raising their arms to protect them, we much mistake their character. Will they again allow a Northern governor to cheat them out of their just revenge? We answer emphatically, no! If the governor of this territory and the administration at Washington any longer attempt to force us to assume the position of outlaws before we can have justice done us, the sooner such a contingency arises the better. We are now in favor of levelling Lawrence, and chastising the traitors there congregated, should it result in the total destruction of the Union. If we are to have war, let it come now! While the memory of our murdered friends, Clarke and Jones, is fresh in our memories, we can coolly and determinedly enter into the contest, let it result as it may. We do not approve of the course of the governor, in calling out the United States troops to enforce the laws of the territory. It looks to us as a virtual admission that the law and order party of Kansas are not strong enough within themselves to enforce the law."

CHAPTER XX.

MARSHAL DONALDSON DECLARES WAR.

Up to the spring of 1856 Missouri had maintained the struggle for the conquest of Kansas alone. Only a few straggling Southern adventurers had come to her aid. As an evidence, I quote from the circular of the branch of the slavery-extension party located in Lafayette County, Mo.:

"The western counties of Missouri have for the last two years been heavily taxed, both in money and time, in fighting the battles of the South. Lafayette County alone has expended upwards of one hundred thousand dollars in money, and as much in time. Up to this time the border counties of Missouri have upheld and maintained the rights and interests of the South in this struggle, unassisted, and not unsuccessfully. But the abolitionists, staking their all upon the Kansas issue, and hesitating at no means, fair or foul, are moving heaven and earth to render that beautiful territory a *free state*."

Early in the spring of 1856 President Pierce came forward still more actively in the cause of Missouri, and issued his proclamation, the effect of which would be to sustain their violent conquests by the federal troops. Pierce, by his territorial appointments, had already done a great deal for this "holy alliance," but no more than he had contracted to do; for Senator Atchison stated, in the company of several persons, on board a boat on the Missouri river, that "*President Pierce had done no more than he had a right to do, for he had given pledges before he received his nomination at Baltimore, that he would give all his influence towards making Kansas a slave state.*" This pledge the President has faithfully kept. Missouri had several other allies, even in the free states, prior to this time; but their valuable assistance the Lafayette circular shabbily ignores.

In the spring of 1856 Missouri received a fresh supply of active allies. Col. Buford, a Southern adventurer from Alabama, brought up the Missouri river, in April, a regiment of young men, from Alabama, and Carolina, and Georgia. These adventurers were armed, and came in military companies. They came for the avowed purpose of making Kansas a slave state by violence, if necessary, and returning after this had been accomplished. Many of them were poor young men, but well connected; dependent members of the decaying Southern aristocracy,—a numerous class, who can be dispensed with by the South unless in case of servile war. But the larger portion of these carpet-bag adventurers were reckless characters, from the vilest purlieus of society; men who had been robbers and gambling loafers, and whose lawless character well suited them for the task they were to perform. As an illustration, these gentry robbed Buford himself of a considerable sum of money while coming up the river; and they got into disgrace, even amongst the Missourians they were called to aid, by their depredations.

Shortly after their arrival in Kansas city, Mo., they were drawn up in military array, in a sort of review. Here speeches were delivered about their mission to conquer Kansas for slavery, and Buford, in order to give his expedition a specious appearance at the East, made a prayer *to them*, which was an odd mixture of hypocrisy and blasphemy. These men were there called to sign a pledge and give an oath that they would not leave Kansas until it was made a slave state; that they would be ready to fight for "Southern rights" when called upon, and that they should never vote anything but the pro-slavery ticket, and should be subject to the direction of their leaders, etc. There was also a business contract between them, the terms of which, as promulgated at Kansas city, gave great dissatisfaction, the young adventurers declaring them different and less favorable than the promises by which they had been lured from their homes. The promise extorted from them, of voting the pro-slavery ticket, may seem unnecessary; but there was a considerable number of the poorer classes, who had been to the territory from slave states, formerly, who had become free-state men.

It must not be supposed that all of this regiment were vicious characters. Some amiable and high-minded young men came with them; but most of those deserted and went back, disgusted with their associates, and sick of the duties entailed on them by the pro-slavery conquest. Some of those who remained were what would claim to be gentlemen at home, but either deeply identified with the slave-property interests, or prejudiced in favor of the institution to such an extent that they were prepared to go any length to accomplish their object.

For some time these young Southerners were quartered at different points in Missouri near the territorial frontier. Here they were sustained partly by means sent to them from the South, and partly by contributions from the people of Missouri. As a great many of the merchants and business men in western Missouri had no interest in the system of slavery, and at heart disapproved of this course of lawless violence, they failed to subscribe their quota, when a tax was levied in Westport, and other western Missouri towns, for the purpose of sustaining the Kansas war.

As Sheriff Jones was unable to attend to his duties, his deputy, Sam Salters, undertook the arduous duties devolving, in the progress of "law and order," on the Sheriff of Douglas County. With a party of dragoons at his heels, he rode backwards and forwards over the county, making, or trying to make, or pretending he wished to make, arrests. One lady ordered him not to come into her house, and threw some scalding water on him when he tried to do so. Some of the men whom he declared that he wished to arrest, had to leave their homes, and sleep in thickets and in prairies, to avoid this legal persecution. Armed bands of the Southerners now began to come into the territory, and not only Salters but all of the territorial officials were soon in full communion with them. As citizens were often molested and stopped by these persons, the following is a pass given by this redoubtable Sam Salters to a law and order man, who found it necessary to travel:

"*Let this man pass i no him* two be a *Law* and abidin Sittisen. (Signed), SAMUEL SALTERS,

"*depy sherf.*"

As will be seen, the deputy sheriff is not liable to any of the anathemas pronounced against the "scribes." Like Jones, he was a man of powerful and robust frame, though much coarser and more vulgar. Jones is not at all remarkable for his scholastic attainments. Both of these men were addicted to excessive drinking; they gambled, and in other respects were far from exemplary.

Amongst the Southerners who came into the territory at the time of which I write, was a Georgian named Fain. This man was appointed by U. S. Marshal Donaldson as one of his deputies. This man, Fain, in spite of the noise he has made in the world, is, so far as education or talent is concerned, a very insignificant character; an apt illustration of the statement once made by a letter-writer in the West, who wished his friends to emigrate thither, "Mighty mean men get in office out here." Donaldson himself, although a federal appointee, is a comparatively illiterate and uninformed man, and, judging from the manner of acting in his official capacity, totally devoid of the legal knowledge necessary to dignify his office. He is an Illinoisian. He is a man past middle age, of coarse, unintellectual face, and, from his looks, ought never to have held a station above that of town constable; he would not have been too well qualified for that.

The committee were in session at the town of Tecumseh, and the First District Court of the United States for Kansas Territory was in session (being the adjourned April term), in the early part of May, 1856. A rumor prevailed that indictments for usurping office, and other state crimes, were being drawn up by the grand jury. Judge Lecompte, at the opening of the court, delivered a most remarkable charge to the grand jury, in which he specified that they should indict those persons for certain offences. He urged the grand jury to do so, and not to be deterred by the fear that the laws of the territory or the process under such circumstances would not be executed; assuring them that *there would* be force to execute them. He also told them they must not hesitate to indict these persons because they were *sincere* in their opinions, and cited the early witchcraft history of Massachusetts, to prove the impropriety of being regulated by sincerity. The following extract from the report of his charge contains its most striking feature, and shows to what uses the federal courts and officers in the territory were put:

"GENTLEMEN: You are assembled to consider whatever infringements of law may come under your notice, and bring in bills as your judgment dictates against those whom you may find to have been guilty of such infringement. Your attention will naturally be turned toward an unlawful, and before unheard-of organization, that has been formed in our midst, for the purpose of resisting the laws of the United States. The exciting state of affairs makes it important that you should deliberate calmly, and above all have respect to the oaths that you have taken, and without fear or favor of any party of men, whether high or low, to mete to all the justice which is their due. You will take into consideration the cases of men who are dubbed governors, men who are dubbed lieutenant-governors, men who are dubbed secretaries and treasurers, and men who are dubbed all the various other *dubbs* with which this territory is filling (and there *are* such men), and will find bills in accordance with the following instructions." [I give below his exact words.] "This territory was organized by an act of Congress, and so far its authority is from the United States. It has a Legislature elected in pursuance of that organic act. This Legislature, being an instrument of Congress, by which it governs the territory, has passed laws; these laws, therefore, are of United States authority and making" [that is, the United States makes laws by *proxy*, employing the borderers of Missouri to make the laws, inasmuch as being away out West it is inconvenient for her to come herself. This is the meaning that I deduce from the judge's opinion], "and all that resist these laws resist the power and authority of the United States, and are, therefore, guilty of high treason. Now, gentlemen, if you find that any persons *have* resisted these laws, then must you, under your oaths, find bills against such persons for high treason. If you find that no such resistance has been made, but that combinations have been formed for the purpose of resisting them, and individuals of influence and notoriety have been aiding and abetting in such combinations, then must you still find bills for constructive treason, as the courts have decided that to constitute treason the blow need not be struck, but only the *intention* be made evident."

Besides these recommendations to indict the persons elected to future state offices under the state movement, the grand jury in question, under the instructions of Judge Lecompte, made the following presentment. It is proper to add that this step was not taken until a force of Missourians and the Buford regiment were around Lawrence, as a marshal's posse, threatening to destroy it:

"The grand jury, sitting for the adjourned term of the First District Court in and for the County of Douglas, in the Territory of Kansas, beg leave to report to the honorable Court that, from evidence laid before them showing that the newspaper known as *The Herald of Freedom*, published at the town of Lawrence, has from time to time issued publications of the most inflammatory and seditious character, denying the legality of the *territorial authorities*, addressing and commanding forcible resistance to the same, demoralizing the popular mind, and rendering life and property unsafe, even to the extent of advising assassination as a last resort;

"Also, that the paper known as *The Kansas Free State* has been similarly engaged, and has recently reported the resolutions of a public meeting in Johnson County, in this territory, in which resistance to the *territorial laws* even unto blood has been agreed upon; and that we respectfully recommend their abatement as a nuisance. Also, that we are satisfied that the building known as the 'Free-State Hotel' in Lawrence has been constructed with the view to military occupation and defence, regularly parapeted and portholed for the use of cannon and small arms, and could only have been designed as a stronghold of resistance to law, thereby endangering the public safety, and encouraging rebellion and sedition in this country; and respectfully recommend that steps be taken whereby this nuisance may be removed.

"OWEN C. STEWART, *Foreman*."

It was at this stage of affairs that an attempt was made against the person of Gov. Reeder, and, through him, against the commission of Congress. Gov. Reeder had been in attendance at Washington with his certificate of votes received, and claiming his seat as delegate from Kansas Territory. His claim, though not decided on, had been considered, and when the special commission was sent out to investigate matters Reeder was notified to attend its sittings as a party to that investigation.

I need not show here that Reeder was intensely hated by the propaganda. His refusal to aid them in their nefarious schemes, and his efforts in behalf of the people of Kansas, had made him a formidable enemy. Threats of assassinating him were current, and the border ruffians, who had already given frightful evidences of their sincerity, declared that he should never leave Kansas alive. Gov. Reeder had been indefatigable in his efforts before the committee, and his knowledge of the territory made him eminently useful to its investigations.

On the morning of the 7th of May Mr. Fain presented a paper to Gov. Reeder at the hotel at Tecumseh. It purported, on part explanation of Fain, to be a subpœna requiring the presence of Reeder at Lecompton to testify before the grand jury. Fain claimed to be deputy marshal. I was conversing with Gov. Reeder when the paper in question was presented, and can state distinctly what passed. Reeder examined the paper, and asked some explanations regarding it from Fain. He then said that he was engaged with the congressional committee on its citation, and that his presence was all-important (as it was). He said that his residence in Douglas County had been too recent and temporary for him to be of any service to the jury in matters of which they had cognizance. The governor added that the paper in question purporting to be a subpœna was altogether irregular, and did not show its authority on its face. He folded it up, and put it in his pocket, telling Mr. Fain that if he could have spared the time he would have complied in any case, waiving the question of privilege and the informalities in the service; but he was persuaded he could be of no possible service to the grand jury, and the interests at stake before the committee were too important to be neglected.

Deputy Fain, who seemed to anticipate such an answer, left the room and returned to Lecompton.

Next day, according to previous notice and arrangement, the committee of investigation was in Lawrence, and engaged in their duties. In the afternoon Deputy Fain, accompanied by several other persons, came into the room, and presented a paper to Reeder, which was a writ for his arrest for contempt of court.

Gov. Reeder begged the indulgence of the other gentlemen of the committee for a moment to a private matter, when he stated to them the affair relative to the subpœna, and claimed his right of exemption from such arrest under the constitution, both as contestant delegate and as cited before this committee of investigation.

The committee, after a short consultation, stated that they had nothing to decide, as they were not a court for the adjudication of such a matter. As individuals the members of the committee expressed their opinion. Mr. Howard, chairman of the committee, said he had no doubt but that Reeder was entitled to his privilege, but that was a point for him to maintain himself. Mr. Howard added that he supposed that this was not an attempt to insult or interrupt the commission. He scarcely thought it could be so. If it was, or the commission was thus to be molested, it had power to call to its aid a sufficient force, and send the party thus disturbing them to Washington under such charge.

Mr. Sherman also took the same position, reading from the constitution, and in a clear and lucid manner explaining the rights of the respective parties.

Mr. Oliver dissented from this opinion. He thought the court in question had a right to arrest Reeder.

Gov. Reeder then addressed Fain in a firm, but calm and steady voice. He was sitting in the chair he occupied at the table of the commission where he had been when Fain entered. He told Fain that he claimed his privilege of exemption for several reasons. His presence was important to the committee. He had reason to believe that the object was merely to take him from the committee, so as to interfere with its labors. He said he had also reason to believe he was not personally safe in Lecompton, as he had received letters containing intimations of assassination. For these and other reasons Reeder told Deputy Fain that he would not go with him; that he did not recognize his right to arrest him; if he did so it must be at his peril; and that in case of loss he would have no cause of action; or of bodily injury, no legal remedy.

Having delivered himself thus, Fain, who was merely the tool of others, and who was altogether incapable of deporting himself in such position with proper dignity, shook his head in a half-persuasive half-threatening manner, and in a weak, childish voice said:

"You had better go — you had better go."

"O," rejoined Reeder coolly, "perhaps I better *had.*" Fain and his companions immediately left the room.

There were about thirty persons in the apartment at the time of this occurrence. It was a small room, some sixteen by eighteen feet. When Reeder gave his decision five or six of the persons present expressed their approbation; but they were immediately called to order by the sergeant-at-arms.

Simple as this matter might appear, and trivial as a cause of public disturbance, it led the way to important occurrences, and had been fully calculated by those who now wished to attack the people of Lawrence and Kansas Territory.

Fain, as I have stated, was a Georgian; and, instead of returning directly to Lecompton to report himself to his superiors, he went down to Franklin, where at that time a band of Southerners, under Capt. Moon, were stationed. There the alarm was given, and soon scouts were sent to Missouri to gather in the Southerners still stationed there.

It was about this time that a great misfortune for the territory occurred. In spite of the past experience, many men in Lawrence and around it persisted in believing that, if all causes of offence were removed, those who menaced the place would not proceed to extremities against it. It was the intention of the free-state men that they should not, if possible, be forced into hostilities until the Legislature met in July. It was known that the territory was not sufficiently prepared for hostilities. Arms and ammunition were lacking, and the men were not drilled.

Before the difficulties above narrated had occurred, it had been determined that Governor Robinson should go to the North and East, and endeavor to secure what was needed to meet the impending struggle. From the information that reached the territory through reliable channels, it was known that the governors and officers of many of the Southern States had given their pledge to the Missourians, who were leading the contest, that they would sustain them in it, come what might. Under such circumstances, and with the prospect of a bloody civil war, Charles Robinson, as governor of the new state, could not but feel the responsibility of exposing those he had thus been called on to protect, to such a hazard, without having assurances that Kansas would be sustained in case of such a death-struggle. The most important part of his mission from Kansas was to get pledges, from those whose influence would give their pledges weight, that Kansas, if she had the nerve to meet the crisis and defy her conquerors, should not be left to perish alone, if the South sent forces into the territory to crush her.

Startling though all these aspects of the case might be, they were its true aspects, and the dangers feared would in all human probability be encountered. To provide against them, without anticipating them, — to array the North against the South, (only to have some guarantee of support in case the South did take the field), — was far too important a consideration to be neglected.

When the threatened disturbance, arising from the attempted arrest of Reeder, occurred, Governor Robinson had just been on the point of starting, so as to transact the business required, and return before July. When the threats of the deputy marshal made the prospect of a fight probable, Robinson declined to go. In this situation his friends urged him to leave, as his mission was important, and it was not deemed likely that any difficulty would grow out of the present affair that could not be averted. Besides the members of the committee of Congress urged him to take with him a part of the testimony. There had been a conspiracy to destroy this, as the border ruffians were determined that it should never leave the territory. Mrs. Sherman, who had accompanied her husband to Kansas, was to have returned in company of Mrs. Robinson, and taken a duplicate of the testimony with her; but, by indisposition, Mrs. Sherman was prevented from leaving, and Mrs. Robinson had the package entrusted to her charge, as she was to accompany her husband.

Thus it was that Governor Robinson was persuaded to leave Kansas at that moment; and yet it was very reluctantly on his part. He did not think the threatened difficulty was one which could not be averted, but he felt keenly at leaving with such a possibility.

But he was not permitted to depart. He had travelled without concealment or disguise, as people have a right to travel on a great national thoroughfare. When at Lexington, Mo., he was violently and illegally seized by a mob of Missourians. Mrs. Robinson travelled with him, and the following is her account of the occurrence, penned shortly after:

"ST. LOUIS, *Tuesday, May* 12, 1856.

"As Governor Robinson and myself were passing down the Missouri river, on our way to St. Louis, and further East, upon affairs of business, we were taken off the boat at Lexington, at the instigation of lawless men, they pretending that Governor Robinson was fleeing from an indictment. He assured the gentlemen, some eight or ten in number, who gathered about our state-room door, opening upon the guard, that such was not the case; that he had heard of no indictment; that his whereabouts, whether in Lawrence or elsewhere, were at all times known; that if the marshal had desired to serve such a process upon him he could have easily done so, and he should have suffered no resistance. He told them also that he would never think to escape for an indictment for any political offence; and, had he been doing so, of all places he would have avoided the Missouri river and Lexington. Upon the statement of a gentleman, that the delay in consenting to leave the boat, as the crowd had found the bar, and were drinking freely, only added to Governor Robinson's danger of personal violence, he said, 'Let me see the crowd, and I can shortly convince them that I am not running from an arrest; then

I can continue on my journey.' To which the reply was given to the effect that he would be in immediate danger of mob violence. It was also insisted upon, as a means of safety, that we pass out on the guard, in leaving the boat, while the exasperated people, a 'cabin full' of them, should be unaware of our departure. A carriage was in readiness to take us to the town. We were quartered in the house of a Mr. Sawyer, who kindly offered his house as a place of safety, the night-guard about the house alone reminding us of the fact that Governor Robinson was a prisoner. I omitted to mention, in its proper place, that the gentlemen upon first coming to the state-room said they had been talking to the crowd for fifteen minutes, trying to persuade them to leave the boat, but that none would be satisfied unless he remained in Lexington until they could learn whether an indictment was out against him; while others cried, 'Drag him out.' To Governor Robinson's suggestion that, if he was running away from an arrest, he could see no grounds for another state to interfere, one of the gentleman replied, 'He did not wish to get into an argument,' etc. Governor Robinson is retained a prisoner, while I am allowed to pass on.

"I make this statement that the true state of the case may be known. SARA T. D. ROBINSON."

Mrs. Robinson, while she is a quiet and unassuming lady, is as resolute as she is high-minded and intelligent. She went on with the testimony, and attended to the other business of her husband as far as she could, and then hurried back to rejoin him in captivity.

Shortly after Governor Robinson left Lawrence, ex-Governor Reeder was also induced to leave. I have little doubt but he was urged to do so by the members of the committee. They regarded him as the stumbling-block, and while this was merely an apology for attack, the members of the commission wished nothing to occur that would put a stop to their important investigation. Reeder left in disguise, and, after being concealed for two weeks in the Kansas City Hotel, succeeded in making his escape down the river as a deck hand on board the boat. His private secretary, Mr. Lowry, accompanied him.

Shortly after, the Commission of Congress adjourned from Lawrence to Leavenworth. On account of the aspect of affairs, which every day grew more threatening, several citizens had requested of them to stay and use their influence to defend the place. Had the military force been placed at their disposal, as the resolution of the House of Congress designed, they would probably have done so. But the executive of the general government had intentionally refused to afford this protection to the committee. It was therefore that the committee left Lawrence while the danger impended.

On the 11th of May, Donaldson, U. S. Marshal, issued the following singular proclamation, which was soon circulated in all the pro-slavery neighborhoods, and in Missouri. No copies of it were sent by the marshal to Lawrence, or to any free-state town or neighborhood, and, as a consequence, but few of them were circulated in the territory.

"PROCLAMATION.

"To the People of Kansas Territory:

"Whereas, certain judicial writs of arrest have been directed to me by the First District Court of the United States, etc., to be executed within the County of Douglas, and whereas an attempt to execute them by the United States Deputy Marshal was evidently resisted by a large number of the citizens of Lawrence, and as there is every reason to believe that any attempt to execute these writs will be resisted by a large body of armed men; now, therefore, the law-abiding citizens of the territory are commanded to be and appear at Lecompton, as soon as practicable, and in numbers sufficient for the execution of the law.

"Given under my hand this 11th day of May, 1856.

"J. B. Donaldson,

"*United States Marshal for Kansas Territory.*"

"P. S. No liability for expenses will be incurred by the United States until its consent is obtained.

"J. B. D., U. S. M."

Prior to the issue of this proclamation, the Southern regiment, who doubtless anticipated it, had come up in armed bands into the territory, and were committing depredations, and stopping and molesting people, and made threats that they were going to destroy Lawrence. On this account, the following letter was called out:

"LAWRENCE CITY, *May* 11*th*, 1856.

"TO HIS EXCELLENCY, WILSON SHANNON, GOVERNOR OF KANSAS TERRITORY —

"DEAR SIR: The undersigned are charged with the duty of communicating to your Excellency the following preamble and resolution, adopted at a public meeting of the citizens of this place at seven o'clock last evening, viz.:

"'Whereas, we have the most reliable information from various parts of the territory, and the adjoining State of Missouri, of the organization of guerilla bands, who threaten the destruction of our town and its citizens; therefore,

"'*Resolved*, That Messrs. Topliff, Hutchinson and Roberts, constitute a committee to inform his Excellency of these facts, and to call upon him, in the name of the people of Lawrence, for protection against such bands, by the United States troops at his disposal.'

"All of which is very respectfully submitted, etc.

"C. W. TOPLIFF,
"W. Y. ROBERTS,
"JOHN HUTCHINSON."

On receiving this letter Governor Shannon held a consultation with the pro-slavery leaders at Lecompton. This council was not confined to the federal officers, although all of these were pro-slavery over the eyes. Buford and Colonel Titus, the one a recently-imported Alabamian, and the other from Florida, and several others of the avowed conquerors of Kansas, were admitted into that executive conclave. The following ambiguous, but discreditable letter was the product:

24

"EXECUTIVE OFFICE, *May* 12, 1856.
LECOMPTON, K. T.

"GENTLEMEN: Your note of the eleventh inst. is received, and, in reply, I have to state that there is no force around or approaching Lawrence, except the legally constituted posse of the United States Marshal and Sheriff of Douglas County, each of whom, I am informed, have a number of writs in their hands for execution against persons now in Lawrence. I shall in no way interfere with either of these officers in the discharge of their official duties.

"If the citizens of Lawrence submit themselves to the territorial laws, and aid and assist the Marshal and Sheriff in the execution of processes in their hands, as all good citizens are bound to do when called on, they, or all such will entitle themselves to the protection of the law. But so long as they keep up a military or armed organization to resist the territorial laws and the officers charged with their execution, I shall not interpose to save them from the legitimate consequences of their illegal acts.

"I have the honor to be yours, with great respect,

"WILSON SHANNON.

"Messrs. C. W. TOPLIFF, JOHN HUTCHINSON, W. Y. ROBERTS."

This harsh and partisan letter from the governor, under such circumstances, could not be regarded as anything short of a declaration of war.

As the citizens of Lawrence were anxious to avert troubles, if possible, a meeting was held, and the following action taken:

"Whereas, by a proclamation to the people of Kansas Territory, by J. B. Donaldson, United States Marshal for said territory, issued on the 11th day of May, 1856, it is alleged that 'Certain judicial writs of arrest have been directed to him by the First District Court of the United States, etc., to be executed within the County of Douglas, and that an attempt to execute them by the United States Deputy Marshal was violently resisted by a large number of the citizens of Lawrence, and that there is every reason to believe that any attempt to execute said writs will be resisted by a large body of armed men;' therefore,

"*Resolved*, By this public meeting of the citizens of Lawrence, held this thirteenth day of May, 1856, that the allegations and charges against us, contained in the aforesaid proclamation, are wholly untrue in fact, and the conclusion which is drawn from them. The aforesaid deputy marshal was resisted in no manner whatever, nor by any person whatever, in the execution of said writs, except by him whose arrest the said deputy marshal was seeking to make. And that we now, as we have done heretofore, declare our willingness and determination, without resistance, to acquiesce in the service upon us of any judicial writs against us by the United States Marshal for Kansas Territory, and will furnish him with a *posse* for that purpose, if so requested; but that we are ready to resist, if need be, unto death, the ravages and desolation of an invading mob.

"J. A. WAKEFIELD, *President*."

These resolutions were forwarded to the marshal and to Governor Shannon.

As I have said, the marshal never sent a copy of his proclamation to Lawrence. The copy that reached Lawrence was sent to me from Lecompton by one of my agents, and was received a few hours after it was issued. I carried it into the chamber of the Committee of Safety, which held a meeting that night. Its meetings were private. Several proposals were made, but the majority were unwilling to do anything. Lieutenant-Governor Roberts and Colonel Holiday were opposed to any defence being made. Holiday urged that it was a busy season, and the farmers could not be taken from their farms to sustain another siege at that season without great loss. Others urged that the merchants and business men had advanced provisions, stores, and goods, during the Wakarusa war, and had got pay only for a small part of it, and could not advance anything more to defend the place.

Dietzler and several other members of the committee were in favor of defending the place against the marshal's posse. The discussion was vague, pointless, and unsatisfactory. There was no one to take the lead. One proposal was that efforts be made to see that three or four hundred men, armed only with pistols and other side-arms, should go to Lecompton, and offer themselves to Donaldson as his "posse," in obedience to the proclamation, and demand from the governor a share of the public arms then at Lecompton.

The committee determined that matters should go on as they were. Roberts declared that he did not mean to go out of the territory, but should stay and be arrested.

I mention these things because they show reasons why the impending stroke was permitted. Several of those who had advocated warlike measures left in disgust. The people, who, as a general thing, wanted the town to be defended, dispensed with the old committee, and elected a new one. The following are their names, composed in part of the first: William Y. Roberts, G. W. Dietzler, Lyman Allen, John A. Perry, C. W. Babcock, S. B. Prentiss, A. H. Mallory, Joel Grover. A few days after its selection, Mr. S. C. Pomeroy arrived from the East, where he had been on the business of the Emigrant Aid Society, and was admitted as a member.

A change of rulers does not always bring a change of policy; this second committee was more pacific than the first, although selected by the people with the expectation that resistance might be made. In fact it was the federal authority employed that acted as a dead weight on them.

Whether it was owing to the proclamation, or preconceived arrangement, Marshal Donaldson's posse grew with frightful rapidity. The whole country was soon in a state of warlike confusion that is, as warlike as a country can be when the demonstrations are all on one side. As the molestation of travellers was frequen another meeting was held, of which Dietzler was chairman, an J. H. Green secretary. This meeting passed resolutions simila to those adopted at the first meeting. These resolutions wer sent to Lecompton with the following letter, which was signed b Robert Morrow, Lyman Allen, and Jno. Hutchinson:

"LAWRENCE, *May* 14, 1856.

"J. B. DONALDSON, U. S. MARSHAL FOR K. T.—

"DEAR SIR: We have seen a proclamation issued by yoursel dated 11th May, inst., and also have reliable information th morning that large bodies of armed men, in pursuance of your proclamation, have assembled in the vicinity of Lawrence. That there may be no misunderstanding, we ask, respectfully, that we be reliably informed what are the demands against us. We desire to state, most truthfully and earnestly, that no opposition whatever will now, or at any future time, be offered to the execution of any legal process by yourself, or any person acting for you. We also pledge ourselves to assist you, if called upon, in the execution of any legal process.

"We declare ourselves to be order-loving and law-abiding citizens; and only await an opportunity to testify our fidelity to the laws of the country, the constitution, and the Union.

"We are informed, also, that those men collecting about Lawrence openly declare that it is their intention to destroy the town and drive off the citizens. Of course we do not believe you give any countenance to such threats; but, in view of the excited state of the public mind, we ask protection of the constituted authorities of the government, declaring ourselves in readiness to coöperate with them for the maintenance of the peace, order, and quiet, of the community in which we live."

To this Marshal Donaldson sent the following reply, in which an officer, under circumstances of the utmost importance, descends to sneering insults and irony, and treats the people, he should have protected, as enemies:

"Office of the United States Marshal,
Lecompton, K. T., *May* 15, 1856.

"Messrs. G. W. Dietzler and J. H. Green, Lawrence, K. T.—

"On yesterday I received a communication addressed to me, signed by one of you as president, and the other as secretary, purporting to have been adopted by a meeting of the citizens of Lawrence, held on yesterday morning. After speaking of a proclamation issued by myself, you state, 'that there may be no misunderstanding, we beg leave to ask, respectfully, that we may be reliably informed what are the demands against us? We desire most truthfully and earnestly to declare that no opposition whatever will now, or at any future time, be offered to the execution of any legal process by yourself, or any person acting for you. We also pledge ourselves to assist you, if called upon, in the execution of any legal process,' etc.

"From your professed ignorance of the demands against you, I must conclude that you are *strangers*, not *citizens*, of Lawrence, or of recent date, or been absent for some time; more particularly when an attempt was made by my deputy to execute the process of the First District Court of the United States for Kansas Territory against ex-Governor Reeder, when he made a speech in the room and presence of the Congressional Committee, and denied the authority and power of said court, and threatened the life of said deputy if he attempted to execute said process; which speech and defiant threats were loudly applauded by some one or two of the citizens of Lawrence, who had assembled at the room on learning the business of the marshal, and made such hostile demonstrations that the deputy thought he and his small posse would endanger their lives in executing said process.

"Your declaration, that you 'will truthfully and earnestly offer no opposition now, nor at any future time, to the execution of any legal process,' etc., is, indeed, difficult to understand. May I ask, gentlemen, what has produced this wonderful change in the minds of the people of Lawrence? Have their eyes been suddenly opened so that they are now able to see that there are laws in force in Kansas Territory that should be obeyed? Or is it that just now those for whom I have writs have sought refuge elsewhere? Or it may possibly be that you, now, as heretofore, expect to screen yourselves behind the word 'legal,' so significantly used by you. How am I to rely on your pledges, when I am well aware that the whole population is armed and drilled, and the whole town fortified; when, too, I recollect the meetings and resolutions adopted in Lawrence, and elsewhere in the territory, openly defying the law and the officers thereof, and threatening to resist the same to a bloody issue, and recently verified in the attempted assassination of Sheriff Jones while in the discharge of his official duties in Lawrence? Are you strangers to all these things? Surely you must be strangers in Lawrence! If no outrages have been committed by the outlaws in Lawrence against the laws of the land, they need not fear any posse of mine. But I must take the liberty of executing all processes in my hands, as the United States Marshal, in my own time and manner, and shall only use such power as is authorized by law. You say you call upon the constituted authorities of the government for protection. This, indeed, sounds strange from a large body of men armed with Sharpe's rifles, and other implements of war, bound together by oaths and pledges, to resist the laws of the government they call on for protection. All persons in Kansas Territory, without regard to location, who honestly submit to the constituted authorities, will ever find me ready to aid in protecting them; and all who seek to resist the laws of the land, and turn traitors to their country, will find me aiding and enforcing the laws, if not as an officer as a citizen. "Respectfully yours,

"J. B. Donaldson,

"*U. S. Marshal of K. T.*"

It is but justice to Donaldson to say that he did not write that letter, for he could not. Some border ruffian scribe, of unusual malignity and literary excellence, most certainly penned it.

In the early part of this difficulty Captain Walker, a free-state captain of volunteers, had been sent with a letter to Lecompton. On his return he was pursued by these Southerners and fired upon. Messrs. Babcock, Roberts, and Mr. Miller, former editor of the *Free State*, went up to Lecompton to see the governor, and try to get the matter arranged. They failed, of course. On their return they were waylaid, when but a short distance from Lecompton, by a band of South Carolinians, who took Mr. Miller prisoner. These men were part of the posse.

Mr. Miller was originally from South Carolina; and, as he had ventured to be a free-state man in Kansas, they made up what they were pleased to consider a court from amongst their own number, and, placing Mr. Miller before it, tried him for treason to South Carolina. After a hard effort some of the Carolinians, who knew him, and felt friendly, contrived to prevent his being hung, although he was found guilty. He got off after losing his horse and money.

It was about the same time that Mr. Weaver, a sergeant-at-arms of the Kansas Commission, was arrested while in the discharge of his duty, and taken across the Kansas river into the South Carolina camp, which formed part of Marshal Farin's posse. Mr. Weaver, when taken, was travelling in company with a dragoon he had met on the way. The dragoon was also taken. They questioned this blue-jacketed and yellow-trimmed hero, as to "What the devil he meant by riding through the country with a d—d abolitionist?" Thinking it now safe, they concluded to let the dragoon go, but kept Mr. Weaver. This gentleman showed his papers, and wished to be released, as he was a United States officer. His papers got a very critical examination before the captain first; then something that passed for a major, and finally every ruffian, gentle or simple, had to have a peep at them. All this investigation did not procure his liberation. He was taken to the head-quarters of the chief Carolinian then in command, a Colonel Wilkes. This colonel hunted up a General Craimes, whom he got to help him in the investigation. After giving Weaver's papers a thorough and critical investigation, the colonel, with his general, pronounced them "all very good," and expressed as their opinion that he ought to be permitted to pass. On the request of Weaver, a pass was given him, so that he could get through all armed parties he would meet. This document was signed "Warren D. Wilkes, of South Carolina." The colonel very considerately suggested to Mr. Weaver that, if he was hailed by any party, he had better answer promptly; otherwise he might be shot.

The following is a copy of another letter sent by the people of Lawrence to Lecompton:

"LAWRENCE, K. T., *May* 17, 1856.

"J. B. DONALDSON, U. S. MARSHAL OF K. T.—

"DEAR SIR: We desire to call your attention, as citizens of Kansas, to the fact that a large force of armed men have collected in the vicinity of Lawrence, and are engaged in committing depredations upon our citizens; stopping wagons, arresting, threatening, and robbing unoffending travellers upon the highway, breaking open boxes of merchandise, and appropriating their contents;

have slaughtered cattle, and terrified many of the women and children.

"We have also learned from Governor Shannon, 'that there are no armed forces in the vicinity of this place but the regularly constituted militia of the territory;'—this is to ask if you recognize them as your *posse*, and feel responsible for their acts. If you do not, we hope and trust you will prevent a repetition of such acts, and give peace to the settlers.

"On behalf of the citizens,

"C. W. Babcock,
"Lyman Allen,
"J. A. Perry."

To this letter the marshal did not deem it necessary to reply.

An armed force was thus concentrating round Lawrence. Their camps and posts were drawing nearer and nearer. Missourians, fresh from different parts of the state, and some of them pretending to be Georgians, were collected close to Lawrence, and threatened the town with destruction. They stole, or, as they expressed it, "pressed" all the horses belonging to free-state men that they could find. A large number of valuable horses were taken around Lawrence in this way. Cattle were taken from the settlers and driven into the camp for beef. Property of all kinds, especially arms, they took whenever they got an opportunity. Mr. Stowell had gone down to Kansas city, Mo., after some fifty breech-loading guns of an old pattern. Queer-looking, alligator guns these were, for we recaptured some of them when the war broke out. While driving through the town of Franklin, on the way back at night, he was stopped by a party of Georgians, under Captain Moon, who searched the wagons and seized the guns. While they were attacking the wagons Mr. Stowell made his escape. This was an unfortunate affair for the people of Lawrence, as arms were scarce.

At the time these guns were taken the fight ought to have commenced. They had been taken, without even the pretence of authority, on the highway, and the Lawrence companies ought to have marched down and retaken them. When the news of the capture was brought up they were prepared to do so. Drums were beat and men mustered, but just as they were ready to start the Committee of Safety took the matter into consideration, and ordered that they should not go down. There were some bitter imprecations in Lawrence that night.

Another more startling event occurred. A young man named Jones, who had emigrated to the territory from Illinois, was attacked, near Blanton's Bridge, by two of these young Southerners, belonging to the posse. Armed parties of these were scouring the county in all directions. Jones had been to a store to get some flour, which he had with him on the horse. He was close to a store at the end of the bridge, when they attacked him; they were armed with United States muskets and bayonets. These arms were Mississippi rifles, as they are called. They were public arms, belonging to the territory, in the charge of Governor Shannon, and with his permission given to these young Southerners and Missourians, who formed the posse.

When Jones was attacked by these two men he dismounted and went into the store. While there they entered and attacked him. A person present in the store handed Jones a pistol, whereupon the men raised their pieces and threatened to shoot him unless he gave it up. The person in the store again got it, when an altercation between him and the two men ensued; Jones left, got on his horse, and started for home. The two men followed him, swearing that the abolitionist should not escape. They fired at him; he fell mortally wounded, and died during the day, or before next morning. The murderers immediately left.

About noon the report of this occurrence reached Lawrence, and excited great indignation. A few young men, amongst whom was Mr. Stewart, formerly from the State of New York, and who had been employed as clerk by the codifying committee, a Mr. Cook, also of New York, Mr. Lenhart, and two others, started for Blanton's Bridge to see about it; determined, if possible, to find the murderers. They were armed with Sharpe's rifles, and some of them had revolvers. They had gone but a short distance, and were just at the California road, a mile and a half from Lawrence, when they saw two armed men riding down the California road in the direction of Franklin. The two roads are at right angles with each other, and the parties were likely to meet at the point where they cross. Stewart insisted on hailing them, and asking if they knew of the Jones affair, as perhaps they were the men. The others demurred to this, when Stewart said, "What did we come for? Are we afraid to speak to these men?" At this the young men, who were all mere boys, marched forward.

When the men came forward Stewart asked where they were going?

"Where we d—n please!" was the reply.

"Who, and what are you?" said Stewart.

"That 's none of your d—d business!" was the reply, and both men, who were armed with Sharpe's rifles, raised them; one of them took deliberate aim at Stewart, saying, "D—n you, I know who you are." The boys instantly raised their guns, and one of them attempted to shoot; his cap bursting, the piece did not go off. At the same instant the two men fired, one of them shooting Stewart through the head, the ball entering his temple and killing him instantly. He reeled an instant and fell dead on the road. All of the young men attempted to fire, but all their guns snapped. The two pro-slavery men rode off rapidly. Mr. Cook, finding his rifle would not go, drew his revolver and started after them, on foot, as fast as he could run, discharging his revolver at them. One of the men, the one who shot Stewart, was wounded in the arm, and dropped his Sharpe's rifle, which he had just loaded. Several of the pistol bullets went through their clothes.

The young men lifted the body of their dead comrade and carried him back to Lawrence. None of the citizens had been aware of their enterprise, or its object, until the body was conveyed through the streets towards the Free-State Hotel. Mr. Eldridge was unwilling that it should be laid there, and it was taken to a house which had been used as a guard-house. Marshal Fain was in the Free-State Hotel at the time.

All this time the citizens of Lawrence had made no preparations for defence, and, as the marshal, who had charge of the posse, was a United States officer, they determined to make none. The people clamored, and wished that the hordes of villains be driven back, but it was overruled. Companies were formed in differen parts of the territory, and some of them marched towards Lawrence, but their services were refused by the committee.

By this time the enemy, still timorous, were concentrating thei forces closer and closer to Lawrence, and ex-senator Atchison with the Platte County Rifles and two brass cannon, was approaching the doomed town from the north, over the Delaware reserve.

During the whole of this preparation against Lawrence, th most urgent appeals had been made to Colonel Sumner to defen the town; not only by its citizens, but by members of the congressional committee, and other influential third parties. Thes were made in vain.

CHAPTER XXI.

SACKING OF LAWRENCE.

The morning of the 21st of May, 1856, broke upon Lawrence through a clear sky. It was neither to South Carolina nor Missouri that the leaders of the Kansas squatters had succumbed. President Pierce by his proclamation had made it treason for the people of Kansas to defend themselves. Federal officers, under the orders of a federal court, led on to Lawrence the army that was thirsting for its destruction. In such a case the people of Lawrence would have been justified in setting all federal law and authority at defiance, in falling back upon their right of self-protection. So, many in and around Lawrence felt. "What is federal authority to us," they asked, "when it is drawn up to rob and murder us?" But the conservative and trusting hoped on. They looked up to the glorious banner of their country, and thought that, under its folds, they surely were safe. "Let us offer no opposition," they said, "and they will have no excuse for molesting us." "Let us yield obedience to these officers, corrupt though they be, and it will place these men under too much responsibility to attack us." Such were the deceptive words that lulled that "eternal vigilance," which is the "price of liberty," to rest. They forgot that corruption, engendered by devotion to party, and a dangerous, aspiring element in our government, had been blotting out true American republicanism.

General Atchison had crossed the Kaw river at Lecompton, with the Platte County Rifles, and two pieces of artillery. The Kickapoo Rangers, under Captain Dunn (for Captain, Martin refused to go with them), reinforced by all the loafers and wild pro-slavery men from Leavenworth and Weston, had marched for the same point. General Stringfellow had crossed from Missouri to Atchison, and reinforced by his brother, the doctor (who is the more eminent of the two), and the infamous Bob Kelly, Stringfellow's law partner Abell, and several other pro-slavery men there, had gone to Lecompton. Colonel Boone, from Westport, with several other pro-slavery leaders from that place, and also from Liberty and Independence, at the head of bodies of armed men, or to take command of companies that had preceded them, marched across the frontiers a day or two before the twenty-first. On the evening of the twentieth Atchison and the Stringfellows had reinforced the different camps under Colonel Wilkes, of Carolina, and Colonel Titus, of Florida, who were camped between Lecompton and Lawrence. At the same time the Missourians and their Southern allies from the eastern frontier were encamped at Franklin, on the other or south-eastern side of Lawrence, under Colonel Buford. The forces thus congregated numbered from five to eight hundred men. Part of these were mounted, part of them on foot. They were mostly armed, Missourians, Carolinians, Georgians, Alabamians and all, with Mississippi rifles and bayonets. These arms were United States arms; they belonged to the territory, and were in charge of the federal appointees of Kansas. Besides the artillery brought by Atchison, there were other two pieces of cannon in the hands of these men. The camp towards Lecompton broke up before daylight on the twenty-first, and, under the command of Colonel Titus, marched for Lawrence.

Shortly after sunrise the inhabitants of Lawrence saw the advanced guard of this army, some two hundred horsemen, drawn up on Mount Oread, on the highest point, some two hundred yards behind Governor Robinson's house. They were armed, as I have mentioned, and also in an irregular way, with revolvers and bowie-knives. These men had halted on the top of the hill, and looked down on Lawrence. The town was perfectly quiet. Its inhabitants were shaking off their slumbers; those already astir were going quietly about their avocations. No guns were planted upon the embankments. No lines of riflemen were drawn up. The cry was, "Peace! peace! when there was no peace." There were but few men then in Lawrence; for, when the committee decreed that there should be no resistance, many of the fighting men left the town, where they would only have been needlessly exposed. The few men then in town were without a tried leader, round whom they could rally. At that moment,

> "A leader in that hapless town
> Were worth a thousand men!"
> * * * * *
> "O, for a blast of that dread horn
> On Fontarabia's deserts blown!"

But it was too late then. When the posse was thus seen collected on Mt. Oread there were some fluttering amongst timid hearts, recollections of bloody threats, and the knowledge of the murderous wishes of their enemies. Groups began to cluster here and there in the streets, and many eyes were turned to the body of armed horsemen on the hill; but there was no demonstration of resistance.

About seven o'clock the posse moved forward from the highest peak to the brow of the hill nearest the town, and Gov. Robinson's house was taken possession of for head-quarters. They then planted their cannon on the end of the hill overlooking the town, and pointed towards it. This was long musket-range from the town, but good range for breech-loading rifles. About eight o'clock, the remainder of the forces from the camps to the west, who were on foot, arrived at the summit of Mt. Oread, and halted there. When the posse first took possession of Mt. Oread a white flag flew over their lines, but soon after a red one — the war-flag — took its place; on this was inscribed, "Southern Rights." Soon after, a United States flag, the "stripes and stars," floated beside it.

As soon as these forces were securely posted, Deputy U. S. Marshal Fain, who was with Donaldson's posse, rode into Lawrence with ten men. These had no guns. It is proper to add that Deputy Fain had been in Lawrence the evening before, alone, and served two writs without molestation; indeed, he never had been resisted in Lawrence. When Fain came into town he summoned several gentlemen to act as his posse: Dr. Jarvin, a pro-slavery resident of Lawrence, John A. Perry, C. W. Topliff,

Wm. Jones, S. W. Eldridge and T. B. Eldridge. These gentlemen assisted him. He then arrested Gen. Dietzler and Judge G. W. Smith. He said he had other writs, but made no more arrests. He staid until after dinner; called for dinner at the hotel, where he, and the posse he brought with him, dined; he left immediately after, neither he nor his companions paying their bill. He returned to the posse on the hill. While these arrests were making, and while the posse he had raised in Lawrence was under his orders, and retained by him, two of the number, Mr. Perry and Col. Topliff, were robbed by the posse on the hill. They lived in a house on the side of Mt. Oread, near which the part of the posse on the hill were stationed. During the time they were waiting for Fain to go through his legal manœuvre, they busied themselves in breaking into a few houses in the suburbs, and, amongst other performances, robbed these gentlemen of several hundred dollars in money, a gold watch, and other property. It is proper to add that only a portion of those on the hill were thus engaged.

While Fain and his small posse were in Lawrence, Col. Buford and the forces from Franklin reinforced them. There was some speech-making on the hill. When Deputy Marshal Fain returned to the hill he briefly addressed the posse, telling them that he had "got through with them, but that Sheriff Jones had some processes to serve, and that they would hold themselves in readiness to go with him."

Sheriff Jones, the man who had been "murdered," "shot in the spine," etc., and over whom the border ruffian journals had pronounced some pathetic obituaries, rode forward in the crowd. It was no wonder that the people of Lawrence now believed the story of his being shot a hoax; for, although he had been wounded, his injury had been exaggerated. Jones was received with enthusiastic cheering.

While Fain was in town he had been treated with great respect by those who had received or assumed the privilege of acting for the citizens. Some one or two of the "Safety Valve," as the Committee of Safety were sarcastically called, vied with each other in showing their willingness to respect authorities. This yielding spirit was generally disapproved by the people, even then, and by several members of the committee. Whether this arose from an over-anxiety about that first law of nature, "Number One," or a too severe conscientiousness regarding the lives and property entrusted to their charge, is doubtful. If the first, it was simply *cowardice;* if the latter, the sequel proved it to be wretched policy. Under the feeling to which I allude, a letter was framed, addressed to the marshal, which ran in the following words:

"LAWRENCE, K. T., *May* 21, 1856.

"J. B. DONALDSON, United States Marshal, K. T.:

"We, the Committee of Public Safety for the citizens of Lawrence, make this statement and declaration to you, as Marshal of Kansas Territory:

"That we represent citizens of the United States, and of Kansas, who acknowledge the constituted authorities of the government; that we make no resistance to the execution of the laws, national or territorial, and that we ask protection of the government, and claim it as law-abiding American citizens.

"For the private property already taken by your posse we ask indemnification; and what remains to us and our citizens we throw upon you for protection, trusting that under the flag of our Union, and within the folds of the constitution, we may obtain safety.

"SAMUEL C. POMEROY, C. W. BABCOCK,
"W. Y. ROBERTS, S. B. PRENTISS,
"LYMAN ALLEN, A. H. MALLORY,
"JOHN PERRY, JOEL GROVER."

It is not worth while to make any comments upon this letter. Every man may draw his own conclusions. It proposes to relinquish that for which the free squatters had always contended, — a position against the Bogus Legislature and its usurpations. The present prostrate condition of Lawrence was owing to a desire to submit to the federal or national authorities; but this was no reason why there should be submission to the territorial laws. Well knowing that the force arrayed against Lawrence was there to sustain the usurpations of which the Bogus Legislature was an essential part, these peace-seeking leaders in Lawrence, in this hour of peril, framed the foregoing document, with the fallacious hope of averting the storm. The position they took may be apologized for by their extreme peril, but cannot be justified; and even then would not have been sustained by the people, and is now utterly repudiated. It is proper to state that several of those whose names are attached to the document declare that it had not their assent. Messrs. Allen, Babcock, Mallory and Grover, repudiate, and declare they did not sign it; some of these admitting that they signed a paper that forenoon, but know of no part of such a document sustaining or submitting to the territorial laws. I have been informed that Dr. Prentiss was not present when it was drafted.

However humiliating this letter, it utterly failed in averting the blow. It was only the prelude to acts of reckless villany.

It was nearly three o'clock when Sheriff Jones rode into town with some twenty armed men. He halted in front of the Free-State Hotel, and called for Gen. Pomeroy. Pomeroy came out and shook hands with him.

"Gen. Pomeroy," said Jones, "I recognize you as one of the leading citizens here, and as one who can act for the people of Lawrence. I demand that all the arms of Lawrence be given up, or we will bombard the town." Jones here took out his watch, and continued: "I give you five minutes to decide on this proposition, and half an hour to stack the arms in the streets."

Gen. Pomeroy said the time he gave was too short; but Jones was not in tune to listen to any evasion; the army on the hill had waited too long already. Pomeroy hurried up stairs, and communicated with the Committee of Safety. Only fancy treating on the point at issue under such circumstances! — Jones, with an army at his back, thirsting for blood and plunder; the committee, who had provided no means of defence, and who had only a handful of men in Lawrence, who, if they attempted to resist, would merely be butchered, unless the invaders were cowards! Pomeroy returned to Jones and informed him that the artillery in Lawrence would be given up; but the Sharpe's rifles and other guns were private property, and that each man had his own gun, and would not give them up upon any order of the committee, and that Jones would himself have to apply for and get these from the persons who had them. Like a prudent general, who takes what he can get as it comes, Jones said, "Very well; give up the cannon." The artillery in question consisted of the twelve-pound brass howitzer, brought into Lawrence so gallantly during the Wakarusa war, and some four other small brass breech-loading cannon, carrying a pound ball. These latter were nearly useless, or could be of comparatively little service in a field engagement, or in defending or assailing any point or town. All of these guns had been carefully concealed a few days before, having been buried under the foundation of a house in town, where they could never have been found. Gen. Pomeroy and Lieut. Gov. Roberts hastened to give them up as a peace-offering; and they were dug up and surrendered to Jones by these gentlemen. Jones desired that they be taken out to the camp outside, and free-state men were called on to do this ignominious service. Numbers of those whom Jones thus asked haughtily refused. Some of the men with Jones threatened to use their arms, and rode at some of the young men who refused, and threatened them with their bayonets, but did not intimidate them into compliance. A few, less resolute, aided the ruffians to remove the guns.

While this was going on, other important events were transpiring. One of the threats Jones had made, if the guns were not given up, was that the "*posse*" would come in town. While the guns were being delivered up, and a few Sharpe's rifles taken, the forces on Mt. Oread, under Atchison, Buford, Stringfellow and Titus, marched down the hill towards the south end of Lawrence, dragging their cannon with them. They formed in a hollow square in the prairie amongst the houses in the suburbs, and there Atchison made a speech to them. The great border ruffian, ex-Senator, ex-Vice President of the United States, was not remarkably sober on this important occasion. For several days he and his confreres had been engaged in a debauch, in which, perhaps, they strove to drown their knowledge of better things. He began his speech with,

"Boys, to-day I'm a Kickapoo Ranger, by G–d! This day we have entered Lawrence, and the abolitionists have not dared to fire a gun." Various reports of this wild speech have been published, but all more or less incorrect. It is an odd mixture of drunken enthusiasm, restraining forbearance, partisan ferocity, and profanity. He declared that the Free-State Hotel must be destroyed, and the printing offices; but told them they must deport themselves as Southern gentlemen, and "law and order" men. He said they must not forget to be gallant, and must respect ladies; but added, "if you find a woman armed as a soldier, and thus putting off the garb of her sex, trample her under foot as you would a snake." He said the people of Lawrence seemed determined not to resist, and that, therefore, it would not do to attack them; but said that if there was the least appearance of resistance, no quarter should be shown. He alluded to the distance the young Southerners had come to aid them in the defence of "Southern rights," and complimented them on their zeal and courage. He commenced speaking on his horse, and then dismounted, and got on a brass cannon, from which he spoke. He was interrupted by the arrival of Jones, who, after the guns had been delivered up, rode out of town. Jones told them that he had orders, from the First District Court of the United States for Kansas (Judge Lecompte), to demolish the hotel and destroy the printing offices. Loud and enthusiastic cheers were given for Jones. Atchison resumed his speech, telling them, "And now we will go in with our highly honorable Jones, and test the strength of that d—d Free-State Hotel!" He said something more, urging them to bravery and good order, and finished by saying, "If any man or woman stand in your way, blow them to h–ll with a chunk of cold lead!"

The army of invasion formed into line and marched into Lawrence. A motley-looking crew they were; many of them had red flannel shirts, with curious border ruffian devices on them, so that they could be recognized by their friends in travelling. This scarlet uniform gave them some little the appearance of the "red coats;" and certainly never did such "tories" march to desecrate American soil, or trample under foot the rights of American freemen. As motley an assortment of banners floated over them. The flag of South Carolina, with a crimson star in the centre, and the motto "Southern rights." Another flag resembled the American flag, in being striped like it; but there were no stars, and in their stead a rampant tiger, — fit emblem of the men it floated over, and the cause it vindicated. Another had white and black alternate stripes, which truly represented the cursed amalgamation of races which is ruining the slave states, and which these nullifying fillibusters meant to introduce into Kansas, and to nationalize. One banner bore the inscription, "South Carolina;" another, "Supremacy of the white race," on the one side, and "Kansas the outpost," on the other. One bore an inscription in the shape of a sorry distich:

"You Yankees tremble,
And abolitionists fall;
Our motto is
'Southern rights to all.'"

When they had passed the Little Redan earth-work at the foot of Massachusetts-street, they were halted, and their cannon pointed up the street. Dreadful rumors had prevailed that the street was mined, and that they would be blown to atoms if they entered it. Several of the young Southerners and some Missourians were for advancing into town; but Buford, calling them back, said, "No one must go in that street now, — there is no saying what these infernal Yankees would do." At this point two spies, who had been staying in Lawrence for several days, stepped up to Buford, and told him, "It 's all right, cap'n, — there 's no mines in the streets. The stories are all humbug." After this, and a little more discussion, the army of invasion moved forward, and soon was in possession of the town. Before the army thus entered, Jones had given orders that all the women and children should leave the town. Several had fled in the morning, on the first appearance of danger, but most of them had remained until now. It was a trying and sorrowful scene to see the people of Lawrence leave their homes and fly from the place. Some of the women were moved to tears, and others would look back, like Lot's wife, and freely vent their indignation. They had not time to move their effects; and, had they been seen taking them off, they would probably have been stopped.

The first place attacked was the printing office of the "Free

State." It was in the second story of a concrete building. There was a store below. One of the ruffian officers entered the store and demanded of the proprietor if there was a mine under the building to blow it up. The merchant assured him there was not, when the interrogator told him that they were going up into the printing office, and that if anything happened he would hold him responsible. The "posse" or ruffians, either or both, entered the office of the *Free State*, and the work of demolition commenced. The press and other articles were first broken, so as to be rendered perfectly useless, and then thrown into the Kansas river. As this was some distance to carry the articles, they got tired of it, and began throwing the remainder in the street. Books and papers were thrown in the street. Many of these men got books they fancied, and kept them. Some of the officers ordered them to take nothing, saying, "These Yankees will tell stories enough about us for this, without our stealing from them." Colonel Zadoc Jackson, of Georgia, exerted himself to prevent the plunder, as did several others; they were prepared for the most desperate war against Freedom and American rights, but they had too much honor, or too much pride, to wish to occupy the position of highwaymen. Unfortunately, these officers were unable to prevent these outrages, or restrain the villains they had gathered up to do their lawless work.

The office of the other paper in Lawrence, the *Herald of Freedom*, was entered by the Carolinians, shortly after their compatriots had commenced the work of demolition in the *Free State* office. The *Herald of Freedom* office is a tall, narrow, concrete building. Into this the gallant "chivalry" were afraid to venture. The dread of mines and infernal machines was a sort of nightmare with them. In order to *be safe* in entering the office in question, they drove some young men, residents of the town, up the stairs and into the building, at the point of the bayonet. How this stupid policy was to demonstrate anything, or afford security, it would be difficult to discover. In the *Herald of Freedom* office the same reckless work of destruction went on. The presses were broken in a thorough and *enlightened* manner, which showed the hand or the direction of a practical printer, the fragments being perfectly useless. Books and papers were thrown out in the street, or stolen. Several members of the posse were marching about the streets with books stuck on the points of their bayonets. Others were tearing books to shreds, but the more prudent carried them off.

The next step in the process was the destruction of the hotel. The enemy planted their artillery in front of the hotel, one hundred and fifty feet distant from it, across Massachusetts-street. The hotel was a very large building, three full stories high besides the basement; it seemed almost impossible that they could miss it. The proprietor of the establishment, Mr. Eldridge, was notified by Jones to remove his furniture in a certain time. This Mr. Eldridge said he could not do. Some of the posse went to work and began to carry articles of furniture out into the street; but they very soon got weary of this, and found a task more congenial. They discovered the wines and liquors, a good stock of which was on hand, and, helping themselves freely to these and to eatables and cigars, the heroes of this gallant campaign were soon in an interesting condition.

The hotel was cleared of people, and Atchison aimed the first gun fired at it. The worthy ex-vice-president was rather too tipsy to win many laurels as a gunner. He stooped over the gun. "A little higher, boys, a little lower — a little higher. That 's it, boys; let her rip!" Bang went the gun, the ball missing the hotel altogether, going clear over it. The next gunner was rather more successful, putting a ball through the top corner of the right. Some fifty rounds were fired, when, finding it slow business, the hotel looking, externally, little the worse for it, they undertook to blow it up. Four kegs of gunpowder were placed in it, but only two of them exploded, and they made little report, and still less impression on the walls; but fire was communicated to the building in several places, and it was soon a magnificent sea of flame.

As the flames hissed and crackled, Jones leaned upon his horse and contemplated the spectacle. His eyes glistened with a wild delight, and he said, "This is the happiest moment of my life."

And now commenced a scene of wild and reckless pillage.

When the citizens of Lawrence had left their homes, those who could locked them; but locks and bolts were small security; when the marauders could not enter by the doors, they got in by the windows. All the money and jewelry that could be found was taken, and also clothing. In fact, they took everything they wanted, or could carry away. Much of what they could not take, they destroyed. Nor was this pillage confined to the rank and file. One Deputy United States Marshal (of whom there are many) carried off a valuable case of surgical instruments worth three hundred dollars. Stringfellow went into a store, and stole two boxes of cigars, remarking, with a laugh,

"This is all the booty I want."

Ex-Vice-President Atchison was also seen with one of these, or another box. With such bright examples it would be needless to enter into a detail of the brilliant exploits of the rank and file. During the early part of the day several young men, attempting to escape, were chased and fired at. Some of them got off, others were taken prisoners; but none were killed, so far as has been ascertained, on the free-state side. One pro-slavery man shot himself accidentally, while the posse was on Mt. Oread, and another was killed by the falling of a brick from the Free-State Hotel. Two others of these men fell violently while galloping after some flying free-state men, horse and man rolling over, one of the men having his leg severely shattered.

Nearly a hundred and fifty thousand dollars' worth of property was stolen or destroyed. Trunks were broken open, and such of their contents as were not wanted were scattered about the streets. Letters, family pictures, and other relics were not respected. Many letters of public men were taken, as they were supposed to be of value, politically or otherwise. Even Mrs. Robinson's letters were stolen by the "chivalry." One gentlemanly Southerner, seeing these, tried to get possession of them to restore them, but did not succeed. The office of the *Herald of Freedom* was fired several times, but, as it had been emptied of nearly all that was combustible, some of the employés of the office would go in and put it out again.

The closing act was the burning of Governor Robinson's dwelling, which stood upon the brow of Mount Oread. This had been plundered through the day, and at night it was set on fire; and the pyramid of flame from the mount lighted up the pathway of the retreating army.

Besides the plundering in town, these men, both before and after the 21st, went about the country, and plundered many houses. It is supposed that not less than two hundred horses were taken, in and around Lawrence. There were also frightful stories of outrages, and of women being ravished. Such cases there may have been, but rare. There were villains in that posse who were certainly none too good for it.

Such was the sack of Lawrence; but, in order that the reader may get a glance of the picture as painted by the actors in the scene, I give their own version in subjoined extracts. The first is from the journal of one of these pro-slavery bravoes, who started for Lawrence, at the secret order of the Blue Lodge, anticipating the marshal's proclamation, which they had learned would be issued. It will illustrate a little of the camp life of these worthies. The writer has a fund of humor for a border ruffian, and, doubtless, under a better state of affairs, would not have been such a bad fellow. His journal was published in a pro-slavery paper.

"*May 14th, and Sunday, too.* — Flattered myself a halt would have been ordered, but no; the cry is, Onward, still onward. Learn that a very important appointment has been made by the officer in command during the previous evening. That the little doctor, in view of his having become the surgeon of the company (though how he became so no one knows), is also appointed commissary of the company. Understand he accepts the same with the spirit of a martyr. The men, evil-minded of course, think the two jars of whiskey, property of the company, tend greatly to his resignation toward the duties of his appointment, as by it he has entire control of all the whiskey, which is a consummation devoutly to be wished for by all. Again in motion; we arrived at the house of a Dutchman, who, although with free-soil proclivities, had whiskey. With one or two others, constituted an advance guard, and assailed the house of said Dutchman for whiskey. After considerable parleying, whiskey produced, and I take the liberty of stating that it was as good as any whiskey I ever tasted in the territory, either from pro-slavery men or others. All hands drink here *ad libitum*. After a very hasty consideration of the supper, we are turned out to drill. Drilling is a perfect humbug, in my opinion. All are straightened out in a line. A fat, good-natured orderly sergeant drills us, — twenty-five of us, green as gourds on the subject of military tactics. Shoulder arms! present arms! and order arms! are strangely commingled in our brains, and the order to do one of the foregoing is responded to by attempts to do a little of all we know. Our marching and countermarching is painful, as we all, from a sincere wish to do right, tread on the heels of the person in front, and are cursed accordingly, regretting seriously our incapacity to be Napoleons. Our orderly sergeant dismisses us amongst the acclamations of the company, and we all make a rash attempt to sleep; but, alas! our attempts prove futile. Hardly do we compose ourselves, so that Morpheus may embrace us, when we are rather roughly informed that we must turn out to fight the enemy. All turn out with their muskets in most murderous attitudes. One half of our force sent towards the creek to reconnoitre; the balance, amongst whom I was, remain in camp to guard the same. After a few minutes of absence, first half returned, and informed the company in general, and the officers in charge in particular, that some two individuals had passed, and had told the gentleman on guard near the road, that he might, if he found it convenient, proceed to Pandemonium; a decided reflection on our company, but said reflection was responded to in a manner calculated to strike terror into unbelievers, and such who could not prove unmistakably their soundness on the Goose. By the firing of all the pistols in the direction that they who had insulted us had gone quiet was once more restored.

"*May* 15. — Having been up all night, am consequently up very early in the morning, and proceed to the breakfast ground, anxious to eat something. Find that a bottle of whiskey was going its rounds with unusual vigor. Take my station, that it might find me in its circle of acquaintances. Whiskey being all drank, the more important matter of breakfast claims our attention, and each has some office to do in this respect. Grinding coffee requiring less culinary talent than anything else, the job is assigned to me. All are very jolly and dirty, and the conversation very lively.

"After breakfast, good-natured orderly sergeant gets us into as near a straight line as he can, and proceeds to drill us again, with, if possible, less success than the previous evening. At the command, right wheel, most of us wheel the wrong way; and the nearest approach to a hollow square that we can attain to is an imperfect oval. Our muskets are seldom, if ever, in their proper position, and prove for an inanimate subject very hard to manage.

"After coursing up and down the prairie to our disgust, and to the acceleration of our digestion, we are dismissed with the melancholy conviction that we are but poorly drilled, although we feel awfully bored.

"Nothing occurs to distract us from our monotonous snail's pace, or attracts our attention, save two dogs, who join us more from interest than glory. At last Buck Creek appears. We think how gladly would we '*pass*' the *Buck* as at '*poker;*' but we are not playing that game now, although, before getting through, we got to '*all fours.*' Buck Creek is a succession of ugly hills and gloomy hollows. We got down the hills and across the creek, but to ascend the other side required a little more exertion. We had not gone far when we succeeded in sticking admirably. Mud being about one foot deep, men fall in it with perfect impunity, seldom going far with a load before they are immersed. That day there were but few of us but deserved the euphonious title of '*stuck-in-the-muds.*' While stuck in the mud we are met by several gentlemen, who read to us Marshal Donaldson's proclamation, calling upon us to aid in support of the laws, etc. The proclamation is received with great glee, and our throats give signal of our hearts' joy. Retire to a little distance to do some shouting on my own hook, and sit immediately behind a horse to gratify my exhilaration. The horse rather unceremoniously kicks me, in the midst of a most glorious yell, and on a portion of my frame that for several days after rendered it a matter of impossibility for me to take a seat. Limping from the scene of my disgraceful kicking, and breathing curses against all horses in general, and this individual in particular, I wend my way slowly to the top of the hill. On my way thither, meet a Chief Justice proceeding homeward. Chief Justice greets us kindly, and, after we assist him to catch a runaway steer, he bids us adieu, thinking that we are a very irregular-looking portion of the regular militia."

Having given the above picture of the "militia" from one who ought to know, I subjoin the pro-slavery account of the sacking of Lawrence, as published in the official organ of ruffianism in the territory. Its main discrepancy consists in its denial of the stealing, for which I scarcely blame the editor.

The following is from the Lecompton *Union*, of May 21st:

"LAWRENCE TAKEN!

"GLORIOUS TRIUMPH OF THE LAW AND ORDER PARTY OVER FANATICISM IN KANSAS.

"FULL PARTICULARS.

"On Tuesday, the 20th, a large force of law and order men having gathered in and around Lecompton, the marshal ordered the different camps to concentrate about two miles this side of Lawrence, so as to be ready for the execution of his immediate demands upon the people of Lawrence. At this order we left our sanctum and proceeded to the encampment, equipped for the occasion, and here begins our notice:

"*Tuesday, May* 20—1 *o'clock.*

"Here we are in camp. Everything looks very warlike. The cavalry, numbering some one hundred and eighty, commanded by Col. H. T. Titus, of this county, originally of Florida, are dashing over the hills at the clear tones of their commander's voice. The infantry companies are being drilled by their different captains, and everybody is in the line preparing for an engagement. But few have an idea of the feeling that possesses one at the martial notes of a drum and fife, or the clear, shrill tones of the bugle, sounding the charge of two hundred troopers. It is enough to make the veriest coward a brave man, and the expiring soldier grasp again his sword.

"This encampment consists of about fifty tents, and upwards of four hundred men. All have made up their minds to fight desperately, in case of resistance. Men never were more determinedly resolved and eager to meet the issue.

"The prison-tent has eight occupants. They all seem contented and satisfied, and say they were never better treated in their lives. Their quarters are comfortable, and they have a plenty to eat and drink.

"2 *o'clock.* — Orders were received to march at three. Tents struck, wagons loaded, and all were upon the move at the appointed time. Three pieces of cannon, with one hundred and fifty additional men, were in the road a short distance off to join us. We encamped about six o'clock near that place where the noted Squatter Convention was held in '54. Here we heard various rumors about fighting; one that three hundred mounted men from Topeka were in our rear, and intended attacking us that night; one that the various propositions made by the Lawrenceites to the marshal were only to gull us, and that there would certainly be a fight. This last rumor was considered credible, and pleased the boys very much. We were not disturbed by the Topekans that night; but early next morning the cavalry were called to escort the cannon to Lawrence.

"At half past four o'clock the cannon were planted without any resistance upon the heights beyond Robinson's house, and within four hundred yards of the big stone hotel. When we first reached there not a human being could be seen. In about one hour there gathered in the streets in front of the hotel some one hundred and fifty men. Some one was haranguing them. Off to the east of the town eleven men came out from a small stone building, formed in front, and marched in town. Several men attempted to leave town, but were cut off by our pickets. These were the only indications of a fight.

"At eight o'clock the infantry joined us. At eleven Major Buford's company from Franklin arrived; and by twelve our forces amounted to eight hundred strong, cavalry and infantry, and four six-pound pieces of brass cannon. About this time great excitement was created by Mr. James Keiser accidentally shooting himself; but the wound was not mortal.

"At one o'clock the United States Deputy Marshal selected a small posse and entered town to make arrests. He selected his posse from the ranks of the Lecompton Guard, commanded by Capt. John Donaldson, who was also honored with the command of the posse, — Donaldson's "Red Shirts," as they are more commonly known, by adopting the red shirt as their uniform, — and reflected credit upon themselves and their commander. They were well drilled, always ready for any emergency, and prompt and obedient in action. Most of them were young men from Virginia, who have left home and friends to offer up their lives to the preservation and establishment of Southern institutions in Kansas. The following are the names of the posse under Donaldson's command:

"Capt. J. Donaldson, R. M. Nace, J. N. Casey, J. W. Ransom, B. Jones, John Shelton, C. H. Grover.

"Only three arrests were made, viz.: Smith, Jenkin, and Dietzler. The town seemed almost forsaken. When the marshal returned, having done all he could do, he released the posse from his jurisdiction, and they were immediately summoned by Sheriff Jones. Mr. Jones, notwithstanding his feeble condition, appeared upon horseback; and, as he rode along the line summoning each company to assist in the execution of the laws, he was received with loud and deafening cheers. His pale countenance and emaciated form, the products of an almost fatal blow from an assassin's arm, made every man irresistibly clutch his pistols, impatient to revenge this foul deed. The very appearance of Jones, who had so often presented himself at the very mouth of danger, and consecrated his life to the maintenance of the laws, sent a thrill through every heart that choked all utterance of their willingness to follow him in the face of any danger. He selected a small posse of mounted men, mostly from the Atchison Guards, commanded by Capt. D. Treville of South Carolina. Col. H. T. Titus commanded the posse.

"Jones had a great many writs in his hands, but could find no one against whom he held them. He also had an order from the court to demand the surrender of their arms, field and side, and a demolition of the two presses and the Free-State Hotel as *nuisances*. The arms were immediately demanded and surrendered. But very few could be found, — four pieces of cannon, one twelve-pound howitzer, and four small pieces, and a few Sharpe's rifles. When they agreed to surrender, our men were marched down in front of the town, and one cannon planted upon their own battlements. Over the largest piece, commanding the Emigrant Aid Hotel, was unfurled the stars and stripes.

"The cannon were then brought out and thrown in front of our lines. During this time appeals were made to Sheriff Jones to save the Aid Society's Hotel. This news reached the company's ears, and was received with one universal cry of 'No! no! Blow it up! blow it up! We will not injure private property; but our motto is, Destruction to everything belonging to the Aid Society! The court has declared it a nuisance, and we will destroy it.'

"About this time a banner was seen fluttering in the breeze over the office of *The Herald of Freedom*. Its color was a blood-red, with a lone star in the centre, and South Carolina above. This banner was placed there by the Carolinians — Messrs. Wrights and a Mr. Cross. The effect was prodigious. One tremendous and long-continued shout burst from the ranks. Thus floated in triumph the banner of South Carolina, — that single white star, so emblematic of her course in the early history of our sectional disturbances. When every Southern State stood almost upon the verge of ceding their dearest rights to the North, Carolina stood boldly out, the firm and unwavering advocate of Southern institutions.

"Thus floated victoriously the first banner of Southern rights over the abolition town of Lawrence, unfurled by the noble sons of Carolina, and every whip of its folds seemed a death-stroke to Beecher propagandism and the fanatics of the East. O! that its red folds could have been seen by every Southern eye!

"Mr. Jones listened to the many entreaties, and finally replied that it was beyond his power to do anything, and gave the occupants so long to remove all private property from it. He ordered two companies into each printing office to destroy the press. Both presses were broken up and thrown into the streets, the type thrown in the river, and all the material belonging to each office destroyed. After this was accomplished, and the private property removed from the hotel by the different companies, the cannon were brought in front of the house and directed their destructive blows upon the walls. The building caught on fire, and soon its walls came with a crash to the ground. *Thus fell the abolition fortress;* and we hope this will teach the Aid Society a *good lesson for the future.*

"Before entering town our commanders instructed each member of his company of the consequences befalling the violation of any private property. As far as we can learn, they attended strictly to these instructions. One act we regret to mention — the firing of Robinson's house. Although there is but little doubt as to the real owners of this property, yet it was a private residence, and should have remained untouched. During the excitement, the commissary, Col. Abell, of Atchison city, learned that it was on fire, and immediately detailed a company to suppress the flames, which was done. Once afterwards, we understand, Sheriff Jones had the flames suppressed, and the boys guilty of the act were sent immediately to camp; but with regret we saw the building on fire that night about ten o'clock. This we saw from camp, and cannot tell who set it on fire the third time. During the firing upon the hotel one of our men was killed by the falling of a stone from the wall.

"Before another week rolls around no doubt the papers will be filled with vastly magnified reports, and the country disturbed with 'loud shrieks for the cause of freedom' by abolition organs. This cry one anticipates, and will not be disappointed at the bloody picture their ready writers will paint for their own purposes; but they are only a faction in the country, and have produced this state of things. It remains to be seen whether that portion of the North and East calling themselves conservative national men, will be led into excitement and extravagances by their 'loud shrieks.' We think the conservative men of the North and East have had furnished them, long since, sufficient data to form correct opinions of the motives governing these men. If every man of them had been killed, every house burned, and total and entire extermination had been the motto of the 'law and order' party, who would be to blame? Impartial decision answers, 'these men have brought the calamity upon their own heads.'

"*We have done what we have done, and would not have anything undone that was done, and shall do no more if let alone;* so let our doings go forth for the inspection and criticism of the nation. In this report we have 'not extenuated, nor aught set down in malice;' but furnished a simple and unvarnished sum-total of facts. As to the 'law and order' party of Kansas, they have but one opinion, but one mind, — *to stand in defence of their laws and their rights at all hazards.*

"We forgot to mention, in our account, that the long conjecture of the Free-State Hotel being a fortress was found to be true. From the surface of the roof the wall extended to the height of three and a half feet, with four port-holes in each side, — making in all sixteen, — large enough to admit the mouth of an eighteen-pound gun. The mouths of the holes were concealed from view by a thin coat of lime that could be easily knocked out when desired. The above statement can be established by several hundred witnesses.

"The 'Red Shirts' raised the first flag upon the Free-State Hotel. They have in possession the twelve-pound howitzer taken from the enemy, and, whenever necessary, can use it effectually. Capt. Donaldson may feel proud of his 'Red Shirts.'"

CHAPTER XXII.

GUERILLA WAR — THE DRAGOONS — LAW AND ORDER IN LEAVENWORTH.

THE day after the sacking of Lawrence, the marshal's posse began to disperse. Those Southerners, who had been disgusted by the outrages of their companions, or who had secured as much plunder as they could take care of, incontinently left, Buford's prayers, their oath, and the necessities of "law and order," to the contrary, notwithstanding. It was on the 22nd that Atchison, with the Platte County Rifles, rode to the southern outskirts of Lawrence, and requested permission of the citizens to go through the town and cross the ferry at that point. To allow the great ruffian and his retreating band the privilege of passing peacefully through a town the people of which were bewailing their lost property, and the smoke from the ruins of the best buildings in the place still ascending, was too much to ask or give; but a few of the leading citizens gave permission. Perhaps they thought that it would take some days or a week to rally sufficient force to Lawrence to defend it, and, knowing that the different sections of the army were still within a few miles of Lawrence, desired to avoid, at the present, a collision with a small part, the destruction of whom would soon bring on them the whole force. Some few citizens, however, when the rumor that Atchison was coming through the town, reached them, seized their guns and went out into the street. Had the notice of their approach not been so short it is more than likely that a fight would have ensued, whether the "committee" authorities would have sanctioned it, or whether the participants would have been "right on the record" or not. But there were only a few men who thus hurried into the streets, and they, finding that there was neither concert of action nor force sufficient, withdrew.

Atchison and his men rode through the streets as quietly as possible, having only one piece of artillery with them. The rank and file looked camp-weary and camp-dirty, and, as they rode along, cast suspicious glances at the citizens. Well they knew that every man of them should have been strung up by the neck, and, although they had humbly begged that they might go through, they seemed to have at bottom a suspicion that so unreasonable a request was hardly likely to be granted. Atchison is a tall, muscular man, his face slightly marked by the ravages of dissipation. As he rode on through the streets of Lawrence, he buttoned his coat and pulled his hat as far over his eyes as possible. A few of the citizens watched the retreat of that wild band of Missourians until they crossed the Kaw and were lost to view in the dense timber that skirts its northern shore.

The day after the sacking of the town, a man named Cox, who had at one time pretended to be a free-state man, and who had acted as a spy in Lawrence, drove into that town from Lecompton, on his way to Kansas city. He had been in Lawrence, and, knowing the peaceable character of the people, supposed that he could enter and leave it unmolested. In this supposition he was not mistaken; but he still had a few guilty fears, though he had ventured into town, and betrayed his nervousness by his sidelong glances at every one, and his frightened manner. The people, generally, paid no attention to him, only regarding him with contempt. Two waggish boys, who saw his trepidation, went to him, and, to have some fun, said, with a solemn shake of their heads,

"Look here, sir, it 's not safe for you to be here; take our advice, and leave."

Quaking with a guilty conscience, he got his buggy, harnessed up, and started off for Franklin as fast as he could make his horse go, trembling with fear all the way; his exodus under such trepidation being hailed by a shout of laughter from a group of observers at the foot of Massachusetts-street. In order to make a plausible story of it, he reported, when he got to Franklin, that he had been driven out of Lawrence by a mob, and fired at. By the time he got to Westport, this furnished food for another declaration of war from Missouri. The Westport paper got up another "war" extra, of which the subjoined is a morsel:

"Fish's abolition hotel may meet with an accident. All nuisances should be abolished.

"There should be no mistake in this matter. *Our Missouri friends must understand that this is but the beginning of the end. We want you still;* and if our citizens are to be shot at, simply because they are true to Southern principles, in the streets of Lawrence in the open day, and that, too, within four and twenty hours after the reception of such a bitter lesson as the pro-slavery men of Kansas (!) taught them on the 21st, we have but one resource left, and that is *to level Lawrence* (*and*, if necessary, *every other abolition settlement in Kansas*) with the ground. We pity the women and children upon whom this unhappy state of affairs falls heavily; but the responsibility must rest with the fanatics who have preached Sharpe's rifles and armed resistance to *our* laws.

"Come, then; we call upon every true-hearted pro-slavery man and son of the South to come up and help us.

* * * * *

"Three times three for *our* gallant Jones."

This merely resulted in keeping a portion of the Westport rowdies in the county, who, under Capt. Pate, of Westport, commander of the Shannon Sharp-Shooters, and Coleman, the murderer, went about the county to the south of the Kaw, committing depredations.

Some of the Southerners, who had been in Lawrence on the 21st, left it intensely disgusted. One physician from Kentucky, who had acted as an orderly sergeant in one company of the posse, abandoned his companions while they were sacking the town. He wept that evening, as he rode through the Delaware reserve, and denounced the whole conduct of his companions, declaring, to a gentleman who rode part of the way with him, that he "knew who was in the wrong now." Another Kentuckian and pro-slavery man, who was in the territory, left it at the same time. The account he gave was published in a Kentucky paper, and part of his version runs thus:

"Mr. Sebree says that large numbers of Missourians are in the territory, and that the supply of them is only limited by the demand. The representation he makes of the men who compose the body of the pro-slavery party, and of their proceedings, is not very flattering to them. He says that decent Southern men, who go there under no undue excitement, are ashamed of them, and he saw some such whose minds on the subject of slavery in Kansas had undergone a complete change. The large company of Southern emigrants, recruited in Alabama by Major Buford, he represents as a miserable set of drunken loafers, many of whom have died in consequence of their vices and imprudence, and all of whom are cursing the men that induced them to go into the country. Mr. Sebree says it is generally conceded that, of the actual citizens of the territory, two to one are in favor of a free state, and that, with the exception of a comparatively small number of brawlers, they are quiet, industrious men, seeking to establish homes for themselves and their families. They have been outnumbered and outvoted by the people from the borders of Missouri, who have been organized for that purpose. These are unpalatable truths for Southern men, but the sooner the truth is known the better. Mr. Sebree thinks that the war has but commenced, and that, in a very short time, thousands of armed men will be in Kansas from the free states."

It was at this time that the free-state guerilla companies sprang up. Finding that armed bands of pro-slavery men were prowling about the territory, a handful of persons, chiefly youths, took the field. One company, under a young printer named Lenhart, was particularly active and bold. Nearly every one of its members had been plundered at Lawrence, or where they lived in the vicinity, some of them of all they had, even their clothes. Other companies also took the field. Capt. John Brown, senior, who lived near Ossawattomie, immediately on the sacking of Lawrence concluded that the war was begun, and that it ought not to terminate. His son, Capt. Brown, junior, had been up with a company of men to relieve Lawrence during the marshal's attack. This company only got to Palmyra when they heard that Lawrence was sacked, and that the citizens had sought to make no resistance. As they were not now wanted in Lawrence, they prepared to return, but part of their number went with Capt. Brown, senior. Several small companies of free-state youths, with no recognized leaders, or with temporary leaders, engaged in the guerilla warfare. To recapture the horses and arms taken at Lawrence was one great object, and many engaged in it with the determination to plunder those who had been in arms against, even if they should not be in arms when they happened to meet them.

One of the earliest of these adventures was the capture of three horses from Capt. Pate's camp. Pate and Coleman had been at Franklin since the sacking of Lawrence. This company went down the road, and was menacing Fish's store, where it was reported that the free-state people had gunpowder. Several free-state men had been stopped by them. While thus camped near Fish's, on the California road, three young men, almost boys, slipped into their camp unperceived at night, and each selecting a horse from the lot of horses tied up, saddled them, and, mounting, galloped off through the lines, the sentinels and others of the party who got the alarm sending bullets whistling after them through the night. They got off with the horses scathless.

Another party of Southerners were going up the Santa Fe road to commit depredations. They had taken one free-state man on the road, and abused him, and had also insulted and intimidated some settlers, and ordered them to leave the territory. Eight of the young free-state guerillas, being informed of this, started to hunt them, and found them, as I have stated, on the Santa Fe road. As there were eighteen of the Southerners, the others did not deem it advisable to attack them. They lay in wait for them where the road passes some thickets, and, as the pro-slavery men rode past, fired at them. Several of the Southerners were killed, and the rest, thinking the ambushed force larger than it was, galloped off. Several horses and some arms were also captured at this time.

Another incident occurred, which made some disturbance at the time. It was called in the papers the "Burning of St. Bernhardt," and was reported as the burning of a pro-slavery town by the abolitionists. Now Bernhardt, in the first place, is not a town, and, in the second place, it was not burned. What is called Bernhardt is constituted by a log house in which a store is kept. The owner had been a pro-slavery man, and took an active part in the difficulties distracting the territory. His store was attacked, about the time of which I write, by one of the boldest bands of young guerillas. There was no shooting done. The proprietor saw that it was no time to resist, and the others, who intended to take what they happened to want, told him to hand down this, that, and the other thing, which he did with as much equanimity and politeness as he could muster. They thus got what arms and ammunition he had, blankets, clothing, shoes and boots, provisions, etc. Having got what they wanted in this way, the lieutenant of the company, a harum-scarum New Yorker, called the owner to the door. Two horses were hitched up close by.

"Look here!" cried the lieutenant, pointing to one of the horses, "Look here! saddle that horse for me. I want him to use till the end of the war."

The obliging retailer of calico and coffee complied, while the lieutenant, a mere boy, watched the proceedings with becoming gravity.

"Look here!" he resumed again, "put the saddle on the other horse; I believe I prefer him."

This was also complied with, the man being glad to get off so easily. This was the "burning" or sacking of Bernhardt.

Another incident I will narrate. The pro-slavery men had stored some of the arms taken at Lawrence, and other articles, including two kegs of gunpowder of their own, at the house of a pro-slavery man. The guerillas heard of this, and made a night attack on it. No one was killed, as the pro-slavery men attempted no resistance. The articles sought were taken. But I need not enumerate instances; such was the state of affairs. Armed guerilla bands of both parties were ranging over the country, and whenever they met there was a skirmish. The marshal's posse had been disbanded. The Missourians had returned to Missouri, where many of the Georgians and Carolinians had also gone; the remainder being in the roving bands of which I have spoken. But few pro-slavery men were at Lecompton to defend it, as the artillery taken at Lawrence was there, with some other guns and horses, as well as other property. The governor got alarmed. He heard the reports of the skirmishes, and from all accounts the free-state guerillas appeared to get the best of it; the pro-slavery men being almost invariably worsted when there was a brush. Another thing disturbed the governor's equanimity. He had a couple of carriage horses. As he had winked at the stealing, or "pressing," of free-state men's horses, he was regarded as an accessory before the fact, and as it was desirable that guilty men only should suffer, two waggish free-state guerillas "pressed" the governor's horses. One of these they dubbed "Shannon," and the other "Pierce," and they forthwith went guerilla-ing on them. This was unendurable. Besides, the governor was quaking in his boots for fear of a regular attack by the Lawrence people on Lecompton. Under these circumstances, the military was called out, and soon dragoon camps were scattered over the country, and the clanking of sabres and the sound of iron hoofs resounded in the valley of the Kaw. The country was not placed under martial law. The bogus laws were recognized by all the territorial officers, who were pro-slavery men, or their tools, and the troops were dependent on the territorial authorities.

It was about this time that the Potawattomie affair happened. It was one of those stern and remorseless acts in civil war which make the delicate and sensitive shrink; but it is wrapped in profound mystery. In the neighborhood of Osawattomie, on the Potawattomie, lived a Mr. Wilkinson, a member of the Bogus Legislature. He and a Mr. Sherman, and a few other pro-slavery men in that neighborhood, had always been violent, bad men. Immediately after the sack of Lawrence these men concluded that the war had begun, and that the free-state people must be driven from the country. Violent partisans, men of reckless character, and covetous of the claims of the free-state settlers who surrounded them, they commenced the work of persecution. Several free-state men were ordered to leave, by letter, and verbally. One man was seized and abused, and threatened that he would be killed if he did not leave, and a cabin was burned. Such was the provocation,—how the rest happened God in heaven only knows. Terrible stories have floated through the newspapers, distorted and misrepresented by those whose interest it was to misrepresent them. From all I can learn, five of these pro-slavery men had assembled in one of their houses to arrange their plans for an attack on one man, whose life they had threatened that night, when a party of seven or eight guerillas, not young men, but stern, determined men, attacked them, and in the scuffle every pro-slavery man was killed. It has been stated that two of them were killed when unarmed and helpless, and that those who took them subjected them to a form of trial, they themselves being the judges, and shot them in cold blood, in conformity with the sentence. If this was so, it was one of those cases at which enlightened humanity will shudder, even though it cannot forget the fearful list of outrages that provoked it, and the state of insecurity which existed when pro-slavery men were permitted to run riot in murder and robbery, and no law to arrest their course. Viewing it in this, its true light, we still shudder, but attach the blame to the corrupt government and perverted official authority, where it belongs. Lynch-law is terrible always; but Kansas was the seat of guerilla warfare, and this was its sternest phase. The frightful stories about mutilation were unfounded, as applied to this affair. A Mr. Sherman, who was killed at that time, was killed by the Camanches, he having gone out to the plains to hunt buffalo. The Indians not only killed him, but mutilated his body; and his friends, when they found the body, brought it home to Potawattomie. The pro-slavery men in the neighborhood took advantage of this circumstance to confound this affair with the other, and charge it upon the "abolitionists," and it afforded a fine theme for war extras along the Missouri frontier. Free-state men, too, believing the worst pro-slavery version of it, held meetings and denounced it.

About this time the committee of Congress were sitting in Leavenworth city. The pro-slavery men were anxious to break up their investigation. Those who had been engaged in the sacking of Lawrence, and who had gone over from the north side of the river, got to Leavenworth. There, also, came Colonel Wilkes and several other Southerners. As they clustered into Leavenworth the town grew more and more warlike every day. Citizens of Leavenworth who were known to be free-state men were notified that they must leave the territory. This was the state of affairs when the following notice was found posted upon the doors of the committee rooms :

"*May* 26. Messrs. HOWARD AND SHERMAN.

"*Sirs*, with feelings of Surprise and Disgust wee have been noticeing the unjust manner in which you have been Conducting this Investigation. Wee wish to inform you that you can no longer sit in this place.

"Wee therefore request you to alter your Obnoxious course, in order to avoid the consequences which may otherwise follow.

"Capt. KEMP — in behalf of the citizens.

"Leavenworth City — 1856."

This passed without note by those to whom it was addressed, but it was significant of what was to follow. On the morning of the 28th of May, the office of the Leavenworth *Herald* issued a reprint of a violent "war" extra of the Westport paper, the design of which was to excite the border men to acts of violence against the free-state settlers of Kansas. In the forenoon of that day a pro-slavery meeting was held, at which Stringfellow and General Richardson were prominent actors. At this meeting it was decreed that all persons who had taken an active part as free-state men must leave the territory. A list of names of those they were most anxious to get rid of was drawn up.

In the mean time the Kickapoo Rangers, and the young Southerners, under Wilkes, armed themselves with the United States muskets and bayonets, put into their hands by the territorial officers, and began to parade the streets in military array. Guards were placed at every avenue of escape from the city, and, as soon as this and other steps were taken, the work of arresting began. It was noon. The committee had adjourned for dinner, and I was proceeding, in company with Mr. Sherman, and some of the officers of the committee, when we saw the band of armed men parading the streets towards the hotel, or boarding-house, where we stayed. There they arrested Judge Conway, who was acting as transcribing clerk for the commission. He had some of the testimony which he was transcribing in his possession, and gave this to Mr. Sherman, who occupied a parlor down stairs. Besides Conway they took the mail-carrier, who carried between Leavenworth and Lawrence, and another man named Baldwin, who had just come to town; neither of these gentlemen's names were on the list which Colonel Wilkes carried. Mr. Sherman stopped at the office of Messrs. Parrot and Miles More. Seeing the armed force coming down a street to the right, and knowing that my name was on the list, and having also learned that it was not the intention that *I should leave the territory*, unless I left by a route which none of us are in a hurry to travel, I took to the left, and avoided them by going through an alley, Mr. Hanscomb of the committee considerately going with me.

The armed band continued on their way down town, and drew up before the office of Messrs. Parrot and More, and arrested these gentlemen. While the prisoners were placed in line, Mr. Sherman, who saw one of the clerks of the commission amongst them, demanded of Wilkes if he had any legal process for making these arrests, or if it was by any legal authority. Wilkes told him "No;" he had a list of names given him, and those he meant to take. The armed party moved on down the street, and arrests were made until they had taken thirty prisoners. These were placed in the upper part of a frame building, and guarded. The prisoners were kept till night, and then, as those who took them had no means of keeping them, they permitted many of those they had taken to get away under a promise that they would leave the territory. That afternoon they entered the committee rooms to find me, but I had escaped through their guards, and gone up to the fort. They informed the committee that they had a certain list of names of men who must leave, and that if they had any need for them they must examine them immediately. The committee, being unable to carry on an investigation, adjourned and proceeded to Westport. The violent proceedings in Leavenworth lasted for some time, and had not been fairly settled up to the close of July.

CHAPTER XXIII.

CAPTAIN WALKER — THE GOVERNOR ON SHARPE'S RIFLES.

THE good people in and about Lecompton have been afflicted, ever since Lecompton grew out of the Bogus Legislature and a fifty thousand dollar appropriation, with a desire to "wipe out" the "abolitionists," who happened to have claims within a few miles of the place. As Lecompton was not a city, except on paper, until late in the fall of 1855, it so happened that much of the country adjacent was taken by free-state men. The effort to dispossess these people caused a great deal of trouble, and their presence was a fruitful source of annoyance. Even Judge Lecompte, who has an interest in the capital named after him, was unable to keep the matter as it should be, although he decided cases in an extra-judicial way before they came up, and threw all the influence of the bench in favor of "law and order," and the interests of Lecompton. When difficulties arise, it is natural, as it is providential, that more energetic minds should arise with them to solve them, and it is equally natural that these should be very thoroughly hated by those in whose way they happen to come.

One of the men whom the pro-slavery party at Lecompton learned to hate very thoroughly was Capt. Walker, of the Bloomington company, a brave Ohioan. The captain had rendered himself conspicuous on several occasions, and the enemies of the free-state party signalled him out for destruction. Shortly after the sack of Lawrence, Colonel Titus, the Floridan, offered three hundred dollars for his head, although it is doubtful if he could have paid this reward if it had been claimed. Threats were also made that his house should be burned down. Most of these threats the gallant captain had disregarded; but, one night, there came an intimation that looked too true for joking; the house was to be burned down that night; so the captain sent out to invite his neighbors to a cartridge frolic. Amongst others, there was Col. Topliff, who had been appointed by Gov. Robinson to drill the military companies and put the volunteers in shape. The colonel was a West Point graduate, and knew all the modes in which men could be trained to shoot each other scientifically, from the old-fashioned sergeant major polka to the Crimea drill.

On the occasion to which I refer some thirty men had congregated at Walker's. A dozen of these were stationed in the house with Walker, and the remainder, with Topliff, were stationed in an empty log cabin close at hand. Captain Walker's house stands at the point where the Lecompton road branches from the California. There is an upright fence about thirty yards in front of the building, which is a log house. Some of the chinking was knocked from the walls of the house on the night in question; but whether to look out at, or shoot out at, will be seen. All remained still about the premises until nearly midnight, and the watchers had begun to get sleepy, or to think it was a false alarm, when some fifteen horsemen came up the Lecompton road. When they got in front of Captain Walker's house, several of them dismounted, and, drawing their pistols and bowie-knives, and endeavoring to sink their humanity down to a point where they would not scruple to "kill an abolitionist," they were just on the point of pitching in, a portion of the party being in the yard, some in the saddle, and some dismounting, when Captain Walker, thinking their demonstrations sufficiently conclusive, gave the command "Fire!" and the riflemen in the house began to blaze away.

Never did the touch of the magician's wand make Harlequin go through more rapid and spasmodic evolutions than did this cracking of Sharpe's rifles, these bowie-knife heroes of law and order. No one gave the command to retreat; but that was quite superfluous; there was a general scattering. One horse fell, shot dead in the gateway, and those inside had to jump the fence. One of these gentry, in this "ground and lofty tumbling," lost half of his coat-skirt, which, with a bottle of whiskey in the pocket of the same, was left hanging to the fence. Another left his hat, and several bowie-knives and revolvers were afterwards found in the yard. In their anxiety to get off, they ran into Colonel Topliff's company, which they did not see, in the dark, until they were close on it. Luckily for them, Topliff had told the men not to fire. As soon as the ruffians saw they had got into another scrape, they again wheeled to back out of it, but not before two of them were captured.

These gentry protested their innocence of any intentions to do wrong; and, when they were taken to the house to give an account of themselves, told half a dozen different stories as to the reason of their present whereabouts, each of them being more improbable than the other, and none of them exactly agreeing. At length, seeing that appearances were too decidedly against them to make much by denying it, they admitted the party had come to burn the house, but swore that they two, individually, knew nothing of it when they left Lecompton, or *they* would not have engaged in anything so discreditable. One of these worthies was a deputy U. S. marshal, and it was ascertained that Governor Shannon's son, who officiated as his private secretary, had been with the party. It was also ascertained that, besides the horse lying dead in the gate, there were some others rendered useless by the operation, and, although the parties engaged kept very quiet about the business, it was understood that several of them were his, and that one man had been severely, if not mortally, wounded.

The dangling coat-skirt, with its whiskey-bottle, having been relieved from the paling, those of the warriors who imbibed drank to the success of the defence in border ruffian whiskey. In the morning the two prisoners were allowed to go, their captors not knowing what to do with them. They were very glad of this privilege, and made liberal promises of amendment. But these worthless fellows repaid this kind treatment basely. By going to the house they had ascertained who took part in the defence, and used this knowledge to predicate writs of arrest. Writs of arrest are not hard to obtain in Kansas when a pro-slavery man wants to arrest a free-state man. As a consequence, Captain

Walker had to flee from his house and his family, and conceal himself in the prairie ravines, or the thickets. Another of the persons present was Judge Wakefield. When the old judge heard that there was a writ out against him he started for Illinois, where he intended to "work in the cause" till the storm blew over. He was arrested at Leavenworth, while on his way, and carried back to Lecompton, but, after a good deal of detention and indignity, got away, as the actors in this affair, even with the judiciary on their side, had not the impudence to appear against him.

Under these circumstances Governor Shannon became impressed with the conviction that it would be a good thing if he could go round amongst the free-state settlers and take their guns from them. This brilliant idea about "putting an end to all trouble," had been suggested several times before by the border ruffians, but it was only now that Shannon was brought to feel its immense importance. He accordingly started in pursuit of arms, *especially* Sharpe's rifles, ignoring the constitutional right to bear arms, and the opinion the settlers might have on the subject. Well knowing that a simple demand of this kind from him would be apt to be treated with contempt by the "abolition traitors," he fortified himself with a dozen of dragoons, and a staff from the chivalry, Colonel Titus being its chief pillar and ornament, his *Fidus Achates*, and legal and military adviser to boot. In taking the field, they did not encumber their progress with ambulance, limiting the range of this peace-giving mission to the distance they could go between times to get hungry. The only articles requiring a commissariat were whiskey and brandy, which were never neglected; each man, however, providing for himself.

The governor went from house to house, searching for guns. The wonderful zeal displayed on these occasions was highly creditable to him. He searched, with a vigor which ought to recommend him for a custom-house officer, in trunks, bureaus, boxes, under beds. No place was too sacred or too mean for him to poke his nose into. He got a few guns in this way; nor was that all. There was a camp of the recently-imported Georgians close to Lecompton at the time, and they, being well advised as to what was going on, followed the governor in his rounds, keeping, however, "afar off," and stealing — no, "pressing" what horses there might be about the premises. As the guns were supposed to be gone, this was a safe business. Amongst the other houses that he entered was that of the murdered Barber. Mrs. Barber had returned to Ohio to see her friends, but the brother of the deceased and other two men were there. Here the governor rummaged through the whole house, as usual, opening every trunk and box save one small box. In this the three men had deposited their Sharpe's rifles (for they happened to have them) when they saw the governor and dragoons coming. This box was hauled out, and the governor was eying it very intently, as if he would have said,

> "Fee faw fum —
> I smell the blood of an Englishman!"

Hereupon, one of the men interfered, and said the box in question "belonged to the Widow Barber, and had been locked by her when she went away, but he would break it open," etc. The governor concluded to let the box go without being broken open; whether the name of "Widow Barber" grated on his ear, and made him willing to go, we can only guess.

Another young man he came across, and disarmed rather slyly. The person in question, knowing that Sharpe's rifles had been pronounced contraband, and happening to have one, started with it to what he supposed to be a place of greater safety. While travelling, on emerging from a bushy ravine, he was surprised to see Gov. Shannon and Col. Titus with their horses drawn up before him. His first impression was to turn and escape, but seeing only Shannon and Titus, and happening to remember that if Shannon dared to molest him, this would afford him an opportunity to shoot him and Titus, which he felt was decidedly too good a chance to throw away, he strode on. They permitted him to pass them, but just as he did so he came on the dragoons, and, being thus fairly caught, flight was out of the question. His rifle was added to Gov. Shannon's trophies of the war, the youth cursing the dragoons generally, and Shannon specially.

Thus it was that Gov. Shannon, during his hunt for Sharpe's rifles, lately, left a streak of glory in his wake that will last long after his brilliant political services are forgotten.

While thus engaged he enquired for many persons whom he was pleased to consider dangerous characters, and especially did he ask for Capt. Walker, whom he seemed anxious to catch. During this "investigation" the governor was often in a situation of which it might truly be said, that if he "was na fou, he just had plenty."

"One day an equestrian, tall, stoop-shouldered, and — well — not *exactly* sober man — rode up to the residence of Capt. Thom, which is situated on the California road, a few miles west of Lawrence. He had several specimens of the recently imported 'chivalry' with him; imposing men, none of them being of less grade than a colonel or a major, and a string of Uncle Sam's dragoons behind them, in dirty blue woollen uniform, with dirty white facings. The leader of the party drew up his horse at the door, and hailed a little girl who appeared.

"'Who lives here?'

"'Capt. Thom.'

"'Who 's Capt. Thom? What is he captain of? — hic — Captain of Capt. Walker's company, eh?' and the long-backed interrogator swayed uneasily on his horse.

"'No, sir; he 's an old sea-captain.'

"'O, yes; where is he?'

"'At Lawrence.'

"'At Lawrence! Lawrence! — hic — Lawrence! What 's he doing there? Gone to raise a company, eh?'

"'No, sir; he has gone for lumber.'

"'Lumber! lumber! What 's he going to do — hic — with lumber?'

"'Going to fence our field, sir.'

"'Ah! yes, yes; well — hic — look here, my little girl; don't you know I 'm Governor Shannon?'

"At this point, Mrs. Thom, who had been at work in the garden, came up, and the little girl, with admirable *naiveté*, said, 'Mother — Gov. Shannon.' Here Shannon cordially offered his hand, but Mrs. Thom said her hands were all dirty; she had been working in the garden.

"'Never mind, ma'am — never mind — I don't care — I don't mind dirt, ma'am, at all — hic — I never do. This is Captain Thom's, I believe?'

"'Yes, sir.'

"'Very well, ma'am, that 's all right — hic — that 's all right. You don't keep any Sharpe's rifles, Mrs. Thom, do you? I 'm out to put a stop to all this business, — hic — I 'm — I 'm determined to have all the Sharpe's rifles. We have — hic — we have law and order in this territory, ma'am, and I 'm' —

"'We 're peaceable people, sir; we have no Sharpe's rifles.'

"'That 's right, ma'am, all right. I — hic — believe you.'

"'Yes, sir; and we want protection. There have been parties — Southerners — about, molesting people and taking horses, sir. Can we not be protected from them?'

"'Certainly, ma'am, certainly. Look here,' turning to that tall specimen from Florida, Col. Titus, 'look here, colonel, I say; I want you distinctly to understand — hic — distinctly to understand, mind — that this good woman and her family are not to be molested. Yes, sir — hic — they are to be protected; mind, this house is to be protected. These are law and order folks, sir; they have no — hic — no Sharpe's rifles.' And with these assurances of protection, and a gallant bow to the ladies that nearly precipitated him from his horse, he wheeled about with his cortege of Southern bravos and United States dragoons, and rode off."

The day following he started determined to find Capt. Walker. "On that day Major Hoyt stopped for a moment at the house of Capt. Thom, and told them to send over a girl to Capt. Walker's to let him know that Shannon and the troops were coming. The little girl in question, Miss Dolly Thom, not more than nine or ten years old, I should think, went over. Capt. Walker picked up his rifle and hid in the ravine. The governor and his troops came, searched, found nothing, and went away. Shortly after they left, and just as the little girl was about starting home, these Georgians came up, and were for taking Capt. Walker's pony, that was staked out in the prairie in the front of the house. With wonderful tact and coolness, the little girl went to the pony and put her arms round its neck, as its head was down.

"'Is that your pony, sis?' asked one of them.

"'Yes, sir.'

"'Well, we must have it; the governor told us we must take it.'

"'It's my pony; you can't have it!'

"Here they threatened her, and one of them, it is said, although I can hardly credit it, presented a pistol. The little girl did not relinquish her hold of the pony, although she was nearly moved to tears. At last one of them said, 'Well, well, sis, you may keep it,' and turned away from her. With great coolness and prudence, she unloosed its halter, put on Capt. Walker's saddle and bridle, and started home with it."

About the same time a more startling occurrence took place. A free-state settler from one of the Western States, named Storrs, had a fine claim on Washington creek. A party of Georgians camped on the creek, a short distance above him. These fellows threatened to burn out and drive off Mr. Storrs. Accordingly, they attacked the house one day, or rather made demonstrations of attacking it, keeping some little distance off, as the house had one or two holes knocked out between the logs where the attack was expected, and five of the neighbors had got into it before the attacking party came up. The house was, therefore, an ugly thing to attack, and the Georgians, who were well armed, but prudent withal, made their approaches with due caution. A widow woman lived on a claim adjoining Mr. Storrs', and, seeing the state of affairs, she got a horse and galloped to Lawrence for help. There was a company of dragoons on Mount Oread, and although they had done nothing towards defending the free-state people, yet Col. Topliff, in the emergency, thought they might be got, and went to the officer of the dragoons. That officer happened to be a pretty good fellow, and so he despatched an orderly and two dragoons, who, with Col. Topliff, and other two free-state men, galloped as quickly as they could to the scene of operations. The Georgians, who were on the look-out, saw their approach, and retreated before they had been observed by them. Meanwhile, the watchers at the narrow portals of that squatter's cabin were keeping a bright look-out. So far they had kept the Georgians at bay, but they expected an attack every moment. As ill-luck would have it, the dragoons approached the house from the same direction in which the Georgians had been last seen. The besieged, who had no idea that the dragoons would come to help them, and who did not expect to see their friends come in that way, cried out, "Halt!" when the dragoons were two hundred yards off; but the party, anxious to be in time, came on pell-mell, at the gallop. "Halt!" was again shouted, but as this also was disregarded, and as those in the house thought the enemy were near enough, they blazed away. In a twinkling, both the foremost dragoons rolled over, horse and man, one of them with a bullet-hole in his arm and another in his leg; both horses were wounded, and though the other dragoon was not shot, he came down with an emphasis that left him stretched for a minute or two senseless. In the summersault his sabre flew out of its scabbard, and the scabbard bent double. As the bullets were coming too thick to be pleasant, Col. Topliff, with his two friends and the orderly, wheeled about and galloped back as hard as they came, the Sharpe's rifle-bullets going "uzz — uzz — uzz;" there is a fascinating music in a Sharpe's rifle-bullet.

Of course they were fully persuaded that the house had been taken by the Georgians, and it was not before next day that the mistake was discovered. Luckily, nobody was killed. It was only a few days after this that Storrs came into Lawrence, telling that the Georgians had attacked his house, and threatened to destroy it. A few neighbors were in the house, with his wife and two young children. The Georgians had stepped out of rifle-shot from the house, and Mr. Storrs hurried into Lawrence for assistance. Almost immediately a volunteer company, of forty-six men in all, started for the spot; eight of them being a mile or more behind the rest, and taking a different road. Before the first party arrived, the Georgians, who had been threatening the house, retired, and went up the Wakarusa to a camp. In the meantime, the party of eight came across a party of five Georgians near the crossing of the Wakarusa, and took them prisoners.

They had with them a camp-wagon and three yoke of oxen. They were brought up to the house of Mr. Storrs, where the whole company had assembled. The leader of these Georgians, a Captain Jenigen, of Georgia, one of Buford's men, evinced some anxiety, and asked one or two what free-state people did with prisoners, in a tone that showed he did not look upon the matter as a joke.

Captain Jenigen was a young Georgian, rather good-looking, although rendered fierce in expression by a red or sandy mustache. He had evidently seen better society than that in which he was found, for his comrades were a hard-looking set.

These prisoners were, on deliberation, set at liberty, with their goods, including a fine horse the captain had, which some of the boys suspected had been stolen, a double-barreled shot-gun, a fancy rifle that the captain said was a family-piece, an ornamental sword, which the captain said had been given him, as a present, by somebody in St. Louis, as his company came up the river. In fact, they got all of their own property back, even their arms. They denied having been at the sack of Lawrence, or having been with those who had attacked Storrs' house. They said they had merely stopped at the camp of these Georgians, on their way down from One-hundred-and-ten to Franklin. It was very evident that they lied in all this. Two kegs of gunpowder were taken from them, two Sharpe's rifles that had been stolen, and one of the breech-loading rifles taken at Franklin just before Lawrence was attacked. Capt. Jenigen was a gentleman, and was evidently surprised at the liberality with which he was treated. He said, as he prepared to leave, "By G—d, boys, is not this carrying the thing too far?" and then he solemnly promised that those arms just returned should never be used against free-state people. He cursed Shannon for a d——d old fool, and said he had left Buford, and was "down on him." He added, with admirable *naiveté*, that he was a gentleman when he was at home. Mr. Storrs and family left their prairie home, and returned to Lawrence for safety, taking all the furniture they could in their wagons. It was a sad scene — that bustling, hurried departure. Once I saw Mrs. Storrs wipe the perspiration from her husband's brow, and say with that inspiring tone — woman's best gift — "Well, never mind; we will get over this yet."

It afterwards turned out that this Capt. Jenigen was one of the hardest cases in Buford's regiment. Next day after we let him go, he robbed a free-state man, on the road, of his horse, watch, and money. The day after, he and his men robbed and abused a teamster. He was subsequently engaged in some of the most lawless outrages, and yet I learn that he is the only son of a respectable family in Georgia.

CHAPTER XXIV.

BATTLE OF BLACK JACK.

TOWARDS the close of May, 1856, Captain H. C. Pate, with his company of "Shannon's Sharp Shooters," went down towards Osawattomie. Their business may be inferred from a statement of the occurrence published in the *Lecompton Union*, by Mr. Brock, the first lieutenant of the company. He says:

"We were going down to the southern part of the territory, expecting to see rattlesnakes and abolitionists, and took our guns along."

Captain Pate, however, pretended to be an officer under Marshal Donaldson. Quite likely they belonged to the "militia," as they had the United States arms belonging to the territory; but most of them, like their gallant captain, lived in Missouri. Captain Pate is a Virginian by birth. He is a good-looking fellow, and a man of intelligence. He has been engaged as an editor in Cincinnati, and has acted as the Kansas correspondent of the Missouri Republican; for which he provided pro-slavery versions of the occurrences in Kansas, he residing in Western Missouri. He is a violent pro-slavery man, and has been engaged in the lawless inroads on the territory ever since he has lived in the Missouri border. He was at the sacking of Lawrence, and distinguished himself chiefly by riding about on a fine horse, he being decorated with ribbons. It would be impossible to speak highly of the moral character of a man who has participated so actively in outrages on an intelligent and moral people. He has the bearing of a gentleman, but is either the tool of a corrupt system, or is a very corrupt man.

Directly the reverse of this picture, in many respects, is a character I must now introduce, — old Captain Brown, or Captain John Brown, Sen. Captain Brown moved to the territory from the State of New York, early in 1855, but he is by birth a Vermonter. He is an old soldier, and was through the war of 1812. Tall and stern-looking, hard-featured and resolute, there is something in Captain Brown's air that speaks the soldier, every inch of him. He is not a man to be trifled with; and there is no one for whom the border ruffians entertain a more wholesome dread than Captain Brown. They hate him as they would a snake, but their hatred is composed nine tenths of fear. Although the captain is a practical man, he is one of those abstruse thinkers who have read much and *thought* more. In his opinions he is inexorably inflexible, and the world generally would pronounce him a "fanatic." He is one of those Christians who have not quite vanished from the face of the earth, — that is, he asks the blessing of God when he breaks his bread, and does not, even in camp, forget his devotions in his zeal against the border ruffians. There is not a more stern disciplinarian in Kansas; he is a regular martinet, and so carefully can he conceal his quarters, that, when you wish to find him when *he does not wish it*, you might as well hunt for a needle in a haystack as for Captain Brown. He is a strange, resolute, repulsive, iron-willed, inexorable old man. He stands like a solitary rock in a more mobile society, a fiery nature, and a cold temper, and a cool head, — a volcano beneath a covering of snow. Whether with reason or not, I cannot say, but he was regarded as a participator, if not leader, in the Potawattomie affair; and, as the border ruffians desired to kill him, an object Captain Pate admits he had in view was "to capture Old Brown."

While near Osawattomie he contrived to seize two of the old man's sons, — Captain John Brown, Jun., who was a member of the State Legislature, and Mr. Jason Brown. These were taken while quietly engaged in their avocations. Captain Brown, Jun., had been up with his company at Lawrence, immediately after the sacking of the place, and at the time the men at Potawattomie were killed. He had returned home when he saw he could not aid Lawrence, and quietly went to work. He and his brother Jason were taken by Pate; charged with murder; kept in irons in their camp, and treated with the greatest indignity and inhumanity. While Pate was thus taking people prisoners, without any legal authority or writs, he was joined by Captain Wood's company of dragoons, who, so far from putting a stop to his violent career, aided him in it, and took from him, at his desire, the two prisoners, keeping them under guard in their camp, heavily ironed and harshly treated. While these companies were thus travelling close to each other Captain Pate's men burned the store of a man named Winer, a German, who was supposed to have been in the Potawattomie affair. They also burned the house of John Brown, Jun., in which, amongst a variety of household articles, a valuable library was consumed. They also burned the cabin of another of the Browns (the old captain has six grown sons), and also searched houses, menaced free-state settlers, and acted in a violent and lawless manner generally.

Not being able to find Captain Brown at Osawattomie, Pate's company and the troops started back again for the Santa Fe road. In the long march that intervened, under a hot sun, the two Browns, now in charge of the dragoons, and held without even the pretence of bogus law, were driven before the dragoons, chained like beasts. For twenty-five miles they thus suffered under this outrageous inhumanity. Nor was this all. John Brown, Jun., who had been excited by the wild stories of murder told against his father, by their enemies, and who was of a sensitive mind, was unable to bear up against this and his treatment during the march, and afterwards, while confined in camp, startled his remorseless captors by the wild ravings of a maniac, while he lashed his chains in fury till the dull iron shone like polished steel.

To rescue his two sons from their captors became the determination of Captain Brown. Like a wolf robbed of its young he stealthily, but resolutely, watched for his foes, while he skirted through the thickets of the Merodesin and Ottawa creeks. Perhaps it was a lurking dread of Captain Brown's rescuing the prisoners that made Captain Pate deliver them to the United States dragoons. The dragoons, with their prisoners, encamped on Middle Ottawa creek, while Pate went on with his men to the Santa Fe road, near Hickory Point. On the evening of Saturday, the 31st of May, he encamped on the head of a small branch or ravine, called Black Jack, from the kind of timber growing there. His camp was on the head of the ravine, in the edge of the prairie, not far from the Santa Fe road, but to the north of it. This camp was some five miles east of Palmyra, and nearly the same distance in a north north-easterly direction from Prairie city. The bottom of the ravine at Black Jack, besides the growing timber, had some deep water-drains or ruts, round which was a thicket; there were also several bogs on the spot where the camp was.

On the same night that they pitched their tents on Black Jack, Pate's company attacked and plundered the town of Palmyra. That night they only got arms and a few other articles. They surprised the household of Mr. Barricklon, who keeps a store in the place, getting into the house before the inmates awoke. There were several men there, but no resistance was offered to Pate's men. Not being satisfied, the Missourians returned next morning and made a more thorough work of plundering. They took one keg of gunpowder, which was in the store, and blew it up in the Santa Fe road, just to gratify their reckless disposition. They loaded a wagon with plunder, and started back for their camp. This was on Sunday morning.

On Saturday night Captain Shore had been out reconnoitring the enemy. Captain Shore is a free-state man, who came from Missouri. He was a member of the State Legislature of Kansas. He is a quiet man, but brave and resolute. He commanded the Prairie city company. The same night Dr. Graham, of Prairie city, along with a Mr. Barringer, went to Palmyra to reconnoitre. They knew that a band of Missourians was somewhere in the neighborhood, but did not know where. About nine o'clock at night the forces, coming to plunder Palmyra, came across these two men and took the doctor prisoner; Mr. Barringer escaped. The doctor was carried prisoner to their camp. They also took a Baptist preacher prisoner, the Rev. Father Moore. He was a free-state man, but came to the territory from Missouri. He was an old man, and was taken while riding down the Santa Fe road towards Westport. Some of his captors had known him in Missouri, and tormented him after they had made him prisoner, with a wicked refinement of cruelty. They knew he was opposed to drinking; so, when they had taken him prisoner, they seized his person, and, putting a tin funnel in his mouth, poured liquor down his throat, — the scoundrels swearing that they would "make the old preacher drunk." On Sunday they took another prisoner, a free-state man, who lived in that neighborhood, an Englishman, named Lymer.

After dinner, on Sunday, Pate's men wanted to go over to Prairie city and plunder it. Pate attempted to dissuade them, but some of them would not be dissuaded. Amongst other things, they had stolen a number of horses from the free-state men. Prairie city is a small place yet, and, fancying that it would be easily taken, and that no resistance would be offered, six of Pate's men started on the expedition. At the time this party approached Prairie city, the people of that place and vicinity were congregated in the house of Dr. Graham, to hear preaching. They could "watch as well as pray," however. There were some twenty men present, and most of them, after the old Revolutionary pattern, had gone to church with their guns on their shoulders. It was one of those primitive meetings which may often be found in the West, with the slight addition of its military aspects; simple and unostentatious garb; easy and primitive manners; a log house, the ribbed timbers of which gave a rough-cast look to the simple scene, with here and there the heavy octagon barrel of a long Western rifle, or the smooth barrel of a shot-gun, were visible where they leaned against the wall, ready for action. The worshippers were nearly through with their devotions, and the closing psalm was echoing through the timbers of that log house, to one of those quaint old melodies to be found in the *Missouri Harmony*, when the sacred strain was snapped by another "Missouri Harmony." A watcher entered, saying,

"The Missourians! — they are coming!"

Never was a congregation dismissed on shorter notice. The holy man forgot the benediction in remembering his rifle. The six ruffians had galloped up, when the congregation, suddenly rushing out, surrounded them. Two of the number, who were a little back, wheeled their horses and galloped off, more than one bullet going whizzing after them; but, thanks to their fleet steeds, or their enemies' hurried shooting, they got off scathless, and got back and told a frightful story to Pate about the other men being killed — "horribly!" etc.

The other men were merely taken prisoners of war. One of them, however, had come very near getting his quietus. A son of Dr. Graham, a boy of about eleven years, seized his father's double-barrelled gun at the first alarm, and hurried out to the fence, the Missourians, who were thus all taken aback, being immediately outside of it. The daring boy, with his Irish blood up, went within three rods of them, and, poking his gun over the fence, took deliberate aim at one of the men, and would have fired the next moment, — for Bub was not enlightened in the mysterious "articles of war," — when a free-state man put aside his gun, and said,

"Bub, what are you doing?"

"Going to shoot that fellow."

"You must n't."

Bub shook his head and began to put up his gun again, muttering,

"He 's on pap's horse."

Bub remembered that his "pap" was then a prisoner in the enemy's camp, if not killed, and he felt that important interests were devolving on him, and must not be neglected. The names of three of the men taken were Forman, Luck and Hamilton; the name of the other I forget. They all lived about Westport.

Through the whole of that Sunday night did Captain Brown's and Captain Shore's company hunt for Captain Pate, but their search was unsuccessful. As the gray dawn of Monday morning, June 2d, glimmered in, they had returned to Prairie city, when two scouts, Messrs. McAlliston and Hill, brought the tidings that the enemy was encamped on the Black Jack, some four or five miles off. A small party was left to guard the prisoners, and the remainder immediately took up their line of march for the enemy.

Of those who thus left Prairie city, Captain Shore's company numbered twenty men, himself included, and Captain Brown had nine men besides himself. They rode towards the Black Jack.

Arrived within a mile of it, they left their horses and two of their men to guard them. They despatched other two messengers, one to Palmyra for help, and another to Captain Abbott's company, some eight miles off, on the Wakarusa. The remainder, twenty-six men all told, in two divisions, each captain having his own men, marched quietly forward on the enemy.

On Sunday night there were sixty men in the pro-slavery camp on the Black Jack. Coleman, the murderer of Dow, and a number with him, had reinforced Pate. Late on Sunday night five or six pro-slavery men left the camp; but, on the morning of the second June, they had upwards of fifty well-armed men in martial array. Three or four wagons had been drawn up in a line, as a part of breastwork, several rods out on the prairie from the ravine, and one of the tents was there. Such was the state of affairs when the outer picket-guard, about six o'clock in the morning, galloped in and reported,

"The abolitionists are coming!"

"Where — how many?" and there were a hurrying to and fro, and seizing arms.

"Across the prairie — there 's a hundred of them," cried the frightened border ruffian, whose fears had multiplied the approaching force by four, and who probably had never stopped to examine carefully or count, but had galloped off as soon as he caught the first glimpse of them.

Captain Pate's position at Black Jack was a very strong one. It afforded shelter for his men, and, except by a force coming up the ravine or stream from the timber at Hickory Point, had to be approached over open prairie, sloping up from the place where the Missourians were posted. When the alarm was sounded, Captain Pate drew up his men in line behind the breastwork of wagons.

When they neared the enemy's partition Captain Brown wished Shore to go to the left and get into the ravine below them, while he, with his force, would get into the upper or prairie part of the ravine, in the bottom of which was long grass. As the ravine made a bend, they would thus have got in range of the enemy on both sides, and had them in cross fire, without being in their own fire. Captain Brown, with his nine men, accordingly went to the right. Captain Shore, with more bravery than military skill, approached the foe over the hill to the west of their camp, marching over the prairie up within good range, fully exposed, and with no means of shelter near them.

"Who comes there? What do you want?" cried Captain Pate.

"When I get my men in line I 'll show you," cried the gallant Captain Shore; and, true to his word, without waiting for or wanting any humbug parley, the gallant band poured in a volley on the Missourians, who were drawn up behind the wagons, the latter instantly returning it.

Volley after volley pealed through the air, and echoed from the ravine at Black Jack away up to the dense timber at Hickory Point. Meantime, Captain Brown had hurried into the ravine on the right of Shore, and, posting his men well, began to discourse the "music of the spheres" from that quarter.

"We 're whipped! we 're whipped!" yelled the Missourians, before the battle had lasted ten minutes, and, breaking from the wagon, they retreated to the ravine and concealed themselves there, some seven or eight of them being wounded. One was shot through the mouth by a Sharpe's rifle bullet. He had been squatted behind the wagon wheel; the ball hit one of the spokes, shivering it, and the border ruffian, in trying the juggler's feat of catching it in his mouth, got it lodged somewhere away about the root of the tongue, or the back of his neck. Another was shot in the upper part of the breast, or the lower part of his neck, the bullet descending, and lodging in his back. Another, Jim McGea, of Westport, was wounded in the most uncomfortable manner. He, with several others, who were also wounded, left their camp by the eastern side and rode away, like other Hampdens, leaving the battle-field; but, O, how unlike Hampdens in anything else!

After Pate's men retreated to the ravine, he endeavored to rally them, and a fire was kept up from the ravine where they lay concealed, and from which they could shoot in comparative security, although the bullets were whistling over their heads at a fearful rate. And soon the position of Captain Shore was found to be hazardous and critical; fully exposed to an enemy who could shoot at his men almost without running risk, they began to give way, and soon they had nearly all retreated some two hundred yards up the slope, on to the high ground where they were out of range. Captain Shore, however, and two or three of his men, went over and joined Brown, where the force lay in the long grass, firing down the ravine. While this firing was going on, to little purpose on either side, Captain Brown went after the boys on the hill. Some few of them had gone off after ammunition; one or two of them were sitting in the grass fixing their guns. Finding that they could not be brought up again to a charge, he led them rather nearer the enemy, and induced them to shoot at the horses of the enemy, which were over the ravine, at long shot. This he did to get up their spirits, as most of them were mere boys, and to intimidate the enemy. He returned to the ravine. The firing was still kept up. It is proper to state that Brown and Shore's men had but four guns of long range; there were only three or four Sharpe's rifles in both companies.

While the firing was going on, one of Pate's men got up and swore he would see to the prisoners. A guard had been stationed to watch the three prisoners, the tent in which they were being the most exposed part of the camp. This guard was in great trepidation. The prisoners had thrown themselves on the ground, and the trembling guard also lay down, taking care to get the person of Dr. Graham between his own precious carcass and the enemy. So matters were when the ruffian to whom I have alluded went to the tent with fierce oaths. Dr. Graham saw him approach with ferocious expression, and, just at that moment, the ruffian raised his pistol, aiming at the doctor, who gave a spring just as the piece went off; the ball hitting him in the side, inflicting a flesh wound. Graham sprang into the ditch of the ravine, and, as he did so, received another ball in his hip. He broke from the camp, and fled, fifteen pistol-shots being fired after him by the person who first attacked him and the guard. He got off without further injury, and joined his friends on the hill.

The firing had lasted three hours. Only two free-state men were wounded. One of these, Mr. Carpenter, was shot in the arm in the early part of the engagement. The other, Mr. Thompson, a young man with a great exuberance of spirits, kept springing up in the grass, shouting and firing his gun, when, on one of these occasions, he was struck by a ball in the side. Luckily it glanced off the ribs, or it would have killed him; as it was it inflicted a severe wound, and two of his friends had to take him off the field. There were now only nine free-state men in the ravine keeping up a fire, and about as many more on the hill, three hundred yards from the enemy, who kept firing at the horses, and occasionally making a sally, but never near enough to do much mischief. Frederick Brown, one of the captain's sons, a half-witted lad, stood on the brow of the hill midway between the two divisions of the free-state force. He was in full view of the enemy, and had got a sword, which he was brandishing in the air, and shouting, "Come on!" as if he had a regiment behind him. His manœuvres and demonstrations had a powerful effect on some of the most timid of the enemy. The pro-slavery men in the ravine were getting discouraged; they dared not venture out of their shelter, and the bullets were making ugly music in it. They knew that the free-state men might receive reinforcements at any moment. In this view of the case they began to drop off. One by one they would slip down the ravine till they were out of range, and then get their horses, which were on the eastern side, and gallop away. The free-state men had no cavalry force in the field, and no men to spare in any shape from where they were, or they would have prevented this. Some one or two of them had started off to get help the moment the party retreated to the ravine. Those who went subsequently pretended to be going for help, also; but there is no doubt their individual safety was the great consideration. One or two went off when they were wounded. In fact all the wounded pro-slavery men had thus ridden off but two, and these lay helpless, looking as if they might "go off" in another way.

The bravest man in the pro-slavery camp was a young Southerner, named James. Whether this was his first or second name I do not know; but he was a gallant fellow. The tent, where they had ammunition, was out of the ravine, and exposed to shot. To this James went, on several occasions, for supplies.

At last Captain Pate sent this James and their prisoner Lymer out with a flag of truce. These walked up the slope together towards the free-state men, who, regarding the white flag as a surrender, ceased firing. When they reached Captain Brown, that personage demanded of James if he was captain of the company. James replied, "No."

"Then," said Captain Brown, "you stay here with me, and let Mr. Lymer go and bring him out. I will talk with him."

Thus summoned, Captain Pate came out; and, as he approached Captain Brown, began to say he was an officer under the United States Marshal, and that he wanted to explain this, as he supposed Capt. Brown would not continue to fight against him if he knew it. He was running on this way when Brown cut him short:

"Captain, I understand exactly what you are, and do not want to hear more about it. Have you a proposition to make to me?"

"Well, no — that is" —

"Very well, captain," interrupted Brown, "*I have one to make to you* — that is, your unconditional surrender."

There was no evading this, and just as little chance to make a fool of old Brown, who, pistol in hand, returned with James and Captain Pate to their camp in the ravine, where he repeated his demand for the unconditional surrender of the whole company; which was complied with. There were only nine free-state men in the ravine, or in sight, when this was done; four of these, by Brown's orders, remained where they had been stationed. The rest, five, Captain Brown included, received the surrender of the arms and persons of twenty-one men, besides the wounded. A large number of arms were obtained, some of which had been taken from Lawrence, and some at Palmyra, twenty-three horses and mules (some of the horses had been killed by the boys when firing at them from the hill), wagons, provisions, camp-equipage, and a considerable portion of the plunder taken at Palmyra, and some of that taken during the sack of Lawrence. One drum, that was taken, was riddled with bullet-holes, and all the wagons were more or less injured by the bullets.

The prisoners being now disarmed were ranged in file by the slender band of captors. The boys on the hill were induced to come in, swelling the free-state force to sixteen; and soon the remainder of those who had been in the battle when it commenced began to crowd in, as did many others. In about half an hour after the surrender, Captain Abbott, who had commanded the company who rescued Branson, and who now commanded a company from the Wakarusa, of fifty men, came up with his company. Brown marched with the prisoners and spoils for his own camp. All of that afternoon men were coming in; but the game was over. Towards night those who had started from Lawrence began to get to Brown's camp. The wounded pro-slavery men were taken to the residence of Dr. Graham, at Prairie city; and the doctor, though wounded himself, attended to them, as did others. It was expected that two of the Missourians would certainly die.

CHAPTER XXV.

BATTLE OF FRANKLIN.

Almost immediately after the battle of Palmyra some motive power that lay behind the dragoons sent them trooping down in the direction where Capt. Brown was supposed to be. But it must not be supposed that all the soldiers sympathized with this persecution of the free-state cause. One subaltern officer met a free-state man, and, supposing he would have means of finding the party, told him to go down and tell Capt. Brown that they were coming. Another officer, who had come upon a fragment of a free-state camp, and who saw their rough camp life and hard fare, swore, on his honor as a soldier, that it looked too much like the days of Marion and his men. He asked how they were off for ammunition, and, learning that they were none too well supplied, slipped five dollars into their hands to get more. Other officers there were who had violent pro-slavery proclivities, and who not only executed their hard orders against the settlers of Kansas, but exceeded them, and acted in a lawless and irregular manner, which would have brought condign punishment on their heads but for the unsettled state of the country and the impossibility of punishing crimes against free-state men.

Bands of roving free-state men began to concentrate towards Franklin, the Wakarusa, Hickory Point, and Bull Creek, on the Shawnee reserve. It was at Franklin the Southerners first began to muster, and they were clustering there before the battle of Black Jack. Buford's men and some Missourians were there for nearly a week in martial array, and evidently in full communication with the other parties coming into the territory and forming in it. They had a brass six-pounder, and a large quantity of ammunition and camp provisions. They had been taking prisoners, and had a free-state man in their guard-house on the night of the 4th of June.

To attack this point, take the ammunition and the cannon, and make the place a dangerous one for those who had thus taken possession of it, was the policy of the companies of free-state rangers.

Franklin lies four and a half miles south-east of Lawrence, near the Wakarusa. It has, on more than one occasion, been used as a camp by the border ruffians, and is the base of operations against Lawrence by bands coming from Westport or Independence, Mo. During the Wakarusa war Franklin was, in point of fact, pro-slavery head-quarters. At the sack of Lawrence it was the seat of a mischievous camp, which formed a rallying point for those who came from Missouri, and at that point the Lawrence supplies were intercepted, and arms, provisions and goods, taken.

It was clearly foreseen that there was likely to be fighting towards Palmyra or somewhere in that direction, but it was deemed advisable not to leave a fire in the rear. It was likewise possible that Lawrence would be attacked again, even by a small party, if the men were to leave it. It was therefore secretly resolved that Franklin should be attacked and disabled. The recent battles and skirmishes had put the pro-slavery men on their guard. There were twenty-three pro-slavery men, partly Missourians, partly Georgians and Alabamians, in the guard-room where they were posted. Sam Salters was with them. Besides these there was a pretty fair sprinkling of the pro-slavery residents of the town.

As it was supposed that the force in Franklin was much larger than it really was, the first determination was to have a sufficient force to meet any emergency. The affair was bungled. The person who had undertaken its management had botched it, or rather had been too indolent to take the proper steps to secure concert of action. The Wakarusa company was to come up and attack on one side, and the Lawrence boys on the other; but they had no means of knowing the movements of the other party, or at what time they were to unite in attack. Neither was any disposition of the forces made so that they could both attack without getting into each other's fire. The intention was to take the gun, but no provision was made to ensure its being got off. A company of dragoons was camped on Mount Oread, only a few miles off, and might come down at any moment.

In Lawrence all was mystery. Those few who knew of it could get no information as to how the thing was to be done, or who were going. After dark, nearly all who had contemplated going supposed that the expedition had been abandoned. A few, however, were determined it should not be; they declared they would go if no others went. "These boys from the Wakarusa will be there, and may get in a scrape, and we must go;" so said some, and some few did go. About a dozen went in one lot, nearly all of them officers of some kind; stragglers by twos and threes went after them.

About sixteen of the Lawrence boys mustered in what would be the suburbs if the place were not altogether rural. Part of these were left to guard the outlet towards Lawrence.

It was as dark as Erebus, and a little before two in the morning of the 4th, when the little party defiled by the ridge on which the town stands, and entered the streets of Franklin. The other company had got a guide, and were to be at the point at the same hour, but owing to the darkness had lost the way, and were stumbling in the ravines to the south of the town, down towards the Wakarusa. The first-mentioned little party, as gallant fellows as ever stood before a breach, calmly walked up the street to the spot where they heard the cannon was, for the purpose of taking it and the ammunition without firing, if possible.

But the cannon was not to be found; in fact, nothing was to be found, or was where it should be. For more than an hour those who had arrived were marching about seeking for something they could not find, or ascertaining the position of the enemy; and before operations had been commenced the pro-slavery men were wide awake and ready. They kept in-doors, which clearly showed their discretion. Those in the guard-house were all on the *qui vive.* They had received notice of what was coming, and had their brass cannon posted in the door and loaded with an affectionate regard for abolitionists.

It was at last ascertained that the guard-house must be assailed, and at it they went. In front of the guard-house they were hailed, and the leader of the free-state rangers demanded that they should surrender. Again they were hailed; again the demand to surrender was made, when the guard fired on them. The rangers poured in a volley; it was returned At this stage of the game something occurred which, with better gunning, might have been serious. That it happened without killing several free-state men is almost miraculous. These were just across the street from the guard-house, and but few shots had been fired, when the six-pound howitzer, the muzzle of which was pointed out of the guard-house, was discharged. It was fired rather obliquely, and missed the party, being also a little too high. What it was loaded with Heaven only knows; probably shingle-nails, horse-chains, or the refuse of a blacksmith shop; for such an infernal noise has not been heard since the siege of Sevastopol, as when the missiles went whistling by.

The firing from both sides continued with great rapidity, the bullets whistling about like hail. The pro-slavery men in the other houses commenced firing on the free-state men, who had assailed, or wanted to assail, nothing but the guard-house. The fifteen, finding it pretty hot, lay down flat in the streets, and the fire continued for nearly an hour — they hoping their friends would come up, when they would make an attack on the guard-house.

Now this kind of work was decidedly interesting. A man of squeamish morality, or weak nerves, or who was "conservative," had better be in his bed. There is something confoundedly radical in a bullet; and, if it be a Sharpe's rifle bullet, it is perfectly fanatical. They *are* musical — decidedly. The boys got divided, — in fact, they were never all together, — and when the firing began it was not safe for anybody to be poking about anywhere, for the bullets were going in all directions. Major Redpath was sent after the other company; but he might as well have been sent after a rifle-bullet, or to dive through the muddy Kaw after a catfish. In spite of the serious nature of the case, the boys in the street could not help laughing at his rashness. He mounted a horse and deliberately rode up the street, where the balls were whistling about too plenty to be pleasant, his horse kicking and plunging, and finally he got in full range with the fire of his own friends, and had to back out; whereupon he dismounted and led his horse down the street again.

One very cautious gentleman, when the firing began, made his exodus on the crawling plan. He said he was "going for assistance," but was not heard from afterwards that day. But nearly all acted with the coolest intrepidity. They loaded and fired with as much exactitude as if they had been on parade; only they were lying flat on their bellies, and had no particular inclination to resume the perpendicular. That is one advantage of a Sharpe's rifle. You can lie as flat as you please, poke out your gun before you, shove in the cartridges from behind, and fire away as long as you have any cartridges left.

It was a most magnificent spectacle, — the sheets of livid fire in the darkness of the night. The streets were momentarily lit up when two or three happened to go off together, but there was no attempt at regularity.

Guided by the firing, the Wakarusa men found their way to Franklin; but, although the flashes lighted the streets of Franklin, this latter company, having had no proper understanding or concert of action, as the balls were whistling in all directions, and as they were as likely to be shot by their friends as their enemies, scarce knew how to advance. One thing, however, they did know, — the Buford men had most of their stores in a place near where they came up. From this they obtained a large quantity of powder, shot, and caps, a lot of provisions, and a few Sharpe's rifles, and some of the old breech-loading alligator guns that had been taken at Franklin previous to the burning of Lawrence.

In this place there were stores of all kinds, and the bulk of what was got consisted of flour, bacon, coffee, sugar, and other "law and order" condiments, which Buford had stored at Franklin for the faithful, little thinking that the "abominable abolitionists" were going to lay their "appropriation clause" (*i. e.* claws) on them.

A wagon was loaded with these, and, as day was approaching, and the United States dragoons might possibly interfere, being within hearing, this company made off toward the Wakarusa, on the road to Palmyra. Two or three wagons could have been loaded if they had been there.

Thus the Wakarusa company attended to the stores, while those in town kept up the fire. This was the only part of the proceeding that was done according to agreement; the Lawrence boys, having brought no teams with them, had not calculated on doing anything but fighting.

The firing in the streets of Franklin ceased. Day was beginning to come on, and reveal the shady outline of timber on the Kaw. The pro-slavery men did not surrender, but dared not return the fire, and the others ceased when they did. In fact, the Southerners in the little guard-house began to "vamose the ranch" when the firing got too hot, the house in question being fairly riddled. When daylight began to come in the enemy had evacuated, save one, who was so badly wounded he could not get away. He died next day. Two Carolinians, a Georgian, and an Alabamian, were wounded, according to the accounts published in the pro-slavery papers, besides Tischmaker, who was killed. They represented that the town had been attacked by a hundred or two hundred abolitionists, and I don't blame them; for fifteen men with Sharpe's rifles can make noise enough for a hundred. The free-state prisoner made his escape from the guard-house in the morning. His clothes had been cut by the bullets of his friends. No free-state man was even wounded; which, from the nature of the engagement, is almost incredible.

And now those in the town were in an awkward predicament. The cannon had been captured and lay deserted at the door of the guard-house; but they could not carry it, of course, and had no team to take it away. Besides, the dragoons were encamped close to the way they must return, and they wished merely to enter Lawrence as quietly as they had left it, and had no desire to take the gun there. Under these circumstances they evacuated the place.

One incident I had almost forgot, which will show the small amount of blood-thirstiness manifested by the free-state men. After the cannon had been discharged a man was bold enough to step out to load it. A free-state man who had crept up was close to him when he came out, and said sharply:

"D—n you, load that gun if you dare!" and, instead of shooting him, which he would have had to do very deliberately, as he was very close, he gave him a smart blow with the butt of his rifle, and drove him into the guard-house, adding:

"D—n you, get in there!"

Bullets whistled about this fellow's ears; but in the darkness he was not shot. Another man came out to load it afterwards, when the bullets whistled about him rather briskly, and one of them took off his ear. That was rather close shooting, and the fellow dodged in, doubtless having *heard something*.

The Lawrence boys left Franklin on the morning of the fifth of June, not exactly in military order. In fact, no one knew when they did go. They melted away with the darkness, and dropped into Lawrence one by one ere the quiet, staid citizens of that place were fairly out of bed, or before the gossips could collect in front of the post-office to inquire, "Ho! did you hear of that affair at Franklin?"

The officer commanding the dragoons on the Oread heard the roar of the cannon, and, springing up, his camp was soon in motion; he telling the orderly to have the men ready, while he ran to the brow of the hill to listen. He could hear the cracking of the rifles in the distance, and could guess what it meant; but very judiciously staid where he was, and permitted his men to stay. After daylight two pro-slavery men from Franklin rode up to his camp, and wanted him to come down with his dragoons, complaining bitterly of the "abolitionists." The officer replied by pointing with his hand down to Lawrence, where the blackened ruins of buildings were visible, and said:

"Look at that! who begun it?"

And now the reader will excuse me for writing of events which transpired rather before the dates of which I have been writing. I mentioned the arrest of Gov. Robinson at Lexington. This was without a warrant. He was retained by violence until Gov. Shannon had made a requisition for him to Gov. Price of Missouri, which Shannon did before any process had been issued by any territorial court against him. The pro-slavery men had determined he should be taken, and Shannon scrupled at no step, and faltered at no irregularity, which could secure this purpose.

Shortly after Robinson was taken, G. W. Brown, Esq., of the *Herald of Freedom*, and Mr. Gaius Jenkins, who had driven down Gov. Reeder in his carriage when that personage escaped, were arrested by a mob at Kansas city, and, without any requisition, carried violently into the territory and surrendered up, by the lawless men who took them, to the authorities of the territory. These two men, after having been detained for a short time in Westport, were taken to Lecompton. Gov. Robinson was taken up the same way until they arrived within a short distance from Franklin, when orders came to go immediately back. At first it was thought that this alarm was needless; but it was well grounded. Two or three companies of men were watching the Santa Fe and California roads, and, had they come on, he would have been rescued to a certainty. He was finally sent up the river to Leavenworth, — was retained there for a week, and while there Stringfellow tried to get up an excitement to have him lynched. Had they made such an attempt, he probably would have been rescued. He was finally sent to Lecompton, Judge Lecompte refusing to liberate him or any other of the political prisoners on bail.

These prisoners were therefore confined at Lecompton in prison-tents, guarded by United States dragoons. The prisoners were Governor Charles Robinson, General G. W. Dietzler, Judge G. W. Smith, and G. W. Brown, Esq. To these were added Captain John Brown, Jr., and Mr. Williams, members of the Legislature.

I subjoin two of the indictments; the first against several persons for "high treason," the other for usurping office:

"UNITED STATES OF AMERICA.

"TERRITORY OF KANSAS, COUNTY OF DOUGLAS:

"*In the First District Court of the First Judicial District of the Territory of Kansas. April Term*, A. D. 1856.

"The Grand Jury of the United States of America, within and for the First Judicial District, Douglas County, Territory of Kansas, sworn to inquire upon their oath, present, that Andrew H. Reeder, Charles Robinson, James H. Lane, George W. Brown, George W. Dietzler, George W. Smith, Samuel N. Wood, Gaius Jenkins, late of the County of Douglas, First Judicial District of the Territory of Kansas, owing allegiance to the United States of America, wickedly devising and intending the peace and tranquillity of the said United States to disturb, and to prevent the execution of the law thereof, within the same, to wit: A law of the said United States entitled an act to organize the Territories of Nebraska and Kansas, approved May 30, 1854, on the first day of May, the year of our Lord one thousand eight hundred and fifty-six, in the county, district, and territory aforesaid, and within the jurisdiction of this court, wickedly and traitorously did intend to levy war against the said United States, within the same, and to fulfil and bring to effect of the said traitorous intention of him, the said Andrew H. Reeder, Charles Robinson, James H. Lane, George W. Brown, George W. Dietzler, George W. Smith, Samuel N. Wood, Gaius Jenkins; afterwards, that is to say, on the seventeenth day of May, in the year of our Lord 1856, in the said district, county, and territory aforesaid, and within the jurisdiction of this court, with a great multitude of persons, whose names are to the said grand jurors unknown, to a great number, to wit: the number of one hundred persons, and upwards, armed and arrayed in warlike manner, that is to say, with guns, swords, pistols, artillery, and other warlike weapons, as well offensive as defensive, being then and there unlawfully and traitorously assembled, did traitorously assemble and combine against the said United States, and then and there with force and arms, wickedly and traitorously and with the wicked and traitorous intention to oppose and prevent, by means of intimidation and violence, the execution of said law of the said United States, within the same, did array and expose themselves, in a warlike and hostile manner against the said United States; and then and there, with force, and in pursuance of such, their traitorous intentions, they, the said Andrew H. Reeder, Charles Robinson, James H. Lane, George W. Brown, George W. Smith, George W. Dietzler, Samuel N. Wood, and Gaius Jenkins, with the said persons so as aforesaid, traitorously assembled, armed and arrayed in manner aforesaid, wickedly and traitorously did levy war against the said United States, and further to fulfil and bring to effect the said traitorous intention of him the said Andrew H. Reeder, Charles Robinson, James H. Lane, George W. Brown, George W. Smith, George W. Dietzler, Samuel N. Wood, and Gaius Jenkins; and, in pursuance and in execution of the said wicked intention and traitorous combination, to oppose, resist, and prevent, the said law of the said United States from being carried into execution in the territory and district aforesaid, they, the said Andrew H. Reeder, Charles Robinson, James H. Lane, George W. Brown, George W. Smith, George W. Dietzler, Samuel N. Wood, and Gaius Jenkins, afterwards, to wit, on the 20th day of May, A. D. 1856, in the territory, district, and county aforesaid, and within the jurisdiction of the said court, with the said persons whose names to the said grand jurors aforesaid are unknown, did wickedly and traitorously assemble against the said United States, with the avowed intention, by force of arms and intimidation, to prevent the execution of the said law of the said United States within the same, and with the intention then and there and thereby to subvert the government and law, and of the said United States, in the said Territory of Kansas; and in pursuance and execution of such, their wicked and traitorous combination and intention, they, the said Andrew H. Reeder, Charles Robinson, James H. Lane, George W. Brown, George W. Smith, George W. Dietzler, Samuel N. Wood, and Gaius Jenkins, then and there, with force and arms, with the said persons to a great number, to wit: the number of one hundred and upwards, armed and arrayed in a warlike manner, that is to say, with guns, pistols, swords, artillery, and other warlike weapons, as well offensive as defensive, and then and there unlawfully and traitorously assembled for the purpose and design of overthrowing and subverting by force and violence the Government of the said United States in the Territory of Kansas aforesaid, contrary to the form of the statute in such case made and provided, and also against the peace and dignity of the United States of America.

"A. G. ISACKS,

"*United States Attorney for the Territory of Kansas.*"

"THE FREE-STATE GOVERNMENT — PRESENTMENT OF THE GRAND JURY.

"TERRITORY OF KANSAS — DOUGLAS COUNTY, SS.

"*The First District Court, Adjourned Session of April Term,* A. D. 1856.

"The Grand Jurors for the Territory of Kansas, Douglas County, sworn to inquire upon their oath, present: that, whereas, by an act of Congress entitled an act to organize the Territories of Nebraska and Kansas, approved May 30, 1854, among other things it was provided in substance as follows, to wit: 'That the executive power and authority in and over said Territory of Kansas shall be vested in a governor, who shall hold his office for five years, and until his successor shall be appointed and qualified, unless sooner removed by the President of the United States.' And by another section of the same act, among other things, it was provided as follows, to wit: 'That the governor, secretary, chief justice, and associate justices, attorney, and marshal, shall be nominated, and, by and with the consent of the Senate, appointed by the President of the United States.' One Charles Robinson, late of the county aforesaid, well knowing the provisions of the aforesaid acts, on the 23d day of April, in the year 1856, in the county aforesaid, and within the jurisdiction of the said court, then and there being nominated and appointed according to the act aforesaid, and without then and there having any lawful appointment or appellation whatever, as Governor of the Territory of Kansas, unlawfully then and there did assume

30*

and take upon himself the office of Governor of the Territory of Kansas, under the false name and style of Governor of the *State* of Kansas; and that the said Charles Robinson afterwards, to wit, on the twenty-third day of April, in the year aforesaid, in the county aforesaid, and within the jurisdiction of said court, did utter and issue a certain Proclamation, as Governor of the State of Kansas, the issuing and uttering of which proclamation, then and there, was an act appertaining to the office of Governor of the Territory of Kansas, and that the said Charles Robinson, without having any appointment or deputation whatever so to do, at the time and place last aforesaid, and on divers times between that time and the day of taking this inquisition, did exercise the power appertaining to the said office of Governor of the Territory of Kansas, to the great disturbance of the peace and good order of the said territory, contrary to the form of the statute in such case made and provided, and against the peace, government, and dignity of the Territory of Kansas.

"C. H. Grover, *District Attorney.*"

Capt. John Brown was indicted for high treason on a different indictment, namely, for having brought a company of men from Osawattomie to defend Lawrence when it was sacked. He and Mr. Williams were also indicted for usurping office (the State Legislature), the form of indictment being the same as that against Gov. Robinson.

Many other indictments were made out against other parties, some of which were taken. I place these indictments in the history of these occurrences because these remarkable documents are so violent, so gross in their assumptions of power and extra-judicial wresting of the constitutional rights of American citizens. Should the principles of republicanism prevail in our country, the day may come when these papers will be looked to with interest and astonishment. To avoid the despotic arrests for "treason" with which tyrannical and corrupt governments have bolstered themselves up in all ages, the fathers of the Revolution declared that treason should *only* consist in levying war against the United States, or in aiding and comforting its enemies, and that there must be two witnesses to an *overt* act. The system in the Territory of Kansas gives unrestrained license to unprincipled men and corrupt officers to crush the only instruments that would render the people dangerous to tyrants. It is worthy of remark here that the names of S. C. Pomeroy and W. Y. Roberts had been on the indictments and the records of the court, but had been scratched off, and those of Jenkins, and G. W. Smith inserted. Perhaps the ruffians thought, after the surrender of the guns at Lawrence, that it would be bad policy to indict them.

CHAPTER XXVI.

NIMROD WHITFIELD — DEATH OF CANTRAL — CAMPAIGNING IN THE WAR OF FREEDOM.

THE governor issued another proclamation. Under its potent authority all armed bands were to disperse and go home. So long as the border ruffians had everything their own way there was neither proclamation nor troops to disperse them; but now the free-state men were rapidly getting the upper hand of them. By the proclamation in question it was declared that the troops should disperse all companies, and if they ventured to assemble again they should be disarmed. Fortified by a copy of this document and a deputy bogus sheriff, Col. Sumner, with several companies of his dragoons, were on the hunt for Capt. Brown. Brown was still in camp, on Middle Ottawa Creek, with the prisoners and spoil taken at the battle of Black Jack.

It was about the same time that Gen. Whitfield fitted out one of the most rapidly organized and best managed expeditions that ever went up into the territory from Missouri. Three companies of seventy men each were raised in the neighborhood of Westport, Independence, and Lexington, in Missouri. That the man who claimed to represent the territory in Congress, on the strength of Missouri votes, should lead up an army of Missourians to invade the territory, was certainly appropriate. The special object of this expedition was to relieve Capt. Pate and his fellow-captives; its incidental object to demolish "old Capt. Brown," and the rest of the free-state guerillas.

With Whitfield there was a fair sprinkling of the wildest pro-slavery leaders in Jackson County, Mo. Capt. Reed, of Independence, a candidate for Congress in Missouri, and a man of some position; the famous, or infamous, Milt McGee, of Westport; Coleman, the murderer; Capt. Jenigen, Capt. Bell, and several of Buford's colonels and captains. Their rendezvous was on Bull creek, some twelve miles east of Palmyra. Having obtained a force of about three hundred men, they marched up the Santa Fe road, and encamped on the 5th of June in a ravine half a mile to the south of Palmyra.

While these men were assembling, couriers had been despatched for aid, as Capt. Brown was likely to be closely pressed. On the 6th of June, immediately after the attack on Franklin, men began to move in small parties towards Palmyra. The movement was not a general one, as some were afraid of the proclamation, and others were of the opinion that there could be no fight. Several companies, or, rather, fragments of companies, marched; — some fifteen men from the Franklin free-state company, most of whom were Western men, nearly all Missourians, Capt. Walker, with a few of the Bloomington company, Capt. Cracklin, with a segment of a celebrated Lawrence company, Capt. Abbott's Wakarusa company, which made the largest turn-out, there being forty-six of its members on the march, and a small company from the neighborhood of Hickory Point and Palmyra. When these got to the point of rendezvous, — the thick timber of Hickory Point, about a mile from Palmyra, — they numbered in all one hundred and eleven men. Besides the officers I have enumerated, there were three or four field officers; but the expedition was not organized, except by council of the officers, as it was deemed advisable to defer this until a junction could be effected with our friends, who were beyond the enemy to the south of Palmyra.

Capt. Brown was in camp, but had only some twenty men, and had twenty-seven prisoners; so his hands were pretty well tied.

Capt. Shore had about forty men encamped at the back of Prairie city; and Capt. Lenhart, with some twenty of the wildest and most daring young free-state guerillas, was a few miles further west. With this company were Cook, Hopkins, and others who have officiated as guerilla captains. This latter force was the free-state guerilla force, and included nearly all the free-state guerillas south of the Kaw. They were a harum-scarum set, as brave as steel, mostly mere boys, and did not consider it a sin to "press" a pro-slavery man's horse. At various times they have made more disturbance than all other free-state men together. They were under no particular restraint, and did not recognize any authority — military, civil, or otherwise — any further than suited their convenience. While they went round the county skirmishing, and carrying on the war against the pro-slavery men on their own hook, and in their own time and way, they were at the same time quite willing to lend a hand in more systematic and important fighting when there was an opportunity. These boys have been most bitterly maligned, and the free-state men, or conservative free-state men, were not slow to denounce them. Resolutions were passed by the sensitively moral free-state people, or the *sensitively timid*, declaring that these daring young guerillas were a nuisance, and that they, the conservative class, did not wish to be held responsible for them. To all this moralizing these young braves turned up their noses, ironically recommending all who were too cowardly to fight to "keep right on the record." For their own part, they regarded the war as begun, and would wage it against the pro-slavery men as the pro-slavery men waged it against their free-state friends.

This was the state of affairs near Hickory Point on the morning of the 5th of June. Whitfield was camped behind Palmyra with near three hundred men. The free-state camps mustered, or mustering, on that day, were about two hundred strong, and two companies were marching from Topeka with fifty more, who arrived the day after.

With a full knowledge of this state of affairs, our companies from Lawrence, constituting part of the force above enumerated, marched that morning on Hickory Point. It was a hot summer's day, and the sun shortly after it rose blazed down in all its force. As we marched through the prairies the men would occasionally be halted, and go through the Crimea rifle drill, to try its operation on ground broken, or rolling, or flat. This and the marching (nearly all our men were on foot) was hot work, and the perspiration rolled down in fearful style. That day's march lay through a perfect Arcadia of natural loveliness. There could not be a more beautiful landscape in nature than was then presented. Coal creek at your feet, with its feathery strip of timber to mark its windings; a gently undulating country, dotted here and there with a bold promontory on the tributaries that meet the Wakarusa from the south; away to the north and east glimpses of the densely-timbered Wakarusa among the breaks of the prairie knolls; and high up against the face of the sky the double-peaked Blue Mound.

I have not seen a finer part of Kansas for the agriculturist than that which lies between the Wakarusa and the tributaries of the Neosha. Indeed, I do not think there is a richer or more beautiful spot on the continent. The prairies are small, and gently undulating; and the streams are so plenty that you are rarely more than a mile from timber. At Hickory Point there is a grove, of many thousand acres, stretching over the hills for miles, and densely timbered.

But there is one feature that the country then presented, and which contrasted the beauty of the scene with the troubled nature of the time. Fields are scarce, but, scarce as they are, many of them were not cultivated. Wild weeds were springing from the deep black soil, which now should have been cherishing the blades of the young corn, or waving with luxuriant wheat and oats.

Another striking illustration of the times, and it forcibly recalled the days of the Revolution, I witnessed, as our two companies marched from Lawrence towards the scene of action near Palmyra and Prairie city. *Women* were at work in the field; delicately-reared, intelligent, New England women, working vigorously and earnestly, trying to get in crops, while their husbands, fathers, and brothers, were under arms to drive the hostile marauding bands from the territory. We also met in our line of march at least a dozen wagons loaded with families and household goods. These were settlers who had come in from Illinois and Iowa. Tired of a country where to live as American freemen is equivalent to being rebels, and in which to be "law-abiding and reverencing the powers that be" is the most abject slavery, those who are most weak in the faith left the struggle of freedom to others, and, having "put their hand to the plough, looked back." Many of them, too, had "seen the elephant," in the shape of those gallant bands of "chivalry," rummaging and pillaging their houses. One team contained the relatives of Jones, who was so cruelly murdered at Blanton Bridge. Could we wonder they were "going back to the states"?

These relatives were a widowed mother and younger brothers and sisters; he who had been so cruelly murdered being their stay and support. Ah! it was no wonder they were flying from the beautiful, ruffian-ridden Kansas!

That a decisive battle was to be fought on that 5th of June was the general opinion, and the chances were certainly in its favor. Our determination was to march as closely as possible on the enemy, and endeavor to effect a junction with the other parties, or plan a point of attack on Whitfield's army, with them; or, if we should happen to fall in with the pro-slavery party on the way, which was as likely to be busy as we were, to throw ourselves in as strong a position as we could, and fight till we could get assistance. But the fates or Col. Sumner had willed that we should have no fight on that occasion.

On the 4th Col. Sumner had started towards Palmyra, to take command of several companies of dragoons then in that vicinity. On the forenoon of the 5th he was in the neighborhood of Prairie city, the whole of the three distinct forces being within four miles of each other, scattered at different points. Col. Sumner was there, under the proclamation to prevent fighting; but his principal business, for the time being, was to find Capt. Brown, and relieve the Missourians who had been taken prisoners at Black Jack. Learning the position of Shore's company, he went and dispersed them, ordering them to retire. It was scarcely likely that he would ever have found Capt. Brown; but he got pretty close to where his camp was; he learned from some of the settlers that the camp was not far off, and said he wanted to see Brown. Capt. Brown, learning this shortly after, sent a messenger to Col. Sumner, saying that if Sumner wished to converse with him, or had any communication to make, he would come out and see him. Col. Sumner sent back the messenger to tell him to come out.

Under these circumstances Captain Brown, thinking it was a conference between military men, went to him (and, while I accord old "Bull of the Woods," as the dragoons style Sumner, all praise as a gallant soldier, I question if he ever acquitted himself as gallantly as Captain Brown). When Brown went out to the prairie he was astonished to find himself a prisoner. Colonel Sumner ordered him to stand by his stirrup and lead them into his camp. He also told him that there was a deputy sheriff with him who had an arrest for him, and added, "Take my advice and surrender yourself; make no resistance."

Under these circumstances the dragoons and the deputy sheriff went into the camp of Captain Brown. So rapidly and unexpectedly did the thing occur that there was no opportunity to secure the arms and horses taken at Black Jack. Only fifteen of Brown's men were in the camp at the moment they entered it; but that camp, Colonel Sumner, who was astonished at it, said afterwards that a small garrison could have held against a thousand men, and, from the peculiar nature of the ground, artillery could not be brought to bear on it. It is not wonderful that both Sumner and the deputy sheriff should come to the conclusion that the handful of free-state men they saw, with nearly thrice their own number of prisoners, was only a part of Brown's force. They believed that a hundred riflemen must be concealed in the thickets around it; consequently, the tone of these gallant officers and gentlemen grew more urbane and polite. Colonel Sumner asked deputy bogus if he had not some writs of arrest.

Bogus looked carefully around him, fixed his timid, irresolute eyes on the prisoners, and the small band Captain Brown had with him, and at the dense and mysterious-looking thickets around him, and said, in a hesitating voice,

"Well, I believe I don't see anybody *here* against whom I have any writ."

"You don't!" said Sumner, indignantly. "What did you tell me you had for? What did you mean by getting my help to make arrests, if you have none?"

"Well," faltered the hesitating deputy "law and order" man, "I don't think there is anybody here I want to arrest."

Colonel Sumner, who is rather blunt and off-handed, and not much of a believer in humbug, gave deputy bogus an objurgatory piece of his mind, which I need not inflict on the reader. He then liberated Captain Pate and the other prisoners. These men had been treated exceedingly well by Captain Brown. They were allowed to use their own blankets and camp equipage, which were much better than anything Brown had; they also were fed while thus held captive much better than Brown was able to feed his own soldiers.

Not only did the prisoners get their liberty, but their horses, arms, equipage, and stores; nearly all that had been taken, and all except what Brown had given to those who came the day of the battle to help, or was in the hands of some others who had been there, and who were not now here.

The guns these men had were, as I have said, United States arms.

"Where did you get these arms?" asked Colonel Sumner of Captain Pate.

"We got them from a friend," was the reply.

"A friend!" growled out old Bull of the Woods. "What friend had a right or could give you United States arms?"

In this dilemma, Captain Pate did, as many a wise man has done before him, evaded the question when he did not feel it advisable to answer it. The arms in question were the public territorial arms, given in charge of the federal officers of the territory, for the use of the territory, and by them given to the Missourians. This not being exactly a story fit to tell, Pate entered into a disquisition on the general subject of his imprisonment, and told Sumner that he was acting under orders of Governor Shannon, and that his being taken prisoner was an outrage.

"That is false, sir!" said Colonel Sumner, sternly; "I had a conversation with Governor Shannon about your particular case, and he declared that you had no authority for going about the country with an armed force."

There was no replying to this, and the enraged and silenced Pate bit his lip. Colonel Sumner went on; he denounced him for his conduct, and told the ruffian commander and correspondent of the *Missouri Republican* what he thought of him, in language more pointed and succinct than complimentary. He wound up his remarks, however, by allowing Pate to take everything his company had, even the public arms. Captain Brown and his company were then ordered to disperse. .Brown spoke of Whitfield's army close by, and said the free-state men could not disband with a hostile invading army at their doors, threatening their lives. Colonel Sumner pledged his word that these should be dispersed, and told the company of Brown that they must not assemble again unless invaders were attacking them.

Colonel Sumner then left Brown's camp and proceeded to the camp of General Whitfield. There he was politely received, and, as the force under Whitfield was too formidable looking to be treated with disrespect, Colonel Sumner was courteous. The officers of the pro-slavery camp deceived Colonel Sumner in a very important particular. They pretended to be all residents of the territory, whereas there was not a tithe of them who could make any pretence to a residence. One company lived on this creek, another company lived on that creek; every man was an "actual resident," to believe him. Now, Colonel Sumner was not particularly well posted as to the geography of the territory, particularly its *modern* geography, so he believed all this, or at least that a part of it was true. As Pate and his men were released, and as Colonel Sumner gave his pledge that he would disperse all parties of the settlers of Kansas who might band together, or arm themselves for defence, or any other purpose, they promised Colonel Sumner, on their "word of honor," to disperse, and not assemble again in arms. Having thus negotiated, Colonel Sumner fell back towards Prairie city, and encamped. Whitfield's camp broke up from their position near Palmyra, they moving down the Santa Fe road, and camping five miles below on Black Jack. It was at this stage of the game that Captain Walker and myself reconnoitred affairs from the high grounds half a mile from Palmyra. The smoking camp-fires of the enemy, which they had just abandoned, were at the head of a ravine a short distance off. Down the Santa Fe road the Missourians were going toward Black Jack, although many of them had halted at a grocery in a grove half a mile from us. The rascals had still scouting parties flying about. They plundered one free-state cabin, and took one of our boys prisoner, while falling back according to the orders of Sumner.

The man thus captured was named Cantral. He had come from Missouri to the territory, and was making a farm near Palmyra. He had a wife and young family. When the battle of Black Jack was fought, Cantral had hurried to the aid of the others, and had been seen with them by several of Pate's men. This was one cause of their hatred to him, and another was the fact of his being a Missourian and a free-state man. These are regarded by the border ruffians as traitors; a most absurd idea, as the poor white men of the slave states have, of course, no slaves; but such is the tyranny of opinion in slave-states that a poor man seldom dares to oppose the slave interest.

Cantral had been over to Prairie city for some butter, and was returning home to his family. As Colonel Sumner was to disperse all parties, he supposed there was to be peace. He was taken near his home and carried down to their camp on the Black Jack.

Two messengers were despatched to the camp of Colonel Sumner to inform him of it, and get his release. And here, as Colonel Sumner is, by the unhappy circumstances, somewhat implicated, justice requires that I give the account of the affair he gave to me. He said that his dragoons and himself had been in the saddle all day, and had just camped when the messengers reached him. General Whitfield and the other pro-slavery officers had pledged him their word of honor that they should disperse, and that there should be no more trouble. Believing that these were honorable men he deemed that Cantral's imprisonment would be merely temporary. He said he would go after him next day, if not released.

That evening Captain Walker and myself carefully scanned the position of the enemy, who were encamped exactly on the battle ground of Black Jack. Now, while this was a strong point to be attacked from the prairie, it could have been assailed most successfully from the ravine, by a party coming up from the creek that here winds through the timber of Hickory Grove. The bottom of the Black Jack hollow, besides being thickety, has water-runs and ditches, and spreads out below where they were encamped, so that a party of riflemen could have come up on each side of the ravine, in a sheltered position, and have got the enemy in a cross fire.

When we returned to camp I urged a night attack with the force we had; but as we had not heard from any of the other camps, and did not know that Brown was disbanded, the others thought it would be injudicious. Messengers had been sent after Captain Brown and the others, but they had not returned. It was deemed inadvisable to make an attack on a force so much larger until our friends could unite with us. The Missourians were encamped about two and a half miles from us. Our camp was put under close and careful guard, and I turned in reluctantly, as did many of my companions, fearing that the dragoons would spoil our sport in the morning.

Early next morning about one half of General Whitfield's army, some one hundred and sixty men, under Captain Reed, of Independence, Captain Pate, Captain Bell, Captain Jenigen, and others, started for Osawattomie. Some twenty of them, with a Captain Sanders, who lived on Washington creek, in the territory, started from Whitfield's camp to go home, halting at a grocery near Hickory Point. Whitfield and the remainder of them started back for Westport, carrying several prisoners with them.

When the morning came I went out again to reconnoitre, in company with Major Redpath; I had a terrible headache, and but a moderate estimate of camp comforts. We had intended to be perfectly still in our camp and await events. If Uncle Sam would drive out the invaders, good and well; if not, we would. But the gods interfered with our peace intentions, and showered down a little incident. While my companion and myself were scanning the face of the country and the passing affairs below us, four horsemen galloped up from the enemy's camp to Palmyra. While they approached we saw two men leave the houses at Palmyra and come toward the timber on our right; the horsemen then left the road and came toward the timber on our left. As the houses at

Palmyra had been pillaged by the pro-slavery bands and deserted by their owners, who were mostly in camp, we naturally concluded that both parties were of the enemy, and the design was to cut us off. We fell back into the timber, and we two posted ourselves at a saw-mill on the creek (also deserted). While there, as was natural for two journalists, we fell into a disquisition, and, for the time being, forgot the enemy. Redpath jumped up in the middle of the argument, cocked his rifle, and cried "Halt!" A man had popped his head above a saw-log. I recognized him as a free-state man, and told my friend to put down his gun.

This man, and another just behind him, were the two we had seen leave Palmyra. They had gone up there in hopes the enemy had been driven off, as they lived there; but their presence had been immediately discovered; the horsemen we saw had been sent out to cut them off, and had turned off toward us on seeing us. The proposal was that we should go back and take them, but our accession of numbers had no arms, and wanted to go back and report. I thought they would immediately gallop back, and that there would be no more of it. Once in camp, I commenced pencilling a letter for *The Tribune* on my knee. A messenger for Lawrence was about starting, and held a fiery horse pawing at my elbow, while I hastily scribbled, I hardly remember what. Before I got through Major Redpath had taken ten men out on a scouting party. They were back in an hour. They had crossed the creek, and, having got near the spot where we had been, saw three of the horsemen; they were no doubt scouring about for us. The men stretched themselves in the long grass before they were observed. When the three horsemen got near, the major started up, cried "Halt!" and gave orders for the men to rise. It is reported that the eyes of these fellows rolled like boiled beans at sight of the ten boys with Sharpe's rifles. They made a virtue of necessity and surrendered.

While the prisoners were placed in file and marched back into camp, the fourth man, their comrade, who had been in sight and observed the performance, galloped over to Colonel Sumner, and told him a cock-and-bull story about "peaceable people going along the road," etc., and the sequel followed.

The prisoners thus taken were Capt. Sanders and two of his men. They were examined and placed under guard. It was about the dinner hour. Cooks, and sub-cooks, and deputy-cooks, were at work trying to make what provisions we had eatable, and it was almost worth a dinner, and better than the dinner they thus prepared, to see them manufacturing corn and flour flippers, and roasting beef over the smoky fires, now turning a flipper or poking a beef-steak, and again wiping the smoke out of their eyes with their dirty sleeves. Just as the dinner was ready in galloped Mr. P. Robinson, a brother of the governor, and reported an armed and mounted force approaching our camp. Instantly the men were under arms and in line. The force was approaching by a road that led into the timber, and ran close to our camp; this road came in on a narrow ridge. The force was divided; a small number (we had received some more men, and numbered one hundred and twenty) were left to guard the camp and the prisoners, and the remainder were posted in two divisions, one on each side of the ravine.

Having disposed ourselves after the Crimea drill pattern, commanding the road, we watched. Another horseman galloped in; the approaching force was Uncle Sam's boys. "Confound them!" muttered several. "Well, we don't want to fight United States troops till they fight us," was the general response; so, with a general anathema of three-cornered fights and third parties, we fell back a hundred yards from the road and lay down. Soon they came. Galloping down the shady road, with their sabres clattering, they swept past us. Little did they think that they were running the gauntlet of a hundred Sharpe's rifles, which could have annihilated them on that rash entry to our camp, but for the loyal reverence to United States authority that beat in every heart, and but for our respect for Uncle Sam's livery which they wore.

Once in our camp, we could hear the hearty laughter of the dragoons. They set the prisoners at liberty, gave them their horses and arms, and, some of our officers having gone in, the officer in command said we must disband and go home. That officer was a pro-slavery man, and rather exceeded his duty. One thing which he said (and which I hope was gratuitous) gave general offence: "You must submit to the territorial laws, or leave the territory." What business had an officer of dragoons with the territorial laws?

After keeping our poor fellows stretched on the grass for an hour, in no very good humor at such an interruption to the dinner hour, Uncle Sam's boys at last thought fit to leave, clattering off as they came, the released prisoners going with them.

I hate these three-cornered, triangular fights, especially when the third party pretends to be equally hostile or equally friendly to both parties, — free-state men on one side, pro-slavery men on the other, and Uncle Sam's men pretending to keep the peace, but not able to do it.

As no one had promised to disperse we concluded that it would not be proper to do so until we were sure that the enemy had left the territory. The determination was to keep a force, sufficiently large to hold these Missourians in check, close to them until they should leave the territory, — to evade Uncle Sam, and fight the enemy should occasion offer. The camp was therefore shifted immediately to a secure spot on Coal creek, two miles from the first camp.

When Capt. Sanders left the dragoons he went down to the lower end of the grove, to Conner's grocery, where the territorial part of the pro-slavery army was. They then rode up the Santa Fe road. They had proceeded up for a considerable distance, and were near the Willow Springs, when they ran against a small circumstance. As I have stated, two companies had started from Topeka when the report of Whitfield's army marching into the territory reached them. One of these companies, about twenty men, with two wagons, were hurrying down the Santa Fe road, when they encountered the pro-slavery men under Capt. Sanders; both parties were of about the same size.

The moment the Topeka boys saw the enemy coming, they drew their wagons across the road, and drew up behind them in line of battle. Their opponents looked bewildered and not at all anxious to fight. They kept at a respectable distance, and by "signs and wonders" and all the peace demonstrations they could make, succeeded in obtaining a parley. They then explained that Sumner had *dispersed* them, and that they were going peacefully to their homes, and did not want to fight. There is no doubt but they would have been much more warlike if they had found a party much smaller than their own; but, under the circumstances, the Topeka boys allowed these meek "law and order" men to pass and drove on that night to our camp on Coal creek.

On that 6th of June a deplorable occurrence happened in the camp of the pro-slavery men who had started for Westport. They had taken with them, amongst other prisoners, Mr. Cantral. When camped at noon on Cedar Creek, some fifteen miles below the Black Jack, where Whitfield's army had divided, they pretended to try Cantral for treason to Missouri, he being a free-state man, and for fighting in the free-state cause in Kansas. Milt Magee, of Westport, took an active part in these proceedings, being chief of the court. Of course Cantral was found guilty. The other prisoners with fear saw Cantral led out of the camp by four men, with whom was Magee. They went towards a ravine close by. Directly after Magee was seen to ride away from the ravine, and just at that moment a pistol-shot was heard, and Cantral's voice crying,

"O! — O, God! they have shot me!"

Another shot was heard, followed by a long, piercing scream, and then another, and all was still. The man who shot is supposed to be a man named Forman, of Westport, who had been with Pate, and who had been taken prisoner that Sunday at Prairie city. He had been most kindly treated while a prisoner in Capt. Brown's camp.

Several others of the prisoners were supposed to have been murdered in the same way; seven dead bodies have been reported found at that place and the next creek where they camped. Two of the prisoners they had, who were supposed to be pro-slavery men, were allowed to leave immediately after Cantral was shot. It was by their account that the friends of Cantral were enabled to find his body, with three bullet-holes in his breast, and bear it to his agonized widow.

CHAPTER XXVII.

SACKING OF OSAWATTOMIE.

It was Saturday night. I had been scouting around the streams and hills to the south of the Wakarusa. I had become convinced that the large force I had seen galloping down the Santa Fe road from Palmyra, on the 5th, while reconnoitring with Capt. Walker, had left the neighborhood, and, for the moment, half concluded that the dragoons were really a good "institution," when, about six o'clock, a messenger came in from Osawattomie, asking for help. When the messenger left, the enemy was encamped eight miles from Osawattomie, and an attack was feared. Another messenger immediately followed the first; this latter had started first, but had been taken prisoner by the enemy. By the intercession of Capt. Bell he got away. He told us that Capt. H. C. Pate, of the Missouri *Republican*, was with them. The captain and his company, taken prisoner at the battle of Palmyra, had been released by the troops, and their arms restored them. The messengers wanted help. It was thirty miles off; besides, there were three companies of dragoons between our camps and Osawattomie. On the assurances of the troops the companies had been preparing to disband.

Col. Sumner had returned to Fort Leavenworth. One company of dragoons was left at Palmyra. There was one down at Middle Ottawa Creek, where John Brown, junior, Jason Brown, Mr. Williams, Mr. Partridge, and other three free-state men from Osawattomie, were held prisoners. Another company of dragoons were stationed close to Osawattomie, having been there during the occurrences narrated in last chapter.

When the appeal for assistance reached our camp that evening there were not lacking those who wished at once to make a night march on Osawattomie; but hoping, trusting faith prevailed. As the representative of the camps, I started for the nearest company of troops. Capt. ——, of Topeka, went with me. The twilight was setting in as we started. Night came on before we entered the deep, thick woods near Hickory Point, but although the path was scarcely visible, we galloped on, for the case was urgent. It might have been about nine o'clock when we emerged on the prairie highlands near the Santa Fe road. Away to the right we could observe the glimmer of a few lights at Palmyra, and soon, as we galloped on, we saw the camp-fires, and by their aid the tents of the dragoons encamped on the skirts of the timber. Within a hundred yards the sentinel hailed us. The usual military preliminaries were gone through, and we were led to the officers' tent. My companion did not alight, and the master of the guard held my horse while I entered the tent. It was small; the fresh, green grass was the carpet; a small camp-pallet lay on the ground; on this the occupant reclined, reading by the light of a lamp. He motioned me to a trunk in the centre. It was Lieutenant Mackintosh, who has the reputation of being an intelligent and gentlemanly officer. He told me, to my question, that Major Sedgewick was at another camp, nearer Osawattomie. When I stated my mission, he replied that he had received some report of the kind, and had sent an express down that morning to the other camps, which were near the spot, informing them of it. I told him of the urgency of the case. He replied that such rumors might not be well founded. I said our friends were at least inclined to believe them; and I then told him my mission fully and plainly. We had been disbanded with the assurance of protection; our friends were threatened by a large force, part of the same we had understood were to be driven out. We had force we could soon rally, and who were ready to march at once to relieve Osawattomie, and I came to tell him that unless they took immediate steps to defend it and drive these Missourians out, *we would*. I was almost sorry that an officer, whom I believed to be a gentleman, should have been so far under the influence of the duty he was sent to do as to question me at this point relative to our friends, the existence of free-state camps, etc. The impending fate of Osawattomie made it painful. I repeated again to him that unless I could carry back some guarantee that all the troops could do would be done immediately, we would immediately march on the point ourselves. He then assured me that everything they could do would be done. He would start immediately for the other two camps, one of which was nine miles below, and the other near Osawattomie, and that everything that could be done would be done, and those men driven back if they were there; he did not wish us to take any steps. I conversed with him while he prepared to leave. He accused the free-state people; spoke of their disinclination to obey the territorial laws,—as if resisting these tyrannous enactments was a sin! spoke harshly of a few of the more impulsive of the Lawrence people, who had treated Sheriff Jones with disrespect in the performance of *his duty!* It was evident that he regarded the bogus law as law, and the squatters of Kansas as a species of rebels. I saw him on the way toward Osawattomie, and returned at the gallop. Our friends were satisfied with the result, concluded to abandon the field, and to trust the dragoons for the present.

The part of Gen. Whitfield's army that had gone down to Osawattomie numbered one hundred and seventy men. They approached the place as rapidly as possible. They had a thirty miles' march, and arrived in the vicinity of the place, or some five miles to the east of it, on the Indian reserve, across the Merodesin. They had sent a spy ahead of them into the place to reconnoitre it. Next morning the company of dragoons, which had been stationed close to Osawattomie, left that place and took a fresh camp day up in the direction of Ottawa creek, several miles off.

I do not mean to insinuate that there was any collision in this case between the officers of the troops and the border ruffians, although the movements, taken all in all, look decidedly suspicious. Of course the border ruffians were soon informed of the movement of the troops and the condition of the town. On that day there were but few over a dozen men left in Osawattomie. Nearly all the residents had claims out in the county, and were at work on them. So rapid had been the movement against them that they did not expect any sudden attack on the town, and although they had heard of the Missourians being over in the Indian reserve, only a few men thought they would attack the place, and it was these who had sent after help. The general impression was, the town would not be attacked, and that these invaders would only surround the town to cut off travellers and supplies on the road. But those who thought so were mistaken. That more prompt steps were not taken to defend Osawattomie is merely another evidence of the slow process by which free-state settlers arrive at a correct conclusion upon border ruffian character.

The blow aimed at Osawattomie can only be attributed to two things. In the first place, it was a thriving free-state town; in the second, the law and order ruffians, or those of them in this part of Whitfield's army, had been unable to get any booty in their recent campaign, and it was hard to leave the territory without it. By their scouts they learned that there were few men in the place, and those few making preparation for defence. Still the ruffians were timid and cautious. They suspected some trick. They thought that the people of the place had by some means obtained information of their presence, and that some force was concealed, and that they would fall into an "abolition ambush." As the evidence they obtained, however, was all to the contrary, they at last ventured to march, leaving a small force at the camp they had made to guard some property.

They approached the town by the road from Westport to Osawattomie, and had to cross the Merodesin close to the town. On the east bank of this stream, which is a large creek or small river at that point, they halted. They were fearful that an ambush lay in the thickets near the ford. At last some of their number, more resolute than the rest, dashed into the stream and crossed over, and the whole party entered the town, which is separated from the stream by a narrow strip of timber. They entered the town rapidly, and the astonished people, the few men in town and the women and children, saw this horde of pro-slavery barbarians take possession of their town almost before they could realize their presence or their object. No attempt at resistance was made by the people; in fact, it was out of the question.

Then commenced a wholesale work of pillage. Dwelling-houses and places of business were alike ransacked. All the horses that could be found, sixteen in number, were taken. The spy who had entered the place the day before, and who had pretended to be sick, and had been kindly treated, led the way from place to place, showing where the best plunder was to be obtained. All the arms, money and jewelry, that could be found, was most anxiously sought and taken. Their object was evidently to take all they could carry on their horses, and to carry the most valuable articles. Trunks, desks, bureaus, and every other place where desirable articles to steal could be found, were broken into. Liquor was obtained and drank freely, while they indulged in the fiercest threats and the wildest profanity.

A few of the more patriotic tried to find the printing press. There was a printing establishment in the place, but it had not yet seen the light. The press had never committed treason, or rendered itself indictable by squeezing a free-soil emphasis on paper; nor had the unoffending type ever been defaced by "abolition" ink; but the pro-slavery ruffians well knew that a printing press is an incendiary machine at best, and that this one was probably in hands not sufficiently alive to the glorious principles of "law and order." They therefore searched indefatigably and vainly. The whole apparatus, press and all, was carefully boxed up and concealed. They threatened several persons, and hunted for the editor, or, rather, he who was to be the editor; but he was not in town. One woman, whom they felt sure knew something about it, or was connected with it, they threatened to hang, if she would not tell where they could find it. She treated their threats with indifference, and they, after having spoken and acted violently and insultingly, had to give it up. They threatened and insulted several other ladies.

In their investigations they entered the house where the press was, but happening to fall in with a case of excellent brandy and some wine, they proceeded to help themselves pretty freely to these "anti-abolition" articles. After drinking freely, they concluded that no "abolition" press could be in a place where there was so good brandy. In fact, that is one way the border ruffians have of judging whether a man is "sound on the goose." A person who does not drink is voted an "abolitionist" at once, without further testimony; and the presence of liquor, especially good liquor and an abundance of it, is considered as a sure symptom, infallibly tending to "law and order."

Not content with robbing stores, and men's trunks, and private dwellings, these chivalrous fellows actually took the women's rings and ear-rings, and some of their apparel. They ought to have had a petticoat apiece as trophies. They attempted to burn the building where the hotel and post-office were, and one or two other houses; but were in too great a hurry to kindle any building thoroughly, and the inhabitants watched them, and extinguished the flames before they could do any damage.

Having got all the plunder they wanted, they were anxious to be off.

"Hurry, hurry!" they said to each other. "These d—d abolitionists are somewhere not far off, and they will be down on us the first thing we know." They accordingly retreated from the ill-fated town as rapidly and unmolested as they had entered it, carrying their booty with them.

When they got to their camp the company divided. Half of them started immediately back for Westport, and the remainder moved off and camped on the lower part of Bull creek, some eight miles from Osawattomie. There they had an adventure.

As might be expected, they kept a sharp look-out for abolitionists. Two days after the sacking of Osawattomie, a couple of their own number had been on a scout, and on their return to the camp, while near it, fired off their guns. The guard in that direction gave the alarm, fired his gun in the direction of the two men, and cried at the top of his lungs, "The abolitionists are coming! —the abolitionists are coming!" Whereupon the whole camp got into a panic, and, without taking time to pack up their effects, started off at the run. There were some horses harnessed to wagons; these were hurriedly taken out, and off the whole party went in a helter-skelter race, outrivalling John Gilpin's. Once or twice one of their number would discharge a pistol or a gun behind him, as a warning to abolitionists to keep off, which had the effect of keeping up the fear of the retreating party.

They never stopped till they got to Battiesville, an Indian station amongst the Weas. The Indian store-keeper, seeing a band of wild-looking fellows galloping up, with arms in their hands, and looking very terrible from fear and excitement, closed his door, and, in spite of all their entreaties, would not let them in.

"The abolitionists are coming!—we want to come in to defend the place!"

The Indian happened to be a pro-slavery Indian, but he was moderately suspicious of the appearance of these "law and order" men; so he grunted,

"Abolitionists, heap, bad!—no come!"

"Yes, they *are* coming!" yelled a score of anxious voices. "G–d blast ye! let us in! They 'll be here in a minute!"

"Come in to-morrow, may be," was the cautious answer.

Time was pressing. There were two or three unoccupied log-houses close at hand; so they made a virtue of necessity and got into them. The chinking was driven out for port-holes, and the doors were barricaded; meanwhile two of the best mounted were despatched in hot haste to Missouri, one to Jackson, and the other to Cass county, telling their friends to come up quick, for the abolitionists with great force were besieging them in Battiesville, and that they would endeavor to *hold out till they could come.*

A party of men did start up to the rescue, and more would have gone if these had not returned and reported it a hoax. This masterly retreat was a standing joke amongst the border ruffians in that quarter, who taunted their comrades about their "holding out against the abolitionists."

CHAPTER XXVIII.

A CHAPTER OF OUTRAGES.

DON'T start, reader, at the ominous heading of this chapter. A chapter of Kansas outrages! Why, there could be a book as big as "Webster's Unabridged," and more frightfully dreary, written on such a subject. I would no more think of inflicting an account of all the outrages against the settlers of Kansas, on the reader, than I would of all the free-soil speeches and "resolutions" passed in the territory. So far, I have confined myself to what I deemed the most important incidents, and those most necessary to give a correct outline of Kansas history. And yet there are a few important matters and decided steps in the Kansas struggle that can be best exhibited by statements found in this chapter.

Governor Shannon had gone down to Westport to see the committee of Congress, still there. While in that place and in the adjoining Kansas city he saw the most extensive preparations for another invasion, in which the free-soil settlers of Kansas were to be "wiped out *this* time." Whether it was owing to fear, or awakening conscience, or resentment at the marked disrespect with which Governor Shannon was treated at that time, is uncertain; but Governor Shannon was, or pretended to be, hostile to this invasion. He returned to Fort Leavenworth by the river, and, having roused Colonel Sumner, the two came over together, with an additional force of dragoons and some artillery. These men he posted on the Shawnee Reserve, in order to keep the invading army out. It was about the same time that the following letter reached Lawrence by the post-office:

"INDEPENDENCE, MO., *Thursday, June* 12, 1856.

"POSTMASTER, LAWRENCE, K. T.: There were some men here

32*

yesterday trying to get men to go with them to the territory for the purpose of going to Topeka to burn it up. Now, for God's sake, send an express immediately to that place, and get the people there to send for the United States troops to protect them. One of the men that were here was named William Donaldson (brother of Postcript Donaldson), and he said that Shannon had left the territory and gone home, leaving Secretary Woodson as acting governor, and that *he* would let the pro-slavery party do as they pleased, and that *now was the time* to burn out, kill, and drive every free-state man from the territory.

"I am a pro-slavery man myself, but I want things done honorably, and give you the warning now. Do not delay, for they will be in Topeka in a very few days.

"Respectfully, JAMES BROWN.

"P. S. — This is not my proper name; but what is said is true."

The dragoons were not remarkably active in ferreting out the parties of border invaders; for the force that had plundered Osawattomie was in the neighborhood of Bull Creek for a week with their booty, and were not molested. Several other bands of these men had returned to the territory, and had camped on Turkey and Cedar Creeks. They were rather cautious in their movements, however, as they were not sure but the dragoons might attack them. A very considerable force had been raised in Missouri to invade the territory once more, but the presence of the dragoons, under Colonel Sumner, acted as a check. The pro-slavery bands were chiefly confined to the Indian reserves close to the Missouri frontier. Here they had no settlers to molest and plunder, and, in the absence of any, began to plunder from the Indians. The Shawnee Indians, having been robbed of corn, hogs and other articles, complained to their agent, Mr. Gay, who made complaint to the dragoons. Under these circumstances the dragoon forces, camped on Cedar Creek, went down to Turkey Creek, and drove out a large company of the invading Missourians. These latter, when they saw the dragoons coming, hauled up their red flag, and prepared for battle. The officer in command of the dragoons rode in, and told them he would give them five minutes to take down their flag and leave. He then posted his cannon. These warlike demonstrations prevailed, and they retreated into Missouri. Another party of them had gone up to burn Palmyra, and when the troops came, they resisted them, and, the dragoon force being weak, had to retreat till they could receive reinforcements, before they could be driven off. This action of the dragoons, and a week of rainy weather, dissipated this invasion. Colonel Buford, whose regiment had been driven out, felt very sore, and complained to Governor Shannon. The governor sent him the following reply:

LETTER TO COLONEL BUFORD FROM GOVERNOR SHANNON.

"EXECUTIVE OFFICE, *June* 10, 1856,
"LECOMPTON, K. T.

"MY DEAR SIR: Your favor of the 18th is received. I wrote to you some days ago, which, I presume, you had not received at the date of your last.

"You can have no difficulty in coming into the territory with bona fide settlers.

"I have resigned my office, and leave for St. Louis probably on to-morrow. As soon as I pass the line, Colonel Woodson will be the acting governor, and, if you have any difficulty with the troops, you will address him on the subject. I repeat that my proclamation has no application to bona fide emigrants coming into the territory. Yours, with respect,

"(Signed,) WILSON SHANNON.

"COL. BUFORD.

"N. B. — I will probably see you as I pass down."

In this letter Governor Shannon alludes to his resignation. He had, indeed, been reduced to the last extremity of political degradation. He was despised and hated by the free-state settlers, and just as heartily despised by the pro-slavery men who now threatened him. He had made himself the tool of the slavery extensionists, at the instance of the administration, and now he had rendered himself, and the administration with him, so odious to a large class of people, that the administration hoped, by sacrificing him, to let him go, like the scape-goat, to the wilderness. Shannon was also threatened with personal violence by the border ruffians. Under these circumstances he left the territory. He would have published his resignation before he went, but Colonel Sumner advised him not to do so until his successor could be appointed, so that there would be no interregnum. At St. Louis Governor Shannon was stopped by General Smith, who advised him to go back again. This he did, publishing a card in the city denying the report of his intended resignation. He returned to the territory to await the political decapitation the national executive had in store for him.

During all this time pro-slavery parties stealthily prowled through the territory, or hung upon the Missouri borders. Outrages were so common that it would be impossible to enumerate them. Murders were frequent, many of them passing secretly and unrecorded; some of them only revealed by the discovery of some mouldering remains of mortality. Two men, found hanging on a tree near Westport, ill-fated free-state settlers, were taken down and buried by the troops; but so shallow was the grave that the prairie wolves dug them up, and partly devoured them, before they were again found and buried.

Mr. Upton, sergeant-at-arms of the committee, was taken prisoner by one of these bands on the road from Westport to Lawrence. They treated him with indignity, and threatened to hang him. Mr. Oliver interfered, and went out to procure his release.

The following statement of Mr. John A. Bailey, which is attested by three respectable gentlemen, his neighbors, is a rather interesting case:

"I have been fourteen months in the territory; came from Pennsylvania. I started last Tuesday morning for Little Santa Fe after provisions for myself and neighbors. I had got as far as Bull creek by five o'clock in the evening, when a man came up and stopped my wagon, telling me to stop there for the night. This man was Coleman, the murderer of Dow. He had twenty men encamped where I met him, among whom I recognized Buckley, Hargus, Jones, Conelly and the Cumming brothers; the two first being also accomplices in the murder of Dow, and all of them in the posse of Jones which took Branson. In the night my horses were stolen, their halters cut. In the morning these men made pretence of sympathy, and said, 'It was too bad for people to steal horses from their friends.' They told me I could find them in the camp at Cedar creek, and three of them volunteered to go with me. I borrowed a pony, and, leaving my wagon with the others, started.

"After going about half way to Cedar creek, we met a large company of not less than two hundred men. They took me prisoner, and ordered me to dismount. After taking me for some distance in a wagon, well guarded, I was again compelled to mount my pony, and the three men who came with me from the other camp held a consultation with the officers of this. I overheard Coleman say, 'There may be treachery used,' but could gather nothing definite of their intentions further, save that these three men, who had volunteered to help me find my horses, were sent to take me to Westport. The company went on over the hill in the prairie. Shortly after they disappeared these men led me off the road a hundred yards into the prairie. They made me dismount, and demanded my money. I gave them all I had, forty-five dollars, without a word. One of them then raised his gun as if to shoot me. It was a United States musket. I told him, if he meant to kill me, he would kill a better man than himself. Lowering his gun, he said, 'I wish you to take off them pantaloons for fear they should get dirty.' I told him they were mine as long as I was alive. He again raised his musket, but while he was in the act of firing, I dodged. The ball hit me in the side, glancing along my ribs, and through the cartilages, and lodging in my back. I fell. He then struck at my head with the butt end of his musket, and missed, only grazing it. As he struck at me the other two men rode off as fast as possible after the company that had gone over the prairie. He struck at me again, when I caught the musket in my hands, and held on to it. He held to the other end, and jumped on my body, stamping on my head and face;

but, as he wore Indian slippers, he did not hurt me much. He then tried to jerk the musket from me, and, in doing so, pulled me to my feet. I still held on to it, and, dealing him a blow with my fist, he let go the musket. He then ran after the others, calling them to come back, but they had gone some distance, and did not hear him. He ran after them, and I ran after him; he commenced running harder, and soon disappeared. I then turned, ran some distance into the prairie, and hid in the grass. Three hours passed quietly, when I left my hiding-place, and wandered toward home.

"At ten o'clock I came to the branch of timber where the road crosses to go to Blanton's Bridge. I there saw two sentries on horseback. I passed so as not to be seen by them, expecting to get across at another place. I heard cow-bells clinking and dogs barking. I thought I was coming to a dwelling; but in a short time I found that the noise moved, and that there was no house there. I then went to the upper end of the grove, hoping to get across there. At this point I heard the same noises. Further up I came on their camp in the timber. It was nearly day-break, and I moved away and hid in the grass, where I could watch their actions. In the morning they were called in by the sound of cow-bells. While there I heard some one cry, 'Are you going to hang me?' I heard no reply to this, except the noise of two rings of the cow-bell. In about five minutes I heard a shot, and, at the same time, something like a boatswain's whistle to lower. (Bailey has been a sailor.) After that I heard six shots fired at intervals of five minutes. I heard no more till night came. I lay in the thicket all day. At night I crawled out and contrived to travel about two miles. My side was so sore I could scarcely walk.

"I walked up to the Santa Fe road, and found that also guarded. I went to the Wakarusa, and remained hid there all day. While there I saw a wagon stopped by five men. I could not see well, as they were at some little distance; but they appeared to be quarrelling. I heard angry words, when there was a shot fired. All was then peaceable, and the men went down the road with the wagon and team. At nightfall I found my way to the house of Dr. Stills, at the Blue Mound. During the three days I was exposed I had nothing to eat, and took nothing but stagnant water; my side was very painful and stiff where I was wounded, and I was very weak. While in the camp where I was first taken, I heard the men there say that they intended to kill and drive out the free-state men from the territory; they spoke very bitterly of the battle of Palmyra, some of them having been in it; they were determined to have revenge. They took from me forty-five dollars in money, and they have my team, wagon, and several other articles in it.

"John A. Bailey."

I subjoin another statement of a person who was driven from the territory. It was published by him in the *Chicago Tribune:*

"Chicago, *Wednesday, June* 11, 1856.

"I wish to make, for the benefit of your readers, a true statement of the manner in which free-state men in Kansas are treated by the mob which has now possession of the territory, and Missourians on the border, as proved by my own case.

"I emigrated to Kansas in March last, and settled in Lawrence, where I took no part in the political troubles by which the territory has been convulsed. In all respects I endeavored to demean myself as a good citizen and an honest man.

"On Thursday, the fifth of the present month, I had occasion to go to Kansas city, Missouri, with my oxen and wagon, for a load of freight, consisting of household goods for an emigrant in my employ, who was with me. On my return with the load I was obliged to pass through Westport. When about a mile, or a mile and a half, from that village, I came upon a camp occupied by sixty or seventy Missourians and Alabamians. Here I was met by a squad of these men, armed with muskets, rifles, and side-arms, who demanded of me to stop.

"'Here's a d—d abolitionist!' was the cry; 'let us have him, anyhow.'

"I produced a *pass*, which had been given to me by United States Marshal Donaldson; but they swore it was a forgery. They proceeded to break open the boxes in the wagon and to scatter the goods about in the road. While this was going on I was sent into their camp, where I was questioned thus:

"'What's your name?'

"'C. H. Barlow.'

"'Where do you live?'

"'In Lawrence.'

"'Where are you from?'

"'Waterbury, Connecticut.'

"'What are your politics?'

"'I am a free-state man.'

"'How much money did that d—d Emigrant Aid Society give you to come out here?'

"'None; I came out with my own money.'

"'Who gave you a rifle — Beecher or Silliman?'

"'Neither. I brought no gun of any kind to the territory.'

"'What the hell did you come out here for?'

"'Why, to get a home, and make money.'

"'And to make Kansas a free state?"

"'That's my intention, now I am here.'

"'Why did n't you go to Nebraska? That's a good country, and you d—d Yankees may have it. But Kansas you will have to fight for, and we'll whip h—ll out of you, but we'll get it, Union or no Union.'

"'That's a game that won't win, I'm thinking.'

"After much more of this sort, interlarded with impious oaths and ruffianly threats, I was asked:

"'If we'll let you go, will you take a gun and march with the pro-slavery party?'

"To this I had but one word in reply, and that was, 'NEVER.'

"Immediately there was a cry for '*The ropes, boys — the ropes!*' These were speedily brought, and a noose was thrown over my head and around my neck, and I was dragged to the nearest tree.

"I exclaimed, 'You do not intend to kill me in this manner, do you?'

"'Yes, G—d d—n your abolition heart, and all like you!'

"I begged, if I was to be sacrificed to their fury and causeless hate, that I might have time to collect my thoughts and arrange my worldly affairs. I was told that if I had any property to dispose of, or my peace to make with God, that I would be allowed just ten minutes for both.

"I gave a man among them, who, I learned, was called Bledsoe, and who seemed to think that I was to be killed without cause, a schedule of my effects, and asked him to send it to my brother-in-law at the East, whom I named.

"At the expiration of the little time given me I was again dragged to the tree, the rope was thrown over a swinging limb, and, in spite of the remonstrances of Bledsoe and of Treadwell, who also began to plead my cause, I was jerked from the ground and suspended by the neck,—I cannot tell for how long, but probably for a brief period only,—when Treadwell, who was called major, and appeared to have command, peremptorily ordered me to be let down.

"I was again questioned:

"'Will you leave the territory, if we'll spare your life?'

"To this I demurred, saying that I had offended no law, nor infringed any man's right.

"The leader again interposed, and told me that, unless I would promise, he could not save my life. He told his men that I was guilty of no crime, except that of being a free-state man; *that* I had a right to be, though he would admit that I had no right to such opinions in Kansas.

"At last, his ruffian followers extorted from me the promise they required, giving me just twelve hours to make the promise good.

"I was then sent with a guard to Kansas city, to see that I did not escape. My oxen and wagon were taken possession of, and I, with less than five dollars in my pockets, was forced to take the next boat and leave the country.

"In conclusion, I declare that I am, and have been, a law-abiding and peaceful man; that my mission to Kansas city was one perfectly lawful and proper; and that, so far as I know, I am driven out of the territory only because of my political opinions — my desire to make Kansas a free state. My case is not a solitary one. Every man of my opinions who falls into the same hands is liable to the same abuse; and this, in Kansas, is called 'law and order.' "(Signed,) C. H. BARLOW."

It was now that the Missourians carried out a new system of warfare. Heretofore their great aim had been to "wipe out" free-state settlers; but it now occurred to them, as a heavy emigration began to pour into the territory in the summer of 1856, that the easiest way to do it, or, at least, the first thing to do, was, to *keep* out those who might want to enter. In accordance with this conclusion, the roads leading to Missouri were blockaded, and emigrants from the free states stopped and sent back.

The subjoined is the statement of an Illinois emigrant who fell into the hands of the ruffians:

"STATEMENT OF JAMES C. BALDWIN.

"Eight families, with twelve teams, started from McLean County, Illinois, for Kansas, on the twenty-second of May. These consisted of the families of John Veteto, two of his sons with their families, Benjamin Draper with his family, John Wooster and family, James Hancock and family, R. Roberts and family, M. Dibble and family. Three teams from Iowa, consisting of two families, overtook them in Missouri, and travelled with them. The men who started from Illinois had four prairie ploughs, and a variety of farming implements, and articles of household furniture, travelling in the style in which Western emigrants usually travel. They travelled unmolested until they reached within four miles of Platte city, intending to cross the river at Leavenworth. On Tuesday, twenty-fourth ult., in the morning, while travelling on the state road, the emigrants were stopped by an armed band of one hundred and fifty men, and most of whom were armed with United States muskets and bayonets, the remainder having shot-guns and revolvers, and two having Sharpe's rifles. They asked the emigrants where they were going, and where they were from. On replying to this the captain said:

"'I suppose you've hearn that we don't allow any movers to go through into the territory.'

"Witness, who drove the first team, replied that he had not, when the captain rejoined:

"'Yes, we stop them all.'

"They then said they would have to search the wagons to see if there were any arms on board. One man from Iowa objected, when they told him he had better be quiet; and one man drew a revolver, and told him to 'hold on.'

"They then searched all the wagons; and, after searching them once, were not satisfied, but searched them again. They took what arms they could find. There was about one gun to a wagon, these being mostly Western rifles, some few being shot-guns, such arms as they happened to have. It was reported that they took money from some of the emigrants. They gave receipts for the arms taken in the following form:

"'Received of —— (so many guns described), to be deposited with the County Clerk of Platte County, to be delivered up at the end of the war.'

"These were signed by two men, who they said were *responsible*. We were detained nearly two hours, when the company increased to nearly five hundred, a large proportion of whom were armed with United States arms. They told emigrants that they could not be permitted to go on, but would be guarded back till they got through the state. After taking the guns, they took a vote as to whether they should allow them to take back their guns with them. Nearly all of the men voted that they should have the guns; but the leaders were opposed to their getting the arms, and overruled the popular vote. The emigrants asked permission to stay in Platte County until they could get over into the territory, but could not be allowed unless they would promise to buy farms and settle permanently in Platte County; in which case they were assured they would be 'taken care of.'

"The evening before this attack the emigrants had been visited by their spies, who asked them a great variety of questions, and told them they would be a great deal of trouble in the territory, and a good deal of it *before they got there*. After taking them they detailed a guard of eight men, under command of Robert Pate, who escorted them back to Liberty, Mo. Here they were delivered up to the leading men of Liberty, among these Judge Thompson. The first guard returned, and the emigrants went out to the back of the town, where they could get water and grass for their teams. They were told shortly after that they could go where they pleased; that they were at liberty, so that they did not go *into the territory.* They staid there two days, when some friendly people advised them not to stay there, for if anything happened, or 'devilment' was done, they would be held responsible for it, and get into trouble. They started back some ten miles on the road toward Illinois; they there rented houses and went into them, and were there awaiting the cessation of hostilities. Witness left the rest of the emigrants and came on on foot. His father was in the territory, and he waited to see him, and also to see the state of affairs in the territory, and what would be the chance of getting into it. He was questioned by several on the road as to 'where he came from,' and replied that he was staying in Missouri (a fact to his sorrow), and got over the river. After he got into the territory he had no molestation."

While the emigration from free states was thus stopped, the fragments of Buford's regiment, and the reinforcement arriving from the South, were entering the territory in small parties or bands. A few of them clustered about the pro-slavery towns and cities, and the remainder camped on the creek here and there, exhibiting but little indication of making permanent improvement or location. They operated as a terror and a scourge. As an illustration of this I subjoin a copy of a letter, written rather later than the time of which I have been writing:

"BLUE SPRING, NEAR TECUMSEH, K. T.
July 24th, 1856.

"MR. W. G. SHERWIN: Dear Sir — We take this method of acquainting you with the sad fate of your friend. Yesterday morning, we — my friend Rooks and myself — were going to Tecumseh, but when about eleven miles from that place, we were appalled by the sight of the body of a murdered man, tied firmly to a tree, near the road-side. He was tied with his back to tne tree, with his hands and feet partially around it. He had been shot just above the left eye, with, we suppose, a rifle ball. A huge hunting knife was sticking in his breast. It had been driven clear through him, and the point was two or three inches in the tree. He was evidently murdered yesterday or the day before. There was a toad-stool tied to the handle of the knife, on which the following inscription was written: '*Let all those who are going to vote against slavery, take warning!*' We went to the nearest house, which was about a mile and a half, and got some help and some tools, and buried him. He was a stranger to all of us, except Mr. More, who says he has been boarding at his house eleven or twelve days. His name was Laben Parker, and he came from Cleveland.

"He had repeatedly said at the boarding-house that he did not intend to resort to force, but, so far as his influence at the polls went, he was going to use it for making Kansas a free state. A company of armed men from South Carolina have been staying around Tecumseh three or four days. A squad of them was down this road yesterday and day before. We don't, any of us, know where his relations live, but, among the papers in his pocket, we find a letter from you, written on the sixth of May, and that is the reason we direct this to you.

"Yours, &c. "MARTIN RULEX,
"J. E. MORE,
"FREDERICK ROOKS.

"*Lane County, Kansas Territory.*"

A systematic and remorseless legal warfare had been waged against the free-state settlers of Kansas. Not only were Governor Robinson and other influential men of the territory held prisoners, and subjected to a severe and degrading confinement, under charge of United States dragoons, but there was a systematic persecution of this kind all over the country, by which every man who took a prominent position, or showed himself to be useful or necessary to the free-state cause, was seized or persecuted by officers in search of them. I subjoin an editorial of a pro-slavery paper on the subject, written at the time of which I write:

"We understand that the grand jurors of Doniphan and Atchison Counties have found true bills of indictment against all the persons acting in the late disorganizing election in their respective counties.

"We hope the other counties will follow suit, and teach the abolition traitors that the laws are now in force, and that all attempts to ruin this country will be strictly dealt with by law."—*Squatter Sovereign.*

But the war in which Kansas was to be conquered was waged in every direction, and no means of securing it to slavery were left untried. The war which Missouri had waged against the free-state settlers in Kansas had aroused the feeling and indignation of their friends in the free states. I deem it unnecessary to take the trouble, or use space in this work to show what that feeling was, and how exhibited. The same sentiment existed in the Southern states. It was a warring of conflicting interests as well as conflicting opinions. Money was raised in both sections to support the struggle, and aid was given to emigration, so that a sufficient number of men of the proper kind should settle in Kansas. And here the Southern states found, as they ever must and will, that the energy and nerve of the free states as far exceed them, and is so much healthier in its exercise, that it would be utterly impossible to cope with them. The violence they had already used had destroyed the specious plea, under which they got Northern politicians to concede so much contrary to their convictions; namely, that they would "dissolve the Union" if the others did not do so and so, and thus they were impelled by the policy they were bent on pursuing, as well as by feeling, to resort to violence. The Missouri river was blockaded. Governor Price, of Missouri, gave the artillery belonging to the state to the bands along the river and on the border, to carry on the war. Batteries were made, and guns planted along the river, and the free-state, or, as they termed it, the "abolition" emigration, was stopped. As the difficulties existed in the territory, and were contemplated before these men left home, they came armed and prepared for the emergency, as they had a constitutional right to do, and as the nature of the case required. They were disarmed, and in many cases robbed and sent back. This violence continued until the river was, in point of fact, closed against emigration from free states. The following choice morsel is an account of one of these outrages, from a border ruffian journal:

"MORE ABOLITIONISTS TURNED BACK.

"The steamer *Sultan*, having on board contraband articles, was recently stopped at Leavenworth city, and lightened of forty-four rifles, and a large quantity of pistols and bowie-knives, taken from a crowd of cowardly Yankees, shipped out here from Massachusetts. The boat was permitted to go up as far as Weston, where a guard was placed over the prisoners, and none of them permitted to land. They were shipped back from Weston on the same boat, without even being insured by the shippers. We do not approve fully of sending these criminals back to the East to be re-shipped to Kansas — if not through Missouri, through Iowa and Nebraska. We think they should meet a traitor's death, and the world could not censure us if we, in self-protection, have to resort to such ultra measures. We are of the opinion, if the citizens of Leavenworth city or Weston would hang one or two boat loads of abolitionists, it would do more towards establishing peace in Kansas than all the speeches that have been delivered in Congress during the present session. Let the experiment be tried."

CHAPTER XXIX.

DISPERSION OF THE LEGISLATURE.

As the fourth of July approached, day after day witnessed some new effort of the pro-slavery party to prevent the state Legislature from assembling at that time. Several members of that body were languishing in state prisons, and others had to keep in places of concealment to avoid arrest. Gov. Robinson, the life and the soul of the free-state men, was in prison. The gallant Lane had a warrant hanging over his head, and dared not enter the territory. Lieut. Gov. Roberts was in Washington city, engaged in the hopeless task of getting the pro-slavery administration to relent in its purpose. Those whom the people had called to public posts, to take the lead and infuse courage and give direction, were thus not at hand at the trying moment.

The Missourians had threatened to bring up another army, and declared that the state Legislature should not meet. They thought that this would be the last step in the conquest of Kansas. Every other power seemed to be crushed out. That the general government would interfere to do this the most sanguine of the ruffians had not hoped. They, therefore, began to nerve themselves for another invasion and another struggle, in which not only should the Legislature be prevented from assembling, but a fatal blow struck at Topeka and Lawrence.

In anticipation of this many active and influential men exerted themselves to induce all the free-state men in the territory to assemble at Topeka on the third of July. For this purpose a mass convention of the people was called to deliberate at that time and place on the condition of the territory. The convention had necessarily no connection with the Legislature; but it was the intention of those by whom the call was issued to have a body of citizens thus around the Legislature, to protect it if necessary.

It was the design, as it was the expectation, of the originators of this movement to have at least two thousand settlers at Topeka during the third and fourth of July, who should be under arms in drill-parade, as is customary in the fourth of July celebrations throughout the country. Several causes interfered to prevent this. At that time there was scarcely a newspaper in the territory. Already had the border ruffians destroyed three prominent presses in the territory by mob violence, the *Herald of Freedom*, *Free State*, and *Territorial Register*, and, although other two had a sort of nominal existence, their issues were prevented by the want of paper, their supplies being cut off by the blockade of the Missouri river. Thus the most direct mode of communicating with the people was cut off. Travelling in the territory was not very safe at that time, as bands of Southern guerillas infested the roads. At the instance of Col. Sumner some influential free-state men had recalled the free-state guerillas, on his promise that he would keep peace in the territory. This had only the effect of recalling the best and most useful of these guerillas; the remainder keeping the field on their own account, and, being the very wildest, they carried on the war more for their individual aggrandizement than the interests of the cause.

In spite of all difficulties, some few active men succeeded in visiting certain portions of the territory and urging the citizens to come to Topeka the third of July. There was one great cause of hindrance even with those who had been notified. Guerillas were prowling about the territory, and were the people to leave their homes they would only expose them to be robbed, and their families to be insulted, perhaps murdered. Many thus remained at home who anxiously desired to meet with their friends at Topeka.

Thus it was that besides the Legislature there were less than eight hundred persons assembled at the free-state capital. Several settlements and towns sent a delegation of one or two persons to see what was to be done, and send word to those they represented if their assistance was to be needed, as it was a busy season.

Many of those who did arrive came unarmed, and perhaps not more than four hundred men could have been mustered in an available force. Besides these causes to reduce the force assembled at Topeka, several persons, who, by their former zeal as free-state men had received no small share of the public confidence, used their influence to prevent an assemblage, urging that the present moment was an unpropitious one, and that if the Legislature was to adjourn it would not weaken or injure the free-state movements. In this opinion they might be right; or it might merely be a want of courage to meet the issue that had to be met sooner or later.

While this was going on the other side was not idle. The first intention had been to assemble a force of Missourians and Buford's men, and once more invade the territory; but the leaders and thinking portion of the slavery extensionists saw the danger of this. They had succeeded by force and fraud, and by the power of the general government, in acquiring power and the semblance of legal authority in the territory, and had thus far kept it. They were well aware that there would be a force at Topeka with which it would be difficult to cope. War, thus precipitated, might rob them of all the fruits of their ursurpations. The battles and skirmishes of the early summer, if the course of victory had not been checked by the federal troops, would soon have liberated Kansas from the Missouri pro-slavery yoke. It was prudent in these men to pause in such a state of affairs, and not stake their all on a throw in which they might gain little, and possibly lose much. So far it was all in their own hands, and it would not do to play rashly merely for the sake of gratifying their personal hate on the free-state settlers. Besides all this the federal appointees in the territory were deeply interested. A lost battle, or a series of losses on the part of the pro-slavery men, would place them in imminent peril. They had forgotten duty, honor, the public safety, and every other consideration, in order to play into the hands of the Missourians and their allies. They had been sent to protect the people of the territory, and, instead of doing so, had, in obedience to the corrupt administration that had appointed them, oppressed and grievously wronged them. In case of reverses to the cause for which they had sold themselves, their situation would have been critically perilous. In these circumstances they conferred with the border ruffians, and urged that there be no fresh invasion at this time, and gave assurance that the federal troops would be employed to disperse the Legislature. From this course everything was to be gained. If the federal troops were resisted, war would thus be begun, and the whole military power of the government would thus be firmly secured to the pro-slavery alliance. Such was the policy determined on, and, under the circumstances, it was by far the soundest policy for them. Our republican government would thus take the first steps towards becoming a military despotism, by overthrowing of civil rights under the constitution. Startling though this might appear, the slavery extensionists were assured that "the step would be taken, and had been contemplated by the administration." In fact, secret orders on this very point had been issued not only to the territorial authorities but from the war department.

A military force was thus assembled round Topeka as the day approached. Col. Sumner, with several companies of dragoons, the Fort Leavenworth force, encamped close to Topeka, on the south of the town. Four companies from Fort Riley marched on Topeka and took their position in the timber of the Kaw bottom, to the north. While this was going on the people were greatly at a loss to know what steps their enemies meant to pursue. An invasion from Missouri had been threatened, and was generally expected, but as the day approached, and no large army from the state was seen marching upon them, they were puzzled. Pro-slavery conventions to celebrate the fourth had been called at different points near Topeka. These had been projected as a means of organizing before the intention of invasion was abandoned; but it soon became evident that no adequate force was assembling there. Rumors were rife that it was the design to destroy the settlements when the people were at Topeka, and, as the Buford guerillas were at work, there was a good deal of probability in this.

On the second of July the people's convention began to assemble. It was soon evident that there would be none of those present who should have taken the lead in an emergency. Gov. Robinson was a political prisoner; Lieut. Gov. Roberts was in Washington; Mr. Minard, Speaker of the House, had not arrived; and it was understood that he had been intimidated and so prevented from attendance, as had been several other members. Under these unfavorable circumstances, a meeting was held by a few of the most influential men; and, as the difficulties were great, and the prospect threatening, the next officer in authority took the responsibility of issuing the following

"PROCLAMATION.

"EXECUTIVE OFFICE, TOPEKA, *July* 2, 1856.

"Whereas I am in possession of reliable information that certain portions of our state are infested with parties of freebooters, robbing our citizens, burning houses, stealing and destroying property, and murdering innocent men; and believing that some of these parties are now approaching the capital, and soon will be upon us to burn our houses, invade the sanctity of our homes, and sack this town; and

"Whereas the law fails to clothe me with proper authority to provide means of defence against such invasions: Now, therefore,

"I, John Curtis, acting Governor of the State of Kansas, feel it to be my imperative duty to call the General Assembly immediately together, that they may, in their wisdom, enact such laws as the exigencies of the case demand. The members of both Houses are hereby directed to meet at eight o'clock, A. M., of the third instant, at the Council Rooms, Topeka.

"Given under my hand and seal this second day of July, 1856.

"JOHN CURTIS,

"*Acting Governor of the State of Kansas.*

"PHILIP C. SCHUYLER, *Secretary of State.*"

In accordance with the above proclamation, both branches of the Legislature assembled on the third of July for special session, the adjournment having been to the fourth day. When convened they transacted a considerable amount of business in the forenoon and afternoon sessions relative to their present condition. It was now evident that there was no other force menacing them except the federal troops. There was too much difference of opinion, and the aspects of the case were too embarrassing and critical to be easily acted upon; and both branches adjourned on the evening of the third, having made no provision for action with regard to the troops, and having merely agreed that they should convene at noon next day, for the regular session, according to the adjournment in March.

On the evening of the second a committee of gentlemen waited on Col. Sumner, and subsequently corresponded with him relative to the warlike demonstrations on the part of the United States Dragoons.

The following is a copy of the letter sent by Col. Sumner to the people assembled at Topeka, through the committee appointed to confer with him:

"HEAD QUARTERS, FIRST CAVALRY,
CAMP AT TOPEKA, K. T., *July* 3, 1856.

"GENTLEMEN: In relation to the assembling of the Topeka Legislature (the subject of our conversation last night), the more I reflect on it the more I am convinced that the peace of the country will be greatly endangered by your persistence in this measure. Under these circumstances I would ask you and your friends to take the matter into grave consideration. It will certainly be much better that you should act voluntarily in this matter, from a sense of prudence and patriotism, at this moment of high excitement throughout the country, than that the authority of the general government should be compelled to use coërcive measures to prevent the assemblage of that Legislature.

"I am, gentlemen, very respectfully, your obedient servant,

"E. V. SUMNER,
"*Col. First Cavalry Commanding.*"

During the third, some of the timid, or *conservative* persons used all the influence they possessed to induce the Legislature to adjourn, in order to avoid any cause of difficulty. It was the wish of the great majority, however, that the Legislature should meet. It was urged by a few determined spirits that the town be at once placed in an attitude of defence, and that Colonel Sumner be notified that the people of Kansas, while they had the utmost respect and loyalty to federal authority, could not permit even that authority to trample upon their rights under the constitution; that *any* power threatening those rights was no better than a mob, and that he must not, on any account, bring his troops into Topeka, or attempt to disperse the Legislature. Had such a position been taken it probably would have triumphed; but it was overruled, and it was determined that no steps for defence should be taken; that the troops should quietly be permitted to trample on their rights in this violent and despotic way, and trust to the patriotism of the country to sustain them in thus making a sacrifice for the public tranquillity. As there was a rumor that many of the representatives had been intimidated by the representations of fearful and nerveless free-state men, the following resolution was introduced to the popular convention by Mr. Wm. Hutchinson:

"*Resolved*, That it is the imperative duty of the Kansas Legislature to meet, as per adjournment, on the fourth instant, and proceed at once to the work of their office, and persevere until our state code is complete; ever recognizing the eminent danger of PUTTING IN FORCE any statute that will produce a collision with the federal authorities; and that no sacrifice, less than life itself, should deter them from this duty, for which they will ever be held responsible by their constituents."

During the afternoon of the third, and the forenoon of the fourth, this resolution was under discussion. Having taken part in that discussion in favor of the resolution, I decline further allusion to it. The utmost interest was manifested in the debate by the people.

Besides this effort to arouse the legislators to a full sense of their duty in the emergency, there was a voice from the state-prisons of Kansas eloquently imploring the Legislature to go on with their work, and pay no attention to any threats, come from what quarter they might. Besides the name of Gov. Charles Robinson, Judge G. W, Smith, Gen. Dietzler, Capt. John Brown,

Jr., Mr. Jenkins, and Mr. Williams (all prisoners of state), were attached to this document, — their severe confinement and threatened peril not having dissuaded them from this patriotic expression, even though it should give their enemies another tongue to use against them.

The morning of the fourth of July, 1856, broke in a cloudy, dappled sky on Topeka; but soon the fresh breezes, which had swept without a bound or limit from the base of the Rocky Mountains, dispersed the canopy of clouds, and left the glowing sun to blaze down through a sky of unbroken blue. The stillness of the morning was broken by a thundering salute from the artillery of the dragoons; a tribute to the memory of a glorious struggle for liberty, half forgotten, and, at the same time, a threat to those who were now struggling in another cause of liberty, in which those rights, purchased by the blood that flowed in "seventy-six," were to be asserted and rescued from encroaching despotism. It was a strange blending of the memory of dead liberty and living tyranny; an exhibition which ought to startle the American people from their lethargy, and make them search, ere it be too late, for the last landmarks of our glorious constitution.

It was about ten o'clock in the forenoon when U. S. Marshal Donaldson, accompanied by ex-Judge Elmore, arrived in Topeka. It had been ascertained earlier in the morning that a conclave of pro-slavery propagandists and territorial officers had assembled in Colonel Sumner's camp, and were plotting mischief against the free-state settlers. As Gov. Shannon had left the territory with the intention of resigning, Secretary Woodson was acting governor. Woodson was with others in Colonel Sumner's camp. It was with the results of this exercise of collective wisdom that Donaldson entered Topeka. The popular convention was in session when the marshal intimated that he had something to communicate. He was invited to the stand, and, having got upon it, he announced in a weak and hesitating voice that he had sundry proclamations to read to them; but that, as he was no speaker (a self-evident fact), Judge Elmore would read them. Upon this, Judge Elmore got upon the stand. He was rather flustered at first, but proceeded more calmly. He read President Pierce's proclamation of February, in which his Excellency declared that the usurping territorial laws of Shawnee Mission manufacture would be sustained by the whole force of the government. Then he read the latest of Gov. Shannon's numerous proclamations. This had been issued a month before; had relation to the dispersion of armed bands, and had nothing to do with the Legislature. The important part of this proclamation was Secretary Woodson's proclamation, the others being read merely as preparatory exercises, justifying or expletive. Here it is:

"PROCLAMATION BY THE ACTING GOVERNOR OF KANSAS.

"Whereas we have been reliably informed that a number of persons claiming legislative power are about to assemble in the town of Topeka for the purpose of adopting a code of laws, or of executing other legislative functions in violation of the act of Congress organizing the territory, and of the laws adopted in pursuance thereof, and it appears that a military organization exists in this territory for the purpose of sustaining this unlawful legislative movement, and thus, in effect, to subvert by violence all present constitutional and legal authority; and

"Whereas the President of the United States has, by proclamation bearing date eleventh February, 1856, declared that any such plan for the determination of the future institutions of the territory, if carried into action, will constitute insurrection, and therein commanded all persons engaged in such unlawful combinations against the constituted authority of the Territory of Kansas, or of the United States, to disperse and retire to their respective places of abode; and

"Whereas satisfactory evidence exists that said proclamation of the President has been, and is about to be, disregarded: Now, therefore,

"I, Daniel Woodson, acting Governor of the Territory of Kansas, by virtue of the authority vested in me by law, and in pursuance of the aforesaid proclamation of the President of the United States, and to the end of upholding the *legal* and *constituted* authorities of the territory, and of preserving the peace and public tranquillity, do issue this, my proclamation, forbidding all persons claiming legislative power and authority as aforesaid from assembling, organizing, or attempting to organize, or acting in any legislative capacity whatever, under the penalties attached to all unlawful violation of the law of the land and disturbers of the peace and tranquillity of the country.

"In testimony whereof, I have hereunto subscribed my hand, and caused to be affixed the seal of the territory, this 4th day of July, 1856, and of the Independence of the United States the eightieth.

[SEAL.] "DANIEL WOODSON,
Acting Gov. of K. T."

"The proclamation of the President, and the orders under it, require me to sustain the Executive of the territory in executing the laws and preserving the peace. I therefore hereby announce that I shall maintain the proclamation at all hazards.

"E. V. SUMNER,
Col. First Cavalry Commanding."

Having got through with this ceremony, all of which was listened to attentively and quietly, the two gentlemen prepared to leave, and the convention resumed its business where it had left off. Marshal Donaldson, who had evidently expected some remarkable indication of public sentiment, or a moral earthquake, to follow his announcements, was evidently chagrined at the indifference with which they were received. He halted in the crowd, and asked if they had any communication to send to Col. Sumner. The President of the Convention, Mr. Currier, asked if a reply from this convention was desired. Donaldson, on consultation with Judge Elmore, replied, "No;" but added that if they had anything to send he would carry it. He was then informed that this convention was not the Legislature, to which the proclamation was addressed, and that the convention had no reply to make.

It was nearly noon. The convention was still busy at work. The hour for the meeting of the Legislature approached, and several of the members of the Legislature had entered the hall. The two military companies of Topeka which had been on drill were drawn up in front of the legislative hall to receive a banner from the ladies. A band of music was stationed at the end of the line, and was making the place echo with martial strains. It was a hot summer's day, the thermometer standing at 100° in the shade, and yet the streets were crowded. It was known that the troops might be expected at every moment, and yet not only men, but women and children, in gala dresses, were near the legislative hall, and in the street in front of the hotel where the convention was held. It was at this moment that a young man hurried into town, and announced to the convention and to the people in the streets that Col. Sumner, with his force of dragoons, was rapidly approaching Topeka in battle array. This announcement caused no visible change in the aspect of things; perhaps there might be a fluttering of some anxious hearts, and a tremulous anxiety at the possibility that the brilliant panorama then presented in Topeka might be in a few moments blotted out in blood. Who could tell what an administration, capable of so much political villany, could contemplate?

Such was the aspect of affairs when the head of the advancing column of dragoons was seen rapidly turning into Kansas avenue, about one hundred yards above the legislative hall,— the popular convention being in the same thoroughfare, which was crowded, between the hall of the Legislature and the place where the convention was held. Col. Sumner and his staff came first; at his right the military band, and close behind nearly two hundred dragoons in three squadrons. The military battle-flag fluttered in the breeze. The dragoons entered the town rapidly, dashing up to the legislative hall, where the two Topeka companies of volunteers were drawn up. As they approached, those companies stood firm. The band played on; a little boy was beating on the kettle-drum, and neither he nor his older compeers stopped playing until the dragoons rode on to them, the horses' noses coming up to the drum-sticks, when Sumner, who was evidently much agitated, leaned towards them with his gloved hand, and begged them to desist for the present. His shrill voice was then heard crying, "First squadron, form into line!" and as the troops, under that and other orders, formed into battle array around the hall, and along the street facing it, the crowds in the street, and those at the convention, saw a couple of cannon posted up the street, on a rise about one hundred yards off, where they had just been planted, with their muzzles pointing down the street, the gunners at their stations, and the slow matches lighted and burning. An army surgeon also came with them, his case of instruments open and ready for use. Three other companies of dragoons at the same time approached the town from the other side, and were only concealed, while the force that entered came up, by the strip of timber along the valley of the Kansas.

It was a brilliant and startling spectacle which was thus presented, — the dragoons with their flashing sabres, the officers giving orders, and the men wheeling into position, and, above all, the star-spangled banner floating from Constitutional Hall, as if in mockery of the scene beneath.

After the dragoons were placed so as to suit Col. Sumner's taste, he dismounted and walked towards the Assembly rooms. Both Senate and House stood adjourned to meet at twelve o'clock, a fact of which Col. Sumner appeared to be aware. He was at once informed that the companies drawn up in front of the hall were there merely to receive a banner from the ladies. He said he did not wish to interfere with their assembling on the Fourth of July. Three cheers were given for Col. Sumner; Mr. Redpath shouted, "Three cheers for Gov. Robinson!" which were given with a will; and some one else cried, "Three cheers for Liberty!" which was also heartily cheered. Col. Sumner entered the hall of the Legislature, and the crowd rushed in behind him and soon filled it. The speaker was absent, and Mr. F. S. Tappan, first clerk, rose and called order by striking with the gavel on the desk. It was scarcely twelve o'clock, and the Legislature had not yet convened, when Sumner entered. He went up to the platform, and they offered him a chair, which he pulled to one side, saying, "Do you want to make speaker of me?" (Great laughter and shouts from the crowd.) Mr. Tappan, in a strong, sonorous voice, proceeded to call the roll, and, as there was not a quorum present, he called the sergeant-at-arms to bring in absentees. Mr. Pratt, recording clerk, then called the roll again, and marked absentees.

Only seventeen answered the call, although there were some thirty-three, more than a quorum, in or about the house.

Considerable anxiety was manifested to have all the members answer to their names, but some were tremulous and timid; perhaps their response would be the signal for violent arrest and severe imprisonment. Those who answered did so boldly, and the little band clustered around the stand, and stood prepared for what might come. Col. Sumner arose from his seat, and said:

"GENTLEMEN: I am called upon this day to perform the most painful duty of my whole life. Under the authority of the President's proclamation I am here to disperse this Legislature, and therefore inform you that you cannot meet. I, therefore, order you to disperse. God knows that I have no party feeling in this matter, and will hold none so long as I occupy my present position in Kansas. I have just returned from the borders, where I have been sending home companies of Missourians, and now I am ordered here to disperse you. Such are my orders, and you *must disperse*. I now command you to disperse. I repeat that this is the most painful duty of my whole life."

Judge Schuyler asked — "Col. Sumner, are we to understand that the Legislature are driven out at the point of the bayonet?"

Col. Sumner — "I shall use all the forces in my command to carry out my orders."

The representatives had dispersed, and Col. Sumner, who did not appear to be particularly enlightened on legislative matters, had got on his horse to go, when he learned that the Senate was still to disperse, and that the Senate Chamber was up stairs. He forthwith dismounted again, and proceeded to Constitutional Hall. He entered the Senate Chamber. There was a quorum present; the hour for convening had arrived, but the President of the Senate had not convened it when Sumner entered. Orders had been issued the evening before to the door-keeper to admit no visitors. The door-keeper allowed Col. Sumner to enter, but told Marshal Donaldson he could not let him in. Donaldson said he was United States Marshal, and had official business. The door-keeper, Mr. Fuller, told him to "show his papers;" he exhibited his commission, and the door-keeper let him pass.

Col. Sumner did not pause to inquire whether the Senate was or was not in session, but proceeded to tell them that by virtue of the orders of the President he was there to disperse them, and ordered them to disperse. Having said so, Col. Sumner looked at them to see how they took his announcement. The members of the Senate were standing in a circle, looking at him respectfully, but they did not move. There was a long and disagreeable pause, which Sumner broke by asking,

"Well, gentlemen, do you consider yourselves dispersed?"

Mr. Thornton, President of the Senate, replied thus:

"Col. Sumner, the Senate is not in session, and cannot make any reply to you; neither can any member of it."

Mr. Thornton then asked if Col. Sumner, after his orders to disperse, would permit them to convene, so as to receive any communication he might have to make.

The colonel said, "No; my orders are that you must not be permitted to meet, and I cannot allow you to do any business."

There was an embarrassing pause. The senators were drawn up in a circle, looking respectfully at Col. Sumner, but never uttering a word, when Marshal Donaldson, who had been standing unnoticed in the corner, began to suspect that "law and order" was likely to suffer, and stepped forward. He confronted the members of the Senate, and holding his hat in one hand, and raising the other, gesticulated with the point of his finger, as he said, in a tremulous, squeaking voice,

"Well, I want all o' you members to promise that you won't meet here again. If you don't," — and here the U. S. Marshal shook his head menacingly, — "I'll arrest every one o' ye — every member!"

The Senate paid no attention to this outrageous proceeding, in which a United States officer threatened with a conditional arrest, in the hope of extorting pledges, the yielding to which might be fatal to the cause of freedom in the territory.

One of the members of the Senate exhibited a *little* of the feeling that such trying circumstances may awaken, and said:

"When my country calls me to disperse, by her troops, I yield to that authority."

Here Hon. Mr. Pillsbury said, "Col. Sumner, we are in no *condition* to resist the United States troops; and if you order us to disperse, of course we must disperse." Col. Allen said that he would suggest to his brother senators that Mr. Pillsbury's statement be considered the expression of the whole, which was assented to.

Col. Sumner then left the hall. When he got out on the street he assured many of those who gathered round him that he did not wish to interfere with the convention as then assembled there; that he had merely been sent to disperse the Legislature, and recognized their right to meet on the 4th of July. Three cheers were again proposed for Col. Sumner, and given. Three cheers for John C. Fremont were then given.

At this point the dragoons were filed off in marching order; three cheers were given for "the Topeka Convention and the State Legislature." Some of the pro-slavery officers looked round rather fiercely when this was given; but Sumner's sharp voice was heard giving the order, "Forward — march!" and just as that military band who, under the American flag which waved from the hall of the Legislature, had committed one of the most grievous outrages recorded in our history, spurred their horses to leave the streets of Topeka, three groans were given for Mr. Pierce, and so deep and loud were they that the sound startled the dragoons, and made them break from line as they defiled past.

CHAPTER XXX.

CONDITION OF CONQUERED KANSAS.

KANSAS was now politically prostrate. Her Legislature was dispersed by federal troops; her leading men languishing in prison. The Missouri river was closed to emigration from the free states, and the tedious and uncertain route through Iowa was menaced, and the only security by that route was by companies, sufficiently strong and determined to take care of themselves. The free-state movement being crushed for the time, or prevented from securing defence for the settlers, there was no legal security for free-state men. The territorial officers imposed by the general government, and the local officers thrust on the people by the Legislature of the Shawnee Mission, were tools of the slave power, and active co-workers in the task of making Kansas a slave state. The leaders of the free-state movement had a prison for a reward. The promulgation of free-state sentiments was branded "TREASON," and the federal troops enforced the usurpation of Missouri and the slave power.

It is a grand fact, that never must be forgotten by the American people, *military power is and ever must be inimical to popular institutions.* Speculating on the political principles of a military officer, who is mainly taught to regard government as a necessary pay-master, and political authority as something connected with promotion, is like trusting to the manhood of a dough-face, or appealing to the tender mercies of the usurer of the tribe of Levi. To expect a delicate discrimination, a nice balancing of social and political rights, a careful watch and protection of the people of Kansas, to flow from the mere fact of turning some six or seven hundred dragoons loose to manage the territory, is simply preposterous. The hope that this expedient would act as a sedative, and secure justice and the country's peace, may be very creditable to a sanguine heart, but the result proves that the remedy itself was stupid, and the mode of applying it still more so.

Drilled to the doctrine of implicit and unquestionable obedience, the troops were incapable of comprehending the meaning or importance of popular rights. Trained to obey regulations which they have had no hand in making, they consider obedience in others the only indication of propriety. With them the words "treason" and "insubordination" are potent and significant, and to them popular liberty and popular rights are unmeaning and worthless things.

Ever hopeful, the free-state settlers earnestly looked to the troops for protection and peace. Attached to the general government, — feeling for it a respect that Western states rarely evince, and Southern states never, — they could not realize their persecution to be systematic and remorseless. The evidence sent through the country, by the committee of Congress, of their wrongs and the gross fraud of the territorial law; the sack of Lawrence and other outrages; the war waged on the settlers of Kansas by the slave power, — all of these colossal evidences of their sufferings, they trusted would work the cure, and that the peace of the country and the well-being of Kansas would promptly receive the only remedies that could meet the case. Alas! they waited and hoped, and were deceived. And now a yawning depth was before them. On the one side political ruin and ostracism from Kansas; on the other security, and peace, and freedom for the territory. Between these there was a *step* — the Rubicon. In that barrier stood not only the slave power in the territory, which is trifling, but the slave power out of it; and there was a corrupt territorial government, corrupt territorial courts, a corrupt general government, and the leap for freedom and security must be on the sharp points of United States bayonets and sabres.

In all the Kansas struggle the slave power has never yielded an inch of ground. A fraud might be so monstrous that even conservative men in the South would deprecate it, but the fruit of the villany was never relinquished. An outrage might be so monstrous that every honest man in the country, North or South, would indignantly speak against it; but the power it gained for pro-slaveryism has been jealously guarded, and its protection made the test of political orthodoxy. Yet, at every step, the squatters have hoped, and from every expedient that was to give the slave power a firmer foothold, they have expected something more impartial. Unfortunate fatuity! The slave power could *only win* by such expedients, and it is *determined to win*. Coarse and brutal though each act in the drama, this was the only means of bolstering the weakness of a coarse and brutal system. Fairness was ruin, impartiality equal to a relinquishment. Thus, on the advent of dragoon government, the people said, "Well, we will be protected. These Missourians dare not come here now. Pro-slavery men will not molest us; and then the evidence which has gone on to Congress will secure us at last our rights." It was the same hoping, trusting, peace-loving spirit. The slimy reptile, slavery, was merely wrapping another coil round its victim. The free-state settlers had been so outraged that they would have been vindicated in the eyes of the world for defending themselves. The first fiery spirits had already sprung into the contest. A mere handful of the free-state party had dared to meet the war declared against them, and "Franklin" and "Palmyra" had attested their courage and superiority. But this had been foreseen, and "the people must be protected, and the *peace* preserved."

Liberty and constitutional right were filched from those of the American people who settled in Kansas, first by demagogues, then by Missouri and her pro-slavery allies; and, lastly, the federal troops secured the fruit of outrage and crime, and did their best to clinch the villany.

The conquest of Kansas from guaranteed freedom to slavery was premeditated, and deliberate; but many of those most influential in accomplishing it dared not avow the policy by which they were inspired. Conservative Southern men, terrified at the charge of "abolitionism," which was hung over their head like a whip of scorpions, dared not question the suicidal policy which was endangering the peace of the country, and inflicting an irreparable blow on republican institutions. Corrupt Northern politicians, greedy for political power, were willing to sacrifice their own honor, as well as the interests of those they represented, for the chance of power and place. For this they struggled to blindfold and deceive those they had robbed of their political birthright; for this they were false to the country that had trusted them, and the constitution they had sworn to protect.

Not content with filching civil rights from the people, these corrupt popular leaders undertook to demonstrate that republicanism is a humbug, by corrupting the popular opinion on which it rests. The term "popular sovereignty" was made the foundation-stone of American despotism, and the weapon by which the people were defrauded of those civil rights on which the prosperity of the state depends was called "allowing the people to settle their *local* affairs for themselves."

The idea of the free-state and slave-state interests quietly deciding "their own *local* institutions for themselves" is as infernal a piece of political rascality as ever imposed on the American people. The two systems are the antipodes of each other. They cannot live together. They cannot breathe together. They cannot *merge* their differences. If Kansas is a slave-state no free-state man can remain; for, in order to bolster up slavery among the population now here, the laws would have to be so oppressive and despotic that freedom could not live under them. This talk of the "people settling the question of slavery for themselves" is merely a pretext under which the antagonistic elements in our government are invited to a warfare on a coveted battle-ground. O, you have but to see the hatred with which men there regard each other, to feel this; the suspicion with which one traveller regards another, to feel its weight! If slavery triumphs, the principle on which our government is founded is virtually overthrown. If freedom triumphs, the greatest evil in our country is kept in bounds.

Murder, rapine, highway robbery, were committed in the name of "law and order," and the appeals of an oppressed people fell unheeded and unanswered on the ears of a corrupt administration. Not satisfied with all the villany that had been done, and all the outrages by which the conquest of Kansas to slavery was consummated, a party, calling itself a *democratic* party, had the hardihood to make these usurpations and crimes the platform on which they stood, and the *argument* by which they dared to appeal to the people for their suffrages. The cry of "save the Union" was raised; that cry under which the stability of our institutions had already received the most fatal stabs. "Saving the Union" had been the blind and the whip under which coercive and unfair legislation was smuggled in; and, having accomplished this, the same cry was raised to cover up the designing schemes of nullification and secession.

The pro-slavery party were jubilant in their triumph. Flushed with a victory in which fraud rather than military power had triumphed, they gave way to rejoicings. The portion of the Southern regiment, stationed at Atchison, joined with the Missourians and pro-slavery men of the territory in a celebration, of which I give the following, from the account of the Atchison pro-slavery paper:

"At the head of the table hung the 'blood-red flag,' with the lone star, and the motto of 'Southern Rights' on the one side, and 'South Carolina' on the other. The same flag that first floated on the rifle pits of the abolitionists at Lawrence, and on the hotel of the same place, in triumph, now hung over the heads of the noble soldiers who bore it so bravely through that exciting war.

"The following are among the toasts drank:

"Kansas: our chosen home — stand by her. Yes, sons of the South, make her a slave state, or die in the attempt! (This toast was received with loud and continued applause.)

"Disunion: by secession or otherwise — a beacon of hope to an oppressed people, and the surest remedy for Southern wrongs. (Enthusiastic cheers.)

"The city of Atchison: may she, before the close of the year '57, be the capital of a Southern republic. (Cheers.)

"Kansas: we will make her a slave state, or form a chain of locked arms and hearts together, and die in the attempt.

"The distribution of public lands: one hundred and sixty acres to every pro-slavery settler, and to every abolitionist six feet by two."

And, also, the following from the proceedings of a celebration of *slavery* in South Carolina:

"Kansas: already stained with the blood of Southern martyrs in the cause of justice and our most sacred rights. May her streams become rivers of blood, and her forests charnel-houses, before her soil shall be contaminated, and her atmosphere polluted, by the free-soil partisans of the North.

"Kansas: it has risen like the ghost of Banquo, to sear the eyeballs of rampant fanaticism; but, ere they clutch it, they must *cross* many *Brooks*, whose *caney* growth will resist them.

"Kansas:

'Strike while the iron 's hot, —
Strike with men and means;
And let the Yankees see we 've got
The right to hold the reins.'

"Kansas: the battle-ground upon which is to be decided the fate of Southern rights *under the Union*."

Alas, these were not idle and unmeaning words! Every line and every syllable have been attested by fraud and crime in Kansas; and, while I write, they are echoed by the complaints of enslaved freemen, the wail of bereaved widows, and the unheeded plaint of political prisoners who languish in captivity, for loving freedom fearlessly and well. Liberty stands aghast at the fearful prospect, and asks, if these things be done under republican rule to-day, what will our popular institutions be worth to-morrow?

But Kansas, though conquered by Missouri and her allies, is not yet subdued. Every vestige of popular liberty and constitutional privilege has, indeed, been stricken down, but a liberty-loving people remain. Until that freedom-loving race has been "wiped out," there can be no peace and security for the power that has thus trampled on their rights, or for the institution of negro slavery, for the sake of which all this villany and wrong has been done. Liberty and independence do not exist in Kansas to-day, but a people loving these is upon her soil. "Truth crushed to earth will rise again." Our political elements have become very corrupt, because we have forgotten principle in remembering party; but there is a shaking in the "valley of dry bones," and, perhaps, the suffering that has been undergone has purchased a watchfulness on the part of the people, worth all the blood, and treasure, and heart-wrung agony it has cost.

Yet it is possible that the war of conquest may be followed by a war of extermination. Perhaps the struggling, liberty-loving TREASON in the territory may furnish the apology for an attack, in which not only freedom, but the *love of freedom*, will be blotted out. The slavery extensionists well know that without this the fruit of their conquest will turn to ashes on their lips. They know this, and God in heaven only knows what the corrupt men who have been the most active participators in this warfare may not attempt. The spirit that has so far triumphed is exhibited in the following paragraph from a border paper:

"Several parties have inquired of us why the law has not been put in force at Topeka, as well as at Lawrence, against abolition newspapers. Topeka is no better than Lawrence; it is also demoralized; but it is not so well known abroad. If both Topeka and Lawrence were blotted out, entirely obliterated, it would be the best thing for Kansas that could happen. The sooner the people of Topeka sound their death-knell the better; they are too corrupt and degraded to live. We would like to be present and raise our Ebenezer in the funeral. It is silly to suppose, for an instant, that there can be peace in Kansas as long as one enemy of the South lives upon her soil, or one single specimen of an abolitionist treads in the sunlight of Kansas territory."

The foregoing is but one of many such paragraphs which might be given. Such sentiments are a fearful indication of the corruption of the popular mind.

But if that war of extermination is begun, it will prove the war of freedom. The suffering settlers in Kansas have been driven to extremity, and are now nerved to fight. Kansas was settled, in great part, by a peace-loving people; a people in whom delicate sentiment, and a refinement which hates the horrors of blood, are strongly rooted. Imagine an over-sensitive Englishman moralizing over the dead body of a Russian whom he has slain in the trenches of Sevastopol, and you have a picture of the free-state settler in Kansas, contemplating the horrors of a civil war, which he would suffer much to avert. They have suffered much, perhaps *too* much to avert it; they appeal from their wrongs to the great American brotherhood to right those wrongs. In the vindication of justice, peace may yet be secured, but without it there will surely be war and bloodshed, and with these the triumph of freedom; for,

> "Freedom's battle once begun,
> Bequeathed from bleeding sire to son,
> Though baffled oft is EVER WON."

Kansas, the Italy of America, the debatable ground, has still much to tempt. Landscapes of unsurpassed loveliness, a soil of unmatched fertility, with the richest natural elements, exhibit the value of the future empire whose fate was tossed recklessly, by unscrupulous politicians, in the scale, to vibrate between the conflicting claims of freedom and slavery.

There is a healthy freshness and vitality in the atmosphere of Kansas as favorable to pulmonary weakness as the table lands of Mexico. As you inhale the vigor-giving breezes, you acquire a nerve and elasticity, in the possession of which you might forget that the rights of American freemen had been subdued, in order that slavery might be planted upon its soil; or, if it cannot make you forget this, it may inspire you with the thought that freedom can reconquer what she has lost. What matters it that free speech, and a free press, are "*treason*" in Kansas? What matters it that the judiciary is the obedient slave of slavery? What matters it though the federal troops hold in their iron grasp the Kansas that Missouri and slavery conquered? There is, thank God, still a spirit and vitality in the American character which will rise above all these obstacles, and will yet write RESURGAM! on the tomb of Kansas Liberty.

MACAULAY'S HISTORY OF ENGLAND; from the Accession of James II. Volumes I., II., III., and IV., 12mo, with Portrait. Muslin, 40 cents per volume.

HUME'S HISTORY OF ENGLAND; from the Invasion of Julius Cæsar to the Abdication of James II., 1688. A new edition, with the author's last corrections and improvements; to which is prefixed a short account of his life, written by himself. Six volumes, with Portrait. Muslin, 40 cents per volume.

GIBBON'S DECLINE AND FALL OF THE ROMAN EMPIRE. With Notes by Rev. H. H. Milman. A new edition, with a complete Index. Six volumes, with Portrait. 12mo, muslin, 40 cents per volume.

"We recommend it as the best library edition extant." — *Boston Transcript.*

"Such an edition of this English classic has long been wanted; it is at once convenient, economical, and elegant." — *Home Journal.*

LINGARD'S HISTORY OF ENGLAND. 13 volumes. 75 cents per volume.

MODERN BRITISH ESSAYISTS. 8 vols. 8vo. Price $12. Embracing the Essays, Reviews, and Miscellanies, of

Macaulay,	$1.75.	Sydney Smith,	$1.25.
Carlyle,	2.00.	Mackintosh,	2.00.
Jeffrey,	2.00.	Alison,	1.25.
Prof. Wilson,	1.25.	Talfourd and Stephen,	1.25.

Any volume sold separately.

JAPAN AS IT WAS AND IS. By Richard Hildreth, author of "History of the United States." $1.25.

The best, most complete, and most reliable work upon this country extant.

HITCHCOCK'S GEOLOGICAL WORKS:

Religion of Geology,	$1.25.
Outline of Geology,	1.25.
Genesis and Geology,	63.

DR. WAYLAND'S INTELLECTUAL PHILOSOPHY. Price $1.25.

DR. WAYLAND'S LIFE OF JUDSON. 2 volumes. Price $2.

THE EARNEST MAN; A NEW LIFE OF JUDSON. By Mrs. H. C. Conant. In one volume, 492 pp. 12mo. With a steel Portrait. Price $1.

To meet the universally expressed desire for a comprehensive and convenient biography of this eminent Missionary which should fall within the means of all, this work has been prepared with the concurrence of President Wayland, author of the Biography in two volumes, and by the consent of the surviving family of the subject of the memoir, — the copyright being held exclusively for their benefit.

PRESCOTT'S
HISTORICAL WORKS.

ATTRACTIVE AS ROMANCES!

In all the qualities that distinguish the great historian, Mr. Prescott stands preëminent. His materials have been collected with great labor and research, and his style of narration is clear, flowing, and elegant. The reader has never to wander, perplexed, through accumulations of ill-arranged matter; perfect order is evident in all these works. The interest never flags; for the author has the happy faculty of seizing upon salient points, and grouping even minute details with picturesque effect.

HISTORY OF THE REIGN OF PHILIP II. OF SPAIN.

By William H. Prescott. With Portraits, Maps, Plates, &c. 8vo. vols. 1 and 2.

HISTORY OF THE CONQUEST OF MEXICO.

With the Life of the Conqueror, Hernando Cortez, and a View of the Ancient Mexican Civilization. By William H. Prescott. With Portrait and Maps. Three vols. 8vo.

HISTORY OF THE REIGN OF FERDINAND AND ISABELLA THE CATHOLIC.

By William H. Prescott. With Portraits. Three vols. 8vo.

HISTORY OF THE CONQUEST OF PERU.

With a Preliminary View of the Civilization of the Incas. By William H. Prescott. With Portraits, Maps, &c. Two vols. 8vo.

BIOGRAPHICAL AND CRITICAL MISCELLANIES.

By William H. Prescott. With a finely engraved Portrait. One vol. 8vo.

Mr. Prescott's works are printed upon fine paper, with large, clear type, and bound in all styles. Price, in muslin, $2 per volume; in sheep, $2.50; half calf, or half antique, $3; full calf, or antique, $4.

In Press:

ROBERTSON'S

HISTORY OF THE REIGN OF THE EMPEROR CHARLES V.

With a Continuation, treating of the Cloister Life of the Emperor after his Abdication. By William H. Prescott. Three vols. 8vo.

Uniform with Mr. Prescott's previous works.

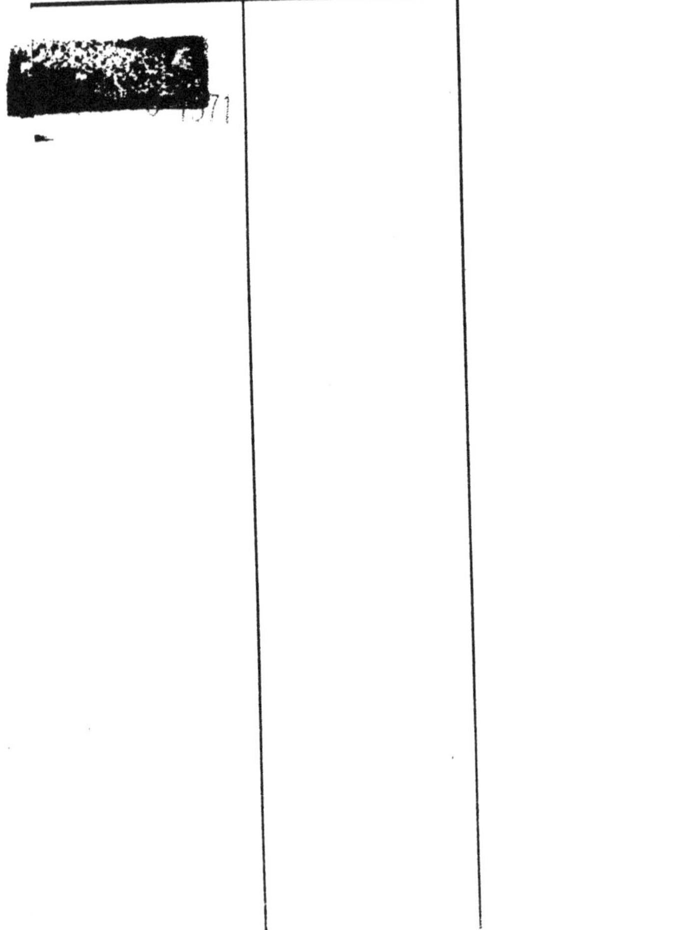

www.ingramcontent.com/pod-product-compliance
Lightning Source LLC
LaVergne TN
LVHW011155110826
845150LV00006B/1228

* 9 7 8 1 4 2 5 5 4 5 7 6 5 *